For my son, Alexander

Sometimes I think the only memories I have are those that I've created around photographs of me as a child. Maybe I'm creating my own life. I distrust any memories I do have. They may be fictions, too.

—Sally Mann, quoted in "The Disturbing Photography of Sally Mann"

But the "theory" is the expression of primal fantasies, and the fable is only a form of knowledge distorted by adults, and in this sense, a deceptive illusion.

—J.-B. Pontalis, *Frontiers of Psychoanalysis*

Contents

Acknowledgments

Without the advice and encouragement of many people, this project would not have found its way into book form. First, I want to express my gratitude to George Monteiro, who forced me constantly to come to terms with my own uninterrogated assumptions about the child and psychoanalytic theory. I would like to thank Humphrey Morris for reading early versions of this book from an analyst's perspective and giving me a sense of where I might begin to chart the psychoanalytic representations of the child. I must also express my profound indebtedness to my friend Cynthia Masse for the fruits of her clinical experience. Thanks go to my sister, Bonnie Burman, for sharing her knowledge of current psychological accounts.

For their invaluable help in responding to this work at various stages in its production I wish to thank Walter A. Davis, Peter Garrett, and Marianne Hirsch. Thanks go to my colleagues Kevin Kiernan, Ellen Rosenman, Larry J. Swingle, and Gregory Waller for their attentive and productive readings. Thanks also go to Linda Krause Worley for her help with Freud's German.

For their generosity and rigor in reading the completed manuscript I am grateful to Mary Loeffelholz and James Kincaid, who reviewed it for the University of Illinois Press.

For moral support and a great deal of good advice I thank Diane Elam.

For their time in helping me retrieve information through the University of Kentucky School of Law library, thanks go to Cheryl Jones and Sue Burch. Thanks also go to Barbara Hale and Janet Layman at the Interlibrary Loan office of the University of Kentucky for their amazing speed in locating necessary materials.

I thank Nikki Swingle for her fine work in helping to prepare this manuscript and Sydney Darby for her assistance.

I am indebted to Research and Graduate Studies at the University of Kentucky and to the University of Kentucky Research Foundation for many forms of financial support, including summer grant funding, minigrants for research materials, and funding my research assistant. Thanks especially go to the Vice Chancellor for Research and Graduate Studies at the University of Kentucky for financial assistance in the production of this book. I am extremely grateful to the University of Kentucky for the release time that made completion of this project possible.

Chapter 4 is an expanded and revised version of "The *Go-Between* Child: The Supplement of the Lack," in *Compromise Formations: Current Directions in Psychoanalytic Criticism,* ed. Vera J. Camden (Kent, Ohio: Kent State University Press, 1989), pp. 99–112.

HIDE and SEEK

Introduction:
Uses of the Child

The factual history of desire is given as a hypothetical
factualness superimposed upon a lost trace. The access to
the truth, Freud boldly said, can only pass through an
examination of its distortions. This is a formidable task,
given that distortion is usually measured against the
truth, whereas for Freud the truth is to be deduced from
the distortion.

—André Green, *The Tragic Complex*

"Kevin!" shrieks the mother in the film *Home Alone,* when
she realizes en route to France that she has left her eight-year-old son
alone in the family house in South Bend, Indiana. In the rush to
leave, she forgot about him. "What kind of mother am I?" she later
wails to a man who admits to having left his own child behind in a
funeral home (a funeral home!) for a day. It is Christmastime, the
flights home are all booked—getting back to Kevin that day appears
impossible. But the mother is indefatigable: she tries stand-by; she
sells her first-class tickets, along with her watch, earrings, and an elec-
tronic translator, to a couple for their seats; she rides all the way from
Scranton to Chicago in a rented truck on Christmas Eve—the trip
winds up taking so long that she arrives home only minutes before
the family's scheduled return flight. The child, Kevin, greets her warily
with the classic look of avoidant behavior ensuing from separation
anxiety. Why did it take her so long? What generated her resistance?
Surely, all the delays constitute the film's representation of parental
(specifically maternal) resistance to the child. Kevin's hesitancy registers her resistance; he knows that he wasn't left accidentally. His
expressed fantasy that his family has disappeared because he wished
them gone recreates the child as agent of the child's passive anxiety
about being abandoned.

In a society that condemns women for aborting three-month-old fetuses, living children are the lowest priority for public funding.[1] This is the split between the imaginary child (concretized as "unborn") and the real child who is a drain on everyone's resources. But the child-protagonist of *Home Alone* overcomes his exacerbating dependence (his older sister advises him, "You are what the French call '*les incompetents*'"). While at the beginning of the film he needs his mother to pack his suitcase for him (which she clearly resents), by the end he has risen to heroic dimensions of self-sufficiency. He has defended the home (read family) "abandoned" by the rest. It is the child who guards the home against outside invaders, at first portrayed as thieves who simply crave the home electronics but who later dedicate themselves to punishing the child. This is because the threat to the family is the child itself (its dangerous aspects displaced in the film onto the thieves) who is never what it[2] should be, never altogether adequate—always in the process of plundering the nuclear family of its self-idealization as purveyor of received gender laws, as storehouse of genetic heritage and guarantor of the transmission of human identity, as producer of a future perfect via an inevitably imperfect child.

As early as 1950, Margaret Mead and Erik Erikson contended that families tend to produce children well suited for the society they inhabit. Thus, Erikson speculated that the protraction of breast feeding among the Sioux produces a combination of generosity and "'hunter's ferocity'" (137). Mead averred that mother-centered childrearing tends to mold "a character suited to lifelong monogamous marriage" ("Mother-Child" 477). But what happens if this logical pattern goes awry? What happens if the child produced by the real family is outfitted for an idealized society entirely at odds with the one it inhabits? Mead has argued that this is precisely what happens in North American society, where with each generation there is a massive disjunction between the perceived past and the proffered future:

> Where each little village, each separate caste or dialect group, in Europe or Asia has been standardized by the experience of the past, faultlessly transmitted to each new generation, the people of America, North and South, East and West, are being standardized by the future, by the houses all hope to live in, not by the houses where they were born, by the way they hope their wives will look, not by the folds of Mother's skirt in which they hid their faces. . . . And this, not because the ideal is so high, but because it is a dream of the future rather than an attempt to reproduce the past. (*Male and Female* 254–55)

There is a fundamental discrepancy as well between the modern Western family's self-representation and the family as it unfolds daily in all of its pettiness and anger and equivocation. The child looks alternately like the sum total of bad social influences and the promise of a new start and a new world. Parental ambivalence is lived out through children caught in the incommensurability of the real with the ideal. Of course, the distinction between the real and ideal is complicated as well by the fact that the ideal interpenetrates the real in a forced coalescence that leaves children and their parents ultimately dissatisfied. Everyone feels "seduced" by these differences between the imagined family and its quotidian manifestations, between its fantasied future generation and the child who reviles the parents for having "used" it. Indeed, the child has been used, sent forth as a sign into the social network where it is expected to assert itself as the bearer of the family's value. The child, finally, must fulfill the promise entrusted to it by the family that stakes its legitimacy upon the success of its child-products.[3] As a result, the family is hostile to the very child to whom it is indebted for its survival. The child's inadequacy is in a sense structurally predetermined. It is necessary, for the fantasy to subsist, to cast the actual child as inadequate instead of recognizing the fantasmatic child as fantasmatic.

Theories of the family and child-development notably continue to posit as though universal a nuclear heterosexual childrearing unit despite the family's widespread reconfiguration, from single mothers and single fathers to gay couple parenting. Psychoanalysts seem to be especially committed to this model even in the face of its dissolution. Indeed, psychoanalysis is heavily invested in genderizing familial roles to achieve its own prescriptive intrapsychic structures and developmental stages. The child's pathology points to the family's pathology. The family's health is what the child must validate. The textbook family will restore a textbook world. A textbook world might restore the textbook family. The textbook child pressures families to *be* the child's origin.

This study's point of departure is the emergence of the child as a social subject in nineteenth-century Western society. Coincident with the child's newfound social status were both the literary emphasis on the child's subjectivity and the psychoanalytic investment in the child as the origin of the adult. While the eighteenth century began to formulate childhood as a trope in antagonism to perceived incursions of industrialization, the nineteenth century promoted the child to a subject in its own right.[4] Thus the Romantics created the "child" as a potential space for the adult imagination, a figure for the recuperation of a preindustrial attunement with nature; as the nineteenth century progressed, this imaginative space was increasingly legitimated as lived experience. The child's relationship to the adult was reshaped from one of dominance and subordination, as well as the distinction between the inchoate and the achieved subject, into a futile encounter between the nostalgic imagination (the bliss of childhood innocence) and a progressive evolutionary mythology. Although the evolutionary conviction remained in place, it was resisted by a counter-current that looked backward in individual and epochal time for its pleasures. Meanwhile, the site called "childhood" was isolated as an extrasocial haven from a growing sense of anxiety attendant on adult-level experience.

That the child could start to appear as a central protagonist in nineteenth-century fiction makes sense in light of a culture that was increasingly complicating its trajectories. Where in Defoe's *Roxana,* for example, the narrator gives birth to numerous children who simply come and go at the narrative's whim, in a Dickensian novel each child is accorded full narrative status. Just as the psychoanalytic project of the late nineteenth and twentieth centuries has been to guide the adult subject backward in search of the infantile, nineteenth- and twentieth-century fiction offers the lure of the child's perspective to a destabilized adult reader who exalts the child for its imagined capacities to transcend and rectify.

While childhood was invested as a sentimental site in the eighteenth and nineteenth centuries, as a field of study childhood has been discovered and canonized in the twentieth.[5] Two widely read works—Peter Coveney's *Poor Monkey,* which surveys the figure of the child in literature and Philippe Ariès's *Centuries of Childhood,* a social history of the development of the idea of childhood—have marked the child as an important area of research for all disciplines.[6] In many ways, however, it is in the arena of psychoanalysis that one finds the raison d'être of childhood as a site of fantasy; even in psychoanalysis's very articulation of the child as an object of study it tells the story not of the child itself but of why the adult talks about the child—what it is that the adult imagination pursues through the child. Indeed, it is possible to read most critical texts that presume to treat the child as a real field of research as so much autobiography. While the same argument might be made about all texts, those both ostensibly factual and those self-acknowledgedly fictional, in the case of the child the extent to which the creative writer and the theorist are writing about themselves is compounded by a tacit confidence in privileged insight into this "space" we all once inhabited.

In the effort to present the "reality" of the child and its perceptions, we cannot help but interpret the child in light of adult motives; we cannot help but interpret *ourselves* through the child. The study of the child thus becomes a perpetual reenactment of the suppression of the actual child in favor of adult imperatives. For Ariès, for instance, the development of the idea of childhood is the means by which he deplores the postindustrial stratification of the classes. Childhood, he concludes, is a narcissistic emanation of the middle class's self-absorption and retreat to the imagined impregnability of the nuclear family unit.

Likewise, Richard Coe, in *When the Grass Was Taller,* sees the separation of spheres into adult and child as the troubled remainder of the Industrial Revolution. These postpastoral narratives that lament falls into differences of all kinds treat the shaping of an individuated child as a signpost to culturewide loss. Lloyd deMause, conversely, with his progressive reading of the child in history, contends that the child hitherto always has been the object of adult projections and reversals and only recently has been dignified as a subject. The "helping mode" is what he labels this new relationship between adult caretakers and their children:

> The helping mode involves the proposition that the child knows better than the parent what it needs at each stage of its life, and fully involves both parents in the child's life as they work to empathize with and fulfill its expanding and particular needs.
>
> There is no attempt at all to discipline or form "habits." Children are neither struck nor scolded, and are apologized to if yelled at under stress. The helping mode involves an enormous amount of time, energy, and discussion on the part of both parents, especially in the first six years, for helping a young child reach its daily goals means continually responding to it, playing with it, tolerating its regressions, being its servant rather than the other way around, interpreting its emotional conflicts, and providing the objects specific to its evolving interests. Few parents have yet consistently attempted this kind of child care. From the four books which describe children brought up according to the helping mode, it is evident that it results in a child who is gentle, sincere, never depressed, never imitative or group-oriented, strong-willed, and unintimidated by authority. (52 and 54)

DeMause perpetrates the same crime that he accuses other adults of committing—projective reversals onto the child. The child is promoted to a little tyrant—note the child who is "strong-willed" and "unintimidated by authority"—and the adult is depicted as "servant" to the child; the child takes over the role of the parent in the deMausian fantasy.

Jacqueline Rose, on the other hand, interrogates "childhood" as a consequence of adult necessity. In *The Case of Peter Pan*, Rose discusses shaping a child-audience for the literature designated "children's." She writes, "It will not be an issue here of what the child wants, but of what the adult desires—desires in the very act of construing the child as the object of its speech" (2). Throughout her account, which is thoroughly undergirded by psychoanalytic theory, Rose emphasizes that the child is posited by the adult imagination as a site of diverse fantasmatic originary moments that ensure the adult's relation to language. While in many ways my study subscribes to Rose's assumptions about the extent to which adult rhetoric about the child is invariably an appropriation and denial of the actual child and also shares her psychoanalytic perspective, I attempt to interrogate psychoanalysis itself as yet another mythmaker, another story of the child that talks about the adult instead, another discourse that employs the child as a vehicle to effect the theory's own adult ends. To uphold one point of view (the psychoanalytic) as real in contradistinction to all the other evidences of false consciousness is to imply that there is a route to the real child via psychoanalysis. I am by no means pretending, however, that the following account of psychoanalytic and fictional children will be free from the same distortions, the same suppression of the child-object I consider. Rather, I want to preface my argument with an admission of its own potential futility, the awareness that despite all efforts to sidestep definitions of the child, such avoidance is itself a theoretical gridlock, in many ways as tyrannical as those I repudiate.

Notwithstanding the impossibility of any effort to speak for or speak as the child, we cannot simply turn away in silence. What needs to be addressed, finally, is not the true nature of the child but the reasons we pursue such knowledge—how we go about achieving it, what it gives us and what we think it will give us. As James Kincaid theorizes in his recent book, *Child-Loving*, this post-eighteenth-century child is the site of eroticizing fantasies that occur as a result of the child's mystification, its utter differentiation from adulthood. Both Kincaid and the sociologist Joel Best indicate the degree to which current stories we tell about child abuse are hystericized. While Best (who explores diverse "threats" to the child) sees the adult/child relation as one of identification whereby the adult projects onto the child her or his perceived victimization by an incomprehensibly menacing society, Kincaid emphasizes the identification between the adult parties, the overt pedophile and the repressed "child-lover" in all of us. It seems to me that both identifications obtain, and, as I hope to show throughout this study, it is in the practice of psychoanalysis that the relationship between adult and child subjects is both foregrounded and complicated.

"Children," writes Neil Postman, "are the living messages we send to a time we will not see" (xi). This fantasy of the child as message precipitates the child into a go-between role; indeed, we find a confusion between the child as message and child as message-bearer. It is impossible to determine the origin and its metonymic trajectory—child as message that acts out as message-bearer or vice versa. Despite how often we are reminded to heed this distinction and not kill the messenger, without the messenger perhaps the message (and this is the scary part) does not exist. This messenger function of the child ensues from a faith in the child's ability to unify what are irremediably separate—first and foremost, the man and woman who produce it. Yet the child cannot be any more successful at permanently dissolving the difference between the sexual couple than it can elevate the real to the ideal.

As a result of the dependency upon the child to elide the differences it contains (in both senses of the term), the child of imaginative literature tends to emerge as a go-between who not only conveys messages between adult parties but cements otherwise disparate agencies. Similarly, the child of psychoanalysis is the linchpin of diverse theoretical debates. The adult subjects, who pursue the origin and meaning of their subjectivities through a past represented as both personal and universal childhood, look to children to perform mediating tasks between otherwise irreconcilable arenas (e.g., classes and sexes) that have resolved into defensively steadfast systems of difference.

While the child acts as a resolving link, it also represents a threat to adult systems of repression that anchor a precarious coherence. It is this status as link—as go-between who cannot help but reveal the chasms, the spaces of difference, the heterogeneities it is the child's mission to elide—that makes the go-between child so perilous. Although the go-between child is used to conceal the gaps, its consequent emergence as the term of denial underscores the inadequacies it supplements. The go-between child must helplessly expose its own self-negating function. Consequently, the child is fated to be expelled from the narrative resolutions it produces, not unlike the sacrificial victim described by René Girard, who contends that the "purpose of the sacrifice is to restore harmony to the community, to reinforce the social fabric" (*Violence* 8). The "sacrifice" occurs in diverse forms: either the child experiences a literal death, like Jo in *Bleak House* and the heroine in *Lolita,* or the child is thwarted in the effort to take part in the sexual unions it brings about, like Maisie Farange of *What Maisie Knew* and Leo Colston of *The Go-Between.* Or, the child is pre-empted by the theories it subserves, like the child of psychoanalysis. In all cases, the child is victimized by the go-between role imposed by adult desire. That such a role cannot be prolonged without betraying its insufficiency foredooms the child to look like a disruption in the hitherto fluid economy of adult relations it has fortified. Like Girard's sacrificial victim, however, the sacrifice of the child is only a transient solution at best. The fictional go-betweens are no more able to preserve the "social fabric" than is the sacrificial victim whose replacement by yet another victim repeats the story of its impossible mission.

This book attempts to find a way of talking about fictions of the child in both literary and psychoanalytic accounts without producing additional self-deceived fictions. This is not to say that there are not other "fictions" of the child, under such guises as historical and sociological accounts. Psychoanalysis, however, is the preeminent twentieth-century discourse about childhood, a discourse that, unlike imaginative literature, refuses to examine the inevitable aporias occurring when adult subjects treat as ultimately knowable a subject-position they have both internalized and forsaken. Although also embedded in ideological productions of childhood, imaginative literature confronts more directly the fantasies that remain defended against in psychoanalysis, perhaps because of its liberation from a scientizing positivism. Finally, of all postindustrial discourses, psychoanalysis is the most deeply dependent on accounts of childhood for its very rationale because the psychoanalytic account of the human subject is that of a subject who was once (and continues unconsciously to be) a child.

Marianne Hirsch points out that psychoanalysis is "profoundly child-centered" (12). Its emphasis on the mother-child relation views the mother only in light of her function as the bearer and nurturer of the child, that idealized object of psychoanalytic inquiry. It is certainly true that psychoanalysis regards maternal subjectivity only in terms of its relevance to the child who is either imperiled by the mother's potential overinvestment (she will never let it go) or underinvestment (she expels the child too abruptly). This child ostensibly revered by psychoanalysis, however, is not the actual child; this child is merely the linchpin of the Oedipal model that fixes fatherhood as the central agency and the child as the proof of the father's procreative and social authority. The idealized child's ensuing connective role defends the father-centered family against the material child's threat to unveil the body of the mother in the reproductive economy.

My study focuses upon a particular trend of masculinist fantasy that is not only a corollary to the failed patriarchal family (undermined, as it is, from within by competing imperatives) but arises as well from a male-centered relationship to both imperfect presents and future perfects. The child as phallus, the central psychoanalytic equation, is a patriarchal fantasy devised in the service of solidifying and perpetuating a gender system in which the woman is marked as lacking the very thing she has most clearly—the child. Thus, while the woman's relationship to the child is metonymic, a relationship of proximity and physical connection, the man's metaphoric relationship is forged out of a combination of social law (legitimacy) and psychological necessity. The phallic-child of psychoanalysis, reconfigured as a "gift" to the woman, is in truth the man's sole link to generation that is otherwise a view from the sidelines of woman's reproductive agency. The Oedipal plot of psychoanalysis arises tellingly as an overcompensation for the man's position in the family, an androcentric narrative that tells of the woman's loss instead of the man's alienation from a family romance that potentially excludes him. As a result, we find an emphasis on the facilitating capacity of the child, a role that could only emerge from a heavily Oedipalized notion of both the heterosexual family and the sexual relation.[7]

Indeed, in *Haven in a Heartless World*, Christopher Lasch bemoans the dissolution of the family and society in the wake of the father's diminishing role. This family, for Lasch, is the cornerstone for a specifically male productivity (within and without the family). This family has been undermined by "the helping professions" who assume "the guise of 'nurturing mother—'" as Lasch notes in his desperation to fix the culprit and reveal the impact of "feminizations" of all kinds (*Haven* 18, 171). Implicit in his argument is the emphasis on the generational link between fathers and sons. Specifically, fathers "spontaneously abdicate in favor of sons-in-law," meekly renouncing their authority (175). If the family is no longer working, it is because the chain of command from father to son is obsolescent; if fathers and sons are no longer central to the family, then the family is a failure. The overtaking of the family by "the forces of organized virtue" has meant the dissolution of the family as such whose very essence is the transmission of power from the father to the son (169). Such circular historiographic elaborations are androcentric hysterical responses to the perceived tenuousness of the father's role. These overcompensations (strong fathers as opposed to simply fathers), as well as notable scotomizations (the possibility of a productive gender-*equal* family), are motivated in historiography by the same compulsions that give rise to the overcompensating go-between child in literature and psychoanalysis, who must not only replace what is missing but defend against the possibility of alternative paradigms of human relationships.

· · ·

In the first three chapters on the child in psychoanalytic theory and practice, I look at the diverse representations of the child in the history of psychoanalysis to show the ways in which the theories that profess to illuminate the child instead mythologize the child. I consider this an essential section of the book in that it undercuts any privileging of psychoanalytic over literary discourse. My discussion of psychoanalysis is organized around theoretical tensions in the field: the distinction between the clinical child and the observed child; conflict versus deficit models; and the ongoing theoretical confrontations between the Freudian emphasis on the Oedipal triangle and the mother-child dyad of object-relations theory. These tensions are rehearsed to clarify my central argument that the Oedipal paradigm is merely a superimposition of a triangular structure onto what remains in all psychoanalytic narratives an imperturbable mother-child dyad.

My aim is not to reproduce for my reader a chronological account of the psychoanalytic representation of the child but rather to investigate the competing ideologies that have produced various narratives about the child. As Walter A. Davis holds, "Psychoanalysis will be adequate to its subject only when it applies its discoveries to its own modes of understanding" (239). Although I cannot offer a solution to the blindness of psychoanalytic theories any more than I can unveil miraculously the "real" child, hitherto perceived through the dark glass of adult distortions, I will attempt to isolate and account for the psychoanalytic disavowals at the same time that I explore the strategies used to subject the child to adult fantasy. I recognize in psychoanalysis the potential to acknowledge more directly the ways in which it conditions the relationship between "adult" and "child" as well as its capacity, in the eventual encounter with its own unconscious, to address, if not the blind spots themselves, its proclivity for scotomization. Child analysis should have dismantled more effectively adult self-constructions. Its exploration of what must necessarily remain opaque (revealing its resistance to illumination in the very effort) should have confirmed for analytic theory the fundamental impossibility of its structure of knowledge, an impossibility that is in fact a component of the structure of Freud's reading of the human psyche. Rather, the development of child analysis has tended to the reverse—it has proclaimed as knowable the adult psyche via its charting of the child and infant.

In chapter 4, I argue that gender transactions in L. P. Hartley's *The Go-Between* expose the deception of psychoanalytic accounts of gender. The way in which *The Go-Between's* child-protagonist simultaneously differentiates and collapses the spaces between the adult characters repeats the psychoanalytic use of the child as the emblem of a "bisexual" economy. Leo's status is finally that of the bisexual subject of psychoanalysis, at once the secret fulfillment of heterosexual desire and an exile from its official program.

I go on to read Dickensian narrative strategies in relation to psychoanalytic narratives. *Bleak House* and *Oliver Twist* illustrate the confusion over the very definitions of adult and child, presenting the child's space as the location where social and sexual hierarchies are threatened with inanition. Using case histories, I address the recovery of the "child" in psychoanalytic therapy, arguing that Dickens's novels and psychoanalytic theory allegorize one another as constructions of childhood. The family invented in analysis, the very family in which the cured subject is entrenched, perhaps is more similar than either subject or analyst would care to admit to the idealized fictional family served up to the reader at the end of many Dickens novels as a regretted beginning to which all just ends must lead.

In chapter 6 I consider James's *What Maisie Knew* as the fictional version of what the psychoanalyst Maud Mannoni calls the "deficient child," the retarded or psychotic child produced by the mother's refusal to subscribe to the paternal order. Maisie as well figures as potentially "deficient"—of a family, of a moral sense—resulting from inadequately negotiated social and familial gender roles and alliances. The novel exposes the idealization of the mother-child relation and the traumatic consequences of its failure.

Nabokov's *Lolita* is the grotesque accomplishment of the adult's narcissistic investment in the child. Such a strategy is endorsed by Lacanian theory, which I see as the culmination of the twentieth century's exaltation of the narcissistic tendencies of the human subject. The go-between child has been reduced to the surface of the mirror between Humbert and Quilty. Humbert's fatal error is surely his refusal to see Lolita as nothing more than a mirror through which he accesses his mirror-image "brother," Clare Quilty. The recognition of the narcissistic predicament, however, which is the text's boastful subversiveness, condones the appropriation of the child as inevitable, whether it be deluded or enlightened. Akin to Nabokov's jubilant self-reflexivity is Lacan's illusory evocation of a Symbolic realm that transcends Imaginary identifications. Inherent in both Lacan's and Nabokov's points of view is the assumption that there is no "real" other within our ken beyond incorporeal self-reflections. The fantasy subtending an insistence upon pervasive mirroring is the denial of alterity. In a gesture more radical than that of Hartley, who petrifies his divisive child as a term between rather than an individuated subject, or James, who excludes his children from the social scene they threaten to expose as fraudulent, Nabokov must "kill" the child who stands between the subject and his own narcissistic embrace. The destruction of the child becomes a means to transcend the mirror that bars access to the recuperation of an intact narcissism.

I conclude this study by relating the examples identified in the earlier chapters to several "fictions" of the child in contemporary culture, including the "repressed" child of sexual abuse who returns as a recovered adult memory, the unconceived child of the Norplant controversy, and the "inner child" movement. These "children" have been fetishized by a culture that invests fictive children while treating living children with comparative indifference. Like the chronic tendency I chart in psychoanalytic and literary fictions to replace the actual child with an imaginary one, the fictive children of contemporary culture inherit the idealizations denied to their material counterparts. The living children cannot help but prove the inadequacy of the child to the projective grandiosity of adult expectations.

• • •

In *The Picture of Dorian Gray,* the artist, Basil Hallward, confesses that the painting is always about the artist. To this extent, my argument is circumscribed by a psychoanalytic perspective, my own ideology. Yet I invite the imaginative texts to "read" psychoanalytic theory in much the same way that to date psychoanalysis has erected a truth-claim against which imaginative literature plays out its frail symptoms. Even in its acknowledgment of the duplicity of conscious discourse, psychoanalytic theory falls prey (rather recklessly) to the very pitfalls it so brilliantly illuminates in the analysand. Recently, I asked an analyst to interpret the import of a specific rhetorical lapsus in a book written by a psychoanalyst—in much the same way that he might interpret a statement by an analysand. He responded that what I requested was impossible because, with the subject of analysis, one has a context (the patient's history, previous analytic sessions, as well as the current session); with the text, conversely, one has no context for the lapsus. Of course, the context in this instance is the text itself as well as the culture that produced it, but here he was invoking as material reality an analytic context that is yet another text, another location where narrative unfolds. The firm insistence on the distinction between the two sites, that of analysis and that of the imaginative text, is what continues to pervade our self-complacent understanding of the difference between the "scientific" terrain of psychoanalytic theory and the "fictions" of the imaginative text. Throughout this book I will invoke momentarily as having truth-value given psychoanalytic theories of the human subject, but such truth-value gains a kind of transience insofar as these theories will be called into question, reversed, recontextualized as they are played out within and between chapters. To argue that they function as springboards would be fallacious because I cannot pretend to offer even that brief solace of a locating device. Rather, when I confess that the psychoanalytic theory of the unconscious is a basic tenet of this text, I am indicating that my theory of the child is entrenched in divisions I cannot begin to isolate, lacking as I do any coordinates for the ground that has been destabilized, uncertain as I remain of the relationship between the "ground" and the "superstructure."

Addressing the tension between what he calls "narrative truth" and the "historical truth" of the "real" event, Donald Spence observes:

> But there is a further problem—the problem of uncontrolled context. If the patient's verbal presentation of a dream or memory is, by definition, incomplete, then we must assume that further context must be supplied in order for understanding to take place. The context may come from the patient, who is elaborating on the remembered dream, or it may come from the analyst, who, hearing the dream report, is unwittingly supplying details of his own to make it somehow coherent. Under the influence of the narrative tradition, the analyst may add a wide range of missing items, always assuming that he is doing justice to the material and merely supplying what the patient would have said had he been asked. Here is where the narrative tradition creates the most mischief because it comes into play between the time the patient speaks and the time the analyst has understood. (28–29)

While Spence is raising important questions about the analyst's own narrative impositions upon the patient's experiential report, he nevertheless holds fast to a faith in an unmediated history that gets distorted during analytic narrativization. My study refuses a distinction between historical and narrative truths. If I present the fictional and psychoanalytic narratives of the child as so many versions of infanticide inasmuch as they unwittingly destroy the child's subjectivity even as they profess to esteem it, at the same time my own account resists an encounter with a material child that I argue throughout remains inaccessible; rather, I address the structure of these representations as well as the fantasies that fuel them. To this extent, I do not attempt to distill from the fictional accounts a historical truth of the guileless victim of adult distortions. In fact, I not only deny the existence of such a child but also cannot identify an authentic child, because the terrain of childhood itself is a mythical country, mapped out by an adult consciousness ceaselessly in search of its subjective experience in another time and place.

Notes

1. See W. Norton Grubb and Marvin Lazerson, *Broken Promises: How Americans Fail Their Children*. For an assessment of the public/private distinction in family law, see also Martha Minnow's "Rights for the Next Generation: A Feminist Approach to Children's Rights," 7.

2. Throughout this study I use the pronoun "it" to emphasize the conceptual as opposed to the material status of this child figure.

3. For an account of the changing relationship between the sentimental and material value of children, see Viviana Zelizer's *Pricing the Priceless Child*. Zelizer argues that in a capitalist society, the "construction of the economically worthless child" is countered by pricing its sentimental value (5).

4. Carl N. Degler sees a noticeable change in the "early years of the 19th century" when "children were viewed as individuals, as persons in their own right" (71). As an example he notes that birthdays begin to be celebrated in the nineteenth century.

5. Philippe Ariès asserts that in Western society the idea of childhood as a social space emerges in the sixteenth century. The relationship to childhood as we know it, however, its sentimentalization and overinvestment, does not occur until the eighteenth century.

6. For the major social histories on the development and elaboration of the idea of childhood and the child, see Philippe Ariès, *Centuries of Childhood*; Edward Shorter, *The Making of the Modern Family*; Bernard Wishy, *The Child and the Republic*; Peter Laslett, *The World We Have Lost*; Lawrence Stone, *The Family, Sex and Marriage: In England, 1500–1800*; Lloyd deMause, *The History of Childhood*; Ivy Pinchbeck and Margaret Hewitt, *Children in English Society*; Carl Degler, *At Odds: Women and the Family in America from the Revolution to the Present*; David Hunt, *Parents*

and Children in History: The Psychology of Family Life in Early Modern France;
and N. Ray Hiner and Joseph M. Hawes, eds., *Growing up in America: Children in Historical Perspective.*

7. Margaret Homans has written about message-bearing daughters in the works of Elizabeth Gaskell. These message-bearers have a different relationship to their respective texts, however, from the ones I consider. As Homans illustrates most convincingly, they are situated at the intersection of the presymbolic maternal language and the paternal symbolic order. Thus, Gaskell's fictional go-between daughters emblematize specifically the woman writer's complicated relationship to patriarchal discourse. The children studied here, on the contrary, are the "offspring" of male writers who not only minimize the role of the mother but also use the child in the service of male-centered Oedipal narratives and social fantasy. See chapters 9 and 10 in Homans's *Bearing the Word.*

I don't like the way you crossed me out.

—Virginia's letter to *The Wall Street Journal* after they crossed out sections of her nude photograph taken by her mother, Sally Mann

When ten-year-old Darrin Davis called 911 to report the white powder embroidering a small mirror in his parents' bedroom, he expected the police to take the drugs from his parents and then "help" them in some vague way as they had promised during antidrug campaigns at Darrin's school. Instead, the police arrested his mother and father and took them to jail. Two years later, when the Georgia Supreme Court found that the police entrance was illegal and the Davises were found not guilty (and handed back their ruined lives), the District Attorney suggested that the Davises had used their little boy as a "pawn" (Curriden and Torpy A16). Conversely, the head of Georgia's ACLU accused the police of using Darrin as a "pawn."

An eight-year-old girl reported her mother and stepfather to her school principal for using illegal drugs. Her parents were arrested and she and her younger sister were removed to the custody of Family and Children Services. This child's principal reported: "She was obviously hurt for having to turn her parents in [but] felt she needed to get out of this environment and help her parents" ("Police say girl turned in" B3). The principal has elaborated for this child a full-fledged adult-level ethical sense along with a firm understanding of her relationship to the future, cause and effect, and so forth. What he believes the child knows suggests the extent to which adults script the child's perspective. On the witness stand, the police in the Davis case claimed that Darrin expressly asked that his parents be arrested. "'That is a lie,'" countered Darrin. "'I did not tell them that'" (Curriden A12). But perhaps the police, invited to Darrin's home, could not distinguish between what the child said and their own projections.

In response to the Darrin Davis case, health professionals noted that although it remains illegal for the police to search a house based on a child's information, a more effective way to limit parental drug use is to threaten to take away their children. "When parents undergo drug-abuse counseling, the strongest weapon in the counselors' arsenal is the warning that unless parents stay with the program, their children can be taken away from them and made wards of the courts" ("Answering a child's call for help"). One Friday in 1993, a Bronx mother reported her ten-year-old son missing when he did not come home from school (Dugger). Throughout the weekend, the mother and the police searched for this child. Not until Monday, upon contacting the boy's school, did they find out that the boy had been removed from the school by the city's Child Welfare Administration. Even the police were concerned that insufficient effort had been made to contact the mother. Here we have an extreme example of state rights over children.

The very popular program "Here's Looking at You, 2000" aims at drug education for small children. Dana Mack has written about the effects of this curriculum on her seven-year-old daughter. One evening, the child asked her parents if they were alcoholics. "'I beg your pardon?' my husband answered, pouring himself a glass of Sancerre. 'You drink wine,' she said, in defense of her question, 'and sometimes you even yell at me.' Apparently, earlier that day a cuddly little puppet named Miranda had told the second-graders a story about her 'Uncle Bud.' Like most of us, Uncle Bud occasionally loses his patience with the younger generation. But only, claims little Miranda, when he has had a bottle of beer." Mack contends that one exercise in this program "fairly extracts family confessions. It invites children to send 'secret messages' to their teacher about 'problems at home.'"

Responding to Mack's criticism of the "Here's Looking at You, 2000" curriculum, Clay Roberts, chief executive officer of the Comprehensive Health Education Foundation, writes in a letter to the editor: "Does [Ms. Mack] really think that we want to turn kids against their parents? Does she really suspect us of urging teachers to spy on their students' families? Does she really believe that the curriculum nefariously wants children to be frightened and unhappy? Why would we do such a thing? What's in it for us?" Indeed—what is "in it" for these agencies that police the family? How otherwise, one might ask, do we instill in small children a sense of the harmful effects of drugs and alcohol? How can we protect children yet not have them "rat" on mom and dad—which ends up dissolving the family in a rather dramatic way? Roberts says that the aim is not to turn kids against their parents—but is he being altogether honest? The law enforcement officers who responded to Darrin Davis's call for help and the school principal who reported the eight-year-old's parents to the police might very well disagree. They might point out to us that if parents are doing wrong, it is the obligation of the child to report them; they might congratulate themselves on jobs well done. Given the moral investment in an antidrug and alcohol environment for children, it would not be surprising to find that many educators do indeed want to turn kids against reprobate parents.

In an odd contrast to these bold intrusions into the family, we find photographer Sally Mann offering up her children as a lure to the public gaze, in a sense *inviting* the surveillance she then excoriates. Sally Mann's remarkable photographs of her three children have come under some scrutiny. For one thing, the children frequently are depicted nude. For another, her children are working for her; given that they are Mann's primary photographic subjects, the question arises, is this exploitation? Although criticized in some quarters, Mann (all the while judiciously consulting with a prosecuting attorney) has avoided any kind of legal action. Alice Sims was not so fortunate. Sims, also an artist, was taking nude photographs of her two small children (ages one and six), photographs that she then had developed through a major drugstore and subsequently integrated into her painting. When one roll of film was noticed at the processing plant in Maryland, a U.S. postal inspector was alerted that "'sexually explicit' photos of children had traveled across state lines" (Hess 31). The inspector, Robert Northrop, instantly on the Sims's trail, contacted the Department of Social Services (DSS), who hustled off the children to foster care.[1] Months after the event, Sims reported that her little boy still "'won't take his underwear off in the bath'" (32). The writer of *The Village Voice* article, Elizabeth Hess, implies that the real pedophiles are the postal inspectors and various excitable members of the DSS. Sally Mann sent a postcard to a friend displaying a nude photograph of her son. As Hess puts it, this photo "also *aroused* the attention of postal inspectors" (emphasis added, 32). I'll bet. James Kincaid suggests that we should be more worried about the self-proclaimed foes of pedophilia. After all, one is suspicious of the sensibilities of people who find pictures of one-year-olds pornographic. At the same time, for Sally Mann to display her child's nude photograph on a postcard and then attack the post office for *looking at* what she aggressively *showed them* seems somewhat paradoxical. We cannot offer the bodies of children for public consumption and expect to control the gaze. Meanwhile, Mann claims to be shocked that pedophiles might be among the audience for her photographs (Woodward 52).

The reception of Mann's photographs plays out the whole spectrum of fantasies about the child and childhood. Thus, we find Janet Malcolm elaborating upon Mann's "tough love" that exposes the tragedy implicit in childhood experience; indeed, Malcolm reads Mann through a Blakean narrative of innocence versus experience—

for example, the angelic child framed by darkness (8). Some people see the vulnerability and innocence of these children; others refer to the truth of childhood sexuality that the photographs unveil. One person suggests that it is the mean looks on the children's faces that unsettles people (Bernays). Different accounts of abuse emerge here— either exploiting your children for profit, offering up their bodies to the appetite of the masses, invading the sanctity of your child's body with your adult gaze. Viviana Zelizer points out that a former belief in the child's productive function within the family has been superseded by an investment in protracted nonfunctional childhoods. Asking the child to do "chores" is okay; bringing in income is not. Consider, for example, the constant vilifications of the parents of child stars who are represented as parasitically feeding off their children's talents.

After the Sims incident, Mann was worried, and so were her children, who expressed fear that "'they'll get taken away'" (Hess 32). Mann hesitated over the release of her book *Immediate Family* precisely because of her fears that children wind up paying for adult fantasy. The *Wall Street Journal*'s reprint of a nude photograph of her little girl with bars across her nipples, genitals, and eyes brought home to the child-model the effects of social disapproval. Said Mann: "'She wouldn't let me photograph her naked for a period of time. . . . That alarmed me, that they could have such power over my child who for six years I had taught to be free and comfortable with her body'" ("Child World" 106). Much more power than her parents, it seems.

But then the current trend is to hold parents legally accountable for their children's crimes. Your child skips school—you can be fined in Arkansas. Your child joins a gang—California might throw *you* in jail. Let us hope you are not on welfare because according to Wisconsin's 1988 Learnfare law, you can lose your payments when your child misses school. More and more states are passing statutes that will make parents responsible for a host of infractions committed by their offspring. The motivation for such laws seems to be that drug use, gang involvement, and adolescent crime (this must be what they're doing when they miss school) will all be diminished if parents have a stake in their children's activities. It need hardly be pointed out that the target of such statutes is for the most part the underclass. Instead of locating responsibility in the class inequities and diverse forms of symbolic violence that structure and sustain the underclass as such, we look to the symptom—the family, where the dejected pulses of a fraught society play randomly. In a self-evident displacement, we pretend that the parents can resolve the social problem children. More interesting still is to hold the parent-blame laws alongside the stories of inveigling children into reporting their parents to authorities. In one narrative the parent is responsible for buttressing civilization in the face of its dissolution; in the other, it is the child who is exalted as hero, bearing the chalice of the dregs of cocaine to the altar of civilization—or the principal's desk.

Note

1. Fortunately, through the agency of the Simses' attorney, the children were restored to their parents the following day.

1

The Child of Psychoanalysis, Part 1

The pejorative use of the word "infantile" betrays the
ambivalence to children of those who are no longer children.
—Paula Heimann, *About Children and Children No-Longer*

Psychoanalysis is the story of the adult's relationship with an
internalized, repudiated, but nevertheless ceaselessly desired child—
not the actual child the adult has been, but rather the "dead" child
mourned by a present-tense self which is constituted on the past this
child at once represents and withholds. In analytic theory, this story
gets worked out through competing schools of thought. In their chronic indeterminacy over where to locate this child, in the reconstructions
of an adult analysand or in the actual child, these schools produce as
theory their respective fantasies about this unknowable subject, unknowable because the child is the ultimate blind spot of the psychoanalytic project of the nineteenth and twentieth centuries.

Despite the centrality of the child to psychoanalytic theory, to date
there has been no extended analysis of the theoretical debates that
proliferate around this child-subject in the effort to codify both the
child's lived experience as well as its future term (in the adult
analysand). Nor has there been an examination of the ways in which
these accounts of the child subserve doctrinal agendas. Such over-
sights in the literature ensue from a general failure on the part of
the psychoanalytic enterprise to account for its own unconscious. As
long as psychoanalysis submits to its unconscious fantasy of the child
as both the origin and guarantor of desire, it will continue to validate its fictions as stories of real life. And, as long as psychoanalysis
hoards its darkest secrets in the mute child-subject, it is fated to repeat its distortions in the form of a lived agenda for living human
subjects, both adults and children.

At the turn of the century, Ellen Key predicted that the twentieth
century would be "the century of the child." Psychoanalysis is the

discourse of this investment in the child. Yet, in many ways, psychoanalytic descriptions of the child are no more *about* the child than are pre-eighteenth-century pictorial representations of children as miniature adults.[1] If the child has gained a central position as subject, it remains nevertheless a highly mythologized object of an adult need to establish origins, both psychological and social. Centered as it is on the attempt to understand the child in the adult, as well as to project the future adult term through the child, psychoanalysis has become most patently the discourse that is only and always an explication of its raison d'être, the relationship between the adult and the child, the conscious and the unconscious. The subject of the fondest hopes of psychoanalysis, the child is also the term that destabilizes psychoanalytic topographic and temporal premises. At the same time that psychoanalysis defines (and captures) the child, its efforts are undermined repeatedly by the failure to locate childhood in relation to an adult subject. The increasing scientization in the sector of infant psychoanalysis (in the form of elaborate technologizations of infant observation) suggests a desperation to maintain as separate and tangible the very child that both forges and subverts psychoanalytic assumptions.

The following exploration of the position of the child in psychoanalysis asks why these various psychoanalytic accounts of the child believe what they do and to what extent they express unconscious desires through a child infinitely conformable to adult expectations. I am not attempting simply to invalidate these theories of the origin of the human subject. Instead, through a close analysis of the discourse of competing psychoanalytic positions, I interrogate what is at stake that is left unspoken, as well as what assumptions precede and produce these representations of the child of psychoanalysis.

As I show in subsequent chapters, the child of imaginative literature overtly foregrounds the child's emissarial role as well as its ultimate failure in this capacity. This go-between child, in contradistinction to the voluntary pimp, is the only subject who does not profit from its own services. In fact, by serving up its own body on the altar of adult desire, the child is simultaneously pimp and prostitute. Although the child is compelled to act as the agent that binds disparate sexes, classes—even the split subject itself—the false coherences it helps to sustain cannot thrive in the face of the child's continued existence. The child upon whom all depend for a happy and harmonious resolution is fated to be vilified (by other characters, or the texts themselves) for its inability to cement the relationships, make coherent the irreparably fragmented. The child hence figures as a remainder excluded by a fraudulent economy that has used it for its own gain. The fantasied child that veils the incompatibilities and the impasses, this child that restores to the social and sexual landscape a prelapsarian intoxication, is supplanted in the very moment of its accomplishment by the actual child who threatens to live on as the reminiscence of that which it formerly elided. The deception of the child of psychoanalysis, on the other hand, is that it is never annihilated altogether because, with the rejection of each theorized child always comes another child to take its place, to promote a theory, to serve an agenda it is the child's mission to displace with the ingenuous appeal of the ostensibly neutral subject who is inviolate, newborn, as it were, in the field of truth.

The Subject of Psychoanalysis: The Adult or the Child

Misguidedly, but from concern, we try to make sense of this
non-sense by either reconstructing the *facts* of infancy
(Winnicott) or its *fantasies* (Klein).
—M. Masud R. Khan, *Hidden Selves*

In the history of psychoanalysis, it is generally understood that Freud concentrated on adults and that he was not interested in children, who were incapable of fulfilling the "fundamental rule" in psychoanalysis to free associate. Freud explained that he preferred adult reconstructions of infancy because "too many words and thoughts have to be lent to the child" (*SE* 17:8–9). The problem with the child, of course, is that the child fulfills more nearly the rule than the rule would like. In short, the injunction to free associate refers to an adult analysand who will inevitably resist doing just that; it is only in opposition to an adult hesitancy that the "freedom" flourishes. It is a freedom that has tasted restraints.

Such works as *From the History of an Infantile Neurosis* have led scholars to conclude that Freud had no particular interest in the child. Even in the case of Little Hans, Freud worked via the child's father, Max Graf, who was himself in analysis with Freud. Freud addressed the child only through the adult—literally and figuratively. Nevertheless, if we think about it, even for a moment, Freud never really theorized any subject *but* the child. In Freud's era, as in ours, the initial response to Freud's theories of sexuality is: how can he impugn the sexual innocence of the child? And next, as if by way of proof, the critic notes: I never felt that way about my parents. This is the horror attendant upon the theory of infantile sexuality, its capacity to cause an adult audience to regress. This is the lure as well. It is telling that the response always slips from the third person to the first, along the lines of the young child's installation into an identity, a name, learning who he or she is second hand, as it were, through being named. The third person is the first role we play. The personal pronoun is inhabited later. Here we have in the adult reader an instant regression to the moment of the construction of identity, a regression prompted by the issue of infant sexuality.

The homology points to the connection between infantile sexuality and human identity. It is the inextricable relationship between identity and the emergence of a subject who is sexed that continues to provoke resistance in readers of Freud, both lay and professional. The pivotal child's question—"Where do babies come from?"—is the point at which these two trends intersect. Where do babies come from means, in the language of pronouns, "Where do I come from," another variation on the movement from the third to the first person. The question couched in terms of babies seems only about sex; the childish query always has been read as a code for an inchoate idea of adult sexual relations, triggered by the sight of the mother's pregnancy, or the family dog's, as the case may be. The question "Where do I come from?" is only about the self-conscious subject, its existence, its origins in nonexistence, a child coming to terms with being and nonbeing. But children never ask that question directly. Prelatency, they ask about babies, other babies, never themselves. During latency, they narrate their necessity in the form of the family romance as an *answer* to "Where do I come from?"[2]

Contemporary psychoanalysis is increasingly drifting away from the sexual materials that are the cornerstone of Freudian psychoanalysis. Again and again, the "sex thing" is the problem. Jung and Freud separated over the issue of the libido—or was it really the question of who wanted to be father, to "father" a discipline?[3] Isn't the contest between father and son in the primal horde finally one about their role vis-à-vis the mother? Isn't this a conflict in the name of identity as much as it is one about sex with the mother? (She makes you a king—look at Oedipus, father of his people, a demigod.) As the psychoanalytic subject progressively is de-erotized, so is the fantasy of a self who is self-identical converted into scientific fact. Stressing the ego at the expense of the unconscious is the overriding agenda of American ego psychology at the same time that the subject of sexuality is neutralized. Ego psychology's emphasis on the "conflict-free" sphere of the ego leads to a psychoanalysis that winds up elaborating a libido-free subject. Entrenching their theories as they do in the growth of the organism, the conflicts generated in the Freudian subject of sexuality frequently are marginalized if not discounted altogether. Kohutian self psychology is the final reversal of everything Freudian in psychoanalysis. *The Restoration of the Self* is Heinz Kohut's title for the book that was to mark in no uncertain terms his break from the disintegrative perils of the sexual and aggressive drives of Freudian theory. Kohutians tell their patients that sexual fantasies are merely erotizations of nonsexual materials. Sexual fantasies, they claim, are about the need for a coherent self.[4]

So why, then, is it that as the sexual content of Freudian thought is increasingly suppressed, the fantasy of an undivided self is advanced as real? What is the connection, and is it possible that the child itself is the linchpin of these theoretical nexuses and divergences? To what extent might the child disguise the theoretical dilemmas, stand in for a latent dialogue that never gets spoken?

It is critical to reassess the truth of that general understanding about Freud, which is that he theorized about adults, that for Freud, the site of psychoanalysis was the adult analysand. Certainly, the adult was the subject of psychoanalysis insofar as Freud treated adult patients. Yet one might argue that the real subject—always, only, inevitably—is the child. Freud insisted that a full-fledged analysis must address the infantile element. His abundance of archaeological analogies, his dream analyses, his insistence that the first event of a trauma must occur before six years of age—all point to the fact that Freud's theory was founded on the earliest years of life. It was not his emphasis on sexuality per se that caused widespread opprobrium; after all, Charcot matter-of-factly had remarked that in cases of hysteria "'c'est toujours la chose génitale, toujours . . . toujours . . . toujours'" ("'it's always a question of the genitals, always . . . always . . . always'") (*SE* 14:14). Moreover, sexologists like Kraft-Ebbing were already being widely read. It was instead the child "thing" that made Freud different and notorious, the child thing both in terms of the founding of a sexuality and the founding of a split subject, in which the unknown is privileged over the known. If heterosexuality fashions itself out of the swamp of polymorphously perverse desires, subjectivity as well is a sleight of hand, a card trick, a temple resting on an abyss, to alter Tertullian.

While the subject of psychoanalysis may be the adult, its object is the child. "Any psychotherapist," Michael Balint maintains, "must always be aware that he will have to deal—in one way or another—with 'the child in his patient'" (*Basic Fault* 90). Out of this discrepancy, this decentering, as it were, of the site of psychoanalytic inquiry, springs the self-narrative of psychoanalysis, constructed according to the self-perpetuating and self-justifying logic of all fantasies. Its primary aim is to maintain the fantasy, just as among the goals of the dream, as fundamental even as wish-fulfillment, is to keep the dreamer asleep.[5]

Even though the child is the central object (on diverse levels) of the psychoanalytic project, psychoanalysis nevertheless goes to extreme lengths to demarcate the realm of the child from that of the adult. Yet the child is the term that calls into question each categorical effort. The child itself is a category that eclipses its own boundaries through its remorseless trespasses into adult terrain. While a faith in the age-appropriate reliability of developmental stages characterizes much of psychoanalytic thinking to date, Melanie Klein offers in place of such positivistic straightjackets her notion of "positions," which emerge in infancy and remain spatial options throughout our lives, changing over the course of time but nevertheless insisting on an irrevocable connection with the infantile. The carefully plotted route of the developmental narrative through oral, anal, genital stages into the "adult" coherence of reproductive genitality is a road on a map from another planet. To argue that the emergence of, say, orality in the adult sexual relation is a perverse token of infantile erotism is to subscribe to the delusion that the body of the "normal" adult shares no points of correspondence with that of the infant. To suggest that children do not inspire erotic feelings in sexually normal adults is to pretend that only perverse adults could find Nabokov's characterization of Lolita sexually arousing or that both textual and reader fantasies of Maisie marrying Sir Claude are set in the distant future of Maisie's adulthood when such a relationship will no longer violate the moral vision of Mrs. Wix's straighteners (the very Mrs. Wix who plots their alliance!). If we adults tend to impose our own sexuality on the child, paradoxically we deny that our sexuality is in any way mobilized (seduced) by the body of the child we invest with our own libido. James Kincaid points to the current national obsession with child molestation as the defense par excellence against what is in fact our culturewide erotization of the child; the pedophile is always someone else. We should consider as well the figure of the pedophile as a device whereby diverse kinds of "misuse" (rhetorically reconfigured as *abuse*) are projected onto a single malignant force. This thief of childhood, this sickest of all deviants who wrests from our children their innocence, is no other than the allegorical type to whom is reducible the pervasive sense of attack.

The Subject of Psychoanalysis: Reconstructed or Observed

He who is both analyst and educator must never forget that the aim of child-analysis is character-analysis—in other words, education.
—H. Von Hug-Hellmuth, "On the Technique of Child-Analysis"

You had to know everything and suddenly what you knew became something else.
—Henry Roth, *Call It Sleep*

In psychoanalytic speculations on the child the ambivalence surrounding the relationship of the child to the adult, the extent to which these domains impinge on one another, leads to the distinction between the reconstructed and observed "child." In theorizing the structure of the human psyche, we run into conflicts that erupt from what seem to be fundamentally antagonistic lexicons[6] of the human being, fantasies of selfhood that are converted into theories validating the origins of one's own self-construction. Hence, a debate emerges around the optimal child-subject of psychoanalysis—the clinical child or the observed child, as Daniel Stern distinguishes them; the psychoanalytic child or the child under observation, according to Jean Laplanche's taxonomy. The clinical or psychoanalytic child is the "child" reconstructed in therapy by an adult analysand and an analyst. Such distinctions mask the more critical unspoken confusion about the temporal and spatial location of childhood.

Certain analytic theories are solely reconstructive, based on the past child reintroduced into the analytic scene (cultivated, in a sense, *for* the analytic scene) by virtue of the regression of the adult subject. This reconstructive enterprise in psychoanalysis entails not only the individual reconstruction of the adult analysand's past; such reconstructions are elicited by the analyst in the context of overarching theoretical paradigms (those derived from personal observation of a number of subjects as well as the "textbook" variety provided by the analyst's own theoretical grid).[7] Thus, developmental models of childhood both derive from and contextualize individual histories. Edward Glover has called this strategy of reconstruction "an oblique reflection from a distorting mirror," meaning that not only are we dependent for the "real" childhood phases on historicized recapitulations but the recapitulations are achieved through "a study of abnormal states," neurotic (or more severely impaired) adult subjects (*Early Development* 5).

Melanie Klein and Margaret Mahler have drawn upon adult experiences (e.g., mourning) and the vocabulary of mental illness (e.g., autism) to describe states of infancy. Emmanuel Peterfreund criticizes such labels as "adultomorphizations" and "pathomorphizations" of infancy.[8] Nevertheless, implicit in his critique is his fantasy that there is a "real" child accessible to adult observation, a child who is undistorted, directly received. By way of example, he suggests that

> the infant's nursing behaviour indicates that some rudimentary distinctions are being made which, when more fully developed, will eventually be classified by adults and called "inside" and "outside" as well as "animate" and "inanimate." It is reasonable to suggest that such rudimentary distinctions, based on elementary classifying systems, are active at birth, built into the organism as a result of evolutionary development, and transmitted by the genetic code. When one observes a nursing infant it is difficult to accept the idea that in the human young the instinct of self-preservation is atrophied.[9] (433)

His rhetoric betrays the truth-claims of his argument, indicates the extent to which it is yet another construction premised on the perspective of the inquiring adult. Superficially, his logic is flawlessly "reasonable," but certain assumptions subtend his "reasonable" presentation of what is transparently (nonsubjectively) available to the adult observer of the infant. "It is reasonable to suggest," he tells us, but according to whom and based on what? Peterfreund's explanation of the infant's "rudimentary distinctions" are derived from his own and others' direct observations; but the deception lies in the very word *observations* that connotes an objectivity denied to the "reconstructionists." His use of the term *rudimentary* conveys with it psychoanalysis's long history of the primitivization of infancy that Freud inaugurated. "Rudimentary" can be understood only in light of the logic of progressive development; "rudimentary" is the adult's way of portraying the child as imperfect in relation to the accomplishment of adulthood. In fact, observationists emphasize that adults lack certain capacities possessed by infants, certain physiological responses, such as the Moro reflex. Yet, because of the child's status vis-à-vis an adult self-conception of developmental superiority (culled from a *discourse* of developmental paradigms that are inextricably bound to the illusion of perfectibility), those characteristics possessed by the child that never become integrated into an adult system are classified as superfluous anachronisms, primitive detritus from a prehistoric epoch.

Peterfreund needs to do more than condemn the approach of the adultomorphizers and pathomorphizers; he needs to argue in favor of an actual biological infant whose world is more directly accessible than Glover's "oblique reflection from a distorting mirror." To justify his critique that Margaret Mahler's approach is a gross distortion, Peterfreund needs to present an alternative that transcends distortion. In short, he has exchanged what he dismisses as a fantasmatic construction of the child for his own fantasy of a sphere unmediated by fantasy.

At the same time, it is worth asking why terms derived from adult experience and pathology would be imposed on the child, as Kleinians and Mahlerians have done. Although the strategy emerges from the conviction that adult illnesses have their roots in typical childhood phases, the result, oddly, inverts the received chronology, makes the child's phases appear to derive from the adult. This confusion that dismantles the chronology in its very elaboration reproduces a central question of psychoanalysis: to what extent does the child's development ensue from (repeat, distort, speak to in some way) adult conflicts?[10] In other words, although it may seem unreasonable to submit the child's experience to the language of adult disturbance, we should not ignore the influence of both manifest and covert adult behavior on the child who is at all times quite literally subjected to parental impressions. The child analyst, Maud Mannoni, goes so far as to represent the child as solely a symptom of repressed parental imperatives. While one could accuse her of overemphasizing the role of adult fantasy in the production of the child, her own theoretical subjection of the child to the adult reflects the impossibility of separating child and adult terms. For example, Mannoni represents her parents as victims of their own infantile fantasies and traumata. Thus, if there seem to be only adults in her narrative, it could be argued equally that there seem to be only children.

Daniel Stern, the foremost American exponent of psychoanalytically informed infant observation, discusses the observed infant as though it is accessible to a scientific gaze uninfluenced by the unreliable realm of adult "creation." He contrasts the observed infant with the "recreated infant [who] is made up of memories, present reenactments in the transference, and theoretically guided interpretations" (14). This recreated infant is offered to us as the sum total of the analysand's fantasies and the analyst's theories, in contradistinction to the observed infant "whose behavior is examined at the very time of its occurrence," as though the "very time" overcomes the potential temporal distortions between the adult and the recollected child (14). In the tradition of René Spitz, Sylvia Brody, and Sibylle Escalona, Stern has attempted to yoke the developmental cognitive psychology of Piaget with the developmental insights of psychoanalysis. As Jean Laplanche points out, however, "Psychoanalytic concepts have to be debased if they are to apply to the actual infant who is under observation. It is simply not the case that one alternative is preferable to the other; they make each other worse" (*New Foundations* 65). Psychoanalysis is primarily about the machinations of the fantasy-producing unconscious whose psychical reality is not only privileged over material reality but also automatically throws into question any attempt to delineate the material from the psychical. The very conception of psychical reality, rather than simply defining a new arena of inquiry, dismantles all former relationships between the human subject and her or his "reality." Any attempt by the psychoanalyst to introduce observational data into psychoanalytic theory in an effort to "contain" the reconstructive insights with what has been witnessed empirically not only rigidifies the position of reality in psychoanalysis but undermines insidiously the reality-claims of the observationists.[11]

Anna Freud, despite her confidence in the insights of the latency-age child, asserts that the preverbal child is inaccessible to psychoanalytic inquiry:

> So far as I am concerned, the study of this darkest of all ages has never been my predilection. I have preferred always as my subject those phases of development where assumptions can be checked against verbalized material recaptured from the unconscious by the analytic method, or against facts which are open to view in the direct observation of infants. Whenever we break through the barrier which divides articulate life from the preverbal period, we find ourselves on uncertain ground, left with conjectures, reconstructions and interpretations which, of necessity, have to remain unconfirmed by the individual with whom they are concerned. In no other realm of psychoanalysis does speculation need to run quite as free, as far, and as wild. (Kris, "Problems of Infantile Neurosis" 25)

By establishing a division between the unavailable "darkest of all ages" and that which can be "confirmed" by the verbal analytic subject, Anna Freud ignores the indeterminate nature of all analytic confirmations, an indeterminacy Sigmund Freud emphasized in "Constructions in Analysis."[12] Her representation of the difference between the preverbal and verbal as "wild speculation" versus that which "can be checked," and "uncertain ground" versus the tangibility of that which can be "recaptured," leaves one with the sense that this inaccessible preverbal epoch can be cordoned off from analytic inquiry insofar as the "real" infant is concerned. This "real" infant, shrouded in darkness, can only be "recaptured" at a later date, through the vehicle of the speaking patient, who then functions as an articulate representative of a prearticulate past. In fact, Anna Freud intimates that psychoanalysis breaks down in the face of an actual infant—at least such is her fear—that the uncertainty of the ground underscores the potential for conjecture, for speculation. Her divisions, then, establish a distinction between the realm of conjecture, wild speculation, and that of the verifiable. The division itself is the fantasy that defends her against the intrusion of the darkness (the arena of instability and the unconfirmed) emblematized and beckoned by the infant experience. What the adult or the older child "recaptures" via regression—this verbalization of the preverbal—is somehow transmogrified in the analytic process into the substantive, the nonspeculative, the truth.[13] Thus, whereas for Stern the distortions emerge in the reconstructive space, for Anna Freud the infant itself figures as the worrisome divergence from verifiable truth, the inhabitant of the darkest of all ages who threatens to mystify as well the otherwise rational gaze of adult inquiry.

Nevertheless, Anna Freud insists that the child is the real object of psychoanalysis. "Some of the doubts and uncertainties governing the field," she writes, "were dispelled with the introduction of the analysis of children. Psychoanalysis moved a step nearer to providing what it had set out to provide from the beginning: a service of child experts" (*Normality* 9).[14] Unlike the preverbal child, the verbal child *enlightens* the field instead of obscuring it further. The hope is that the latency-age child will clarify once and for all the hypotheses derived from adult analyses. She goes on to report that "child analysts . . . offer . . . welcome confirmations of analytic assumptions, as they had been expected to do from the outset" (*Normality* 10). So, whereas the infant destabilizes psychoanalytic assumptions, simply because the infant so clearly must be *spoken for,* which invites one to *say anything,* the verbal child obediently confirms adult assumptions, which is hardly a surprise since this is to tell us no more than what every parent knows: the child, even the delinquent child, tends to fulfill parental desire, whether that desire be conscious or unconscious.[15] This sounds as though her true subject is the child, a position she further underscores when she offers as the goal of psychoanalysis the provision of "a service of child experts." Yet, in case we be misled, it is important to understand *why* Anna Freud concentrated on the child, what she wanted from it, and what she intended by this highly ambiguous "service of child experts." In short, what would be the point of a service of child experts? Whom, in the end, would they be serving?

As Anna Freud freely admits, "In many cases the child itself is not the sufferer . . . only the persons round it suffer from its symptoms or outbreaks of naughtiness" (*Psycho-Analytical Treatment* 5). Thus, the child experts serve the child, in the sense that they make the child a more tolerable family member; but, of course, it is the rest of the family who reap the rewards. The child itself very well might not be suffering. Is the treatment, then, *for* the child? Well, perhaps, if one thinks of the child as an adult in the making, the child's future is being provided for. In support of child analysis, Melanie Klein remarks: "The analysis of adults proclaims its value by removing difficulties which interfere with the patient's life. . . . In child analysis we are preventing the occurrence of difficulties of the same kind or even of psychoses" (*Psycho-Analysis of Children* 121). Child analysis, therefore, at least as conceived by both Anna Freud and Melanie Klein, the two major purveyors of child analytic technique and theory, is really always about serving the adult, whether it be the future adulthood of the child-subject or the adults who suffer as a result of their child's misbehavior.[16] This is not to say that these two analysts intentionally overlooked the needs of the child in favor of either the real adult parties or some hypothetical future adult; rather, I am arguing that because of the fundamental impossibility of analyzing the child qua child, unobscured by adult criteria, from the first their theories were fated to reflect, in the form of certain discursive distortions, the structure of their defenses. Thus, if their primary enterprise involves the elaboration of a representable child-subject, just what the child *cannot* be for them emerges in light of their resistance to that which does not, on some level, serve the adult.

The inability of psychoanalysis to locate its child-subject (reconstructed or actual) as well as the failure to differentiate between the needs of the adult and the needs of the child, in conjunction with denying the insinuation of such complexities into the imperturbable structure of their theories, give rise to a fantasmatic position of the child of psychoanalysis. It is not psychoanalysis alone that serves the family under the guise of serving the child; it is the child as well (in the name of its own illness) who is appropriated to serve adult needs. These disjunctions, between the mental health of an adult subject and the developmental navigations of the child, between the pathology of the family and the pathology of the child, are elided in the production of a theoretical go-between whose actual function is to preempt the questions arising from its own ambiguous status. It is the go-between path itself, between a manifest commitment to "cure" a child (real or reconstructed) and a latent compulsion to serve adult exigencies (including those of psychoanalytic ideologues) that the fantasmatic child is compelled to camouflage in the process of its mapping.

Anna Freud offers an alternative approach to preventive psychoanalysis—the "psychoanalytic education" of parents (*Normality* 4). Her notion is that if parents are inculcated with analytic tenets, patterns of childrearing might be restructured. While Freud's instructional schedule for parents includes the avoidance of seductive behavior, relaxation of moral strictness—standards that *seem* reasonable enough—this is nevertheless a subtle form of what Jacques Donzelot calls "policing the family." Indeed, one cannot help but ask once again *who* is the subject of her theories—the adult or the child? Although the modification of adult behavior ostensibly is intended to reduce the stresses on the child, the adult is being monitored as well. For example, cautioning the parents not to engage in sex in front of their children is an immediate circumscription of adult sexuality, a restriction placed on the spaces in which sexuality may appear, as though subsequent to the sexual production of the child, potentially nonproductive sexuality must be redefined, reassigned to an extra-child sphere, whereby the act and its product are utterly dissociated.

As for therapeutic treatment of neurotic children, Klein predicts that "a great number of those people who later end up in prisons or lunatic asylums, or who go completely to pieces, would be saved from such a fate and be able to develop a normal life" (*Psycho-Analysis of Children* 374). A society scoured clean of the socially dehiscent elements of the criminal and the insane, a society otherwise going "completely to pieces" is also the agenda of other theorists of the child. Maud Mannoni has attacked this reforming impulse as being antagonistic to true psychoanalytic tenets. She suggests that some analysts, particularly American analysts, slip into the arena of social welfare (*Backward Child*). René Spitz hysterically founds his theory of infant caretaking upon the threat that "disturbed object relations in the first year of life, be they deviant, improper, or insufficient, have consequences which imperil the very foundation of society" (*First Year* 300), and Selma Fraiberg warns us that "these bondless men, women, and children constitute one of the largest aberrant populations in the world today, contributing far beyond their numbers to social disease and disorder" (25). More than a fantasy of perfectibility is being voiced here. Society is seen as endangered and these dangers are traced to the child's "deviance" from the proper developmental path. It is the desire to constitute the proper as such that drives both theories of universal childhood phases and universally applicable strategies of childrearing. If childhood often is figured as the "foundation" of society, then society must protect itself through vigilant supervision of that foundation that imperils *the* foundation, any foundation. Thus is "founded" a science of the proper path, an a priori correction of a priori criminal deviance. The route to the correction of the child is through the adult caretaker, and it must be through the home, the family, that the psychological professionals monitor a social future. As Hermine von Hug-Hellmuth, the first specialist in child-analysis, observed, "If the parents themselves were analysed, in all probability fewer children would be in need of analysis" (305).

Jacques Donzelot traces the strategic emergence of child psychiatry to "the need to find a base, a ground in which to root all the anomalies and pathologies of the adult, in the form of a presynthesis; to designate a possible object of intervention for a practice that no longer wanted to limit itself to the management of confined individuals, but sought to preside over the whole social enclosure" (131). The fantasy of this "base," real(ized) in the figure of the child, is the justification not only for treating the child prophylactically but for treating the child in the adult as well. As Donzelot indicates, the child is exploited as a pretext for invading and "presid[ing]" over the family. In fact, the child functions explicitly as a go-between in the service of the "psy" professions, as Donzelot calls them, giving them access to the family through the socially promulgated and sanctioned value of protecting the child. The child plays the double-agent who emblematizes family discord while it functions as origin (of social unrest) and product (of familial breakdowns). The child transgresses the nuclear shell of the failing family as an excrescence that marks the inadequacy of that shell to contain its tortured contents. The child figures the breakdown of the nuclear family to the extent that it registers its inability to remain nuclear; at the same time, the "psy" professionals count on the child as their only route into the otherwise self-enclosed isolationist family.

Notes

1. See Philippe Ariès's *Centuries of Childhood.*
2. The family romance, as defined by Freud, is the child's fantasy that she or he is someone else's child—often the lost or kidnapped heir of royalty. See "Family Romances."

3. In *Dire Mastery*, François Roustang addresses the father/son and sibling rivalries that characterize the politics of psychoanalysis.

4. See especially Kohut's *How Does Analysis Cure?* for his in-depth repudiation of Freudian drive theory.

5. In *The Interpretation of Dreams*, Freud writes: "Dreams are the GUARDIANS of sleep and not its disturbers" (*SE* 4:233). J.-B. Pontalis, in *Frontiers of Psychoanalysis*, distinguishes the opposition between the sleeping and dreaming functions of the dream: "Thus it would appear that the dream strives for permanence, for a suspension of the wish, and not for the achievment of satisfaction; in this case, the object of the wish would be the *wish itself*, whereas the object of the wish to sleep is the absolute, the zero level of appeasment" (36).

6. I use the word *lexicon* to indicate that these theoretical divergences are in evidence at the level of the very language employed. Does one say "patient" or "analysand" or "subject"? Primarily, we are dealing with the differences between humanist, structuralist, and poststructuralist discourses. These diverse discourses, however, reflect worldviews.

7. Donald Spence argues that these narrative paradigms control the nature of what the analysand offers and what the analyst hears.

8. Peterfreund particularly attacks Mahler's concepts of an undifferentiated infant, which he criticizes as an adult perspective. He rejects as well her theorization of "normal autism" and "normal symbiosis" in the infant, which are premised on adult pathology. See Mahler's *On Human Symbiosis and the Vicissitudes of Individuation*. See also Fred Pine's attempts to defend Mahler's approach from the charges leveled by Peterfreund (46–53). Jeanne Lampl-De Groot was among the first critics of the Kleinian strategy of "transposing backwards" superego development as well as pathomorphizing childhood experience. Interestingly, Lampl-De Groot repeatedly founds her objections on what she perceives as "confusing the rudiments or part of a thing with the completed whole" (416). Like Peterfreund, she perceives the child as an adult work-in-progress. In fact, the tendency to adultomorphize and pathomorphize originated with Freud, whose sexual theories of childhood are founded upon just such transpositions.

9. Infant observation plays an increasingly central role in current psychoanalytic theories of the child. The observationist trend in the United States is indebted to ego psychology for its particular psychoanalytic premises. This makes some sense in light of ego psychology's stress on the adaptiveness of the human subject.

10. This issue is particularly highlighted in reference to the mother/child relationship, but it is further argued that the child acts out the parental conflicts, those that inhere in the individual parent her/himself as well as the familial conflicts. See, for example, Therese Benedek's argument that "the parent meets in each child in a particular way the projections of his own conflicts" ("Parenthood" 405) as well as Walter Davis's treatment of the role of the child in revealing otherwise suppressed familial disturbances (243).

11. It is important here to distinguish between direct observation of infants and analyses (as well as observations) of articulate children. While child-analyses have been carried out for many decades, the "scientization" of infant observation is more recent. For many years, psychoanalysts informally observed their own and others' children. Later, D. W. Winnicott used observations gleaned from his pediatric practice to inform his theories. At the same time, more "scientific" psychoanalytic observational studies of the infant were being carried out by René Spitz, Sybille Escalona, Sylvia Brody, and Peter Wolff; it is this scientific group that has given rise to the current infant observationists who are increasingly dedicated to the use of extensive technical apparatuses in laboratory environments. Daniel Stern in the United States and Colwyn Trevarthen and Lynne Murray in Britain are major figures associated with this technologized quasi-cognitive/behaviorist trend. Certainly, the study of the infant is problematic because these theorists swing between an overtechnologization of the infant-object and the projection onto the infant of an adult subjectivity with adult-level affect. Even in the case of direct observation of and active engagement with a speaking child in an extra-analytic milieu, the problem remains of observer distortions and/or interventions. As Albert J. Solnit (himself a proponent of direct observation) has pointed out: "For example, much of the data about patterns of close mother-child interaction can be obtained only in action research—research carried out while the observer is supplying a needed intervention as a trusted, helping person. The field of observation is contaminated further by the care, guidance, and support provided by the participant observer, but the data gathered usually are not available to an outsider, a nonparticipant observer" (5).

Finally, it is important to make clear that I am only discussing the psychoanalytic treatment of the child. Certainly, observational studies of children have been the focus of psychology for many years. In light of the influence that behavioral and cognitive theories have had on psychoanalytic approaches to childhood, however, it is at times difficult to demarcate entirely the perspectives.

12. See chapter 4 of Stanley Leavy's *The Psychoanalytic Dialogue* for an illuminating discussion of the role played by confirmations in psychoanalysis. Leavy argues that "it is irrelevant to psychoanalysis whether the recovered past is grounded in an objectively recognizable event or not. Paradoxical as it may seem, the only sure reality of the memory of the past is fantasy" (103). Donald Spence addresses at length the distinction between constructions and reconstructions in analysis: "So long as the analyst devoted himself to *uncovering* or *reconstructing* what had happened in the patient's early life, he could not be accused of influencing the treatment with his own fantasies and preconceptions. The word *reconstruction* suggested authenticity, making contact with what had actually happened; the word *construction,* on the other hand, carried implications of creating something new and opened the door to influence and sugges-

tion" (176). Elsewhere, Spence explains that "the difference between narrative and historical truth parallels the difference between *construction* and *reconstruction* in the interpretive process" (165). Ernst Kris and Harold P. Blum, on the other hand, have written that Freud used "constructions" and "reconstructions" interchangeably. See Kris, "The Recovery of Childhood Memories in Psychoanalysis" (65), and Blum, "The Value of Reconstruction in Adult Psychoanalysis" (39).

13. In fact, Anna Freud herself treated predominantly latency-age children (although, through the Hampstead Nursery and other "half-way" facilities for children orphaned during World War II, she saw a number of very young children as well); in contrast to Melanie Klein, she believed that prelatency age children were nonanalyzable because they could not form a transference.

14. In her 1921 landmark publication on child-analysis, Hermine Von Hug-Hellmuth referred to "analyst-educators," thereby emphasizing the prescriptive component of treating children.

15. Alice Miller, importing Winnicott's concept of the "true" and "false" selves, argues that children construct "false" selves in order to conform to adult needs.

16. In the case of Anna Freud, it is important to note that often she considered the parents the enemy against whom she waged war in the battle for the child's welfare. She makes it clear, however, that it is not really for the sake of the child that she confronts its family. Rather, she needs to enforce her own program of what the child should *be*. Indeed, these children often seem to function for her as go-betweens between the tyranny of the family and her own correct(ive) values. Winnicott as well congratulates himself on his stealth in appropriating the child from the mother: "I managed to get the mother to believe in me while I actually got in between her and her daughter" (*Paediatrics* 94). We need to remember such comments when considering the influence of Winnicott on theories of mothering and mothers—especially their usefulness for a feminist agenda.

The use of *in vitro* fertilization has given rise to diverse questions related to but nevertheless differentiated from abortion. In brief, *in vitro* fertilization is a process whereby the sperm fertilizes the ovum in a test tube. The transfer of this pre-embryo to the woman's uterus occurs at the four- to eight-cell stage of development. Because so many transfers need to be made before the woman is impregnated successfully, a process of freezing the pre-embryos, cryopreservation, has been developed to spare the woman repeated and painful surgeries. It is specifically the status of this cryopreserved "subject" that has come under scrutiny.

For example, when one couple divorced before a successful pregnancy was achieved, there ensued a virtual custody battle over the frozen pre-embryos. The woman in this case wanted the opportunity to make use of the pre-embryos while her ex-husband argued that this would violate his procreative right *not to* father children. The Tennessee Circuit Court held that because "human life begins at the moment of conception" it is in the "manifest best interests of the children in vitro, that they be available for implantation," thus granting custody to the woman for future implantation (Langley 1221).[1] The court went on to complain that "allowing the cryopreserved embryos to remain frozen for a period of more than two years was 'tantamount to the destruction of these human beings'" (Langley 1221). As one critic observes, the court "ignored the Tennessee criminal abortion statute which recognizes no legal status of a fetus during the first three months of the mother's pregnancy" (Langley 1221). A Louisiana statute bearing on the issue of human embryos argues that "disputes between parties should be resolved in the 'best interest' of the embryo" (qtd. in *Davis v. Davis* 590n). Elsewhere, a pretrial decision in a contest between the gamete donors and the fertilization facility characterized pre-embryos as the "property" of the donors and allowed the case to go forward as a contract dispute. Certainly this tension between the child as parental property and the sentimentalization of the child's personal rights is nothing new. In fact, here we find postindustrial strategies of sentimentalizing the child directly confronting the underlying conviction of parental property rights. The fact that these warring representations are being validated juridically only serves to show how irreconcilable these subject positions (child vs. adult) remain in our postsentimental era of late capitalism when such incompatible values emerge discretely yet in concert in every Western nuclear family. Furthermore, to believe in the child as one's own product is in direct conflict with the state's investment in protecting the rights of its citizens. One might go so far as to argue that, at their root, such battles are not over whether the child is property—but rather *who owns* this property, the parents or the state. It seems as though the state's sentimentalization of the rights of the pre-embryonic "juridical person" is a dissimulating tactic whereby the predations of capital's frame of reference are groomed tastefully in the discourse of fundamental rights. Thus the establishment of the "foundation" of the subject is increasingly critical if one needs to know whose rights might be appropriated and when—certainly if the "when" *is* the "who." From this perspective, the preamble to the Missouri abortion statute that proclaims "unborn children have protectable interests in life, health, and well-being" is a tactic for spreading the breadth of the state's net to capture not only viable subjects but all potential subjects as well (qtd. in Langley 1231).

If we review the above contests as essentially property centered, we can then see what all the fuss is about. In the instance of the abortion controversy, most prochoice advocates argue that the contested terrain is the woman's body and her proprietary rights. Let us look again, however, from the point of view of the state's vested interests in amassing juridical subjects. From the moment the fetus (or preembryo, for that matter) has "rights" in contradistinction to those of its progenitors, this "subject" is both subject of and to the state by which, in return for its "inalienable" rights, its subjectivity promptly is alienated into state property.[2]

Notes

1. This decision was reversed upon appeal. In the interim between the trial and the appeal, Mary Sue Davis decided not to have the pre-embryos implanted in her own uterus; instead she wanted to donate them to another childless couple. Junior Davis, himself raised by a single mother, originally argued that he did not want his child raised by a single parent and, in the case of donating the pre-embryos to a married couple, he worried that "the recipient couple might divorce, leaving the child . . . in a single-parent setting" (*Davis v. Davis*, Supreme Court 604). According to such logic, no child should ever be conceived because all risk (through divorce or death) being single-parented. We can see here a striking instance of how adult fantasy is projected onto children.

2. Certainly, the Iowa court ruling in the case of Baby Jessica, where property law was repeatedly cited as precedent, illustrates transparently the equation of the child with property.

2

The Child of Psychoanalysis, Part 2

The Origin of the Child/The Originary Child

The fallacy of such constructs lies not just in their
"scientistic" reductionism, but in their complicity in
the dream of origins.
—Walter A. Davis, *Inwardness and Existence*

The child figures in analytic theory as both a fantasmatic past
and an idealized future. As fantasmatic past, the child is the locus
for current self-articulations projected backward onto the child as
origin in the form of an "infantile neurosis"; or the child plays the
victim of parental desire (seduction theory) and/or its own desire
erupting from the phylogenetic reservoir of Oedipal race-lust. The
future the child proffers is, on the one hand, the individual future
of the analytic subject whose child-past is resurrected in the quest
for a normative future; in the correction of the exhumed child inheres the fantasy of a new and better "future" for the subject trapped
in an interminable past to which the failed child has clung. When
explored to its logical conclusion, such a perspective denies altogether
the presence of the adult subject, who is simply a site inhabited by
repressed and potential "children." Alternatively, the future is imagined in terms of the actual child who is an adult-to-be; childhood,
from this viewpoint, is interrogated and prescribed insofar as it is the
determinant for a successful or neurotic adult/generation.

The neurotic is characterized by Freud as a subject who repudiates
the past at the same time that she or he is bound to it. "The neurotic person will try to make the past itself non-existent" (*SE* 20:120).
The neurotic's dilemma is precisely that she or he is living in the past
as though it were the present. The analyst's mission, thus, is to en-
trench the distinction between the past qua past (thereby mitigat-

ing its effects) and contemporary reality, in order to usher the patient into the present. Yet, particularly in the case of deficit-model
analysts,[1] there is the sense that the analyst too fantasies trying "to
make the past itself non-existent" by correcting it, by treating the
analytic scene as a direct (not figurative) experience of the child-past
that is revised not only theoretically but *literally* like the raw material of, say, a book-in-progress. D. W. Winnicott observes, "In so far as
the patient is regressed . . . the couch *is* the analyst, the pillows *are*
breasts, the analyst *is* the mother at a certain past era" (*Paediatrics*
288). The fantasy supporting such a theory is that the adult subject
can be outfitted with an altogether new past, that the child can be
reevoked, reparented, corrected, and subsequently reintegrated into
what amounts to a new subject with a revised history. While Freud
and the conflict-model theorists certainly hold that the past persists
in the form of the unconscious, which at all times intersects with
the conscious experience of the present, the deficit model goes further in the sense that the past can be *presenced*. The internalized child
always is accessible in its original form to the present observer, as
though this child were temporally *actual* rather than a reconstruction—and, as a result, open to restructuration qua child.

The attempt to locate the origin of adult experience in the child
becomes, in various psychoanalytic accounts, the transformation of
the necessarily fantasy-laden search for origins into the scientized
"evidence" for the early onset of subjectivity.[2] Otto Rank's theory of
the trauma of birth provides a blueprint for the subject's anxiety, taking for granted a prenatal self-consciousness. Phyllis Greenacre dismisses such "wild" constructions of the prenatal infant as "fantasies
of patient and author, in which psychic constellations belonging to
a considerably later period of development are projected backward
and make it appear as though the fetus lived a full and thoughtful
life" (*Trauma* 15). Nevertheless, Greenacre herself argues that birth
experiences leave "somatic memory traces" (*Trauma* 7), going so far
as to speculate that "dry labour" is the origin of "a body-phallus identification" (*Trauma* 22). As Greenacre admits, it is difficult to locate
the precise moment of differentiation between the biological and psy-
chobiological organism. Perhaps it is this very difficulty that invites
a tendency on the part of the theorist to project backward—not only
because it is impossible to prove or disprove any notion of the subject's prehistory, but also because the assured knowledge that the infant (or fetus) will in fact become a human subject precipitates the
observer into hasty conclusions.[3] Melanie Klein's conviction that the
superego arises in the first year, Daniel Stern's theory of an originary

"core self," the discovery of various "evidences" of prenatal subjectivity all make sense in light of a discipline founded on the central formative role of primitive experiences on the subject. On the other hand, we find a number of object-relations theorists (particularly Margaret Mahler) highlighting a nonsubjective, undifferentiated period in the infant, a model that proceeds from yet another trend of fantasying on the part of psychoanalytic theory. Daniel Stern argues that the theory of the infant's undifferentiated state holds meaning only in light of an adult self-conception as differentiated (70, 105n). Thus, if the desire to project backward an adult self-consciousness onto the child dominates one strain of analytic theory, conversely, the alternative trend that posits an undifferentiated phase, "omnipotent fusion," as Mahler calls it, is fostered by the notion that an adult fantasy, that of fusion with the object world, emerges from the original desubjectifying fusion with the mother (9).

Observationists insist on an unmediated relationship between the infant and reality. Stern believes that "infants from the beginning mainly experience reality. Their subjective experiences suffer no distortion by virtue of wishes or defenses, but only those made inevitable by perceptual or cognitive immaturity or over-generalization" (255). Not unlike their faith in their own objective readings of the infant, observationists cast the infant in the role of a reality-experiencing subject; further, this infant possesses adult capacity for *consciously experienced* affect, a capacity demanded by adult theorists who depend on the infant to corroborate their own projective identifications. Their identifications not only transmute the observed infant into a specular double; the theory as well is informed by the confusion between the sensibilities of the adult and the child, the theorist and her object. As a result of mistaking unconscious identifications with the children they observe for objective reports, we wind up with a fantasy of the clear-sighted child struggling in the face of malevolent parental agents. If the mother were adequately attuned, we learn repeatedly, the "true self" of the child would thrive. These adult theorists, hence, identify strongly with the child victim whom it is their mission to rescue from adult persecutors. This child knows all that they know but cannot protect itself. The identifications of the analyst, with the adult or child position, are invariably at the core of psychoanalytic accounts of the child. The first important observationists, Spitz and Brody, reveal a high degree of identification with the child, perhaps because such identification is imperative to their faith in their interpretations of the child's experiences. Winnicott and his followers, as well, are noteworthy for their ostensible empathic attunement to the child's feelings, whether

it be an actual child or the child in the adult.[4] Heinz Kohut's self psychology emphasis on the analyst's empathic attunement to the
analysand reiterates the small child's fantasy of the mother's responsibility for any experience of unpleasure.[5] Freud, on the other hand,
at least after his assertion of the Oedipus complex, theoretically occupies the parental position (along with all the prohibitions deployed
by such a position) in relation to an insatiable, desiring child.[6] Anna
Freud cautiously distances herself from the instinct-driven child she
portrays. Klein's child, too, is greedy and ruthless before the aim-in-
hibiting effects of civilization.

The Language of the Child

> For the child, more than for the adult whose sexual function is
> truly "in working order," nothing is sexual, everything is sexual.
>
> —J.-B. Pontalis, *Frontiers of Psychoanalysis*

In the treatment of a neurotic patient, the question of regression
versus fixation has been raised ever since Freud's treatment of the
"Wolf Man." Freud argued that, as a result of a traumatic event, the
patient had regressed to the anal stage of development. Thus, a routine consideration for the analyst is whether the analysand has regressed to a prior developmental stage from a more advanced one or
has become stuck in an early stage she or he has never outgrown.
Such a distinction is of particular relevance to the position of the
child in psychoanalytic literature because the very terminology of
regression and fixation casts the adult as temporally undermined by
internalized *temporal* modes of expression and experience. Either the
past insists in the subject in the form of a fixation—an adult body
concealing a child's orientation—or the past reclaims the subject,
dragging, say, the Oedipal-level child, backward into the netherworld
of the anal stage. Hence, the regressed adult is someone who has the
psychical capacity of a later stage but lives in a prior one. The task
for the analyst is markedly different in either case. The analyst either leads the subject through the phases not yet negotiated or she
or he reintroduces the subject to the repressed and abandoned past.
The adult subject, depending on whether the problem is regression
or fixation, is reunited with the past on the one hand, or drawn into
the "future" of a childhood not yet accomplished.

Yet, in either instance, the question inevitably becomes: what age
is this patient? The neurotic patient, whatever the diagnosis, regres-

sion or fixation, is not an adult in the psychoanalytic sense of the term. As Phyllis Greenacre puts it: "The term *infantile neurosis* may be used in two somewhat different senses: one, meaning the outbreak of overt neurotic symptoms in the period of infancy, i.e., approximately before the age of six; a second, meaning the inner structure of infantile development, with or without manifest symptoms, which forms, however, the basis of a *later neurosis*" (*Emotional Growth* 50). Greenacre is pointing to the inevitable temporal complexities of attempts to articulate with any precision the relationship between the chronological and psychological ages of the subject. To say of the adult patient that she or he is suffering from an infantile neurosis is to situate the adult as a child emotionally; nevertheless, the "child" in the analytic space remains hypothetical, a hole in time that is created as much by the analyst, who is assuming origins, as it is by the patient, who is yoked to this internal but "speaking" (symptomatically) child. The "real" child of neurosis, the child who is symptomatic *as* a child, offers in this light a reassurance to the analytic investigator, a positive proof that there is such a thing as the temporal coincidence of neurosis and the child. Nevertheless, to call what the adult experiences an "infantile neurosis" remains problematic at best in terms of the adult's relationship to a child that persists as either "real" or "imaginary" (a historical versus a fantasied past). Moreover, we need to consider the analyst's position *in* and representation *of* that relationship. To raise the question of whether the analytic subject is regressed or fixated demands a idealization of maturational timing, a conviction that the child has certain needs and is primed for given experiences at particular points in its negotiation of developmental landmarks.

Anna Freud deserves credit for her recognition of the inaccessibility of the very young child and the consequent speculation-generating effects in the analytic observer. Other analysts, however, have ignored such perspectival limitations, superimposing on the child what Ferenczi calls the "language of the adult."[7] Edward Glover criticizes the trend and exposes its unconscious fantasy that children are "somehow 'nearer' to the unconscious," more archaic, like the child itself, which, via the slippage characteristic of all metaphors, has been co-opted *as* unconscious (*Early Development* 297). In truth, however, the strategy of adultomorphization not only makes the child the avatar of the unconscious but represents the unconscious as somehow childlike. To say that the less repressed child lives *in* the unconscious is no more than a tautology because the distinction between child and unconscious has been stripped of its valency. Or, perhaps the distinction never existed insofar as psychoanalysis has posited the unconscious. As Freud pointed out early in his career, "What is unconscious in mental life is also what is infantile" (*SE* 16:210). Perhaps the unconscious implicitly has meant always no more and no less than the preverbal child, a child who strikes the adult as a tangle of drives.

The child is associated with a kind of pleasure in the body and its drives that in the adult has been repressed, sublimated, rerouted in some way. Alice Balint notes that "in the nursery we can . . . indulge without blame the instinctual wishes to see and touch the sexual organs, and the naked body generally, or to observe the various bodily functions" (*Early Years* 6). All this unattenuated delight becomes exiled, under the auspices of "civilizing" influences, to the unconscious arena. Yet the problem with equating childhood with what in the adult becomes unconscious instinctual impulses is that it implies that the child *experiences* these impulses in the same way the adult does. The child's pleasure precedes its prohibition, the very prohibition that lends the drives their urgency and shame. To "see and touch the sexual organs" might not suggest to the child the same sexual significations registered by the adult, for whom the sphere of the sexual includes its circumscription.[8] The level on which these organs are "sexual" for the child cannot begin to be ascertained through adult taxonomies that are founded upon the segmentation of the body into zones of pleasure and disgust.

Much has been written about Freud's seduction theory and his subsequent recanting.[9] Whether or not Freud did dismiss out of hand the role of actual seduction in the wake of formulating the Oedipus complex, or whether he continued to acknowledge the external factor of real sexual abuse (as I believe he did),[10] is not, in the current context, as relevant as what "seduction" of the child by the adult might mean beyond the physical relation.[11] The question that arises from the distinction between an adult sexual intrusion into the child's world and the child's sexual fantasies projected onto the adult is, as Laplanche and Pontalis argue, a question of the "origins of sexuality" itself. Erik Erikson attempts to dismantle the logic that mistakes the child's sexuality for that of the adult: "To conclude, as Diderot did, that if the little boy had the power of a man, he would rape his mother and murder his father is intuitive and yet meaningless. For if he had such power he would not be a child and would not need to stay with his parents—in which case he might simply prefer other sex objects" (87).[12] Yet, like Diderot's, Erikson's analogy remains "intuitive and yet meaningless." Although he dismisses the relevance of equating the affective/erotic experience of the child with that of the adult, he fails to explore the full implications of the logical aporias stultifying all adult readings of the child. This oversight is most apparent in his own narrative digression into the scenario of the boy-in-the-body-of-a-man who, just like a "normal" adult male, pursues substitute objects of desire. Erikson's exposure of Diderot's fallacy goes beyond an interrogation of adultomorphizations. He uses Diderot as a springboard to construct yet another reductive allegory in which the child's experience is appropriated by an adult perspective. In fact, Erikson's allegory in no way differs from Diderot's; it is based on the selfsame fantasy of a child who only acts like a child because it is confined to a child's body. While he condemns Diderot's confusion of the child's circumstances and motivations with that of the adult, Erikson himself confuses the eruption of sexuality in the child with its adult manifestations. His "story" elides the distinction between the origin of sexuality and an adult sexuality that both encompasses the structure of its origins and diverges from it, the divergence itself being an inextricable component of adult sexual fantasy. This example in Erikson of repudiation of a position according to a conceptual framework that eventuates in its strategic repetition is pervasive in psychoanalytic theories of the child, which all, in one way or another, wind up replacing one approach that mistakes the child for the adult with yet another.

Theorists frequently identify language as the site of the difficulty. Daniel Stern opens his book *The Interpersonal World of the Infant* with an anecdote offered to the reader as the source of his privileged insight into the infant's "world":

> When I was seven or so, I remember watching an adult try to deal with an infant of one or two years. At that moment it seemed to me so obvious what the infant was all about, but the adult seemed not to understand it at all. It occurred to me that I was at a pivotal age. I knew the infant's "language" but also knew the adult's. I was still "bilingual" and wondered if that facility had to be lost as I grew older.
>
> This early incident has a history of its own. As an infant, I spent considerable time in the hospital, and in order to know what was going on, I became a watcher, a reader of the nonverbal. I never did grow out of it. (ix)

This recollected epiphanic moment seems more like a screen memory for another, repressed, origin of his later interest in the child. The "founding moment" narrative device sounds suspiciously like a displaced primal scene fantasy of origins. What is compelling about

Stern's account is the manner in which he has carved out a fantas-matic "bilingual" domain where the child and adult intersect: this mythical seven-year-old, granted privileged insight into both arenas, is just that—mythical. Because of the immense transformative effects of adult language, the seven-year-old looking at the infant might well be as far removed as the adult, even if he maintains the fantasy of proximity (which Stern evidently did). The seven-year-old's theory of some kind of special communion with the child is repeated by the adult analyst who is now telling the reader that, in contrast to other analysts who "seemed not to understand it at all," *he* has retained access to this special "pivotal" domain. I use the word "domain" here because this is Stern's own term for stages of the "self" that emerge in the child temporally but then are located spatially. Thus, it is an enchanted "domain" Stern claims to inhabit, a domain, spatially and temporally, hovering somewhere between childhood and adulthood, a domain inhabited by Stern alone who, as a result of his privileged history, is the only adult who has access to the child.

What Stern offers, nevertheless, through a kind of circular reason-ing, is yet another explanatory story to account for a theory grounded in itself. The theory that one can be "bilingual" in the way he sug-gests leads to and issues from a theory of a child whose language can be interpreted by an adult, a child whose entire "interpersonal world" can be accessed by Stern's own theoretical "domain." Stern is by no means the only theoriest of infancy who projects his own subjectiv-ity onto the infant. His anecdote simply clarifies the way such rela-tionships, between the intrapsychic fantasy and theoretical construc-tion, operate. These internal "object relations," between one's own fantasied infant- and child-positions and introjects of adult caretak-ers, persist in the adult unconscious as unacknowledged arbiters of clinical judgments as well as affective ties; such is the nature of trans-ference. Furthermore, if we take seriously the inevitability of trans-ference, which is among the founding assumptions of psychoanaly-sis (a "foundation" that perpetually decenters identity and desire), then we must recognize the extent to which the relationship between the theory and its object reproduces that subsisting between the an-alyst and analysand, the object of the theory occupying the silent and blank analyst-position itself.

Ferenczi characterizes the relation between the adult and the child as a "confusion of tongues," but Jean Laplanche argues that the use of the word "confusion" is to confuse the issue. Rather, Laplanche suggests that there is an "inadequacy of languages," by which he means that the respective positions from which the child and the adult "address" one another are on entirely different planes (*New Foundations* 130). The adult is empowered over the child; the child is dependent on the adult. The adult actively takes care of and protects the child while the child has no choice but to respond passively.[13] The child does not quite understand the language of the adult but, as Laplanche remarks, nevertheless is compelled to "inhabit" it (*New Foundations* 125). The adult does not (really) understand the language of the child but supposes that, having been a child once, she or he has access to the language of the child.

In "Fantasy and the Origins of Sexuality," Laplanche and Pontalis point out that the crucial question for psychoanalysis has been whether the child's sexuality originates in the child or is superadded to the child through adult mediators. In his later book, *New Foundations for Psychoanalysis,* Laplanche argues that it is the "enigmatic signifier" as such that is "seductive" (126). He explains that "the *enigma* is in itself a *seduction* and its mechanisms are unconscious. . . . The 'attentions of a mother' or the 'aggression of a father' are seductive only because they are not transparent" (128). What he calls *"primal seduction"* is "a fundamental situation in which an adult proffers to a child verbal, nonverbal and even behavioural signifiers which are pregnant with unconscious sexual significations" (126). For Laplanche, then, what definitively distinguishes the language of the adult from that of the child is its opacity, not only to the child, but to the adult as well. The child is "traumatized" by an adult discursive field that is pervaded by the double entendre, the repressed sexual text always inhabiting and thereby distorting adult meanings. This leads us back to the question of what conditions the field of sexuality for the child; it appears to be that sexuality is founded in the advent of repression itself. According to Laplanche, the frightening subliminal messages of the adults inaugurate what we recognize as sexuality in the child (its adult features). It is not the direct confrontation with adult sexual activity that confuses and traumatizes, then, but rather the enigmatic component—the place where sexuality diverges into the unspeakable.

For Freud's child-subject, Hans, sexuality as it emerges in language is founded upon an original reversal in the parental accounts of sexual difference. When Hans asks his mother if she has a "widdler," she responds, "'Of course'" (*SE* 10:9–10), an assertion that later will be called into question—for Hans, by his father (31), as well as for the reader, by Freud (32). Neither Freud nor Hans's father offers in place of the mother's "widdler" another anatomical marker; rather, the effect of their disavowals (what else can we call them?) is not only to invalidate the mother's sexuality and her own account of her sexuality; it is to mark sexuality as a place of parental indeterminacy, an arena where the mother's story and the father's diverge. Sexual difference, as a result, gets founded for the child out of the incompatibility of parental versions. These "lies" cancel each other and make of gender difference two irreconcilable perspectives; one can take the word of the mother *or* the father, never both. In this sense, gender difference as lived by each sex is transacted according to the child's affiliation with the word of the mother or the father.

André Green maintains that the language problem characterizing adult/child relations constitutes the child's initiation into hermeneutics. "The father and mother say this or that, and act in this or that way. What they really think, what the truth really is, he must discover on his own" (2). The child is forced into the position of an interpreter who lacks the requisite code. What thus precipitates the child into the adult world is the very duplicity of language that cleaves in the child a split between self-presence and indirection, between, as Lacan phrased it, "being and having," the immersion *in* versus the once-removed that is the Symbolic register. It is in the pursuit of what the father and mother "really think," their actual "truth," that the child is exiled forever from its prior fantasy of an unmediated relationship to experience and enters (is *seduced* into, by the tantalizing, perplexing, and traumatic enigma of it all) the realm of adult signifiers inexorably severed from any real(izable) signified. In the very instant of the disruption, the *infans* is lost forever because, despite its proximity, the prior grounds of apprehension have been shaken irreparably; that world of the *infans* simply no longer makes sense from the perspective of the new register.

Laplanche addresses a similar disengagement of language from experience in *Life and Death in Psychoanalysis* where he discusses the psychic origins of the "lost object." Before the baby is aware of the gap between need and its fulfillment, Laplanche suggests, the object— milk specifically—is not differentiated from the organism. Once differentiation ensues, however, the need for milk must be vocalized in a demand (20).[14] Yet that selfsame milk can never be what it was for the baby once its apprehends the difference. The milk that came without demand, the milk that was not yet an object, becomes a lost object. In this light, it would be impossible for the child introduced into adult language to recapture what it had before the transition that has shaken its very foundations, has made of the child a subject of an alien tongue, and at the same time throws into question its felt transparent relationship to the world. As one can see, the child in the midst of language acquisition is a different entity entirely from both the preverbal child and the thoroughly verbal child. This particular child is at once an exile from a prior space and a foreigner in the new one.

Dorothy Burlingham elaborates on the tenuousness of the child's position: "The infant learns thus to live in two different worlds simultaneously: in a 'real' world of his own, shared with nobody, in which words are superfluous; and in another, adult, world, in which this kind of observation plays a minor part, in which secondhand experience is handed down to him by the parents, and in which words are added to the images of things and to the facts" ("Empathy" 766). This particular "infant" Burlingham depicts is the language-acquiring child. Daniel Stern represents the acquisition of language as a kind of eviction from an edenic plenitude: "With its emergence, infants become estranged from direct contact with their own personal experience. Language forces a space between interpersonal experience as lived and as represented" (182). Whereas Burlingham represents the transition from the preverbal to the verbal arena as a negotiation between the direct and mediated experience, Stern sees the change as a most profound alienation. Certainly, Stern's perspective here seems very similar to that of Lacan, who contends that the child's installation into the Otherness of language (and, in turn, the constitutive insertion of that Otherness into the child) founds human subjectivity through an insuperable alienation. But Stern imagines that the "direct contact" is *real*, whereas Lacan treats it as imaginary. According to Lacan, from the very first the child has inhabited language—it just did not know it. Stern, conversely, imagines that there are two realms: one in which the child's experience of its world is unmediated, euphoric, intact; and another in which this perfection is lost through the duplicity of symbolic representations as well as through the consequent estrangement.

In fact, all constructions based on the distinction between the child's and the adult's languages (including Laplanche's and Lacan's, and even my own, for that matter) rely quite heavily on an a priori assumption of a lost direct relationship to the Real. Any concept of estrangement, Otherness, alienation, mediation depends for its signification on a fantasy of undisrupted wholeness. To argue about whether or not the child is conceptually undifferentiated from the maternal matrix, or whether it has or does not have unmediated experience before the advent of language, or even whether this direct relationship is authentic or imaginary is not meaningful in the long run, because all these positions, whatever form they might take, whatever observational or reconstructive evidences are adduced in their

defense, are all self-acknowledged as external to the child they produce in a very literal sense. Certainly they recognize that it is the
very division between the child and the adult, which it is their intention to explicate, that makes understanding impossible. Thus the
difference is always presented as structurally a priori to the a posteriori theorization of that difference. And yet, to define the child as
different is to erect criteria that inevitably generate a difference-cen-
tered theory.[15] It is from within this very difference, finally, that we
postulate a world without difference.[16]

Notes

1. Freud's model of the psyche is a conflict model, meaning that psychological problems arise from a conflict between psychical agencies. The
deficit model, on the other hand, posits an essential deficit in the intrapsychic economy. Michael Balint's "basic fault" is an example of a deficit model theory.

2. Christopher Bollas revises Winnicott's idea of true self into "inherited personality potential," which comes into the world with "the dis-
positional knowledge of the true self"—what Bollas terms "the unthought
known" (*Forces of Destiny* 10). Functioning for Bollas as a primary repressed unconscious with a superaddition of personality (the constitutional factor), "the unthought known" marks Bollas's attempt to strad-
dle the problem of installing a fullblown subject in the place of the
neonate. The problem he confronts is how to lend to the infant the seeds
of personality without naming it as such, how to establish a vocabulary
for the infant that includes adult self-descriptions without imposing on
the infant an adult subjectivity. This task may very well be impossible.

3. The "search for origins" has led ego psychologists such as Greenacre, Hoffer, and Hartmann to posit the priority of the biological subject
whose organic maturation precipitates psychic developments. Hence, the
muscular development of the infant subtends emotional displays of aggressiveness. This emphasis on the biological adaptiveness of the human
subject is among the basic premises of American ego psychology. Hartmann posits a "conflict-free sphere" of the ego, which includes "auton-
omous" ego functions such as memory, spatial organization, and so forth,
adjacent to but highly differentiated from the libidinal and aggressive
drives.

4. Alice Miller draws on Winnicottian theory for her book *Prisoners
of Childhood*, where her insights are heavily informed by an uninterrogated installation into the victimized child's position. She goes so far as
to recount a familial situation she only observed from a distance, but
she nevertheless offers "to describe it as it was experienced by the child"—
as if this were possible! (65). Elsewhere, she presents her formula for ideal
childrearing practice: "Our world would be very different if the majority

of babies had the chance to rule over their mothers like paschas and to be coddled by them, without having to concern themselves with their mothers' needs too early" (89). I hardly need point out how similar this is to deMause's fantasy of the child-as-tyrant.

5. For an excellent assessment of the disavowals underlying Kohutian theory, see Nikolaas Treurniet, "Psychoanalysis and Self Psychology." For Treurniet's description of the child-identified fantasies of this approach, see especially p. 84.

6. I develop further the question of whether one identifies with the position of the adult or the child in the chapter on Dickens.

7. Ferenczi was addressing specifically the adult sexual abuser's misconstructions of the child's "language of tenderness"; nevertheless, I think that the question of "language," the adult's or the child's, applies equally well to psychoanalytic theory and practice, where language, specifically "the talking cure," is foregrounded.

8. In *Primary Love and Psychoanalytic Technique,* Michael Balint distinguishes between the "end-pleasure" of adult genitality and the "foreplesure" of the child. Such a distinction seems to me important in more ways than Balint himself addresses. The nature of pleasure itself is transformed dramatically between these two phases; a pleasure lacking an endpoint necessarily is accompanied by different affects and psychical representations from a pleasure that is constituted with a sense of its own termination.

9. See Masson, *The Assault on Truth;* Holland, "Massonic Wrongs"; Laplanche and Pontalis, "Fantasy and the Origins of Sexuality"; Laplanche's *Life and Death in Psychoanalysis* (chaps. 1 and 2) and *New Foundations for Psychoanalysis;* Peter Gay's *Freud: A Life for Our Time* (90–96, 122n, 143, 252, 583); Baranger et al., "The Infantile Psychic Trauma"; Emanuel E. Garcia, "Freud's Seduction Theory"; and Julia Kristeva's "Place Names" in *Desire in Language.*

10. In fact, his account of the "Wolf Man" makes it clear that actual seduction continued to play a crucial role in his understanding of the etiology of neuroses.

11. Helene Deutsch uses the term "seduction" to define the "normal" libidinization experienced by the child at the hands of its caregivers, including physical warmth and "unconscious seductive acts of the loving mother as she cares for his bodily needs" (269). Thus, "seduction" for Deutsch constitutes the Oedipalization of the child.

12. It is worth noting that Freud himself drew upon Diderot's example in order to support his claim that the Oedipus complex was intuitively acknowledged long before he theorized it (*SE* 23:192).

13. By using the terms *active* and *passive* to describe the relationship between the adult and child, Laplanche repeats the error I note above, namely, to insist upon adult relational distinctions without taking into account a potentially alternative child's subjectivity and agency.

14. Demand is not the same thing as the infant's crying to be fed in

the sense that, before differentiation of objects, the infant does not know that it cries for something in particular that will satisfy its need.

15. While it might sound as though I am stating the self-evident, it is important to note that the distinction between the child and the adult (as well as the taxonomy of childhood—infant, older baby, toddler, etc.) is a relatively recent concept. According to numerous child-historians, the idea of childhood as a separate sphere did not exist before the sixteenth century. I cannot help but wonder, however, if the social historians as well are immersed in a postlapsarian construction of human history. See Philippe Ariès, *Centuries of Childhood;* Edward Shorter's "Comment by Edward Shorter" in response to deMause's *History of Childhood;* Bernard Wishy, *The Child and the Republic;* David Hunt, *Parents and Children in History;* Peter Laslett, *Household and Family in Past Time;* and Ivy Pinchbeck and Margaret Hewitt, *Children in English Society.*

16. Michael Balint addresses "the problem of language" arising in the analytic session, when the analyst is attempting to revive preverbal experiences that have been laid down in the unconscious without benefit of post-Oedipal adult grammar. "As far as we know, the unconscious has no vocabulary in our sense" (*Basic Fault* 97).

The custody battle over "baby Jessica," officially named "re Baby Clausen," ensued when Daniel Schmidt and Cara Clausen discovered they had *lost* something in common. It was the loss of the child that gave the couple a relationship that took shape over this child's (absent) body, a body subsequently contested through the narrative of custody and paternal rights. Not until Daniel Schmidt discovered that he had fathered a child did Daniel and Cara determine to reunite; indeed, there had been virtually no relationship before the revelation of Schmidt's paternity. Interestingly, this is just how Daniel Schmidt characterized the one-night sexual encounter with Barbara Schlicht that produced his first daughter, Amanda: "There was no relationship" ("Schmidt v. DeBoer" 259). In response to questions as to why Schmidt had made no effort to meet Amanda, he claimed that he did not want to disrupt her life. Nevertheless, as attorney Suellyn Scarnecchia made clear, Schmidt was indeed willing to "disrupt" little Jessica's life. Schmidt protested, "I'm not disrupting Jessica's life."

> Q You don't think taking Jessica away from the two people who have raised her for two years is a disruption, sir?
> A No, I do not. Not when they were ordered to give her back a long time ago when she was not even quite a year old in Iowa court. Three times.
> [. . .]
> Q All right. Now, I understand that you never made a claim for custody of Amanda. But it's also true, isn't it, that you never made a claim even for the right to visit Amanda?
> A That's correct. As I stated before,—
> Q (Interposing) Let me just ask you to answer my questions, Mr. Schmidt.
> A That's what I was trying to do.
> [. . .]
> Q Now, you were not married to Amanda's mother; correct?
> A That's correct.
> Q And you were not married to Cara Clausen when Jessica was conceived; correct?
> A That's correct.
> Q All right. So, Jessica is your second child born out of wedlock; correct?
> (Quoting Reporter's Transcript, Feb. 8, 1993, "Schmidt v. DeBoer" 264–66)

As we can see, the issue of disrupting the child's life is about the father's construction of the "relationship" to the mother as much as anything else. Daniel Schmidt does not consider himself relevant to Amanda's life because "there was no relationship" to her mother, Barbara Schlicht. Conversely, it is the "relationship" he has forged with Cara (after-the-fact) that positions him as significant in Jessica's life.

In the Washtenaw County District Court trial, the only best-interests-of-the-child trial that took place, Daniel Schmidt's history of neglected paternal responsibilities was a central concern. He had failed to pay child support for both his son from a prior marriage and his daughter born out of wedlock; as a result, his wages were being garnisheed. Current research indicates that fathers' relationships with their children depend considerably more on their level of marital satisfaction than do mother-child relationships.[1] Schmidt's behavior, accordingly, is typical of the postdivorce father. Consequently, we can see how for the father the child might come to symbolize the sexual couple.

Baby Jessica signified the potential restoration to Daniel Schmidt of everything he lacked: the reputation of good father and a legitimate relationship with a woman who hitherto had been merely a casual lover. He would become the member of the very idealized family he said his daughter needed. The language of authenticity pervading the Schmidts' claims to their biological child, an authenticity displaced onto the child's need for her "natural" parents, was transparently in the service of Daniel Schmidt's longing for social legitimation. Somehow the news media picked up on Schmidt's motivation; by narrating the battle between the Deboers and the Schmidts as the appropriation by rich childless couples of working-class bodies,[2] the media were indirectly but powerfully responding to Daniel Schmidt's sense of social marginalization in relation to the normative American family. In response to questions concerning the traumatic sequelae of taking the baby from the people who had raised her, Cara Clausen argued that her daughter would somehow know instinctively that Cara and Daniel were her real parents.[3] This expressed logic of innate biological attuneness to the natural parents reiterates the overarching fantasy of the "couple" shaped *as a result* of the child whose conception produces the couple as couple.

Over the course of the custody battle paternal rights were supervening. Cara's maternal rights were not restored until a year and a half into the legal process—and then only because she was Daniel's wife. That the courts deemed Daniel Schmidt's rights of property more important than the mother's rights or the child's best interests reveals almost by accident the extraordinary social investment in the father's role in conception.[4] On the one hand, fathers appear to be powerless and insignificant in the face of the mother's substantive acts of reproduction; to counter her perceived power, the law abandons both her body and its product in order to shore up the father's centrality. On the other hand, we might argue that despite the role of the womb in reproduction, the mother's relationship with her child is always mediated through paternity. Thus, the father can decide whether he wants to acknowledge or disregard his child, while the mother anxiously waits. Actually, both readings obtain inasmuch as the father assumes power (legal) through his disempowerment (biological), a disempowerment that is simultaneously empowering (he can take or leave his children). The inability of the father's body to carry the child leads to his exclusion from the pregnancy and even to the possibility of his not knowing of the pregnancy (as in the case of Amanda). Nevertheless, the not-knowing ensues from the not-asking—are you protected? did you get pregnant? are you carrying the baby to term? What Daniel twice earlier experienced as privilege (not knowing about Barbara Schlicht's pregnancy, not supporting Travis) became his story of vulnerability—if only he had known sooner about Cara's pregnancy. Somehow, his avowed insignificance in the lives of his older children (he didn't want to "disrupt" Amanda's life; he somehow neglected to pay many years' worth of child support for his son) is transformed into his victimization—he was not consulted before Jessica's adoption, his name wasn't registered on the birth certificate. Our society's construction of the mother-child relationship is always in the service of the father's central role; the primary goal is to sustain the paternal metaphor. As I will illustrate in the following chapter, even when the mother-child relationship is apparently overvalued, we find at the core of such overvaluation both another means for securing the father's power and the fear of its diminishment.

Notes

1. See Kerig, Cowan, and Cowan, "Marital Quality and Gender Differences in Parent-Child Interaction"; Dickstein and Parke, "Social Referencing in Infancy: A Glance at Fathers and Marriage"; Gable, Belsky, and Crnic, "Marriage, Parenting, and Child Development."

2. Karen M. Thomas writes: "Some who watched the legal battle say that the case became a rallying point for newly politicized birth mothers, raising issues of class and motherhood" ("Adoption: Laws and Emotions," *Dallas Morning News,* August 10, 1993). Available in LEXIS, Nexis Library.

3. See Lucinda Franks, "The War for Baby Clausen" (62). Franks points

out that antiadoption groups "maintain that adopted children suffer deep emotional scars and are condemned to be 'amputees,' missing a piece of themselves, which they look for all their lives" (59). The use of the language of castration to describe issues of identity is transparent.

4. The dissenting opinion in the final ruling makes clear that this ruling was based in property law (*In Re Clausen* 687).

3

The Child of Psychoanalysis, Part 3

The Perfect Couple: The Mother-Child Dyad

I'm not half as bad as I seem. I'm only what you've made me.
—Child's reply to her mother in *Homestead on the Hillside*
by Mary J. Holmes

Most analysts incorporate into their theories a variation on the "fall" into difference. For Sigmund Freud, it is the recognition of gender difference, as crystallized in castration anxiety. For others, the "fall" comes with the imposition of civilizing agencies on the little instinctual savage. As different as their approaches are in other regards, Melanie Klein and Anna Freud certainly have this latter perspective in common. Kohut and the self psychologists treat all disruptions as arising from inadequate parenting; in fact, the core fantasy here seems to be that, given perfect parental and environmental conditions, no one ever need experience that traumatic fall from narcissistic intactness. This core illusion in Kohutian psychology is no more than a fantasy-generated corrective to the tragic destiny of humankind implicit in the Freudian model.[1] All these theories reveal adult self-conceptions and the ways in which they are projected onto, worked out, and narrativized through the child.

The prelapsarian state in many psychoanalytic accounts is portrayed as the inviolable unity constituted by mother and child. The mother's body is hailed as the ground not only of infantile oneness, bliss, closure—in short, all euphemisms for originary pleasure the child must forfeit—it is also the never-ending sustenance for psychoanalytic fantasy. Lacan focuses on the intrusion of the mother's desire into the perfect mother-child unity; the revelation of her desire is concomitant with the "birth" of the child into language. Winnicott, Fairbairn, Mahler, and other object-relations theorists posit an early undifferentiated state succeeded by the apprehension of a "not-me" world of objects. It is the individuation from mother (as well as the mother's emotional retreat from her child) that thrusts the child into the deviousness of the object world. Repeatedly, the mother-child relation is treated as central to the formation of the child both developmentally and pathomorphically.

Mary Shelley's *Frankenstein* gives us the worst-case scenario of the mother-child relation. The "mother"-scientist abhors the monstrousness of the child the moment "she" sets eyes on it. The "child"-monster hates her with equal intensity for her refusal to acknowledge her own accountability in producing the child *as* monstrous. But the mother renounces culpability; indeed, she revises altogether the story of what went wrong. Frankenstein tells Walton: "During these last days I have been occupied in examining my past conduct; nor do I find it blamable. In a fit of enthusiastic madness I created a rational creature and was bound towards him to assure, as far as was in my power, his happiness and well-being" (199), odd sentiments indeed for the creator who promptly abandoned his creation. The monster, on the other hand, argues that he would not have become a murderer if only his creator had loved him. A recent episode of a television police drama told the story of a mother who lies to protect her son after he murdered his father because to acknowledge her son's sociopathy would be to expose the failure of her mothering.

Although psychoanalysts insist that they are no longer blaming mothers for ruining their children's lives, in many ways mother-blaming continues to be an inextricable component of current analytic practice. Self psychology in particular is based on the premise that the analyst must compensate with her or his own empathy for the unempathic mother. Several years ago, I attended a conference on "The Psychic Life of the Infant" where for two days I listened to accounts of how the mother fails her child. Extraordinary emphasis was placed on the mother's level of attunement to her infant. Depressed mothers, for example, produced diverse pathological effects in their infants. When I suggested that we seem to remain invested in holding the mother responsible for everything that goes wrong in the life of her child, I was promptly advised that no one was blaming the mother—it wasn't her fault if she was depressed. Of course, her depression has significant and irremediable consequences for her child— but it's not her fault. Any account that is reducible to idealized/de-idealized splittings (and that is most assuredly what psychoanalytic representations of the mother continue to be—even if her "bad guy" persona is now reconceived as the antihero victim of her own angst) is suspect both as a gross simplification and as a screen for otherwise inexplicable origins and outcomes of the child; this splitting of the mother into two different entities is, as I will elaborate, a strategy for suppressing both the central role of the father and the father's potential inadequacy. Indeed, the penis/phallus distinction implemented by Lacan is no more than another desperate solution to the felt gap between the cultural role and the material body. Yet perhaps the role (represented as phallus) is as insufficient as the penis-bearing body itself. Perhaps it is this potential revelation that the mother must conceal.[2]

The "attachment" of psychoanalytic theorists to what are rapidly becoming *a*typical models of the family is an interesting phenomenon in itself because it suggests a high level of resistance and denial. It is not, moreover, just psychoanalysis that remains entrenched in outmoded paradigms of the family; it is our culture as a whole, whose increasingly sentimentalized visions of childhood speak of a certain desperation to maintain as actual a rather short-lived family system in the history of the family.[3] Notwithstanding the similarity between the culpable Winnicottian mother who is insufficiently immersed in her children and the contemporary weak and erring mother who *inadvertently* deprives her child of sustaining attunement, these representations have somewhat different origins. The Winnicottian program as well as John Bowlby's emphasis on attachment between mother and child were articulated *within* a society that more nearly attempted to live its expressed values.[4] The current disjuncture between the expressed values and the actual family underscores the element of fantasy in not only the fulminations of public officials against the dissolution of "family values" but also in the ostensibly more rational accounts of social scientists. Bad parents increasingly are being reconfigured as abused children (a strategy that somehow redeems them); working women are blamed for slighting the family that can no longer survive without their financial contribution.

In defense of Winnicott's representation of the mother, Judith M. Hughes writes, "What he intended, and accomplished, was to insist that the mother, whom Fairbairn epitomized in terms of treating, or failing to treat, her child as a person in his own right, should herself be regarded as a person in *her* own right" (175). The question remains: to what extent is this expressed right of the mother in fact no more or no less than the right of the male psychoanalyst to speak for her. Indeed, it is the degree to which Winnicott speaks for the mother, constructs for her a "normative" experience and function (all the while kindly tolerating her reasonable failures), that makes his the most pernicious of psychoanalytic accounts of femininity. If we find in Winnicott the comforting pediatrician who empathically embraces our mishaps and assures us we are "good-enough," we should look again. It is in the specificity of Winnicott's mother that we find the normative housewife—the blandly smiling mother of the Beaver—as well as Donna Reed and the host of sitcom mothers who ushered in a generation's worth of expectations.

In "Love for the Mother and Mother-Love," Alice Balint observes that the child expects utterly selfless love from its mother. Even the adult hangs onto this expectation of the mother whose infantile imago persists unconsciously. Further, the fact that we are all children in actuality as well as fantasy lends yet another twist to the theorization of the mother-child relation. Balint notes that even "practically healthy people" persist in this irrational demand of their mothers (253). Thus, if the child *as* child has unrealistic expectations of the mother, what of the adult "child"-as-theorist? In what ways might the infantile fantasy condition the adult point of view, especially when that adult is in the profession of speculating on mothers and mothering? Are psychoanalytic accounts of the mother no more than legitimized versions of the infantile fantasy of the mother-child relation? Or, perhaps they are end-products of a fantasy that arose from the loss of *something,* later specified as the mother.

Madeleine Baranger, Willy Baranger, and Jorge Mario Mom hold that Klein's description of the child's absorption with its mother and her breast is "optimistic" in the sense that "it is preferable to have a relatively localized persecutor against which the subject may take protective measures, than to be at the mercy of nameless, placeless dangers whose nature remains unknown" (124). In much the same way, it seems preferable (safer) for analytic theory to "blame" the mother for the defects in the child than to remain in the dark as to the origins of mental disease (or even mental health, for that matter). It is safer, finally, to focus on the mother as the origin of everything in the child (from character formation to eventual object choices) than to resign oneself to the impossibility of policing the future of the subject.[5]

Assuredly, psychoanalysis's foundational dependence on the mother-child dyad has scotomized all along other (very common) alternatives for the child's upbringing, which suggests that the resistance to the multiplicity of influences acts as a founding moment of developmental theory. Like Baranger et al.'s characterization of Klein, there is a tendency to depend on a "localizable persecutor."[6]

For strategic purposes, omnipotent power is attributed to the mother in the production of the child; an overestimation of her agency in the formation of the human child allows the prescriptive element of psychoanalysis to function as an ostensibly mitigating influence on an otherwise out-of-control mother.[7] As Barbara Ehrenreich and Deirdre English amply have illustrated, the turn-of-the-century attention to the child was followed by a deep concern with, and effort to harness, the mother's formative agency. Thus, a subtext for all the following *descriptions* by psychoanalysts of the mother-child relation is a *prescriptive* imperative.

Masud Kahn writes that "Winnicott was the first among analysts to point out the obvious fact that a mother cherishes, enjoys and *creates* her baby" (*Paediatrics* xxxvii). Serge Lebovici and Joyce McDougall chart the case history of a highly disturbed little boy, Sammy, in order to show to what degree the child figures as a symptom of maternal fantasies. The mother's loss at the age of nine of her masturbation doll, they explain, recurs in the loss of her son to an institution when he is nine years old. Maud Mannoni as well sees the child as always responding symbolically to the mother's repressed desire. According to René Spitz, the mother's "molding influence makes it inevitable that her own discord will be reflected in the child's development—and reflected, as it were, in a magnifying mirror" (*First Year* 205). Spitz's use of "molding" suggests the extent to which he imagines the mother's agency in light of the infant's route through the vaginal canal. His representation of the mirror relationship between the mother and the child is reversed by Winnicott, who comments, in response to Lacan's mirror phase, that it is specifically the mother's face that functions as a mirror for the infant (*Playing and Reality* 111). The question necessarily becomes: who is mirroring whom?

The mother and child repeatedly exchange subject and object positions. While, for Spitz, the child is the mother's "magnifying mirror," that speculum emerging from the maternal matrix, which conveys with it the picture of its origins, Winnicott attributes the mirroring function to the mother who in turn *produces* that which she reflects. The reflection glimpsed in the mother's face is internalized by the child as self-image. Stern, too, in his discussion of the mother's affective attunement, portrays her as an adequate or distorting (and very much *informing*) mirror for the child. It becomes impossible to determine priority in the generation of affect and subjectivity between the mother and child. "The empathy of the mother for her child," explains Therese Benedek, "originates in the experiences of her early infancy which are *reanimated* by the emotions of the current experience of her motherhood" (395, emphasis added). Janine Chasseguet-Smirgel believes that the woman regains, through her relationship with her child, her lost primal unity with her own mother (35). The child infantilizes the mother in the sense that it "reanimates" her experience as a child vis-à-vis her own mother. Hence, the child functions as a "mother," both as origin of the mother's motherhood and as the maternalized object of the mother's projections.

Again, we have returned to the issue raised earlier about the extent to which the child, who is theorized as origin, problematizes all such temporal coordinates by virtue of the fact that the child itself, as a temporal location, is only recognized as such after the fact, in the adult's removal from a position retrospectively defined as *prior*. Thus, what the child might revivify in the mother, more than the dormant residue of her own archaic mother-child relation, is her repressed relation to ontology (repressed by psychoanalytic theory as well), those traumatic negotiations at the nexus of activity and passivity, where the human subject is situated as both creator and created, a subject of self-initiation and precipitant of external initiatives. Klein's version of the relationship between the infant and its objects provokes such derision and outrage among her many critics precisely because her system is immersed in and arises from these chronic subject/object slippages. In one attack on her work, for example, Edward Glover states, "Admittedly it is always hard to prevent anthropomorphism from creeping into psychological terminology, but *the liberties Melanie Klein takes* with metapsychological terms lead to the creation of a kind of slang in which *it is no longer possible to distinguish* between mechanisms, psychic imprints (nuclei or institutions) and unconscious presentations (including fantasies)" ("Examination of the Klein System" 85, emphasis added).

Klein elaborates a phantasmagoric landscape in which the child figures as no more than the container for part and whole objects, the incorporation or projection of which, at any given point in time, depends implicitly on prior incorporations, on how those objects, who "are" the child, interact. Glover invokes a positivistic taxonomy in his repudiation of Klein's "slang." When Klein began to deviate from "standard" psychoanalytic usage, these standards were only in the process of formation and implementation. Hence, Glover's distress seems to result from his fear that the new science was being undermined radically from the start. His insistence on efficient topographic divisions of the psychic landscape—"mechanisms," "psychic imprints," and "unconscious presentations"—responds to Klein's "sloppy" neglect of the substantive demarcations between the essential child and the child as sum of its objects, what psychic functions inhere in the child, and what enters the child from outside.[8] I must confess that reading Klein is at times an unsettling experience and tempting, as a defensive gesture, to ridicule. The complexity of her "system" can be dismissed as inconsistency; the absence of any clear-cut developmental hierarchy can be vilified as a fundamental incoherence. The indeterminacy of her "positions" versus clearly defined linear developmental stages leaves one spatially and temporally dislocated. Yet perhaps this is the point. Perhaps these dislocations and reversals are what happen as well to the adult speculating on the child. In the confrontation with the ultimate impossibility of determining cause and effect, mirror-image and subject are "localized" in the theorization of the mother-child relation, as though the resolution of that relation, emblematizing as it does the ambiguities, will resolve as well into historical/chronological determinacy. To render tangible, perspicuous, controllable the mother-child relation, to regulate that relation, is to domesticate the ontological tenuousness that relation at once stands for and obscures.

Emphasis on the mother-child bond predominates in object-relations theory. Any disruption in the mother-child "fit" (Balint, *Basic Fault* 22), or failure on the part of the mother to provide "good-enough mothering" (Winnicott)—a failure that ensues from her inability to enter a semipsychotic state Winnicott calls "primary maternal preoccupation"—is said to figure in the child as a kind of "deficit," a hole marking the space where the mother is not. Such a parasitic model of the mother-child relation suggests that the mother must merge with her child to the extent that she is self-less; Alice Balint's characterization of the infantile fantasy of motherhood has been elevated to theory. Not only is she expected to be self-less, there is a time limit on her immersion in the child. If she hangs on too long, disaster is inevitable. Joyce McDougall advises us that "if the baby is destined to become the mother's sole object of libidinal and narcissistic satisfactions, there is a high risk of early perturbation" (*Body* 82). Yet Winnicott claims that the devotion of the "ordinary good mother" is "made possible by her narcissism, her imagination, and her memories, which enable her to know through identification what are her baby's needs" (*Paediatrics* 245). Clearly, there is a line drawn between a mother's healthy narcissistic investment in her child and the pathology of narcissistic dependence. Implicit in these, at times, rather murky distinctions is the expectation that the mother who, if she is to be a good mother, must transcend the boundaries of self and other in order to be sufficiently attuned to her child—for a few weeks post birth. At the end of that time, she is supposed to return dutifully to her separate subjective sphere. This fantasy of a mother who can redirect her narcissism so effortlessly arises from psychoanalysis's own underlying warring imagoes of the mother as plenitude and the mother as insatiable maw. The theory reenacts the upheavals of the Kleinian child, who negotiates the vicissitudes of the greedy, sadistic paranoid-schizoid position and the reparative and fearful depressive position as it shifts between fantasies of the mother as something to be eaten and the mother who will bite back. Marianne Hirsch convincingly argues that psychoanalytic theory is in many ways committed to *forging* the tension between mother and child that is then construed as *necessary* for the subject's constitutive separation from the mother, "placing those who theorize into the position of the child and placing the mother into a position of otherness" (171). It is precisely this forged antagonism between "mother" and "child" positions that we need to understand—not only how it works, but what ends are served.

The central position of the mother-child dyad in non-Kleinian object-relations theory is related to an increasing de-erotization of the human subject.[9] The object-relations analyst W. Ronald D. Fairbairn subordinates altogether the erotic drive.[10] "The conception of fundamental erotogenic zones," he writes, "constitutes an unsatisfactory basis for any theory of libidinal development because it is based upon a failure to recognize that the function of libidinal pleasure is essentially to provide a sign-post to the object" (33). Sexuality facilitates the object relation; the object relation does not occur as a result of the sexual urge. Actually, in Freud's own work, the position of sexuality, inborn or superadded to the infant, is not so clear. This is the problem that he negotiates as he moves from the seduction theory to the Oedipus complex. Although he indicates, as Fairbairn claims, "fundamental erotogenic zones," he suggests additionally that they need to be triggered somehow by external factors. These zones are innate to the extent that they are aroused when manipulated. At the same time, they are destined to be manipulated by caretakers who cathect those zones as well, and thus reproduce on the body of the child their own sexual geography. Freud claims that "by [the mother's] care of the child's body she becomes its first seducer" (*SE* 23:188). Followers of Freud, on the other hand, have tended to present as unambiguously innate the infant's erotogenic zones. Fairbairn says that this is a case of putting the "cart before the horse," that, conversely, the object is preeminent and the autoerotic activity of the child is simply a means by which it can fantasmatically regain the object (33).[11] He goes so far as to insist that "the more satisfactory his emotional relations with his parents, the less urgent are his physical needs for their genitals" (122).

What Freud called the "dissolution" of the Oedipus complex is enacted in a rather astonishing way on the theoretical level in object-relations theory, which has "dissolved" the central role of the Oedipus complex in the intrapsychic economy of the individual. For Fairbairn, the child's sexual investment in its parents is really an unhealthy displacement of unfulfilled emotional needs. While Fairbairn nevertheless continues to acknowledge, however attenuated, the sexual component, Kohut discounts it altogether. Kohut's final repudiation of classical Freudian analysis is marked by his reappraisal of the Oedipus complex as a purely neurotic manifestation. Sexuality itself is represented as deviant.

Fairbairn unwittingly shows us how such a strategy unfolds. After referring at length to the pre-Oedipal child as "he," he goes on to observe, crucially: "It will be noticed that in the preceding account the personal pronoun employed to indicate the child has been consistently masculine. This must not be taken to imply that the account applies only to the boy. It applies equally to the girl; and the masculine pronoun has been used only because the advantages of a personal pronoun of some kind appear to outweigh those of the impersonal pronoun, however non-committal this may be" (123). Why Fairbairn goes to such lengths not only to call attention to his use of the masculine personal pronoun but to justify his usage in a way that is patently unjustifiable, vague "advantages" being adduced over any concrete explanation, is mystifying, to say the least. Despite his self-characterization as "non-committal," the use of the masculine personal pronoun is unabashedly "committed"—to a rhetorical convenience, to a particular gender position. This digression from his theorization of the Oedipus complex comes at the reader in a rather striking way—boldly—in the center of the main text, not subordinated to the footnotes as a tangential clarification—suggests that this "tangent" is in fact central to his main argument. He continues: "The child finds it intolerable enough to be called upon to deal with a single ambivalent object [the mother];[12] but, when he is called upon to deal with two [mother and father], he finds it still more intolerable" (124).

Object-relations theory repeats the child's position as elaborated by Fairbairn. This is a theory that finds it "intolerable" to deal with more than a single object, hence its extraordinary valuation of the mother-child dyad. Further, as Fairbairn inadvertently indicates, what is truly "intolerable" about two objects (like two personal pronouns) is the way they install the child in gender difference. At the same time, to reduce rhetorically the child to a putatively undifferentiated "he" is to lend to the mother-child dyad the lineaments of an amorous relation. Thus, one might argue, such a marked genderization of the child as the opposite sex actually entrenches gender division in the Fairbairnian version of object relations. The reduction of the real female child to the male personal pronoun suggests, however, that "she" is no more than "he"; she *is* he. Furthermore, the amorous relationship figuratively induced in the representation of all mother-child relations as female/male is inevitably counteracted by the fact that, between the mother and infant of non-Kleinian object-relations theory, there is no sexuality that is not pathological. Thus, the mother-child relation that takes over for gender division as it works itself out through the defiles of the Oedipal system is a fraudulent depiction of a heterosexual relation drained of sexuality, a strategy that ultimately annihilates gender as difference. Such are the advantages of the personal pronoun.

Forty years later, Jessica Benjamin as well runs into trouble when she justifies her use of the personal pronoun, in a footnote this time: "I will generally avoid confusion by calling the infant 'he.' In those paragraphs where I refer to the infant alone and therefore the referent for the pronoun is clear, the infant will generally be 'she'" (14n). The "confusion" avoided is the confusion between the "she" who is the mother and the "she" who may be the infant. Again, for what are apparently the most logical of reasons, we wind up with a mother-infant dyad that imitates the heterosexual relation. Elsewhere, Benjamin characterizes mother-child attunement as "a dance of interaction in which the partners are so attuned that they move together in unison. . . . Reciprocal attunement to one another's gestures prefigures adult erotic play as well" (27). The problem with Benjamin's account of the mother-infant relation is that she imagines a full-fledged subject in the infant-paramour. Thus, Benjamin's erotization of the mother-child bond is premised on two "adult" subjects of sexuality. It is through the projection of adult-level sexual subjectivity onto the infant that Benjamin finds the origin of adult eroticism. What is overlooked in all accounts that trace adult sexuality to the mother-child paradigm is the *in*equality of the mother and her child. Given the plethora of developmental discrepancies as well as the signal fact that the mother is a self-conscious subject and the infant is not, it is odd indeed to look for an originary *relationship* in the mother-child dyad. Benjamin's subjectification of the infant is indebted to the Sternian model.[13] She writes: "The baby who looks back as he crawls off toward the toys in the corner is not merely refueling or checking to see that mother is still there, but is wondering whether mother is *sharing* the feeling of his adventure" (31). How Benjamin (or the observationists she draws on) know so much about the infant's "subjective" experience remains unclear.

In his description of the mutually gratifying "dialogue" (*First Year* 42) between mother and child, the ego-psychologist René Spitz observes:

> Perhaps one might say that object relations which gratify both mother and child are relations in which an interplay of forces operates in a way to complement each other in such a manner that not only do they offer gratification to both partners, but the very fact that one of the partners achieves gratification will produce a gratification for the other also. *It will not have escaped the thoughtful reader that this last statement would be an equally fitting description of a love relation and even of the mutual feelings between man and woman in the sexual act. But then, as I have said above, what is the love relationship if not the crowning fulfillment of object relations?* (*First Year* 205, emphasis added)

Hence, if his representation of the mother-child relation looks a great deal like the sexually charged relations between men and women, it is simply because the mother-child unit is the prototype for all such future love relationships. However, Spitz's articulation of the superficially self-evident trajectory from cause to effect dissolves under scrutiny. If the adult sexual relationship is based on the object relation inhering in the mother-child dyad, at the same time his account of the dyad plunders the vocabulary of adult love for its tropes. He cannot help but construe the mother and child as an effect of adult heterosexuality and, by the same token, the discourse of adult love is immersed in a fantasy of the mother-child relation as a prior originary term. As a result, Spitz's argument invites more than a strict reversal; the structure of his logic is produced by the vicissitudes of the relationship between past and present—a past conceived as auguring the present and a present invested with a sense of its heritage that is received *as* present by virtue of the past it ingests and subordinates. It is tempting to contend that the insertion of the mother-child relation into the rhetoric of adult love is merely the retrospective reconstruction of an earlier period. Nevertheless, not only would such a strategy replicate Spitz's brand of an uninterrogated linear model, but it would deny that the adult self-description comes from *something,* if not necessarily from the mother-child relation it appropriates as founding moment. It would posit the *present* as origin, overlooking the multiplicity of temporal, spatial, and experiential assumptions that forge the present as such. There is something in the mother-child relation that makes it appear, to an adult observer, like adult love.

Repeatedly, in psychoanalytic literature, the mother and child are referred to as "partners" or as a "couple," and it is to Spitz's credit that he recognizes the implications of this language.[14] One reason the mother-child "couple" assumes such foundational significance for object-relations theory is the mother's role as primary caretaker. But perhaps she is positioned as the primary caretaker (and, as a result, as the child's first love object) in part because of an unspoken ideal of adult sexual relations that *desires to find its origins* in an omnipotent embrace, which it names "maternal." In turn, that adult ideal is reproduced by the childrearing techniques it fosters. As Freud himself (nostalgically) remarks: "A mother is only brought unlimited satisfaction by her relation to a son; this is altogether the most perfect, the most free from ambivalence of all human relationships" (*SE* 22:133).

Indeed, the mother-son relationship is not only the paradigm for adult heterosexual love; according to Robert Stoller, whose work on the distinction between sex and gender won acclaim in the seventies, it is the origin of homosexual love as well. Stoller argues that the mother's obsessive and protracted bond with the male infant inhibits the boy's normal process of disidentification from femininity. While the mother's love for her child is constitutive of "normal" sexuality, there is always the danger of her own desire entering the picture. Thus, it would seem that the heterosexual paradigm depends on containing the mother's power to be a desiring subject; she must efface her subjectivity in order to be the perfect *object* of desire.[15] Only in this way might the little boy's own sexual agency (curiously equated by Stoller with heterosexuality) be activated. As I will argue in the next chapter, L. P. Hartley's account of "deviant" sexuality shows what happens to a boy in the grips of what his novel represents as the mother-figure's phallic prerogative. According to the novel's mother-hating subtext, when the mother has possession of the phallus (when she is an active desiring subject), she desexes (unmans) the male child. As long as male sexuality is viewed as penetrating agency in relation to passive femininity, any desire on the part of the mother might be demonized as a castrating force. Certainly, such a conviction is implicit in Stoller. Just as Hartley will portray homosexual "deviance" as no sexuality whatsoever, Stoller's feminine boy is not an active subject desiring male partners; rather, this is a boy whose sexuality was thwarted by the intrusive and overbearing desire of the mother.

What is it about the idea of the closeness of the mother and her child that emblematizes for the adult observer her or his own experience of love? Moreover, why do we tend to see the individual manifestations of that relationship as falling short of an ideal? Where must the ideal come from if not from the real relation it more often than not rejects as insufficient? Winnicott's "good-enough" mother is always only "enough"—not the plenitude of the "good" the "enough" depletes. It seems to me that the criticism of the mother arises from her idealized (and desubjectified) role as a component of a union. This union does not really symbolize mother *and* child but the intact, undifferentiated child. Implicit in the theory of an undifferentiated stage is the child's cleavage from the mother and banishment into the world of separation and difference that establishes the mother as a separate subject in her own right. To discuss her as lost, as subsequently differentiated from the child she nurtures, is to recapitulate the child's perspective in the theory (the very perspective the theory offers as real) and hence to view her alternately as a lost plenitude and a rejecting object. "Enough" is not "all," which is precisely its incapacity. Ferenczi's theory of our species' phylogenetic desire to return to the sea whence we emerge, bizarre as it might strike one, is the logical culmination of the unveiled fantasy of a lost past more perfect than the mother, a past for which she is a poor substitute:

> This motive [of the sexual act] may well be the striving to restore the lost mode of life in a moist *milieu* which at the same time provides a supply of nourishment; in other words, to bring about *the re-establishment of the aquatic mode of life in the form of an existence within the moist and nourishing interior of the mother's body.* In accordance with the "reversed symbolism" already met with several times, the mother would, properly, be the symbol of and partial substitute for the sea, and not the other way about. (*Thalassa* 54)

Ferenczi's vision of our instinctual oceanic drive, the aim of which is the dissolution of all boundaries, a oneness that embraces the whole world, is but the most extreme expression of the implications of Oedipal thinking. While analytic theory tends to point to the connection to the mother as the source of human desire, the argument often is qualified by an understanding that the ideal experience of that relationship is hallucinated. Implicit in the admission of the illusory nature of this origin, however, is the assumption that the illusion must come from somewhere—and where else but the mother-child relation itself? Thus, Ferenczi's version of plenitude, the return of the species to its oceanic origins, for which the mother is a "symbol," a "partial substitute," seems to be an attempt to escape the circularity of the imperfect mother-child relation functioning as a model for perfection.

Finally, what does the construction of such an ideal (in the sense both of the mother-child union and the sexual relation) suggest about our perception of the child? Chasseguet-Smirgel's belief that the mother's relationship with her child functions in her unconscious as a substitute for the most ideal relationship of *her* life, her bond with her own mother, suggests that ideal love is *only* experienced by the child, a decentering of adult love that thus conditions both experience and fantasy. Returning to Spitz's model of love as "the crowning fulfillment of the object relation" inaugurated in the mother-child dyad, we can see, in light of Chasseguet-Smirgel's theory, that such a fulfillment is specifically the sexual connection with a mother-substitute; this sexuality is redirected physically at the same time that it is unconsciously aimed at the original object. Thus, either to locate the paradigm of the love relation in the mother-child bond or to locate it in the adult experience that filters its view of the primary bond through its own terms is to ignore the decentering process that positions love wherever it is not. The very distinction between affectionate love and sexual love, always such an obstacle in the theorization of the child, is no more than a futile attempt to delineate a space for an unmediated object relation, unadulterated by the fantasmatic refuse of another space in another time.

The Oedipal narrative, which is about rivalry and intrusion, is plotted as the story of the child trying to usurp the position of the same-sex parent vis-à-vis the opposite-sex parent. Yet throughout psychoanalytic theory courses an antagonistic pre-Oedipal narrative, which tells of how the intruding parent (*always* positioned as the father in this version) ruptures the primal bond with the originary parent (always the mother). In light of this narrative, the theory of Oedipal-level rivalry is no more than a repositioning of the child into the space of the outside term—a displacement of the simplest kind. In its identification with the paternal law, the child quite literally assumes the guise of rival, the original of whom is the father. Hence the Oedipus complex itself is merely a dissimulating tactic employed in order to safeguard a consciously acceptable version of an adult sexual couple as primary, when all along the fantasy persists of the primacy of the mother-child couple that both succeeds and antedates (both materially and fantasmatically) the adult heterosexual couple.

A strategic emphasis on the needs of the very young child, whose interests psychoanalysis seems to subserve in its elaborations of ideal childrearing practices by the mother, distracts the theory from its unconscious compulsion to advance increasingly closed models of human love. If non-Kleinian object-relations theory has overinvested the mother-child bond, the origin of its path is in Freud who proclaims that "the finding of an object is in fact a refinding of it" (*SE* 7:222). Where Freud imposed libidinous sexuality upon what until then was represented as the sexually disinterested mother-child relation, what happens in object-relations theory is that the sexuality inhering in the primary bond annuls adult sexuality in its projection forward of what now manifests as a sexually neutral paradigm. The erotic drive itself, henceforth (even in the adult), is reduced to a purified object relation between a bodiless mother and an innocent child.

Perhaps the potential for the desexualization of the human subject can be traced to Freud as well, at least insofar as his theory has been appropriated by object relations. We need to reassess altogether the Oedipal system as well as the pre-Oedipal factors motivating object choice. In "On Narcissism," Freud gets himself into grave difficulties when he attempts to distinguish between anaclitic and narcissistic object-choices (*SE* 14:87–91). The anaclitic relationship, preferred by men, is the Oedipal-level accession to external objects of desire, propped on the earliest object relation with the mother. The narcissistic object-choice (most often women's), on the contrary, arises from the subject's supervening need to be loved. Nevertheless, since the man desires the narcissistic woman precisely because of his identification, through her, with his own forfeited narcissistic self-sufficiency, the anaclitic object-choice winds up resembling narcissism compressed under a fragile veneer of anaclisis.[16] Thus, the Oedipal-level achievement of object relations collapses into narcissistic doubling. As a result, anaclisis itself is really *about* how the fraudulent triangle "leans on" (etymologically, the meaning of anaclisis) an essential dyadic fantasy. In order to manufacture a triangular relationship out of the little boy's desire for his double in narcissism, in a theoretical sleight of hand Freud installs the narcissistic female as both projected subject and external object of male desire.

Indeed, in all psychoanalytic theories we find triangular configurations only thinly veiling foundational dyads. Both the Oedipus complex and its theorization act out the split into two parental objects of the originally fused mother and child. The father assumes the displaced aspects (the lost glory) of the child constituted by its bond with the all-powerful body of the mother, all-powerful precisely *because* of its relation to the child. Although the father in psychoanalysis functions putatively as the prohibition to the recuperation of this perfect union, the prohibitive role is merely the projection outward of the child's internal loss. It is in becoming a subject that the child "loses" the mother; the father retroactively is held accountable for this loss, a loss that is of course a gain. The father becomes, as a result, not only the representative of the lost power of the mother-child bond, he is also the reservoir of the child's presubjective status inasmuch as he has a connection with the mother that the child has forfeited. That which has been stripped from the child now coalesces in the father in the form of an organ of access to the mother's body. Is it possible that the father in psychoanalysis is really no other than the child?

Something of One

What is at stake here is the right adults assume to confiscate,
"for the child's own good" of course, a certain sexuality that
knows neither where it is bound nor what it wants.

—J.-B. Pontalis, *Frontiers of Psychoanalysis*

The pre-Oedipal father enters the picture only insofar as he has to assume the discarded features of the mother-child union; in this way object-relations theory manages to suppress any *difference* intruding through the third term in the very gesture of constituting the third as such. As I will show, the Oedipus complex as well is no more than the superimposition of a triangular structure on what steadfastly remains a dyadic relationship. Because the mother-child relation is the arena where psychoanalysis repeatedly confuses material and psychical reality, the real parents with their symbolic dimension, it is useful to consider what fantasies are being concealed through an overcompensatory dependence on the cultural essentialism of sex roles and child care. Even Lacan, with his celebrated emphasis on the role of language in the constitution of human subjectivity, nevertheless insists on the material body of the mother in the production of a desiring subject.

In the Freudian account of psychosexual development, *both* mother and father alternately function as *both* object and intruder. The intrusive term is originally the mother's "deviant" anatomy as such. Consequently, even in the Oedipal triangle, there are not three roles but two. There are only the mother and the child, and the father is simply the site of what becomes the mother and child's lost "phallic" attributes. Vitally, it is the mother's body that disrupts the idyllic mother-child economy. The three terms of the Oedipal triangle are the child, the object of desire, and the rival. As René Girard has argued, however, the object of desire assumes its value through the rival's insistence (*Deceit*). Moreover, the rival only gains her or his status through the coveted object. It is the body of the mother itself that produces difference, desire, and rivalry—she is the scene of the crime, the terrain where the fantasy of perfect, indivisible, symbiotic love unfolds; the postsymbiotic loss and expulsion into a world of difference; the eruption of absence (of the child, of the phallus) into the prior plenitude; the battleground where the very terms of her geography are contested. The child, in its dismemberment from her body, is the original for the detachable phallic term. Lacan says that the child, echoing the mother's desire, progresses from wanting to *be* the phallus for the mother to wanting to *have* the phallus that will reunite the child with her body, will make her body "whole" once again as it was before the symbiotic relation was sundered ("The Meaning of the Phallus" 83). The phallus thus comes to occupy the place from which the child has been expelled, a place where it never was. The child itself, then, is the original of the role the father will come to play only secondarily, as mere bearer of the penis.

Joyce McDougall reports a patient's fantasy that his "internal mother-image [was] as an 'abyss,' a 'chasm,' a 'void,' coupled with the idea that his role as a child was 'to keep her filled,' or at times to act like a cork that would keep her enclosed" (*Mind* 99). What was originally a seamless body, a motherchild, is fragmented into pieces, the mother's body and the child's. The mother's body that completed the child is now apprehended as the gaping absence that requires the child to fulfill *it*, the child's dependent need having been projected onto the mother. It is at once the void and the cork that the child stands for and in for, the phallus that is known by the space it refuses to, can*not*, occupy. The void *is* the cork. While in Freudian theory the child symbolically compensates the mother for the lack of an organ, in the Lacanian model the child symbolizes her lack.

The work on retarded and psychotic children by the Lacanian analyst Maud Mannoni, whose clinical examples show the practical application of Lacanian theory, reveals the indefatigable insistence in all psychoanalytic theory (no matter how antiessentialist) on the material value of phallic possession—and in turn its material absence inscribed on the body of the mother. Lacan contends that the mother's expectation that the child should *be* the phallus for her is constitutive of the child's emerging subjectivity. Mannoni suggests that the development of psychosis in the child ensues from the mother's refusal to relinquish her phallus-child to its own desire (*Backward* 61). Nevertheless, if the child functions as a "cork" that both satisfies and forecloses the mother's desire at the same time that it extinguishes the child as a desiring subject in its own right, it is a "cork" that is inserted into the maternal matrix more by phallocentric thinking than by any kind of original maternal fantasy. Although mothers and their children tend to validate phallocentric paradigms via their complicity in the fantasy of the child who sustains the mother's desire, it is because the social spaces of desiring hole and phallic cork preexist them and await like vacuums the bodies to occupy the spaces. The site of desire, thus, is the site designated by psychoanalytic phallocentrism, not the bodies that succumb to the prearticulated spaces like so many straw men.

How the spaces come to be gendered is a complex issue, perhaps unanswerable insofar as the analyzing subjects remain enthralled by their subjection to the body/symbol nexus that is lived as gender identity. In an effort to account for how the infant cognitively assimilates gender, Donald Winnicott writes, "In the vast majority of cases a penis must be the infant's fantasy of what a man might have. In other words, we have said no more by calling it a penis than that the infant may have a fantasy that there is something like a breast and yet different because it is associated more with the father than with the mother" (*Paediatrics* 63). This account seems in part to define what Lacan originally meant by a "phallus" that is not a penis. In light of Winnicott's description of the penis as "the infant's fantasy of what a man might have ... [that] is something like a breast and yet different," one can see how the penis would come to signify for the child what previously has been fantasied only in terms of where the breast is not. Crucially, it is the infant's aggressive, invasive behavior toward the breast, what Winnicott refers to as its "reaching impulse," that imaginatively outlines a place for the real penis to occupy (*Paediatrics* 63). Even in its original cognitive foundation, then, the penis is that which will fill an empty place—the place where the breast and its psychic derivatives end and another term is demanded.[17] In this light, the breast functions as an original plenitude from which the phallus (used here to mean the fantasy of the not-breast) diverges. Moreover, it is the penis that installs itself in the place of the phallus; it is the answer to the question: where does the breast end? It is the link between the breast and the realm beyond. Yet, in an extraordinary reversal of the infantile pattern, a pattern in which it is the penis that is "missing" as it were from the psychic landscape, it is the body of the mother that is marked as lacking.

Castration would seem to find its roots in an originary absence of a term beyond the breast, a term that devolves on an organ, the father's anatomical term of difference, for lack of any other representation. In order to justify the value of the penis which, Winnicott argues, is simply a secondary organ in the child's universe, a reversal occurs whereby the lack of the phallic term is projected onto the body of the mother, a body that threatens, with its omnipresent breast, to resist difference, division, separation. If the child's need to "invent" a penis arises from its aggressions against the breast, then the imaginary phallus and its scion, the real penis, function as infantile defenses against reincorporation into the body of the mother. The child, henceforth, in its aggressive advance toward separation and individuation, identifies itself with that not-breast term. What is most noteworthy in McDougall's discussion of the cork-child is the implied wish that the child-as-cork is nevertheless distinguishable from the maternal matrix: the cork figures the mother's need of the child, who is defined as that which can sustain her as whole. The child has reversed into its opposite the dread of her already being the whole world of which the child is merely an element.

While the conflict model attempts to discriminate between the pre-Oedipal child's perception of a third term intruding on its dyadic relation with the mother and the Oedipal child's self-representation *as* intruder, the object-relations model remains at the pre-Oedipal level. Only the father figures as the intruder to the symbiotic bond with the mother—and in the theory itself, which relegates the father to a subsidiary role. It is as if the theory were trying to deny the intrusive influence of *any* third term in the ideal mother-child dyad it exalts and promotes. As Judith M. Hughes points out, "Not only did [Fairbairn] deprive the father of his crucial status in the oedipal triangle; he relegated him to a derivative position" (100). This is not to say that the dyadic structure has not been implicit all along in Freudian theory; rather, object-relations objectifies as theory the tension between a dyadic structure and a triangular superaddition, a tension that has from the first destabilized the Freudian Oedipal story.

Fairbairn explains at length how his theory of object relations actually reverses the Freudian assignment of the psychical impact of the Oedipal and pre-Oedipal experiences.

> For Freud, the Oedipus situation is, so to speak, an ultimate cause; but this is a view with which I no longer find it possible to agree. So far from agreeing, I now consider that the role of ultimate cause, which Freud allotted to the Oedipus situation, should properly be allotted to the phenomenon of infantile dependence. In conformity with this standpoint, the Oedipus situation presents itself, not so much in the light of a causal phenomenon as in the light of an end-product. It is not a basic situation, but the derivative of a situation which has priority over it not only in the logical, but also in the temporal sense. This prior situation is one which issues directly out of the physical and emotional dependence of the infant upon his mother, and which declares itself in the relationship of the infant to his mother long before his father becomes a significant object. (120)

According to Fairbairn, the "Oedipus situation" is itself a disruptive (intrusive) term in the developmental progress of the child. Tellingly, he indicates that to foreground the Oedipus complex in the psychical structure of the child is to foreground as well the role of the father, who is not "a significant object" during the formative period of the infant's intrapsychic economy. Thus, granting preeminence to the Oedipus complex lends the paternal third term too much significance.[18] Michael Balint refers to the "intolerable strain" imposed on the infant as a result of "any third party interfering," which echoes Fairbairn's observation that it is "intolerable" for the child to handle two objects (*Basic Fault* 17). Winnicott justifies at length his preference for single instead of multiple caretakers.

> But at the start a simple *contact* with external or shared reality has to be made, by the infant's hallucinating and the world's presenting, with moments of illusion for the infant in which the two are taken by him to be identical, which they never in fact are.
>
> For this illusion to be produced in the baby's mind a human being has to be taking the trouble all the time to bring the world to the baby in understandable form, and in a limited way, suitable to the baby's needs. For this reason a baby cannot exist alone, psychologically or physically, and really needs one person to care for him at first. (*Paediatrics* 154)

Critical to Winnicott's argument in favor of a single caretaker is the maintenance of this "illusion" whereby a fusion is effected (or at least not undermined) between the hallucinated world and the presented world.[19] In psychoanalytic theory, the mother plays a large part in the infant's hallucinations inasmuch as the hungry infant hallucinates the unavailable breast.[20] The mother herself, or her ministrations, constitutes the infant's world as such. So, one might argue, it is to foster in the infant the illusion that mother and child are one unit that Winnicott favors a single caretaking mother. Winnicott is famous for observing that "there is no such thing as a baby... if you show me a baby you certainly show me also someone caring for the baby." Winnicott's point is that children are born into and thrive within relational contexts; at the same time, however, we have here a glimpse into Winnicott's own investment in fusing mother and child as a continuous subject (*Paediatrics* 99). He seems to fear that multiple caretakers would rupture the fluid maintenance of the illusion generated and maintained by the simple dyad. The actual dyad, a mother caring for her child, creates the fantasmatic dyad—indivisibility; this, finally, seems to be Winnicott's goal. Consequently, this dyadic relationship is about *one* not *two*—it is about the infant being encouraged in the illusion that inside and outside are continuous. It is the threat of the discontinuity between inside and outside that ushers in the single caretaker as an *antidote* to "the world's presenting." Multiple caretakers would offer multiple, heterogeneous versions of a world that necessarily would fragment the idyllic hallucinatory coherence of the infant's world. Subject and object, the very lived experience of difference, would intrude (like the reality-bearing father) on a world characterized by continuity and undifferentiation.

It is possible that the child itself functions as Winnicott's transitional object—indeed, the transitional object of all object-relations oriented theories.[21] The purpose of the transitional object is to smooth the route for the child between the me and not-me, specifically between the child-mother unit and the child as individuated subject. To the extent that the child negotiates the space between the continuous world and the discontinuous world where "me" arises as the solution to the "not-me" world of space and objects, the child likewise functions for the theory as a transitional phenomenon that is used to bridge the untenable heterogeneity resulting from the temporal and spatial disruption of the self-presence of the subject. This heterogeneity, represented as the child's confusion in the face of multiple objects, is rather the projection of the adult's experience of multiple *internalized* objects which, by their very divisiveness *within* the subject, rupture a continuous experience of the world. The transitional object is superior to the parent because of its constancy. Similarly, the *child* fantasied by Winnicott (the psychoanalytic child who hallucinates the continuity of inside and outside) is superior to the adult *because* of this child's apparent continuity—in contrast to de-centered adults. Perhaps, after all, Winnicott himself occupies the space of his own hypostatized pre-Oedipal child whose insistence on a single primary object maintains the illusion of a coherence between inside and outside that is shattered in the triangularization of real object relations.

Also imported into the analytic setting by Winnicott is the dyadic mother-child structure as paradigm. He offers a "holding environment" to the patient in the same way that the mother's reliable ministrations hold together, intact and harmonious, the potentially fragmented infant. Specifically, it is the object *relation* with the mother, an external coherence subsequently introjected, that sustains the infant in its undisrupted sphere. Winnicott writes, "The analyst lets the patient set the pace and he does the next best thing to letting the patient decide when to come and go, in that he fixes the time and the length of the session, and sticks to the time that he has fixed" (*Paediatrics* 67). Winnicott overtly assumes the role of mother for an infantilized patient. Freudian analysis, on the contrary, always assumes a triangularization of the analytic scene because it accounts for the "presence" of other (fantasied) objects that conduct a constant sotto voce conversation. Freud, in short, accommodates a third term; there are the real analyst and the real patient, as well as the transference that invites a host of imagoes into the room. What in Freudian terms is a reliable space, the analytic scene with its fixed place and time, becomes for Winnicott the mother's always empathic and sustaining embrace. In fact the analyst is superior to the "good-enough mother," and the analytic "holding environment" is by far more stable than the merely adequate home situation of the infant. Analysis is thus a kind of "transitional" experience, like the comforter itself; it is the ideal (because unchanging) representative of the actual maternal object and her caregiving milieu. The Oedipal complexities of the imagoes of Freudian transference have been refined to a fused relationship, with no external interference. As we can see, Winnicott's characterization of the analytic setting replicates his fantasy of the stability of the ideal infant experience.

Although highly criticized for its brash arbitrariness, Lacan's "short session" gains a new dimension when contrasted with the Winnicottian program. The short session destabilizes the analytic experience. The analysand never knows when she or he will be ejected summarily from the *locus amoenus*. As a result of the erratic session lengths, the analytic space becomes unreliable, a site of loss, confusion, uncertainty, rejection. The underlying fantasy of object-relations therapy is that the analyst can embody the mother in her most perfect incarnation—a mother that never was or could be but nevertheless is hypostatized repeatedly. The treatment process, with its emphasis on the artificial, retrospective creation of a previously defective mother-infant relation and its provision of environmental stability to fortify the psychic structure of a subject raised in turmoil, acts out the dyadic fantasy that has generated (and is reenacted by) the theory. Lacan's short session refuses the dyadic fantasy; its structural disruptions, the capriciousness of an analyst who seems to be anything *but* nurturing, interrogates not only the analysand's fantasy of mental health as relational and situational stability but also the fantasy-colluding strategies of analytic practice to date.

Yet Lacan as well is caught up in the dyadic fantasy that positions the father, or any disruption of the mother-child relation, as an external and divisive third term that precipitates the child from the plenitude of an undifferentiated totality in and with the body of the mother. Lacan isolates weaning as the retrospectively constructed site of loss.[22] Again, the relation with the mother is primordial in the psychic formation of the subject. Although Lacan argues that weaning is represented only after the fact as the experience of "the lost unity with oneself," he nevertheless depends on the material relationship with the mother that grounds such an imago in the subject's unconscious (*Complexes* 44).[23] While he attempts to avoid Winnicott's lapses into characterizing fantasy as reality, the infant's illusion as both origin and end—of the human subject, of analysis—Lacan's theory of the subsequent localization of weaning as the moment of severance from the body of the mother, which then gives rise in the subject to the positive Oedipus complex,[24] ultimately is rooted in the prior dyad, usurping its imagoes from a given material real. This is the mother's "universal" position as primary caretaker inducing (universally) a human subject who internalizes weaning as the moment of loss.

Lacan's theory of the ego's emergence in a specular relation with an idealized image (the mirror stage) is based specifically on the mother-child relation, since it is during the differentiation from the mother that the child seeks a specular relation as a substitute for the fantasied union. The supervention of the specular Imaginary stage by Oedipal triangularization deceptively appears to transcend a dyadic substructure. Yet, like the specular substitute, the Oedipal substitute as well is yet another manifestation of an essentialized dyad.[25] For Lacan, the mother plays two roles, "food to absorb and at the same time the breast that reabsorbs one" (*Complexes* 56), the same two roles enacted by the infant itself, who can both be "absorbed," like a cork or a phallus, and "absorb"—at the breast. This originary symbiotic relationship in which both infant and mother play the same double-role is the blueprint for self-sufficiency that materializes in the Oedipal drama as *two* parents instead of one. In other words, what manifests in the Oedipal triangle as three subjects—the mother, father, and child—not only derives from the primary dyad but possesses no additional features; the triangle, hence, as theoretically elaborated, evolves from a splitting of the mother into two objects with no *actual* intervention of a differentiated paternal term. In this sense, the phallic mother fantasy of the child gets transmitted covertly into the Oedipal structure in which her originary self-sufficiency is ruptured into separate objects; the Oedipal triangle entails, as a result, no more than a double-anthropomorphization of the mother's fantasmatic characteristics.

This is exactly what Fairbairn concludes when he reassesses the Oedipus: "*A sufficiently deep analysis of the Oedipus situation invariably reveals that this situation is built up around the figures of an internal exciting mother and an internal rejecting mother*" (124). Here we find the unabashed revelation of the fantasied world without fathers;[26] while conflict theorists like Freud might repress the implications of their descriptions of the mother's body, Fairbairn frankly admits that her attributes inform *all* gender positions. Fairbairn's objective in eliminating the father as an actual term of difference is to deplete the parent-child relation of sexuality and aggression; hostile to a drive-based theory, it is important for Fairbairn to minimize the apex, as it were, of the drives.

Yet this mother who is *all* is a phallic mother who diverts the psychoanalytic gaze from seeing the phallus head-on. This phallus, then, is the Medusa at whom we cannot look without fatal consequences. The Medusa is the ultimate transvestite of psychoanalytic thinking— a man decked out like a woman dressed like a man (all those snakes). He will castrate you—but only because you witnessed the origin of his power; indeed, the castration happens through the glimpse of the powerlessness at the heart of the deception. The power is only sustained, as Lacan tells us repeatedly, behind the veil—that veil being femininity itself. We run into trouble, consequently, when we say either that the mother is all or that psychoanalysis is phallocentric, because the mother of psychoanalysis is not a woman and the phallus of psychoanalysis is veiled by the mother's body. The point here is that the phallic mother is at the core of psychoanalytic constructions of gender—the woman disarmed, the phallus protected.

In "God and the *Jouissance* of the Woman," Lacan argues that the fantasy of romantic love is repeatedly characterized as "One" instead of two *relating* subjects because love is mythologized as fusion (138–39).[27] Yet here we find Lacan himself, paradoxically, mythologizing the mother-child relation as ultimate origin. What Lacan fails to come to terms with is the degree to which the Oedipus complex, actualized by rivalry and identification (the two primary features of the narcissistic specular relation of the mirror stage and the Imaginary register), is only tenuously superimposed on this obfuscated core dyadic scene. Even though he recognizes that the rivalry originates in the Imaginary register and is reproduced by the Oedipal Symbolic, he does not address the possibility that the Oedipus complex is no more than a fantasy of a triad camouflaging a dyad. Specifically, it is a triad conceived *within* a dyadic system. Jane Gallop points out that Lacan's definition of the Symbolic entails recognizing the Imaginary *as* Imaginary (instead of transcending that position altogether). I am suggesting, however, that even insofar as the Symbolic is theorized, it remains no more than an *effect* of an Imaginary regime that is recast momentarily as Symbolic in order to serve theoretical and fantasmatic exigencies—namely, to posit a place beyond the identificatory level that nevertheless strands the subject in an Imaginary *mistaken* for the Symbolic.

Maud Mannoni's work with "deficient" children illustrates all too well the theoretical scotomizations of her mentor, Lacan. Mannoni's emphasis on the pathogenic mother's rejection of the paternal order, her refusal to function for the child as the mouthpiece of the father's Law, points to the gender fantasy subtending psychoanalytic theory that is the source of psychoanalysis's inability to accede to the kind of Symbolic gender-differentiated thinking on which it stakes the Oedipus. Because neither Lacan nor his disciples can disengage the material bodies of the parents from their unconscious symbolizations, they themselves remain embedded in the Imaginary register without recognizing it as such. The material body of the woman is inextricably connected to the social Imaginary of her function, just as the material body of the man is mistaken for the Symbolic dimension of the paternal order. Throughout Mannoni's work one confronts a subtext that reads like a diatribe against gender slippage. In the following encounter between Mannoni, her child-patient, and its mother, Mannoni is so intent on establishing gender regulations that she overlooks entirely the profound connection made between mother and daughter. Mannoni explains to the child:

"When a Mummy gets cross, there is a father inside her saying, 'Bring our daughter up well, take care of her.'"

Carole [the child] got up and pressed her face against the window. The mother wept. "Sometimes I get cross for nothing," she said in self-accusation.

The child left the window, a vacant expression on her face, as if she were sleep-walking, and threw herself on her mother, hugging her passionately. "You are my good Mummy."

The child was able to voice these words because I had appealed to the presence of the father in the mother. (*The Child, His "Illness"* 142)

It is just as likely that the child is responding not to "the presence of the father in the mother" but instead to the mother's anguished acknowledgment of her parental failures. Yet, Mannoni imagines that she is witnessing the insertion of the paternal order into the mother/daughter dialogue. Mannoni's abiding conviction that child psychosis results from the mother's resistance to paternal Law leads to an explicit distortion in the service of theory. Inadequately defined gender positions, for Mannoni, produce deficient children, a theory she derives from Lacan's capitulation to socially prescribed values of gender. Lacan's fantasy of reliable gender categories (gender that is worked out predictably on the social and familial planes), his representation of a world where women *speak* to their children their own obeisance to phallic law, confuses bodies with language. Far from revealing the body's subjection to the word, as Lacan would pretend, Lacan posits a language that knows only a very particular body designated by psychoanalysis as castrated or not.

The child of psychoanalysis, consequently, is forced to perform the impossible task of sustaining a fantasy of material difference at the same time that it marks all bodies, both male and female, as phallic. This phallic myth is no more than an overcompensation, a phallus that is founded on the fantasmatic plenitude of the originary maternal body, a phallus that eventually is displaced tenuously onto the father and the organ he offers as a substitute for all that he cannot be in and to the relationship between the mother and child. Lacan argues correctly, I believe, that there is only one term here, the phallic term; but what he fails to recognize, what is brought out so explicitly by object-relations theorists, is that the sole point of reference is the body of the mother as it fuses with the body of the child. The overestimation of the male term is a consequent negation of the latent fear of the father's (and hence his organ's) "insignificance."

While Lacan understood the central fantasmatic role of the phallus in the emergence of gender in the social and discursive arenas, he nevertheless himself falls prey to the Imaginary tricks of a signifier that pretends to set up a difference that all the while is premised on sameness. As Madelon Sprengnether points out, Lacan's form of "subversion" takes place "within a larger structure of containment" (195). Psychoanalytic fantasies of the child are an effect of the compulsion to submit gender to a single category (phallic)—acted out *as though* differentiated. Such a repudiation of sexual difference is ultimately the strategy of the pervert, who disavows the mother's "castration," the "castration," that is, of the child from the symbiotic mother-child bond.

Freud makes clear in his essay "Fetishism" that the pervert's desire is not only to deny castration but to deny gender difference altogether. Joyce McDougall reasons that the perverse structure is founded on the child's disavowal of the fact that "the genitals of his parents are different and complementary, that he is forever excluded from the closed circle" (*Plea* 76). Yet the child is at once included and excluded. It supports the parental embrace as a possibility until the moment of its occurrence, when the child is dismissed from the sexual scene that now repudiates the child as origin. The child itself functions as the fetish, the substitute for the maternal phallus, in that its function is to foreclose sexual complementarity. The child-as-phallus is the agency that effects the conversion of both parents into the same gender. The child itself thus becomes no more than the perverse symptom of the disavowal of gender.

A perverse organization is manifested, furthermore, in the mother-child dyad overtly treasured by object relations—depended on more surreptitiously by all psychoanalytic schools of thought. About one of her perverse patients, McDougall theorizes that the "oedipal situation with its accompanying anxieties had never been faced; it was simply circumvented"; through disavowal and "'play'" the subject could "deny the primal scene through inventing a counterfeit couple," by which she means the subject and his or her masochistically obliging partner (*Plea* 41). Yet isn't the program of the perverse patient the selfsame strategy employed by object-relations theory? It circumvents the Oedipus at the same time that it offers in its stead the preeminent perverse "counterfeit couple" of psychoanalysis, the indivisible mother and child to whom all futures trace their origins.

If the pervert denies the Oedipal situation, so do object-relations theory and Kohutian self psychology. If the pervert suffers from an inability to address the role of the father's penis, certainly object-relations theory disavows the role of the father in the caregiving milieu. As I have argued, the exclusion of the father by object-relations is merely the ultimate disciplining of gender by the psychoanalytic project to date. It is in object-relations theory that we find, by accident as it were, the manifest expression of the phallicized interpretation of the mother's body that is repressed in the Freudian sexual economy.

Although Freudian and Lacanian theories profess to underscore the role of the father because of their emphases on Oedipal-level experience, they too exclude the third term through submitting feminine sexuality to an overarching and, as I have argued, *overcompensating* phallicized anatomy that disguises the primary mother-child "body" on which it is founded. If it is the task of the pervert to insist on a single gender, so too is it the unstated necessity of psychoanalysis to dramatize at length gender assignment when all along difference is circumvented. This single gender, however, based on the mother-child dyad, is transformed from a primary feminine sexual economy into a phallic economy that winds up signifying no more than its own absence. Its absence is reconfigured as its presence inasmuch as the phallic center of psychoanalysis is sustained through the appropriation of an originary erotic model it articulates *as* erotic and *as* originary *in its own terms*. It is not, furthermore, that the originary feminine sexual economy of the mother-child relation is the foundation that the phallocentric *conceals;* rather, the fantasied relation between the mother and child is seen *through* the fantasy of phallic sexuality. It is because of the precarious constitution of the father's role, of the penis's value, of the phallus as desirable and powerful, that the body of the mother must be disciplined to care for her child within certain guidelines. The imposition of a masculinist psychoanalysis on mothering is analogous to affixing a phallus to the body of the mother.

The position of the child I explore in the following chapters on its literary manifestations, as a go-between that at once reveals and collapses the space it measures, is similar to the role the child is asked to play in psychoanalytic theory; here, the child is "treated" (and I use this term in its analytic sense as well) as the central term of an object relationship that is presented as primordially two but is in fact only *one* whole object, as the theory of the undifferentiated mother-child unit so clearly illustrates. Indeed, the covert mission of object-relations theory is not only to collapse the triangle into the dyad but further to represent a dyad that looks suspiciously like a single object—hence the persistence in characterizing the adequate mother as an adjunct to her child.

The psychoanalytic child functions for the theory as a device that obfuscates the superaddition of a triangular relation to a dyadic subtext. The psychoanalytic child is the culmination of a series of displacements, projections, and disavowals that seek to locate the child as temporally before and after the parental couple, which consequently becomes no more than a symbol for the child it is *about*. At the same time, however, the child is always inevitably about the adult insofar as the adult sees her/himself as this former idealized child and destined to be once again (as the idealized potential future of the species the child represents).

The child seems to heal the relational disturbances that haunt the underside of the happy monogamous couple; nevertheless, the child highlights the differences between the manifest and latent fantasies that motivate the sexual relation, what the couple aims for consciously versus their unconscious agenda. The panacea the child proffers is laced with cultural dis-ease, a desperation and an incapacity to trust in our lived values, an inability to distinguish between projected cultural fantasies and a "scientific" account of the origins of the human subject. The go-between child acts out our inconsistencies, dreadfully shows us where they lie even as we employ this child as a distraction. Thus, the child tells us not only of the concealed fantasy but of the structure of that concealment.

While on the social level the child is the origin of social maladies, and on the psychoanalytic level the internalized and repressed child is the cause of adult pathology, at the same time the adult parent precipitates the child into that deviant path—but of course the adult is merely the final term of the child, the "product" of a series of deviations who is bound to "reproduce" the same. What, then, happens to the actual child, caught at the intersection of social fantasy and individual desire? The child figures alternately as a criminal or perfectible future, a deviant or idealized past, a constantly transforming and transformed term through which the psychological individual intersects her or his instinctual desire with social fantasy. The actual child, then, is the go-between child who repeatedly is interrogated, denied, idealized, reconstructed, vilified, corrected by a psychoanalytic praxis with a social agenda, by a society with an unconsciously motivated agenda. This child of psychoanalysis is not a subject, nor even a signifier but rather a *space* where mutually divisive signifiers unfold. It is an expectation, it is a blind spot, it is a field on which desire deceives itself and isolates false objects. It is that which must be suppressed in order for the terms it supports to be lived as real.

Whereas the psychoanalytic child manifestly is the treasured object of an ongoing theoretical enterprise in its service, the child of self-acknowledged fictions more explicitly follows the path of all dangerous impulses into the nether world of repression. The idealized child of psychoanalysis overcompensates for the distrust and horror with which it is associated, in contrast to the ambivalent child-figure of imaginative literature who receives more directly at the hands of its text the ambivalence it generates.

As I turn to self-acknowledged fictional accounts of the child, I am concerned that despite efforts to the contrary, psychoanalytic theory will haunt my readings as a universal truth. So, let it be said here that my own understanding of psychoanalysis (its various theories as well as its historical relationship to a seriously taken child subject and a bourgeois nuclear family dedicated to the production of these subjects)[28] is that if the category/concept "childhood" were to expire tomorrow, psychoanalytic models of the human subject would be unimaginable. In this sense, the novels function as extensions and interpretations of psychoanalytic theories of the child because theorists and novelists share historical and cultural contingencies. That being said, so do I. My readings of these various uses of the child have as much to do with my own situatedness—as the child of divorced parents (like Maisie), as the mother of a child, as the child of a primary caregiving mother and all the fantasies to which that position gives rise, as the mother of a child with *two equal* caregivers and my isolating and appalled sense of how rare this model continues to be in the United States. Indeed, my relationship with *all* the texts explored is informed by my own embeddedness in the nuclear family and its consequent intrapsychic effects that orchestrate exactly what and how I see. Nevertheless, it is my hope that through my efforts to tug out of place the patched-over places—those spots that, if lifted, offer us glimpses of the incoherent that rupture otherwise implacable edifices of knowledge (about child development, about human object relations, about victimization, about sex, about love)—then in the mere inspection I might invite attempts to revise currently received assumptions about the role of the child in Western society.

As I will show in my final chapter on what I call the "speculative children" of contemporary culture, it is important to address our uses of the child because, as the twentieth century has progressed, these fantasies have become increasingly desperate (for adults) and dangerous (for both adults and children)—perhaps in response to despair over the disjunction between fantasy and reality as well as the need to suppress and/or displace aggression. The site of innocence so care-fully narrativized for the child since the eighteenth century has been co-opted by adults who deny both responsibility and agency as ev-eryone strives to enter the no-fault position of the child.

Notes

1. Nevertheless, Kohut insists that *he* focuses on "Tragic Man" as op-posed to Freud's concern with "Guilty Man" (*Restoration of the Self* 132).

2. Consider Freud's definition of the fetish, the substitute for the ma-ternal phallus that conceals the revelation of castration. It is as this dou-ble function of the fetish that the mother-figure serves psychoanalysis, as I will show in more detail at the end of this chapter.

3. See Edward Shorter, Philippe Ariès, and Carl N. Degler for a sense of how historically recent are both "separate spheres" and the nuclear family.

4. At the same time, we need to avoid the kind of historical nostalgia that tends to create a distinction between a fallen present and an idyllic past. So, for example, to say the family was indeed in better shape in the 1950s is not true; rather, the country had more confidence in the nuclear family that was being shored up. Feared dissolution of the fami-ly as the result of political trends seems to be nothing new. Antebellum fiction, for instance, stressed the breakdown of the family as the conse-quence of abolition *or* slavery. Thus, Harriet Beecher Stowe's *Uncle Tom's Cabin* as well as Harriet Jacob's *Incidents in the Life of a Slave Girl* showed the deleterious effects of slavery on the white family; conversely, Mary Virginia Terhune and Caroline Lee Hentz, representing the Southern point of view, use slavery to symbolize the Southern investment in "family."

5. Anna Freud herself openly admitted the futility of reversing recon-structed data and applying it predictively (*Normality* 191). But she was not one to lay at the feet of the mother the multitude of the child's ail-ments, current and future. While she granted the mother a powerful in-fluence, she asserted nevertheless that "she cannot produce either neu-rosis or psychosis" (Kris, "Problems of Infantile Neurosis" 62). There is an enormous difference between influencing the child's psyche and pro-ducing it. It seems only reasonable to believe that a primary caretaker will have considerable effect on a child's development as well as on its relationship with the rest of its environment. On the other hand, to hold the mother accountable for the production of the child in all respects, beyond the economy of the womb, is a brand of overburdening along the lines Alice Balint has suggested.

6. Baranger et al. do Klein an injustice, however; perhaps, reading Klein in light of future generations of analysts who failed to differenti-ate between a real mother and an introjected object, she equates Klein's localized persecutor with the "real" mother. Klein's localized persecutor,

however, is only a localized imago that, in the Kleinian universe, has little or nothing in common with an actual mother. In the end, Klein's universe dismantles the affiliation between real and introjected objects to such a degree that infant development seems a rather hit or miss affair. Sylvia Brody attacks just this element in Klein: "The implication is that what mothers really do with their infants, and really feel for them, is of little avail in helping the infants in the inevitable struggle with wild emotional impulses against their mothers and themselves. Yet theoretically, if the fantasied good or bad mother is more important to the infant than the real one, then the actual behavior of the real mother is of minor importance" (61). It was not that Klein altogether discounted the formative role of the environment. Her case histories repeatedly illustrate how traumatic events generate childhood anxiety and neurosis. But instead of focusing on the mother as the single representative of "environment" in the child's life, Klein sees that a child's world is influenced by diverse factors, including siblings, world events (Klein treated a number of wartime children), or accidental circumstances, such as a child stumbling in upon parents having sex.

7. Anne Dally, in *Inventing Motherhood,* contends that the syndrome of blaming the mother worked to the advantage of men in postwar economy in England and the United States; during World War II, she points out, many women entered the job market, and making them the sole agent of their children's futures was a strategy to drive them back into the home and out of jobs needed by men (88–91).

8. Judith M. Hughes refers to Klein's "downright sloppiness" (89).

9. I have taken the distinction "non-Kleinian theories of object relations" from Toril Moi ("Patriarchal Thought and the Drive for Knowledge" 190). I find it useful in that, although Klein was the "founder" of the British object-relations school, it is impossible to include her formulations of a conflict-ridden infant in the deficit narrative that succeeded her.

10. Despite Fairbairn's de-emphasis of Oedipal thinking in his writing, the object-relations analyst, Harry Guntrip, found him far too Oedipally oriented during his own analysis with Fairbairn; Guntrip wound up leaving Fairbairn for Winnicott! For an account of Guntrip's analyses, see "My Experience of Analysis with Fairbairn and Winnicott."

11. This is similar to the reversal motivating attachment theory, which places instinctual gratification (the oral incorporation of milk) as secondary to the contact with the object. The erotogenic factor is dramatically minimized.

12. Like Klein, Fairbairn believes that the child internally "splits" the mother into exciting and rejecting objects, hence the use of "ambivalent."

13. Benjamin's combination of observationist confidence in infantile subjectivity and classical Freudian theory that problematizes such subjectivity is a useful example of the perils of trying to reconcile these trends.

14. Winnicott calls the mother-child unit a "nursing couple" (*Paediatrics* 99). For further examples of such characterizations, see Ilse Hellman, "Simultaneous Analysis of Mother and Child" (380), and Dorothy Burlingham, "Empathy Between Infant and Mother" (778).

15. Jessica Benjamin discusses the degree to which the idealization of mothering is done at the expense of woman's sexuality and agency. See especially chapter 3 of *The Bonds of Love*. It is important to note, further, that to be a sexual subject in psychoanalysis is to be an agent.

16. According to Freud, what draws the anaclitically oriented man to the narcissistic woman is the lure of his own forfeited narcissism (*SE* 14:89). Sarah Kofman addresses at length the inconsistencies in this essay in her book, *The Enigma of Woman* (50–65). Elizabeth Grosz as well discusses the extent to which the man's object-choice is likewise narcissistic but argues that Freud is aware of the convergence. She goes on to stress that, if one follows Freud's logic closely, one finds that the woman's desire is in fact anaclitic while the man's is narcissistic (130–31).

17. Of course, the question arises, how can the child construct a term outside of the breast when the breast is its only (primal) term? According to Melanie Klein, it cannot; she contends that the penis (both its "good" and "bad" incarnations) is premised entirely on the breast. See especially "The Oedipus Complex in the Light of Early Anxieties."

18. The absence of the father in the bourgeois household has led, in psychoanalytic theory, to an extreme emphasis on the mother-child relationship during the pre-Oedipal stages. Social contingencies consequently have solidified into transcendent psychological "truth." More noteworthy even than an attempt to ground social arrangements in transhistorical intrapsychic necessity, however, is the condemnation that one finds in so many psychoanalytic accounts of multiple caretaking as an alternative. Not only has the social trend produced a given brand of developmental theory, but the theory itself goes so far as to validate this trend as optimal. There has been some literature on the role of the pre-Oedipal father; but, always he appears as a "substitute" for the mother—thus perpetuating a dyadic model. See, for example, Dorothy Burlingham's "The Pre-Oedipal Infant-Father Relationship," John Munder Ross's "Fathering: A Review of Some Psychoanalytic Contributions on Paternity," and Kyle Dean Pruett's "Oedipal Configurations in Young Father-Raised Children." While Burlingham argues that the father often is an acceptable "substitute," Ross insists on the importance of the father's reality-bearing presence "who offers ways out of a child's arresting entanglement with the mother" (321). Nancy Chodorow, on the contrary, emphasizes the mother's position as a member of a familial constellation, who brings to bear on the relationship with her child these multiple affiliations (including her tie to the father). Walter Davis states the matter forcefully: "Alone with the mother, one is actually with the wife of a particular husband/father, inserted into a complex relationship which usually reveals its terms only when one recognizes the role of grandpar-

ents, siblings, and other relatives" (243). Selma Fraiberg as well remarks on the presence of these extra-dyadic influences she calls "ghosts in the nursery," although she, like many others, lapses into a "blaming the mother" perspective. See "Ghosts in the Nursery" in *The Selected Works of Selma Fraiberg* (100–136).

19. Notice that Winnicott needs to remind his reader that the "infant's hallucinating and the world's presenting" are not identical ("which they never in fact are")—as though we might not know this! To what extent might this odd qualifier be a signal for Winnicott's own worried preoccupation with disruptions of all kinds?

20. As Laplanche and Pontalis remark, it is not "the real object, but the lost object; not the milk, but the breast as a signifier, which is the object of the primal hallucination" ("Fantasy and the Origins of Sexuality" 15n).

21. Winnicott theorizes that in its individuation from the mother, the child utilizes a comforter (generally a soft object, such as a blanket) to bridge the chasm from the fused relation to the mother to its status as a separate subject. See "Transitional Objects and Transitional Phenomena" in *Playing and Reality.*

22. Erik Erikson as well considers the timing and management of weaning central to the subject's future object relations.

23. "L'unité perdue de soi-même."

24. The positive Oedipus complex is the arrangement wherein the child loves the opposite-sex parent and is rivalrous with the same-sex parent; the negative manifestation of the Oedipus reverses this paradigm.

25. "Le mouvement de l'Oedipe s'opère, en effet, par un conflit tri-angulaire dans le sujet; déja, nous avons vu le jeu des tendances issues du sevrage produire un formation de cette sorte; c'est aussi la mère, ob-jet premier de ces tendances, comme nourriture à absorber et même com-me sein où se résorber, qui se propose d'abord au désire oedipien" (*Complexes* 56).

26. The Oedipal reading of a theory that wants to eliminate fathers hardly needs to be pointed out.

27. This is only one reading of Lacan's use of "One," which I borrow from Jane Gallop (*Daughter's Seduction* 79). For an excellent account of the philosophical and mythological history of the One, see Jean-Joseph Goux's "The Phallus: Masculine Identity and the 'Exchange of Women.'" Goux traces the phallic myth to Osiris's simulacrum as well Plotinus's understanding of the One as "fertile power" (47).

28. It is worth noting that the nuclear family was as foundational in the theories of Marx and Engels as it has been for psychoanalysis. As Jeffrey Weeks points out in *Coming Out,* their blind emphasis on the traditional division of labor between the sexes is fixated in a bourgeois perspective of gender and the mother's central role in caretaking (144).

4

The Go-Between Child: Falling into Difference

The child bear[s] the full brunt of the open or secret
conflict between family members, thereby assigning him
the sole function of bearer and messenger of the parental
unconscious.

—J.-B. Pontalis, *Frontiers of Psychoanalysis*

When one is made into two, there is no going back on it.
It can never revert to making one again, not even a new
one.

—Jacques Lacan, *Feminine Sexuality*

L. P. Hartley's 1953 novel *The Go-Between* shows just how traumatic adult sexuality can be for the child, specifically the child whose
job it is to serve the sexual couple. Popular among the psychoanalytic community from the 1930s through the 1950s was the theory
that a traumatic event or situation would derail the young subject
from the "anatomically inborn and inevitable fate of both sexes"—
heterosexuality (Feldman 74). Homosexuality, the theory held, was
a kind of "detour" (Feldman 75).[1] Yet despite the avowed confidence
in the "inevitability" of the heterosexual program, the trauma-theo-
ry makes clear how uncomfortably tentative gender might be. The
pivotal traumatic event in Hartley's novel precipitates the child out
of the developmental trajectory of the sexual relation into an asexu-
ality that seems to be a code for "deviance" of some kind. The bisexuality implicit in the child-protagonist's position (caught as he is
between his desire for the "father" and the "mother") reveals with
distressing clarity that in the gender-fluid stage of preadolescence the
child can go either way, as it were. The trauma plunges the child haplessly into a gender narrative that the novel laments as a misfire. Because of the position of the novel's child, Leo Colston, in relation to

not only his own gender-affiliations but also his constitutive role vis-à-vis the adult sexual relation, it is important to look at this paradigmatic instance of the go-between role of the child who produces and is produced by fantasies of gender.

Once upon a time, Hartley was a precanonical British writer.[2] As it stands now, I hope that I can count on at least some of my readers having seen the 1972 Joseph Losey film with its image of desiccated and wasted adulthood fumbling back in time for what marked both the beginning and end of Leo's life—the lush summer of his thirteenth birthday. It is precisely because of this novel's relation to time that I consider it out of chronological sequence, before the novels of the nineteenth century to which it looks back as longingly as Leo Colston does to his mythologized boyhood. In this context, the succeeding chapters on Dickens and James will treat the child that haunts Hartley's text as a grounding "authenticity" that eludes the crass styles of the twentieth century—a century of people who have vulgarized childhood, sex, and the relationship between the two, a vulgarity anticipated by Henry James, a class revulsion shared by Hartley.

Hartley's novel is about its own anachronistic status insofar as it tries to recuperate an era of self-esteem for the British "empire," when what Martin Green has called "the children of the sun" (men like Hartley and his privileged public school/Oxbridge set born around the turn of the century) reposed naive confidence in the permanence of national and class prestige. Like many other "cold war" novels, *The Go-Between* turns to childhood in retreat from what Robert Hewison describes as "the difficulty of coming to terms with the post-war present" in which England ceded its status as an imperialist power to the dreary bureaucratizing chores of the welfare state (*In Anger* 91). Now, titled owners of country houses showed their houses to American tourists in order to meet expenses. Now, just about anyone could gain class credentials by attending schools (Harrow, Eton, Oxbridge) hitherto reserved for those of high birth. While the class nostalgia of someone like Hartley seems transparent, as does his need to sing his class saga as a narrative of childhood lost, what is less evident is how all this gets bound up with the issue of sexuality, and "deviant" sexuality at that.[3] Further, how does what the psychoanalytic paradigm would predict to be "deviant" emerge in Hartley's account as no sex at all? Indeed, Graham Greene's sexually traumatized child of his 1936 short story "The Basement Room" ends up just like Leo—alone, apparently traumatized out of any kind of sexual relation.[4]

Certainly much work has been done on the factors that predisposed psychoanalysts to marginalize and then try to "cure" nonheterosexual sexualities.[5] Homosexuality poses a threat to a bourgeois investment in the nuclear family and its tacit laws of sexual constraint. Yet, as Martin Green has emphasized, homosexual activity was pervasive among Hartley's peers, the very people we find predictably conservative when it comes to class difference and even such nineteenth-century bourgeois fantasies as the innocent and vulnerable child. Nevertheless, Hartley's trip back in time, while it clearly delights in a certain lost grace, represents even this past as a postmortem for the golden age—and the childhood he recuperates is one of anguish, tragedy, loss. One could dismiss his account as the standard stuff of primal scene fantasies and leave it at that. The horror and/or death that ends childhood signifies sex—either the child's sexual awakening or the revelation of its sexual origins—or, more commonly, both. But the sex in the novel not only does not awaken Leo, it precipitates him into a lifelong latency. *The Go-Between* offers a striking illustration of how psychoanalytic uses of the child to confirm its narrative of gender identity do more to disrupt than sustain the heterosexual fantasy.

The Phallic Child

Jacques Lacan observes that "in the case of the speaking being the relation between the sexes does not take place" ("God" 138). Heterosexuality strives to make two into one, denying the intersubjective "relational" experience; furthermore, what there is to speak of is phallocentric, premised only on the male term. There is no relation because only one sex is articulated and a relation necessarily denotes more than one.

Then what of the child produced by this "union," this nonrelation? Lacan philosophizes that *"there is something of One,"* which "is set forth in [Freud's] concept of Eros, defined as a fusion making one out of two, that is, of Eros seen as the gradual tendency to make one out of a vast multitude" ("God" 138). Yet isn't the "something" derived from the two-become-one very specifically (literally) the child-representative of the sexual fantasy? Isn't the child in fact installed in the space fantasy has veiled, a space that paradoxically is disavowed? We might say that like Aphrodite, the child springs from the oceanic landscape of love where identities merge and dissolve, the very desubjectifying condition of love engendering love's subject.

The child is supplementary in the sense that it adds to the sexual relation; a third party joins the parental couple. Yet, in an ironic twist, the "supplement" subtracts as well, in a single stroke effacing both itself and the difference between the parents. Even though the child becomes an emblem of the parental unity, it is an emblem that must be expelled from the sexual scene the moment it appears. This is because the child necessarily reveals the very space of difference it is bound to mystify. Its unifying function belies the insuperable gap it traverses.

If the idea of the sexual relation is founded on a gross deception, so then is the child proceeding from a relation that cannot happen. We know from what Freud tells us of the sexual theories of children that they originally think the baby is born from the cloaca, as a fecal equivalent, and that the female child grows up to imagine she will give birth to her own penis. In short, the child is never itself. Rather, it is inevitably the product of a series of equations founded on distortions. Because of its position vis-à-vis human sexuality, the child can never be any more than what is unspeakable about the sexual relation.

Because the child is the representative of the longed for "fusion" of the sexes, it in turn figures the duplicity of its own referentiality. Either it plays its role as fecal product, reducing sexual difference to the undifferentiated bottom, or it supplies the missing penis to the woman who, as a result, becomes—what?—just like a man. Or finally, and more familiarly, the child represents the wished-for convergence of man and woman into a single undifferentiated sex, because the child is the mark of the denial of sexual difference.

But when I say that the child plays the phallus par excellence, what can I mean? Especially when one considers that this very phallus is what Lacan designates as marking the place of sexual difference. Nevertheless, Lacan insists that the phallus can only play its role as veiled ("Meaning" 82). Like the snake-infested Medusa's head, the phallus manifests the opposite of what it disguises—castrated genitals. Thus, if the phallus rises up in the place where the sexes diverge, it is only to mystify the other of phallocentrism (the woman without a penis), whereby it negates sexual difference, proclaiming its decree: there is no sexual relation; there is only something of One. There is only the child who is born to traverse the renounced gap between the sexes, destined at once to figure and supplement the censored space of difference. The child is fated to be the go-between.

The real child is not the phallus but the adult acts as though it is; for the adult, the child is the link to her or his generational and gender positions, as well as the origin of sexuality as such. The phallic child, the psychoanalytic symbolic equation, is an adult construct. Hartley's novel unwittingly exposes the stratagems of the psychoanalytic equation that the novelistic fantasies reenact. Here we find an adult restored to his repressed sexual past through the agency of the child who emblematizes both the beginning and the end of sexuality, who performs that sexuality's form and function.

The relationship between the adult and an internalized, hitherto reviled, child is acted out directly in the Prologue to the novel. Upon discovering his childhood diary, the sixty-five-year-old narrator, Leo Colston, tells us that it "refused to disclose its identity"; the child-voice sequestered therein remains a mystery, a sealed-off perspective with which the adult projectively identifies him (3). It is not the diary, the site of the child, that refuses, however; it is the adult who refuses to speak to a past that haunts him as a result of the Herculean effort of silencing. "I did not want to touch it [the diary]," the adult narrator tells us twice, as though the touch is sordidly genital, a masturbatory touch, an otherness that is the self (4). Certainly the past represented by the twelve-year-old Leo is a sexual past, specifically a primal scene experience. Nevertheless, in a metonymic sidestep, the diary comes to stand for the child and the child for the sexual scene— as though what in the past happened *to* the child, the child has now *become*.

These two perspectives, that of the child and that of the adult, motivate the novel, and it is the novel's job to attempt a reconciliation, specifically, between the child who is the product of the primal scene and the adult who has failed to assume (re)productive agency. "'Where above all is the Virgin, with her shining face and long curling tresses, whom I entrusted to you?'" the adult Leo imagines his twelve-year-old self interrogating him (17). Where, in other words, is the sexuality in your story, the young Leo is asking.[6] The trust in a reproductive future (linked figuratively with fictional creation) is what has been betrayed by the adult who stagnates in a latency-age brand of sexual deep-freeze. As Anne Mulkeen has noted, the novel looks through "two pairs of eyes (actually the same pair, fifty years apart) so contrasting in their viewpoint" (98). It is precisely this enormous perspectival contrast ensuing from the adult narrator's fifty-year flight from a renounced child, a child endlessly rehearsing a story no one hears, that enables the novel to analogize so remarkably the phallic obligation conferred upon the repressed child of psychoanalysis. Because of the integrative failure, this child has all the power (and individuated identity) of an altogether different subject.

Leo is a prototypical phallic child in that he conspicuously functions as a sexual liaison. For the month preceding his thirteenth birthday, Leo Colston, renowned at his prep school for his occult code- and spell-making talents, is a guest at the country estate of a school friend's wealthy family. During his stay, Leo acts as a messenger between his friend's older sister, Marian, and her lower-class lover, Ted Burgess, a tenant farmer. The traumatic culmination of his go-between activity is to witness the pair making love on the dirt floor of an outhouse.

The Oedipal triangle is almost parodically evident, with Marian in the position of mother, Ted the father, and Leo the child traumatized by the primal scene, the future anterior of his own conception. Leo identifies the various members of his newfound world with the gods of the Zodiac. Marian plays the Virgin while Ted, her lover, is Aquarius, the Water-Bearer, and the Viscount Trimingham, Marian's fiancé, is associated with Sagittarius. Leo himself is pronounced Mercury by Trimingham, who is the first of the group to employ Leo as a messenger.[7] The child revels in his membership in the Zodiacal community and initially appreciates his role as their envoy.

The novel foregrounds Oedipal relations. Leo goes so far as to refer to Marian as his "fairy godmother," and it is Marian's lover, Ted, who offers to unfold for Leo the mysteries of "spooning," assuming the father's role, and cementing the triangular relationship among the three.[8] Yet, Ted turns out to be a false father who will not fulfill the promise he made/showed. When Leo presses him to keep his side of the bargain (go-between service in exchange for the story of the sexual relation), Ted demurs. Ted evades the father's responsibilities even as he exacts the child's wage from Leo. Another triangle is formed by Lord Trimingham, Marian, and Leo. Moreover, underlying the first two is Leo's "real" parental scene including his real mother and his dead father. On a superficial level, we might conclude that Leo is seeking a father to replace the deceased one and a "mother" in the form of a young woman who can serve as a more appropriate object of displaced sexual desire. But Marian is in many ways a more masculine figure than her male partners, and the triumvirate of fathers all fail miserably in the paternal function. The real father has abdicated altogether by dying, while Trimingham is disfigured, figuratively castrated, and Ted, who hoards the truth of generation, the discourse of the sexual relation it is the father's function to supervise and transmit, takes his own life. Hence we have too many dead fathers and a central female character who plays the mother like a man.[9] Martin Green has noted "a distrust of the major masculine roles" among the English aesthetes of Hartley's generation (60). Indeed, it is Leo's untiring dedication to his pursuit of traditional gender role (models) that makes him so pitiably susceptible to his "tragic" awakening.[10]

The Go-Between has at once too many parents and no parents at all, the overabundance signifying the underlying absence. Beneath the sturdy edifice of the Oedipal structure itself might we find the absence of any family system whatsoever? And isn't the story of the child longing for the parent of the opposite sex and fearing the retribution of the same-sex parent yet another fiction installed in the space of desire that gives a form and a name to what always threatens to explode into polymorphous perversity? The very rigidity of the Oedipal system suggests that it cements roles in order to fix what is otherwise mutable, the slippage of sexual and generational identity. It is as a result of this instability the child brings to the Oedipal system that the Oedipus desperately appropriates the child according to its terms; the child's disposition is fundamentally bisexual (between gender) and the child throws age as well into question through recapitulating for the adult an always available personal space that has been repressed as history.

André Green perfectly (and shamelessly) expresses the psychoanalytic fantasy of the mother's relationship with her phallic child: "The child is born of the desire that the mother has for [the father], when she asks herself what becomes of the erect penis that has ceased to be in her. This void, which it leaves after its withdrawal, continues to accompany each stage as more room must be made in her belly for the child that she will see only when the process finally separates him from her" (200). He goes on to observe that this fantasmatic production of the child, its insertion into the space of the erect penis, "privileges the trace over the event" (200). Thus, in Green's terms, the child is a "trace" of an event that is structurally mystified as a result of the transformative symbolizations: sexual act into erect penis, erect penis into fetus, fetus into separated child who thus symbolizes itself as the penis it cannot be for the mother, and, finally, the sexual act itself of which the penis is merely a representative copula. Thus the child undergoes progressive deferrals from central to marginal position, stranded in the end as the representation of a representation.

To position the child *as* the phallus is, strangely enough, a means for maintaining the hoax of the Oedipal structure. If the child seems to be an unwitting guest at the Oedipal table of mother and father, a guest for whom a last-minute place must be set, the child is as well the founding moment of the Oedipus, the term that impassions the other two—offers mother and father to each other as related *to* (each other) instead of related *through* (the child). Like psychoanalytic theory, the novel pretends that the child really *is* a phallus, that the Oedipal pair, Marian and Ted, really are dependent on the mediation of Leo, that what the (repressed) thirteen-year-old figures for the sixty-five-year-old is imagination, productivity, virility—in short, the phallus. As the aged Marian reminisces to Leo many years later, "'you were our instrument—we couldn't have carried on without you'"; but at the same time, she declares that she and Ted were "'made for each other'" and asks Leo, "'wouldn't you feel proud to be descended from our union'" (309)? The fantasy of being "made for each other" is dismantled summarily by the confessed necessity of an "instrument," without which the relation could not have "carried on." In fact, the adult Leo is "descended from [their] union" to the extent that his adult life has been a protracted response to the literal sexual union in the outhouse which has culminated in a "dead" child, the traumatized witness of his own obsolescence. Thus, for Marian to confess the relation's dependence on the instrumentality of the child is to confess nothing—as long as the child is a function of, rather than a term between, the sexual partners. Leo is told by a coachman that his weight in the coach "'won't make any difference,'" but that is just the dilemma, is it not (100). The point of the go-between child is to facilitate that which subsequently looks like it can happen without her or him. Difference is just what the go-between must efface—spatial difference, sexual difference, class difference—"Puck or whoever he is who has produced this miracle will vanish gracefully from the scene" (261). Not only is the Oedipal plot of psychoanalysis a strategy whereby the child is expelled from its central position (in the mother-child dyad) to the marginal role of intrusive third term, but the establishment of the child in the phallic role is a means of rejecting the vulnerability and impermanence of the penis in favor of a phallus that cloaks the real of the sexual relation as rooted in difference, separation, contingency, loss.

The Zodiacal identifications represent Leo's attempt to master the Oedipal positions, the only means by which he can determine his own location in the Symbolic register. Perhaps the emphasis on the child's desire to locate himself Oedipally sheds some light on what the Oedipus complex might mean—to the child, as well as to its psychoanalytic purveyors. It is the arena in which the child is structured as the phallus that adults *control*. While the child requires the Oedipal drama to assume a psychosexual "role," the adult couple needs the Oedipus in order to create a missing phallus. Where Leo gains an identity (as Mercury) through delivering the messages between the sexual couple, in turn Marian and Ted gain a relationship. R. E. Pritchard writes that "Young Leo 'is' Mercury, like the mercury in the thermometer [that he checks daily], the involuntary recorder of heat," suggesting the extent to which Leo functions as the index of the sexual relation, the heat between the sexual couple that he unwittingly produces as he registers it as somehow outside his agency (50). Later, he overestimates his agency; he imagines that "by removing myself [as go-between] I had removed the danger" (225).

Mercury's Greek counterpart is Hermes, who is a phallic god, bearing the caduceus. He is related to the phallic herm that arises at the intersections of roads, the very herm to which Lacan alludes in "The Meaning of the Phallus" (80). Like the herm, the phallus stands at what Edward Casey and S. Melvin Woody have described as the intersection of "the natural and the signifying" or, more specifically, at the place where sex is alienated into language and men and women are divided according to the presence and absence of the penis (106).

One could say that on a superficial level, Leo is analogous to the very penis connecting the sexual partners, the human organ that literally unites them. The text indicates that before Leo's arrival on the scene, Ted and Marian's meetings were rare. Leo is the "inter" of their discourse, both sexual and verbal, bearing the love letters that determine future assignations. The terrain between the Hall and the Farm, rich and poor, woman and man, is collapsed in the person of the courier, the very mediating child who paradoxically yearns for the taxonomy he throws into question.[11]

If Leo is really no more than a penis, a signifier of the phallus (that plays a literal intersecting role), he imagines himself a phallus, what Lacan has described as "an abstract, heroic, unique phallus, devoted to the service of a lady" (*Four Concepts* 39). Early on, he wants to *be* the phallus for the mother (Marian). In reference to his "duties as Mercury," he tells us that "I felt I was doing for Marian something that no one else could" (110). Later, he wants to *have* the object of her desire: "deep down I couldn't help wanting what she wanted," the possession of which would make him desirable as the powerful purveyor of the phallus, finally in control of the meanings that now simply impinge on him (148). The phallus conceals the castration (sexual division) for which it stands, just as Leo's four-mile journey between Marian and Ted is intended to dissolve the space it measures. Leo's situation is as self-negating as that of the phallus he both enacts and subserves.

Originally, the child is a willing participant in the sexual fantasy of union. There is a space between the sexual couple the child offers to foreclose. But a question arises about both the magnitude and location of this space. Let us return to the fantasy of Joyce McDougall's patient (discussed in the previous chapter) whose "internal mother-image [was] as an 'abyss,' a 'chasm,' a 'void,' coupled with the idea that his role as a child was 'to keep her filled,' or at times to act like a cork that would keep her enclosed" (*Mind* 99). The difference between the sexual couple that Leo volunteers to fill is akin to this cork that the phallic child represents to both himself and his mother—the thing that will replace the missing phallus or at least seal off the gaping manifestation of its absence (as a veil of sorts). "I knew I ought to be more explicit about the messages," Leo admits, "but how, when my lips were sealed" (197). Leo is at once the sealed message—what might be spoken (the truth of the sexual relation), what might come out (of the mother), and the seal itself—the repression of the sexual relation, that which seals the mother shut as impenetrable, desireless, self-sufficient. One can see in this instance that the absence constitutive of femininity is perhaps merely a displacement onto the female body of the lack inhering in the sexual relation itself. The phallus thus becomes emblematic of the presence of the sexual relation that the penis so briefly serves to cement. It is the phallus (as fantasied penis) that represents both the permanence and the evanescence of the sexual relation, the phallus that is the site of conjunction (it can only play its role as veiled)—and it is the child who comes to stand for the representative phallus.

Hartley emphasizes that this summer is in many respects a turning point for Leo. In his pubertal passage from twelve to thirteen, he is at the same time introduced into the rarefied world of the wealthy and the mysteries of adult sexuality. He is also, crucially, progressing from the childhood realm of magic to the adult system of reality and its attendant social laws. About the day of his thirteenth birthday, Leo elaborates:

> Now that I was thirteen, I was under an obligation to look reality in the face. . . . Looking back on my actions since I came to Brandham, I condemned them all; they seemed the actions of another person. . . . All the time at Brandham I had been another little boy, and the grown-ups had aided and abetted me in this; it was a great deal their fault. They like to think of a little boy as a little boy, corresponding to their idea of what a little boy should be—as a representative of little boyhood—not a Leo or a Marcus. (271)

Clearly, Leo is trying to outgrow the go-between position and achieve a subjectivity in contradistinction to the "terms of another person" (257). It is in the assertion of a separate identity that Leo is thwarted by Marian, who is disinclined to release him from his job as her Cupid. As a child, inhabitant of the imaginary Zodiac, Leo is happy to unite the sexual couple and function for them as the signifier of the relation. As an adult, however, Leo renounces this role and, in renouncing it, has evaded generational law—for which he pays a price. It is Marian's backward tug into the now reviled go-between role that fixates Leo at the junction of the real and the fantasmatic, the adult and the child, the Symbolic and the Imaginary. He cannot go to war (which Leo associates with manhood), nor can he write, a procreative act. Perhaps what Leo minds most about the sexual relationship between Marian and Ted is the diminution entailed in his descent from messenger of the gods to mere sex organ. When Ted and Marian coerce Leo into continuing on as what they jokingly characterize as their "postman" (120), Leo resolves to become instead an "editor" (134). As long as Leo delivers the messages intact, he remains undifferentiated from the message he bears. It is in the effort to become more than the message that Leo is driven to suppress its contents. Similarly, in Jane Campion's recent film *The Piano*, when the child actively refuses the go-between service imposed on her by her mother and gives the package to the wrong man, disaster ensues. Shame, death, sterility follow in the wake of the refractory go-between child.

The novel is as much about class identifications as Oedipal ones and, perhaps because of its desperation to maintain in the face of disintegrating forces both Oedipal and social order, it reveals the unconscious links between the two arenas. When Leo realizes the nature of Marian's relationship with Ted, he fears a breakdown of the social hierarchy to which he is dedicated. He is fiercely concerned about the subtleties of the language and styles distinguishing social status. His own father is dismissed as a failure, a bank clerk, an emblem in the text for embarrassing middle-class habits (e.g., wearing his slippers to breakfast), a position Leo rejects in favor of the Maudsleys who accede to Zodiacal brilliance as a result of their effortless money and manneredly casual etiquette. This is Leo's version of the family romance, in which he identifies with these new fantasied, omnipotent parents in place of the despised reality constituted by his real parents. The primal scene in the outhouse, where class difference succumbs to gender difference, is as much a failure on the part of the parents to be godlike as it is a revelation of the sexual underside of human experience.

In order to maintain his "role," Leo needs people and things to remain inflexibly fixed in their respective functions—and classes.

Being middle-class himself, the very in-between-ness of his status depends on the opposition of rich to poor. From the moment Leo recognizes the actual nature of Marian's relationship with the tenant farmer, he wants it to cease. Rather, he would prefer Marian to be with Lord Trimingham, a more apposite class connection. Leo explains that "order would have been restored: social order, universal order," a wish that reveals the contingency of the "universal" on the social and vice versa (261).

We are left with the sense that the reason young Leo's notion of promise of the twentieth century is so traumatically misplaced, the reason "universal order" has broken down, is because of the insuperable, deadly power of sexuality to dissolve all differences, all hierarchies—at the same time that it maintains as irrevocable the isolation of the subject. Leo's dilemma ensues from the impossibility of his position, which is to elide difference (figured as the sexual couple) at the same time that he strives for distinctions. Like the psychoanalytic solution to the paradox of the sexual relation, Leo craves an imaginary difference founded on an essential sameness. He demands a single term that conditions its own opposite as mirror image.

> There were two arches: the arch of the sky beyond the cricket field, and the arch of the sky above; and each repeated the other's curve. This delighted my sense of symmetry; what disturbed it was the spire of the church. The church itself was almost invisible among the trees, which grew over the mound it stood on in the shape of a protractor, an almost perfect semicircle. But the spire, instead of dividing the protractor into two equal segments, raised its pencil-point to the left of the centre—about eight degrees, I calculated. Why didn't the church conform to nature's plan? There must be a place, I thought, where the spire would be seen as a continuation of the protractor's axis, producing the perpendicular indefinitely into the sky, with two majestic right angles at its base, like flying buttresses, holding it up. (144–45)

Instead of symmetrically bisecting the sky, which would reveal difference as two equal terms, or rather just a single term unfolding on either side of the dividing line, the spire obtrudes asymmetry into Leo's fantasied harmonious universe where he figures as both the vehicle whereby disjunction is fused and the symmetry-desiring subject himself; hence, Leo's subjectivity is a by-product of his go-between function.[12] Like Freud, who originally described the evolution of feminine sexuality as symmetrical to male development, Leo represents difference as more of the same.

Eventually, he attempts to transcend his status as go-between. Leo's

original childhood eagerness to "fill the gap" turns into his desperation to define and separate, to differentiate his identity from the sexual partners. Yet, while the novel ostensibly illustrates the necessity
for the child to "outgrow" the position of the term between, it shares
Leo's inability to construct authentic difference, difference that does
not proceed simply from hierarchic patterns of domination and subordination. Leo's, as well as the novel's, fantasy of social and universal order entails the exclusion of subversive terms. If the novel laments Leo's impossible position as a go-between, its submission to
an idealized standard repeats the strategy of the sexual couple that
incorporates the copula-child as the repression instead of the revelation of difference.

The breakdown of social and sexual order in Leo's world reflects
Hartley's own dismay with the increasing diminution of the grand and
heroic in modern life. In his 1967 *The Novelist's Responsibility,* Hartley
condemned the commonness of contemporary life and literature:

> Many of us remember how the idea of the Little Man grew up in
> the thirties—and indeed before that, with H. G. Wells and Charlie
> Chaplin. He was a cousin of the Common Man and had much in
> common with him, except that the emphasis was laid on "little"—
> perhaps in reaction against Nietzsche's Super Man, who has been
> deservedly discredited. The Little Man was a poor, puzzled creature,
> pushed around by everyone, and he became almost a symbol of
> man in the modern world; a non-descript person, and essentially
> *little:* nothing much, either good or bad, could be expected of him.
> Well, the novelists, or some of them, got hold of him and he be-
> came their hero—he was not good-looking, he was not clever, he
> was not brave—like the heroes of old: his point was that he had
> no heroic qualities in the accepted sense at all. (10)

Like his beset protagonist, Leo Colston, Hartley morbidly witnesses
the retreat of a golden age of heroism, of moral valor and honorable
codes of conduct, into the outhouse where bastards are produced to
usurp the place of the dying generation of those of pure and noble
blood.[13] It is not surprising that Freud's drama of Oedipus, a story of
heritage and usurpation (by the third term—the common man)
emerges at the turn of the century amid diverse narratives of the dissolution of all golden ages.[14] In a letter to Professor Richard Gill, in
which he discussed the real life counterparts of his fictional country
houses, Hartley lamented the passing of this lifestyle:

> I don't think it's surprising that these great houses affected the
> imagination of novelists—they had so much personality and splen-

dour. They are losing it now, in England at any rate, because so few of them are really lived in by their owners,—who share them with the National Trust and make an income out of showing them to the public, with the result that they are half museums, and the life has gone out of them. They are no longer monuments of personal grandeur. (531)

Like Ben Jonson, three centuries earlier, Hartley focuses on the image of the country house to mourn the passing of an lost age of imperturbable class distinctions.[15] While the novel pretends to attack the standards of social difference purveyed by Leo's friend, Marcus Maudsley (one cannot wear made-up bow-ties; one must not call women "ladies"), Hartley's underlying commitment to a lost gentility resists his stab at irony. Leo expresses, through the central episode of the cricket match between the Hall and the village, what he sees as the alternatives: "it was . . . a struggle between order and lawlessness, between obedience to tradition and defiance of it, between social stability and revolution, between one attitude to life and another. I knew which side I was on, yet the traitor within my gates was not so sure" (147).

Although he recognizes the arbitrariness of Marcus's class regulations, his attention to the distinction between the pretentiousness of the wealthy but title-less Maudsleys and the titled but impecunious Lord Trimingham asserts a nostalgia for a bygone era of "personal grandeur," of which Trimingham is the degraded final gasp. In fact, Trimingham's willingness to offer his title for money (through Marian) haunts the text as a source of social collapse. Of Mr. Maudsley, Leo tells us that "he left behind him a whiff of office hours and the faint trail of gold," the faintly repugnant odor of trade being diffused by the irresistible "trail" (141). For Trimingham, Marian herself is the "trail of gold" (she is, after all, the queen of Leo's promised Golden Age) who (mis)leads the unwitting lord into the den of foul office smells, where people toil for their prestige. Trimingham is operating under a deception, the text seems to warn us, if he imagines that his alliance with Marian (the alluring but deceitful bearer of financial security) will resurrect intact that mourned golden past when authentic lords were linked indissolubly to their landed wealth. Marian herself comes to figure class infraction, through her connection with Ted as well as the duplicitous hope she holds out for a restoration of the aristocracy. In her converges all the textual scorn for pretended rank and sexual temptation. She tempts Leo and Ted with her sensuality, just as she lures Trimingham with the beautiful mirage of a recuperation of status.

All Leo's reassuring schoolboy demarcations threaten to disintegrate around him. And Leo himself is part of the problem. He is a pretender among pretenders. He is the middle-class boy who will not reveal to the wealthy Maudsleys that he does not in fact own a summer outfit; and yet the Maudsleys as well are mere pretenders to Trimingham's birthright. Certainly Marcus spends far too much time explaining "U" talk and manners to Leo for him to be thoroughly "U."[16]

The gender identifications are equally fraudulent. Ted, introduced as the epitome of phallic brawn, is oddly feminized both because of his class position and his enthrallment with Marian, who is herself almost a caricature of the phallic mother. Leo's description of the bicycle she has purchased for his birthday centers on the "great height of the saddle, which, pulled out to its fullest extent for Marian to ride, disclosed a shining tube of steel six inches long" (289). While the pacifism of Leo's dead father is represented as somehow emasculating, at the same time Trimingham, the war veteran, the Zodiacal Archer, is imaginatively castrated as well. The sexual indeterminacy of the adults reenacts Leo's own slippage as the symbol that conditions the sexuality it obfuscates. Leo's ostensible mission is to cement sexual and social roles as he clarifies his own; instead he winds up exposing the inadequacy of his function to his intent.

In the Epilogue, the older Leo explains that he "missed that experience [of war], along with many others, spooning among them" (294). As the child "pivot" of the illusions of the sexual relation, Leo has been petrified in conjunction with the simultaneous fulfillment and evaporation of the illusions, thereafter incapable of assuming a subjectivity apart from being the support of a fantasmatic system (246). Leo confesses that he aspired to be a writer but, apparently lacking sufficient drive, instead became a bibliographer; the creativity of writing is too intimately linked with a sexuality he has rejected. Leo has been desexed and, when one considers the circumstances, what else could happen to the child who was expected to collapse sexual division? The desexed progeny of the sexual relation becomes the concretization of the drive to reduce two into One, to eliminate sex altogether. Being neither on the side of the man or the woman, Leo ends up outside sex, the inevitable result of a sex-repudiating fusion. As I will show, Leo's status is finally that of the bisexual subject of psychoanalysis, at once the secret fulfillment of heterosexual desire and an exile from its official program.

Oedipal Manners

As far as Leo is concerned, the lovers have repudiated social law as rooted in the prohibition of incest. In fact, the novel describes the ultimate incest fantasy in that the child precedes the sexual coupling, a conjunction that amazingly depends on the child's intercession. In this way the child can become the cause of its own creation; it is "incestuously" incorporated into the very parental sexual activity from which it is subsequently excluded. One analytic patient described his disavowal of the primal scene thus: "'Although my parents had three children, including myself, *I never imagined that they had sexual intercourse*. I thought that *I* was the only link between them, as if we had formed a V of which I was the apex, and not a triangle'" (Guttieres-Green 456). One might speculate that the literary go-between indicates to what degree we imagine the child preexists its own conception. If, via a series of displacements, the child has come to represent the fantasy of fusion, it is in connection with the elaboration of this fantasy that the child comes into mythical being. The birth of the child is coincidental with conception or, more mystifying still, to conceive *of* the child is to conceive the child. The question of origins exceeds the question and instead becomes asymptotic. Wordsworth's fond assertion that the child is father to the man suddenly seems to be a grotesque evocation of a chain of genealogical distortions.

Edward Casey and S. Melvin Woody write that "the incest taboo is only the nexus at which these two dimensions of human existence, the natural and the signifying, most conspicuously intersect" (107). The post that marks the nexus of animal sexuality and human law is the herm, the phallic bar, and Leo Colston is the "*post*man" whose function is determined by the law he signifies. Ted Burgess is the man of nature who looks out of place in clothes, engaging with Marian in a purely carnal (anticulture) affair. But it is Ted with whom Leo identifies most nearly ("I could not injure him without injuring myself") (293). What is finally the most dangerous force in the text, more dangerous even than the narcissistic arch-temptress Marian who leads men to social compromise and physical death, is nature itself. Subsequent to the revelation of the Marian-Ted relationship, the beautiful environment of Brandham Hall turns ghastly. The sun, Leo's putative ally, is now desiccating the prior lushness, which Leo describes as "the helplessness of nature to contend with nature," a paradox that aptly illustrates the devastating effects of the eruption of a duplicitous sexuality into the presexual arena of the child (119).[17]

Much like Laplanche's characterization of the intrusion into the child's universe of the "enigmatic signifier," the novel figures sexuality as *essentially* deceitful; the only sex in the novel occurs illicitly, behind the scenes. As Laplanche argues, it is not sexuality that traumatizes the child, however, but its mystified representation by the adult, the child's dawning realization of another language that never says what it means, a language divorced from reference precisely *because of* an inexpressible desire that annihilates all prior connectedness. "It seemed, like many things that grown-ups said to one another, the opposite of the truth" (251). Like Leo's sudden recognition of two "natures" that struggle with one another, the child's entrance into adult sexuality marks a confusion between a transparent sexuality without desire (the pleasure of the body) and a desiring sexuality. When Leo stumblingly negotiates the facts of life through Ted's vague references to "spooning" horses who are "in the family way," he is thwarted by Ted's repeated enlistment of "nature" and the "natural" as all the cause and answer he can adduce (123–25). Again, it is the emergence of this new form of the "natural" on Leo's horizon that renders *unnatural* his previous perspective of the natural world. As he complains about the spire's decenteredness, "Why didn't the church conform to nature's plan?" (145). Nature has deceived him, revealed suddenly a devious underside that subverts the reliable harmony with which Leo always has associated it. It is in this shift from the same word to a new meaning that all the old meanings dissolve. "If only grown-ups would be more explicit!" Leo thinks in vexation (228).

The prenatal figure of the child culminates in its own conception during the primal scene encounter in the outhouse. It is at this juncture that the go-between is superannuated. The "two bodies moving like one" seem to have closed the gap of desire (290), and Leo is abruptly deferred from the space between to the periphery of the union. It is a death-evoking scene in more ways than one. Certainly, Leo's self-aggrandizement as the phallus is blasted. No longer the "linchpin" he imagined (225), he sees himself where he used to "be"—representing the unconquerable space between the bodies that can only move as or *"like"* one—but always irremediably are *two*. In that epiphanic glance, the child must necessarily (traumatically) come to terms with his own mythical status—he is compelled to see where he is *not,* where he never was, now that he has been relegated to a position outside of a space he never filled.

Death is portended in other ways as well, in the act of sexed reproduction, the death blow to human immortality. Leo's earlier denial that Marian would "spoon" echoes every child's protest. To be the product of sexuality implies flesh-bound mortality to the child who dreams of spontaneous and incorporeal generation. Thus, in witnessing his own conception, Leo apprehends the lineaments of his destiny—in the dust of the outhouse, where culture recedes back into nature.

In Winnicott's famous mid-1960s analysis of "The Piggle," the little girl, Gabrielle, has nightmare fantasies of a "black Mummy" that points to the child's dawning recognition of her origins in sexed reproduction—hence her mortality. For the young child, death is imagined as both a prior (prebirth) term and an inevitable future: "[Winnicott]: I then interpreted. I took a risk. I said: 'It's the mother's inside where the baby is born from.' She looked relieved and said: 'Yes, the black inside' . . ." (24). Black is the void, the nothing constituted by the womb that produces the child's body as finite: "When I say good night to her she often buttons up my cardigan so that my yams don't get 'dirty and dead.' She has been very preoccupied with 'dead' lately. I said once: 'Soon your yams will grow.'—She: 'And yours will die'" (64). While, in this instance, Winnicott seems to ignore Gabrielle's connection between birth and death, later he formulates it himself.

> Gabrielle: "When will your birthday be? I want to give you some presents." In the setting I found myself ready with the idea of linking birth and death.
> Me: What about my death day? (124)

It is on his birthday that Leo witnesses the primal scene encounter between Marian and Ted, which is to be his death-day as well, in more senses than one. First, the adult Leo strongly suggests that this episode ruined his life, rendered him incapable of creative activity (literary and sexual). Moreover, the death-day is implicit in the birthday, death both in the sense of nonbeing (the birthday locating the site of the emergence of the subject into life) and as a future term to which the subject must return. As Gabrielle shows us, it does not really matter to the child (or to the adult, for that matter) which direction one takes toward death because death temporally surrounds the subject. The birth-day *is* the death-day insofar as it records a finite emergence and disappearance of the subject.

As a result, the child becomes for the adult an emblem of time itself, at once the past it marks as origin and the future it offers to adult desire. It wasn't really the good old days that Hartley was after through the child—no, it was time itself, at least some understanding of how time works; how it is that one can have been born into a world that looked and felt one way and yet now be entirely different, even when it is the same place. This use of the child as a guide through time, the sense that through examining the child one might learn something about how time works, characterizes *Lolita* as well, a novel written by a man quite traumatically robbed of his past. Leo observes: "there was a picture of a lady and a gentleman bicycling gaily along a country road, looking at me and at the future with surprised but pleased and confident expressions" (191). As though comprehended as child and future in the same glance by the imaginary couple, Leo cannot be "seen" outside of his relation to the future that the child is compelled to locate for the adult. If the couple sees Leo "and" the future as though side by side, it is because the child, serving as a guide, shows the couple where the future lies. The child's own subjectivity is inaugurated by the adult determination of his position, a position the child "volunteers" to live; he not only yields to the role, he participates in his objectification by the adult fantasy.

The phallus as emblematized by the child is generational immortality as well, the indefatigable progress of the individual as humankind. In "The Meaning of the Phallus," Lacan writes that "by virtue of its turgidity, [the phallus] is the image of the vital flow as it is transmitted in generation" (82). Not only does Leo represent the "future" of society, he is also the "future" of the sexual couple—what they hope to "be" when they become One—a child. In fact, Pritchard suggests that they do not consummate their relationship until the encounter in the outhouse (54). If this is indeed the only time the couple has sex, what Leo witnesses is the moment of conception itself. His presence at this decisive event indicates the degree to which he stands for (and in for) the contact of bodies. As "future," then, the fantasmatic child is annihilated into the past (the real child) in the very instant that the "future" is fulfilled.

Freud himself was preoccupied with the question of a transcendent future through procreation. The following passage is taken from one of his own dreams:

> At last we came to a small wooden house with an open window at one end. Here the guide set me down, and laid two planks, which stood in readiness, on the window-sill so as to bridge the chasm which had to be crossed from the window. Now I grew really alarmed about my legs. Instead of the expected crossing, I saw two grown-up men lying upon benches which were fixed on the walls of the hut, and something like two sleeping children next to them; as though not the planks but the children were intended to make the crossing possible. (*Basic Writings* 429)[18]

Recalling his descent into an Etruscan grave containing two adult skeletons, Freud interprets the hut as his grave. He goes on to observe, in reference to the children, that "perhaps my children will achieve what has been denied to their father . . . a fresh allusion to the strange romance [Rider Haggard's *She*] in which the identity of a character is preserved through a series of generations" (430).[19] In the beginning of the dream, Freud watches his pelvis and legs being dissected, which suggests a kind of castration (even though Freud never says as much), an operation from which he miraculously recovers, considerably weakened, however. If we follow the dream to its logical conclusion, then the deterioration of his legs becomes associated with death (the ultimate castration) and only his children, phallicized as planks, can continue the journey—in short, live. For one's legs to fail, to be unable to carry on, or to be mortal, is to be castrated. Via the plank-stiffened bridge-children, Freud dreams that he can transcend the grave and circumnavigate castration.

If we were to reduce this dream to a single wish, it might be: I wish my children could be for me the phallus. Observe, moreover, the fact that instead of the crossing, Freud finds two adult men next to whom lie children who will make the crossing possible—but the crossing to where? To the adult men? And how exactly do the children come to replace the planks laid down by the guide? The children represent the relationship between Freud and the adult men, Etruscan skeletons in the day's residue, but simply men in the dream. Lying side by side, adult and child, Freud perceives not the men as the stand-ins for the planks but specifically the children who lead not only out of the grave but to the adults beside whom they sleep, the adult men to whom they are in this sense indissolubly linked. But the adults are premised on dead men and, in this sense, the children are as much dead as alive, their "sleeping" state a denial of the death to which they allude as insistently as a generational afterlife. They are caught between the positions of grown-up and child, the future and death. The children are not at first absolutely children but rather "something like," as though to suggest that the bridge that will lead the adult past the vanishing point of his own mortality is not exactly a child but "something like" (the future) that the child comes to stand in for. Hence, the child can never be just a child; instead it is "something like" something else, something *beside* itself imposed on it by adult projections and displacements—immortality, the phallus.

Leo describes his entrance into the Zodiac as: "Without knowing it, I was crossing the rainbow bridge from reality to dream" (80). Where Freud's crossing is accomplished via his children who function as the bridge, Leo himself "crosses" into a dream (it is at this point that Freud awakens) that he is *more than* a bridge for others—the mother, the father, the analyst, Freud. In the intersection of the father's dream and the child's we can see that the dreaming (or fantasying) subject refuses to locate *himself* as bridge; rather, others facilitate the dreamer's progress. Thus, Leo owes to Marian his ascendance into the Zodiac, only later to learn that it was the other way around; Marian's lofty position is conferred by Leo, and Marian's relationship depends on her messenger—her bridge who thought *himself* conveyed on the wings of the Virgin goddess. Further, the child-Leo functions as a bridge for the adult-Leo who asks to be carried back through time (out of the efficient, affectively cauterized, world he calls reality) into the dream landscape (the realm of the repressed) of his childhood. To get to the child, he must be taken by the child, emblematized as diary. The child, in this sense, is a bridge to itself.

But this language of messages and bridges is adult language superimposed on a child-character who acts and responds according to adult expectations of childhood. Thus, even the child's perspective is a fraud, a skillful sleight of hand whereby the adult reader gets the child without having to talk to him. At many points, the narrator advises the reader that he is editorializing somewhat upon the child-Leo's experience because Leo did not know what he was feeling until afterward! How similar this is to the reconstruction of childhood in therapy and the conviction that the adult can speak so much better for the child than the child for itself. Thus the bridge between the child and the adult is no more than a "dream" (Freud's bridge-children being just that, the dream that directed him toward a vision of immortality through children) that begins and ends with an adult consciousness from which the "real" child is excluded; otherwise, the bridge, founded on a fantasy of childhood and its relationship to mortality and sexuality, would not sustain anything at all—let alone a sexual relation.

One analyst has reported a female patient's transference complaint that "'there's still something wrong between you and me. I can't bridge the gap'" (Friedman 95). The analyst analyzes this "gap" as the failed bond between the analytic subject and her mother, reproduced and reexpressed in her transference onto the analyst. But perhaps the bridge additionally refers to the transferential bridge itself, the span flung across the temporal space between an infantile relationship to the mother and a contemporary relationship to the analyst. Perhaps the subject is trying to define not only the imaginary structure of the transference but also her incapacity to install herself on either side of the bridge that might appear to begin with the adult subject but finds its materials in the interred child. The question becomes: how does one build a bridge with materials that are on the other side of the gap? One needs to get back there before the bridge is erected—yet one cannot cross the as-yet unbridged gap. As the adult Leo acknowledges, his interrogation of the past involves an "exhumation" of the child, overcoming an entire life spent mastering "the undertaker's art" (17). This process of "exhumation" necessitates listening to the child's voice that he lacks the intrapsychic equipment to hear. He needs to speak to the child before he can hear the child. He needs to "exhume" the child *before* he can resurrect him. Thus, the novel becomes the journey back to the child, instead of the child's firsthand account.

Leo's subsequent return to the scene of the crime, as it were, his visit to Marian, his encounter with her grandson, and his concluding epiphanic vision of the Southwest prospect of Brandham Hall (hitherto repressed) is meant to suggest his final reconciliation with the child. Nevertheless, this child is imaginary, the product of a novel. In his creation of the story, the narrator bears the child, and likewise, through his production of the child, the literary text is "born." Similarly, the creation of the child through the transference necessitates the production of a transference through the agency of the child's infantile affects. The gap, so immense—between the past and the present, child and adult, parent and analyst—can only be bridged through a conspiracy of "the suspension of disbelief," in which a mutual faith (of analyst and analysand, of the narrator and the reader) "suspends" itself across an unconquerable divide. Like the analyst and the analysand who agree to assume that something of the past has been "transferred" into the present scene, the reader of *The Go-Between* accepts on faith that what we are getting is the "reality" of the child's perspective.

The Bisexual Phallus

The Go-Between is really an allegory of the bisexual subject and reveals the extent to which bisexuality as sexual position(s) functions for psychoanalysis as an allegory of heterosexuality. Leo's in-between status as well as his transient allegiances and identifications (with the two men and the woman) suggest that the production of bisexuality is a confusion (even indecision) about where to locate oneself in the heterosexual drama. Both J.-B. Pontalis and Judith Butler make the point that bisexuality is not about a fusion of feminine with masculine desires but rather is about two desiring subjects (both heterosexual as Butler observes) functioning in a single body (Pontalis 85; Butler 60–61). Leo's dilemma acts out conspicuously the problem with any notion of primary bisexuality (both its fantasmatic aspects and its inevitable failure).

According to Freud, the human child is originally bisexual in the sense that it fantasies sexual satisfaction with both mother and father. The subsequent achievement of heterosexuality ensues, in the case of the little girl, from her vilification of her castrated mother and, in the case of the little boy, from a supervening narcissistic cathexis of his penis. Compellingly, it is castration anxiety in both instances that precipitates the subject from its primary bisexuality. Like the bisection of Aristophanes' intact man/woman subject into male and female, the recharting of desire according to a heterosexual matrix structurally incorporates a sense of its loss. Leo's eviction from sexuality as an adult replicates Ovid's story of Hermaphroditus. As Pontalis notices, Hermaphroditus is represented as a child, hence his fear of Clytie's advances. Clytie's prayer that "'May no day ever come / To separate us!'" is achieved with all the unsatisfactory literalness of the fisherman's wife's three wishes. "No longer / Two beings, and no longer man and woman, / But neither, and yet both" is the final term of the ultimate bisexual, the hermaphrodite, who is not at all the perfectly achieved union of the sexes but instead a creature excluded from sexuality, the dénouement of heterosexuality's impossible narrative. Pontalis writes: "The acquisition of a double-power (father-mother, boy-girl) turns into impotence; the fusion of the couple into one leads to death and sterility. A bisexual is sexless" (84). The very dangers the bisexual fantasy seeks to transcend, those of separation, isolation, death, remorselessly afflict the bisexual through exile from the social-sexual world. Yet, heterosexuality is founded on the fantasy of a bisexual conclusion, never attained, always aimed for. It is his confrontation with not only the fantasmatic unconscious of the heterosexual relationship but with its bisexual underside that immobilizes Leo—now the ultimate bisexual, the hermaphrodite caught in his own disidentifying embrace.

Such an embrace throws subjectivity into question to the extent that one's subjectivity is inextricably linked to one's gender identity. Leo's desire, at cross-purposes with itself, torn between being the object of the man's and the woman's desires, is derailed from a trajectory of any kind, the desiring trajectory that assigns aims and their objects. The child is always in danger of being derailed in this way, warns the novel, warns psychoanalysis as well whose hidden agenda has always been to define as structurally essential the gender performances it takes as originary instead of cultural. Psychoanalytic accounts of how the subject becomes gendered read like an adventure story of narrowly missed disaster. I would argue, however, that the primary catastrophe for psychoanalytic theory would be the revelation of the sterile conclusion of its own heterosexual story.

The central role played/veiled by the phallus in psychoanalysis is the locus of the bisexual hoax that sustains the psychoanalytic elaboration of heterosexual desire. Like the myth of bisexuality that logically culminates in the interdiction of desire, the fetishization of the phallus causes two different entities drained of difference to look like one—and one whole object to look like two. As Lacan has illustrated so clearly, the myth of the heterosexual union is founded on its own resolution into One. Yet, what Lacan does not address (a problem in which he is complicit) is the enormous effort at dedifferentiation involved in the resolution. The phallus that is not a penis, that rises above (so to speak) its mundane organic status, is the site of the fantasy that a "relation" takes place, a "relation" between two heterosexual desires mediated by (forged by) their mutual "relation" to a phallus that is better than an organ simply because the organ fails in its essential mission—to keep united two bodies. As Shreve observes in *Absalom, Absalom!* "when the brief all is done you must retreat from both love and pleasure" (323). The point of the phallus is to deny the separation, which inevitably leads us back to the separation between the mother and the child. It is on the body and the being of the child that devolves the necessity to be the phallus not only for the mother but for the heterosexual relation itself, as well as its pivotal role in the psychoanalytic economy. It is because the child must assume the guise of a phallus that the child is marked by the bisexuality the phallus disavows by its vaunted maleness. Its bisexual attributes are displaced onto the child, who is consequently bound to act out not only its indebtedness to the phallus but a conjunctive space that the story of the phallus refuses as a viable space of desire; the phallus needs this space precisely in order to engineer its collapse. Thus, the child who gives body to desire (ultimate desire, the bisexual convergence of male and female) simultaneously repudiates desire's unifying mission because the child insists on the space of separation that desire scotomizes.

The child will remain installed in the position of the phallus as long as we pretend that the relation between the penis as organ and the phallus as signifier is purely metaphoric. Despite Lacan's denial of the derivation of the latter's symbolic status from the materiality of the former, he depends on his own fantasies about the penis and its functions for the theorization of the phallus. "By virtue of its turgidity," he tells us, the phallus is an apt symbol of generational reproduction. But isn't he talking about an organ here? Surely it cannot be a signifier alone that can be described as "turgid" as well as instrumental in human reproduction; certainly this is a signifier dependent on an essentialistic confidence in an objectively material body. Dorothy Burlingham argues that "we may assume that the child's whole body symbolizes for the father part of his own body, i.e., the penis, its erection" ("Preoedipal" 39), an insight that does much to clarify this confusion in Lacanian theory between metaphor and organ as well as an overcompensatory insistence on a salient delineation between the two. The real confusion here seems to be between the penis and its erection, the erectability of the penis being privileged over the organ itself, lending the organ the effect of being *more than* its materiality but at the same time inextricably linking it to a materiality on which such an erection depends.

Although the phallus is the symbolic term of the penis, it nevertheless emerges from a certain valuation of the penis, an emphasis on the role of the penis in generation. While the body of the mother is inescapably determined by the psychoanalytic paradigm to be the child's first caretaker, the body of the father is what gives life. The child, the product of reproduction, itself standing for "generation," is fated to be confused with the phallus that produces it because the child is the term to which the phallus points. It is the child who lends the phallus a meaning the phallus lacks without the life-giving and sustaining qualities that the child confirms. Elizabeth Grosz reads Lacan's description of the penis as that which "functions as a symbolic object (an object of exchange or union) between the sexes" (121). What then are we to think about the equation of the child and the penis in not only the psychoanalytic account of the feminine sexual economy but in the psychoanalytic unconscious itself? Since the child is what the woman brings to the sexual relation (her primary object of exchange), is it not arguable that it is what the woman produces rather than what the man possesses that functions as the fundamental object of exchange in the psychoanalytic unconscious? Certainly, it is Marian who *owns* Leo to the extent that he follows her bidding; it is her will that everyone (Ted and Trimingham as well as the family honor/line) finally subserves. To this extent, the novel forcibly reveals the woman's control over the object (the penis-child) that courses between the sexes. Yet, somehow, in the novel as in the theory, the regime of the phallus overwhelms the initial power of the mother. It is the child's connective (phallic) service that is represented as that which binds the sexes—rather than the "mother" (Marian) who "creates" him as a link. The penis takes the credit for the womb's productive agency. Yet the child does not wind up benefiting from its putative agency. Hartley's novel is the story of how the equivalence between the child and the phallus is structured and lived as real and how, finally, the child must pay with its life (coded in the novel as creative adulthood) for the sake of maintaining the fantasied status of the phallus as life-giving. If Leo must disappear in the wake of his own conception, so too must the child relinquish its subjectivity in favor of the progenitor father-symbol, the phallus that cannot function without the child-pretext.

The illegitimate children of Charles Dickens give us the child-phallus equation as the remainder of what compulsively effaces itself as the origin of the child. Thus the phallic child's interminable mission, to find its parents, marks the child as the only proof of the penis while at the same time, through the child's illegitimacy, calling into doubt the existence of the very organ it emblematizes. Such confusion (over the "origin" of the phallus) gets played out in Dickens as a *narrative* confusion over whose story is being told—the adult's retrospective reconstruction of its origins—or the child's eye view of an adult story it yearns to enter. It will take Nabokov, Hartley's contemporary and an author Martin Green extols as the only successful "dandy author," to see the interminability of the Oedipal jokes in not only the nineteenth-century models of childhood but in Hartley's confused form of angry nostalgia imaged as ruined childhood. Nabokov is another author addicted to nostalgia for a home that eludes him (literally and figuratively)—prerevolutionary Russia.[20] While both Nabokov and Hartley use the child figure to work out their relationships to irretrievable "homelands," Nabokov explores more self-consciously how such efforts are pathologized.

But now I turn to Dickens and then James as examples not only of the heritage Hartley has tried to recuperate with the false note of all such repetitions but also to illustrate that the interminable indeterminacies of the relationships between parents and children, family and society, as well as the retrospective narratives that cast adults as failed children, have precursors in Dickens's circular "histories" and James's urgent effort to locate familial guilt.

Notes

An early version of this chapter, entitled *"The Go-Between* Child: Supplementing the Lack," appears in *Compromise Formations: Current Directions in Psychoanalytic Criticism,* ed. Vera J. Camden (Kent, Ohio: Kent State University Press, 1989).

1. I am grateful to Elaine Showalter for suggesting this way of thinking about the go-between implications of the novel. For other discussions of the trauma theory of homosexuality, see George W. Henry, "Psychogenic and Constitutional Factors in Homosexuality," and Ian Stevenson and Joseph Wolpe, "Recovery from Sexual Deviations through Overcoming Non-Sexual Neurotic Responses."

2. I am importing here Richard Ohmann's term for contemporary works that, in light of their critical reception among the canon-making establishment, are clearly marked out for future canonical status. See "The Shaping of a Canon."

3. Edward T. Jones circuitously suggests that Hartley himself was homosexual. He quotes from Hartley's friend, Francis King: "'Had he been a man less scrupulous about not offending convention or shocking his friends, there is no doubt that, like E. M. Forster's, his books would have been very different'" (qtd. in Jones 20). King goes on to observe that Hartley's *The Harness Room* was the most revealing of his works. *The Harness Room* explicitly deals with homosexuality.

4. The relationship between Greene's story and Hartley's novel was noted by Richard Allan Davidson.

5. See Weeks's, *Sexuality and its Discontents* and *Coming Out,* David Greenberg's *The Construction of Homosexuality,* Foucault's *The History of Sexuality,* Showalter's *Sexual Anarchy,* Freidman's *Male Homosexuality,* Silverstein's *Gays, Lesbians, and Their Therapists.*

6. We can see the ambivalence about femininity already emerging here. At the same time that "Where is the Virgin?" is a code for the heterosexual love missing from the adult story, representing such a love as Virgin seems to undermine the heterosexual motive.

7. Astrologically, Mercury is the ruling planet of Virgo, the Virgin.

8. Peter Bien calls Marian a "substitute mother" (182).

9. Bien reads the novel as unproblematically Oedipal, which is a bit facile insofar as the novel self-consciously employs its idea of the Freudian "constellation." Alan Radley criticizes Bien for reading Leo as an Oedipal-level child. Radley proposes, conversely, that Leo represents Freud's pubertal subject. First of all, Radley premises his reading on an assumption that Leo is the equivalent of a "real person," a typical young adolescent with all the attendant sexual and social confusions. Given one of Freud's central tenets, that the unconscious is indifferent to age or time, such an interpretation is in many ways antipsychoanalytic.

10. Green furthermore points out the pervasive contrast between "coarsely heterosexual" fathers and their homosexual aesthete sons (62–63).

11. Consider furthermore the reversal inherent in Marian and Ted's social positions in that the woman is allied with wealth and social power while the man is installed in the inferior, lower-class role—yet another disorienting, "improper" rearrangement of the categories Leo must negotiate.

12. Pritchard insightfully explores Leo's fantasy: "What Leo unconsciously seeks is perfection, impossible for any adult or fallen human being, a serenity and plenitude, whereby all nature within and without is in harmony with his will and desire: the obstacles of material and social 'reality' will disappear, as the Golden Age returns" (51).

13. Jones addresses Hartley's conflicting representations of social hierarchies: "*The Go-Between* . . . implicitly questions the cruelty of the British social structure and the insensitivity of the upper classes—paradoxically in the act of seeming to vindicate them" (152).

14. Consider, for example, the emergence of manifestly dystopic science fictions and science fantasies in the late nineteenth century such as *The Time Machine, She,* as well as the novels of Jules Verne.

15. See Raymond Williams's analysis of Jonson's "To Penshurst" in *The Country and the City* (27–34).

16. For a revealing account of the emphasis on upper-class (U) and non-upper-class (non-U) by upper-class writers like Hartley, see Irving Kreutz's "L. P. Hartley, Who Are U? or, Luncheon in the Lounge."

17. As Pritchard remarks, "Leo thinks that [Marian] *is* the heat; the heat is both her devouring passion and her destructive will" (50). Thus, the destructive heat that parches the landscape is understood by Leo to be Marian herself.

18. Brill's translation more adequately represents the grammatical confusion in the original German: "Anstatt des erwarteten Überganges sah ich aber zwei erwachsene Männer auf Holzbänken liegen, die an den Wänden der Hütte waren, und wie zwei Kinder schlafend neben ihnen" (*Gesammelte Werke* 455–56). If the sentence ended at "*schlafend,*" it would read that the men were "sleeping like two children." It is the "*wie,*" or "like," that complicates the sentence, suggesting that the figures are not at first recognized as children but rather as "something like." It is because there is no noun following the "like" that such an effect occurs.

19. The day's residue for the dream, Freud tells us, was reading Rider Haggard's *She.* Intriguingly, Hartley, in his letter to Richard Gill, explains that the original of the Maudsleys' Brandham Hall was Rider Haggard's home (531). *She* is a story about woman's horrific connection to immortality through her possession of the womb. While this meaning remains latent in the novel, Freud's dream paradoxically makes it manifest.

20. See Michael Long's reading of Nabokov's nostalgia in *Marvell, Nabokov: Childhood and Arcadia.*

5

The Dickensian Child: Finding a Narrative Home

While the mission of Hartley's go-between child is to implement and witness his birth, the Dickensian child is compelled to found the happy family into which she or he can be born, a goal especially analogous to that of analysis itself. Inasmuch as the termination of analysis is signaled by the patient's transcendence of the transference, the family system has been set in order and the patient has been installed in the real family instead of what was hitherto a fantasmatic universe populated by the stuff of unresolved Oedipal conflicts. With the assumption of the correct position, in becoming the real child of historically real parents, the subject is restored to a family never before known as it really was. As Alice Miller puts it, "This is not a homecoming since this home had never before existed. It is the discovery of home" (21). Further, with the recognition that the analyst is simply the analyst rather than a character out of the Oedipal scene's dramatis personae,[1] the patient has escaped captivation by the child's point of view. The family constructed in analysis, the very family restored to the "cured" subject, is perhaps more akin than either subject or analyst would care to admit to the idealized fictional family offered up to the reader at the end of many of Dickens's novels as a regretted beginning to which all just ends must lead.

But it is specifically, critically, this child's voice that analysis entices and treats, the adult's voice always dismissed as resistance. Perhaps the glimpse of the "interminability" of the analytic process over which Freud half-despairingly pondered toward the end of his life was the half-seen vision of the impossibility of determining which subject is speaking, the adult or the child, and, more perplexing still, whether the adult or the child is the actual subject of psychoanalysis. At the end of the classic 1948 film of psychoanalysis, *The Snake Pit,* the analyst asks the patient how she knows she is cured. Ingenuously, she delivers the conclusive statement of analytic lore: "Doctor, I'm not in love with you anymore." But while her analyst may be satisfied with the ostensible evidence of her investment in contemporary love-objects, the viewer cannot help but wonder who it is she now loves in the analyst's place. If it is her husband, as the film indicates, who, we might ask, is he if not yet another substitute for a primary (Oedipal) love-object? In fact, the analyst himself comes to look like the primary object for which the *husband* substitutes. Furthermore, while the film assumes that it was the deluded child-cum-hysteric who mistakenly loved the therapist and the adult who phase-appropriately loves the husband, how can the analyst (who has been for months in the process of engaging in dialogue the child element) distinguish the adult's speech from the child's?

At the conclusion of *Bleak House,* the reader is intended to recognize Woodcourt as the reasonable adult choice for a husband in contrast to what would have been the child's erroneous selection of father-substitute John Jarndyce. Yet, how then do we account for diverse hints that Woodcourt is as much a father for Esther as is Jarndyce, as well as latent narrative dissatisfaction so tenacious that it subsequently reconceives the Esther/Jarndyce relationship in *Little Dorrit* with an altogether different conclusion?[2] The tension in the novel is as inevitable as the confusion inhering in an analytic scene devoted to distilling the child's speech from the adult's. An early version of *Bleak House*'s account of the illegitimate child, *Oliver Twist,* more awkwardly (hence more recognizably) negotiates both the fantasied relationship between adults and children and the retrospective story of origins it is the child's task to confirm. Indeed, the story of *Oliver Twist* is quite similar to the wish-fulfillment daydream Freud described in "The Relation of the Poet to Day-Dreaming":

> Take the case of a poor orphan lad, to whom you have given the address of some employer where he may perhaps get work. On the way there he falls into a day-dream suitable to the situation from which it springs. The content of the phantasy will be somewhat as follows: He is taken on and pleases his new employer, makes himself indispensable in the business, is taken into the family of the employer, and marries the charming daughter of the house. Then he comes to conduct the business, first as a partner, and then as successor to his father-in-law. In this way the dreamer regains what he had in his happy childhood, the protecting house, his loving parents and the first objects of his affection. You will see from such an example how the wish employs some event in the present to plan a future on the pattern of the past. (49)

Yet, the Dickensian version reverses the chronology of the fantasy insofar as the family the child gains at the end retrospectively founds a past; it is in the end that the pattern is forged for the beginning. Such a reversal obtains because the narrative is located in *adult* fantasy that artificially resuscitates a child's perspective. The question of whose fantasy is "speaking," the child's or the adult's, is as pertinent to the Dickensian narrative as it is to analysis. It is in twentieth-century psychoanalysis that we find the elaboration of the Dickensian project of trying to recuperate a child's voice through adult fantasy. It is in the Dickensian project that we find the structure of the fantasy of origins that is the foundational narrative for psychoanalysis.

From the End to the Beginning: Analysis

The therapeutic strategy is eminently archaeological. The superficial neurotic symptom alerts the astute analyst to subterranean etiological layers en route to the original site of trauma. Freud, whose archaeological metaphors start as early as "The Aetiology of Hysteria," rehearsed this particular account of psychoanalysis to the end of his life: "But just as the archaeologist builds up the walls of the building from the foundations that have remained standing, determines the number and position of the columns from depressions in the floor and reconstructs the mural decorations and paintings from the remains found in the débris, so does the analyst proceed when he draws his inferences from the fragments of memories, from the associations and from the behavior of the subject of the analysis" (*SE* 23:259). Originally, Freud's search entailed early and repressed material events in the life of the child. Later, he pursued fantasies of events that did not necessarily occur.[3] In Freud's revision of trauma as erupting from psychical as much as material reality, there is a consequent revolution in the status of the child. What was once a passive, abused victim of adult perversion now becomes the locus of fantasies of seduction. The analyst-explorer who once pursued the tokens of a historical reality hunts instead the origins of a lifelong fictional narrative, the original fantasy that spawned a life of misreadings. According to the seduction theory, the child who speaks in analysis is the source of truth; under the rubric of the Oedipus complex, however, the child is rather the voice of the *proton pseudos*, the first lie.

Analysis is inevitably a process of reversal, of starting with the end product, the neurotic adult, and pursuing that patient backward in time to infancy. Heinz Kohut comments that "the unrolling of the transference during analysis tells us the childhood story in the reverse order" (*How Does Analysis Cure* 23). This recollected infancy, however, is necessarily a reconstruction on the part of both patient and analyst who impose the language of adult desire upon the speechless child. If the child speaks in analysis, it is only in translation, translation not of one language into another (for language is just what the infant lacks) but rather a structuration of prediscursive experience through language. But if the archaeologist can hold in her hand the ancient artifacts, palpate the actuality of their shape and weight, she or he is nevertheless beholding this site from a different site altogether—regardless of how accessible and tangible the objects under study, she or he appraises the ancient world from her position in the contemporary. When the patient offers up infantile secrets, they are not only repeated in the language of the adult, they are being interpreted from the adult position. The child of psychoanalysis, with its abundant store of traumata, is a reconstructed child who speaks in the adult tongue and is received by an adult audience. Hence, there is always a corruption of the tale the child has to tell; there is always a corruption of the child. The child in the adult analysand can never be known *as* child, before the influence of adult perceptions. Like the dream object of analysis, organized by the day's residues of daily life, distorted by the censorious agency of the super-ego, and then reassembled by the process of secondary revision, the subject of psychoanalysis is always in a sense decentered, apprehended through the terms of an-other—the child submerged in the adult and the adult overlaying the child.[4] In his discussion of the "contributions" of adult analysis to child analysis, Charles Brenner describes the extent to which the adult patient brings the analyst a child to be analyzed: "When one analyzes an adult patient, one deals first and foremost with the child that patient once was. . . . At every step in our analytic work . . . we find ourselves confronted with a child. It is an elderly child, as children go, a child who is sometimes as old as we ourselves are, but it is nonetheless a child. Paradoxical as it may sound to say so, it is still true that every adult analysis is a child analysis" (228-29).

Thus analysis always pursues the beginning from the vantage point of the end, the process being not only one of a recapitulation of origins but of origins altered by the adult's apprehension of them, the contemporary neurosis itself a founder of origins. In the analyst's pursuit of the origins of neurosis, the starting point of therapy is the adult neurotic who invites the analyst along a journey, the conclusion of which is the imagined beginning. Analysis is invariably the art of retrospective reconstruction, of not only real past events but fantasmatic events, the origin of trauma in the discourse of psychoanalysis being always the juncture of historical and psychical reality.

The psychoanalytic process, since Freud himself, has been characterized as a narrativization of the patient's life story. Freud's case histories read like stories in which narrative time (the order in which events are recounted) diverges from chronological time. Donald Spence, in weighing the truth value of any given analytic interpretation or construction, avers that considerations of aesthetic "truth" should supersede any preoccupation with historical accuracy. Roy Schafer has described both the analytic process and its theoretical self-representation as narratively akin to archetypal modes of comedy, tragedy, romance, and irony, a subject I will take up later in this chapter.

In *Project for a Scientific Psychology,* Freud describes the etiology of a hysterical patient's agoraphobia, a combination of events that illustrates well the indeterminacy of origins in the psychical arena: "On two occasions when [Emma] was a child of eight she had gone into a small shop to buy some sweets, and the shopkeeper had grabbed at her genitals through her clothes. In spite of the first experience she had gone there a second time; after the second time she stopped away. She now reproached herself for having gone there the second time, as though she had wanted in that way to provoke the assault. In fact a state of 'oppressive bad conscience' is to be traced back to this experience" (*SE* I:354). Although Emma developed no symptoms from the first experience when she was sexually molested, a much later trip to the store, at the time of puberty, was traumatic. She saw two shop assistants laughing, imagined that she was the object of their derision, and escaped in horror. In the first scene, the child, having no knowledge of adult sexuality, responds indifferently. In the second scene, however, the now pubescent Emma experiences a psychic overlap of the two scenes. Jean Laplanche quotes Freud: "We invariably find that a memory is repressed which has only become a trauma *after the event* [here is the heart of the argument: we try to track down the trauma, but the traumatic memory was only secondarily traumatic: we never manage to fix the traumatic event historically . . . in situating the trauma, one cannot appreciate its traumatic impact, and *vice versa.*]" (*Life and Death* 41; Laplanche's emendation).[5]

As important as the attempt to locate the origin of trauma is the relationship between this origin and the subject of psychoanalysis, the analysand who, in the grips of neurosis, is always reliving the trauma. But which trauma exactly—the historical event, or the subsequent fantasy that ignited the historical event, or the interaction of the two? In a sense, the neurotic lives in a perpetual present of the traumatic moment, a moment that itself exceeds temporal dimensions. Analysis, then, tries to situate the subject in time and space at the same time that it is a science premised on the dissolution of these very boundaries; it is founded on a psychical reality that is perforce a subversion of the chronological event.

From the End to the Beginning: Dickens

Like the analytic process, the Dickensian narrative works backward in time, pursuing an end that is a beginning, a beginning that is in fact a correction of origins—the happy family. I am referring primarily to Dickens's stories of the illegitimate child whose purpose is so explicitly to reconstruct retrospectively its own origins. The illegitimate children under consideration, Oliver Twist and Esther Summerson (with emphasis as well on Jo who is freighted with the dangerous cast-off features of Esther), are not only the products of illicit love affairs, they have no knowledge of their true parentage. One has the uncanny sense of children who give birth to their parents because, according to the narrative chronologies, parents succeed children. These two novels are driven to create parents for children who can miraculously exist without them. This is especially the case in *Oliver Twist*, which gives the reader the acute impression of suitable (albeit vague and long-deceased) parents being superadded at the end of the novel as a rather tenuous narrative device.

Bleak House inserts us into a world turned topsy-turvy. Children have assumed adult positions, and adults depend on them for financial and emotional support.[6] Parents rear children as unpaid employees, as extensions of themselves and their personal goals. Mrs. Jellyby requires the secretarial skills of her daughter Caddy for her African project. Mrs. Pardiggle, that stern and overbearing philanthropist, bestows pocket money on her young boys only to wrest it from them for donation to her various charities. Mr. Turveydrop allows his son to marry Caddy Jellyby with the condition that the couple maintain him in genteel indolence. The combination of the oppressed Caddy and the deformed Prince Turveydrop produces a defective child, deaf perhaps to signal a rejection of parental exigencies, parental desire that overwhelms the voice of the child. Children of these self-involved parents are invariably damaged and old before their time. Mrs. Pardiggle's children are described as "weazened and shrivelled," while Peepy Jellyby is a veritable map of the cuts and bruises of parental indifference (116). As one woman remarks to Esther, Mr. Turveydrop "'wouldn't let his son have any name if he could take it from him,'" which is precisely the point (204). Children are refused an identity differentiated from parental objectives. Passing on the name from parent to child installs the parent in the reproductive chain, confirms both parent and child as historicized members of the community; but in *Bleak House* we find a profusion of parents who attempt to deny any such position that necessarily subordinates the individual to the race. As a result, the respective activities of Mrs. Pardiggle and Mrs. Jellyby seem all the more ironic, when one considers the discrepancy between their missionary zeal (the effort to make a mark on the world at large) and their rejection of that other more naturalized historic project—childrearing.[7]

Old before their time (more "wizened" children), the Smallweed children have been incorporated into the designs of their parents and grandparents; they are replicas rather than offspring (284). As the narrator observes: "There has been only one child in the Smallweed family for several generations. Little old men and women there have been, but no child, until Mr. Smallweed's grandmother, now living, became weak in her intellect and fell (for the first time) into a childish state" (298). The developmental progression of the human being is reversed in this pattern of wizened children and regressed adults. The generations produce not young children characterized by future potential and hope but inbred self-images, dwarfed like the Smallweed family by a past that repeatedly consumes the present.

Harold Skimpole, who blithely calls himself a child, goes so far as to request two young people, Esther and Richard, to pay off his debts. But if Harold Skimpole is an example of the child's incapacity to discharge adult responsibilities, what then do we make of the child, Charley, who has the care of her two younger siblings? In Charley we find a mismatched conjunction of adult and childlike attributes: "There came into the room a very little girl, childish in figure but shrewd and older-looking in the face . . . wearing a womanly sort of bonnet much too large for her and drying her bare arms on a womanly sort of apron" (222). Clothed in the vestments of the adult, laden with adult burdens, the child's face is curiously out of place, a grotesque intrusion into the adult arena of something for which society has allotted neither the financial resources nor interest.

We are introduced to no children who are as carefree as Skimpole, as oblivious to life's exigencies. We find no children quite so self-absorbed as the novel's primary child, who indifferently betrays his patron for the sake of his own gratification. Likewise, the loss of intellect that denotes a childishness in the Smallweed grandmother is by no means characteristic of the novel's child characters. Thus, the very terms "adult" and "child" are stripped of not only traditional signification but are even conflated by a text that has trouble determining the distinction.[8] If there are no children in the Smallweed family, neither do there seem to be children in the text at all, at least not *childish* children. While the novel clearly condemns the adult community for the deformations of its young, it seems equally blind to an actual child underlying its abundant protests of sentimental outrage.[9] For, with its diverse presentations of wizened children, of children grown old before their time, we lose all sense of the real child to which Skimpole is being compared or the childhood to which grandmother Smallweed regresses.

In its effort to define the child in opposition to a duplicitous and jaded adulthood, the novel lapses into a failure to differentiate clearly, into a marked confusion between the two terrains. The analyst Paula Heimann complains about the "distinction [in language] between the factual and the hostile reference to the child" (340). Thus, we alternate between the positive attribution of "childlike" and the insulting "childish," a discursive indecision that Heimann argues "betrays the ambivalence to children of those who are no longer children. They either denigrate childhood or sentimentally idealize it by attributing creativity exclusively to the child" (340). Clearly, such latent repugnance is part of what informs the Dickensian text's chronic reversals. The child *as* child is idealized while the child in the adult is vilified for a self-indulgence that saturates both ethics and morals, a strategy that allows the text to separate positive and negative attributes of the child. The potentially unsympathetic aspects of the child are displaced in Dickens onto adults who "contain" for the text its suppressed hostility to the actual child.

The fact that childhood and adulthood are superficially distinguished, at the same time that the texts covertly drain these positions of their nominal and ideational valence, does much to explain why it is easy to ignore what is a dramatic subversion of the parent/child cycle in both *Bleak House* and *Oliver Twist*.[10] While, on a plot level, the reader is introduced to Esther's parents (Lady Dedlock directly and Hawdon via his handwriting) before we meet Esther, they only become her parents retrospectively, as it were, for both the reader and the characters. What do we make of the fact that Lady Dedlock believed that she did not have a living child? Even if she is literally Esther's mother, the textual world is not entrenched in the biological categories of relation. Rather, the text can create parentage in the same way that it produces characters—arbitrarily. Dickens gives the impression that one's parentage is open to infinite rearrangement, that it is always possible to find the right parents—that one's parents can be *chosen.*

The question for Oliver throughout is how he can find contentment in light of the conditions of his birth, presumably the offspring of a poor unwed woman—in other words, of low financial and moral origins. Obligingly, the text will tailor for him a family suited to his needs: good people (erstwhile reputable denizens of the middle class who have been led astray for textually legitimized reasons) who, however, are dead. This death compensates for their transgression, because in order to remain good parents the tarnished parents should be as good as dead. In a single stroke Oliver's parents have been created and effaced, leaving us with the fantasm of a happy genesis.

The relationship between Oliver and his mother is simply the elaborate erection of a coherent history in the face of instability and uncertainty. The discovery of Oliver's parentage is based on nothing more than the combination of circumstantial evidence and the reader's anxiety to provide Oliver with a family. Consequently, Oliver himself functions as the emblem of what can only be termed the fantasmatic production of the child. This child finds his origins in the narrative conspiracy of textual and readerly desire. Seventy years later, Freud was preoccupied with the same questions he saw raised by the relationship of the small child to its ontology. Freud's description of the young boy's effort to frame his own coming into being through the birth of a little sister closely replicates the chronological indeterminacies of *Oliver Twist* and *Bleak House.*

Hans, the subject of Freud's case history, "Analysis of a Phobia in a Five-Year-Old Boy," provides the instance par excellence of the pursuit of origins that leads backward from sign to event, the tail-end of origin becoming in fact, epistemologically speaking, the origin of origins. Hans dislocates temporally the reproductive sequence. He refuses to go into the street because of his fear that horses drawing loaded carts might fall down beneath the weight. While Hans's father believes that the loaded carts represent the pregnant mother and falling down represents childbirth, Freud recognizes that, more to the point, the image of falling down reflects the child's dim awareness of coitus, specifically "'making a row with its legs,'" as Hans describes his fantasy image of the prone animals (*SE* 10:52). Literally a case of the cart preceding the horse, Hans's sexual cosmos situates pregnancy before coitus, an exact reenactment of the child's epistemological development. Certainly, the child in this case witnesses the fact of pregnancy (the loaded cart) before he has access to its cause. Hence in terms of psychical time, his fantasied chronology is absolutely on target.

More interesting still, however, is what Freud failed to observe—that the structure of Hans's fantasy reproduces the chronology of the phobia itself. According to the child's logic, the image of his pregnant mother arouses his curiosity as to where babies come from; thus the sight of the pregnant body becomes for Hans the origin of the horrific knowledge of adult procreation—because it was the pregnancy that drew him in the first place (like the horse-drawn cart) to the place of terror where the horses fall into a tangle of labor and sexual intercourse. It is a journey into the place before existence, before all knowing and being, that the child refuses, retreating in the face of his obscure but surprisingly astute recognition that this place (receding behind him as event at the same time it looms in his future as knowledge) threatens him with oblivion. If the parents make a row with their legs after the mother has been laden with a baby, it is because the mother's oversized belly is a signifier of that sexual event that preceded both the pregnancy and the child who is himself signified by the pregnancy and the sexual event as at once historically and potentially nothing whatsoever. Hans's fear of the nothingness of preexistence is so pronounced that, despite his parents' correction, he insists on recalling his little sister as a visible member of a family journey when at the time she existed only in utero. Of course, it is only after the birth of his sister that Hans correlates the manifestation of pregnancy with a baby, suggesting that it is the baby that signifies the pregnancy that signifies the procreative act, a retrospective reconstruction that culminates in Hans's own understanding of himself as end-product of events that preceded him.

Hans's father writes to Freud that "'once [Hans] knocked on the pavement with his stick and said: "I say, is there a man underneath?—some one buried?—or is that only in the cemetery?" So he is occupied not only with the riddle of life but with the riddle of death'" (*SE* 10:69).[11] But death appears to Hans in much the same (dis)guise as birth, as something concealed beneath surfaces. One gathers that at this point in his development, all surfaces are seeming duplicitous to Hans. The sidewalk pavement is as sinister as the cemetery ground because the lesson, which by now Hans has mastered quite well, is that both birth and death are hidden from view. Dead people disappear from the surface world yet are nevertheless present underground, just as unborn babies *are* before they exist; both, as we can see, take up *space* before and after they exist in *time*. Surfaces are always liable to sequester some surprise in Hans's experience—and he does not want to be taken unawares.

Both Oliver and Esther reenact the process of the child's self-discovery as a subject that anticipates its generational history. The texts literalize the child's epistemological development from simply being, outside the reproductive cycle, to the awareness of history—which leads concomitantly to the knowledge of death, displaced onto the death of the parents. Esther and Oliver are not just illegitimate; their origins are obscured entirely. As far as their textual lives are concerned, they are just there—on the scene when the curtain opens. Because the reader knows only what Esther knows about herself, her situation more clearly illustrates the child's experience of being always already. According to her personal memory, one day she was "there," with a woman who called herself godmother, who denied blood relation, but was in fact her aunt. The choice of "godmother" itself suggests that Esther's only mother (creator) was a fairy tale figure, or even God himself, a disembodied parent characterized at once by immateriality and immortality. Esther's godmother tells her: "'You are different from other children, Esther, because you were not born, like them, in common sinfulness and wrath. You are set apart,'" which sounds suspiciously as though Esther were free altogether not only from original sin, but from origin itself (33). At the same time that Esther's birth is an exaggeration of "original sin," it denies the story of origin.

The Subject of Sex

For Oliver, the story of his birth *is* the story of death as well, just as for Hans sexuality and temporality fuse. Dickens writes: "A father, sister, and mother, were gained, and lost, in that one moment" (463). J.-B. Pontalis addresses the relationship between sex and the temporal grounding of the subject: "If little Fritz asked how a human being was made, he would be said to have shown sexual curiosity. If he asked 'how much time does tomorrow take to come?', he would be said to be at the metaphysical age. Yet both questions, both 'conceptions,' go together" (100).

The death of his parents cements Oliver's new position as a death-bound mortal, the offspring of an *immoral* act that has become in his case curiously transmuted into *immortal*. Inasmuch as the "crime" of their unwed union was socially repressed (by Leeford's wife, who tore up the will; by Agnes's father, who changed his last name and moved to another town), the *immoral* act led to the fantasmatic *immortality* of its product. The sexual act, underscored *as* sexual precisely because of its severance from the social tie that contains sexual acts as social practice, cannot be accommodated as productive when it does not submit to social conventions. Thus, its child-product, cast loose from social containment, illustrates the transformation of the not-happening (immoral) into the not-being (immortal).

Illegitimacy in this context begins to sound like *unreal*. As Bumble proudly asserts about Oliver's name: "'I inwented it,'" just as the parentless child seems to have been "inwented" out of whole cloth (51). But is not the invention of the textual child equivalent to the social invention of all children? When one considers that the birth of the child is always patently a social and socializing experience in which the child is registered as a statistical member of the community and a name is promptly appended to a creature who would be otherwise unidentifiable, it appears that the invention of Oliver's name by a beadle is no more an invention than any process whereby the infant child is appropriated by adult discursive and juridical systems.

Jean Laplanche and J.-B. Pontalis observe that in the infant "we have a subject who is presubjectal, who receives his existence, his sexual existence, from without, before a distinction between within and without is achieved" ("Fantasy" 5). The infant's assumption of subjectivity is concurrent with the assumption of sexuality. Sexuality qua sexuality is constituted at the moment in which the rupture occurs between the self-preservative function on which the sexual drive is based and the sexual drive proper.[12] The infant's sexuality is received from without in the sense that the child is stimulated by external objects, stimulation that ignites heretofore protoerotogenic zones. Hence the distinction between within and without is subsequent to subjectivity because it is mobilized by the achievement of a subjectivity-conferring sexuality.

The sexualized child, constituted by a sexuality that has diverged from self-preservative functions, is created and defined by adult objects—invented, therefore, in more ways than one. Not only is the child precipitated into human sexual life by external stimuli, the adult sexual community is ever impinging on the child's polymorphous and pregenital sexuality (always *seducing* the child) by translating it and treating it as though it were adult.[13] In response to the question of who is the subject of psychoanalysis, the adult or the child, the confusion in part arises from the infant's protracted condition of presubjectivity.

Subjectivity nevertheless is imposed not only on the developmental child but also on the retrospective analytic child. This retrospective child can only be identified and reclaimed via adult subjectivity. The question arises: how can the adult subject recognize an earlier version of the self when that self was not yet a subject? How can the adult recapitulate the relationship between her/himself as child and the parents when that child in question was not yet differentiated from external parental objects? While the ignorant child discovers origin in what succeeds it, in the token of the mother's pregnancy or, more generally, in its own self-consciousness that precipitates the predestined query, Where do babies come from? the child of knowledge finds origin in its past—a past founded and articulated in the moment of knowledge that is necessarily a posteriori.

Crucially, that "predetermined" question posed by the child as to the origin of babies is always essentially about the child itself. The inevitability of the question makes one wonder if there is something about the formulation of the question that is itself constitutive of subjectivity. Consider that in asking the question about the origin of itself as *another*, the child is at once precipitating itself into the future of its own adult sexuality (how will *I* too make a baby?) and propelling itself back into its own preexistence, the space of "where" from which it emerged.[14] The difference between inner and outer in this instance is analogous to the distinction between past and future because the subject's ability to erect boundaries between itself and external objects seems somehow contemporaneous with the conceptualization of where the subject begins and ends in time.

Laplanche and Pontalis postulate that Freud's concept of the primary process is

> a myth of origin: by this figurative expression Freud claims to have recovered the very first upsurgings of desire. It is an analytic "construction," or fantasy, which tries to cover the moment of *separation* between *before* and *after*, whilst still containing both: a mythical moment of disjunction between the pacification of need (*Befriedigung*) and the fulfillment of desire (*Wunscherfüllung*), between the two stages represented by real experience and its hallucinatory revival, between the object that satisfies and the sign which describes both the object and its absence: a mythical moment at which hunger and sexuality meet in a common origin. ("Fantasy" 15)

The story, or "myth," of the developmental stages of the child is about what structures and organizes the experience that Laplanche and Pontalis call "prestructural"; the use of the term "prestructure," however, indicates to what extent the imposition of time (origins) and space (inner/outer) on the infant is just that—an imposition, a compulsion to adapt thrust upon that which otherwise evades adult strategies of containment.[15]

Oliver Twist and *Bleak House* implicitly raise and answer the question: where do babies come from? That is, finally, what Esther and Oliver all along aim to discover. While for Esther and Oliver the question is posed in the first person, the texts ask in the third (where do they [these children] come from?) repeating the disjuncture between the simultaneously self-subjectivizing child and its projection into the role of an-other. If Esther and Oliver seem to be "inwented," however, by texts that fashion them from nothing and only subsequently confer parentage, at the same time it would be as accurate to say, given the order of events, that the parents are invented by the children.

John Jarndyce confesses to Esther that he "'dreamed when [she was] very young of making [her his] wife one day'" (859). Jarndyce's Pygmalion dream of creation, of fashioning the child into the wife, is nevertheless countered by Esther's dream of transforming the guardian and would-be spouse into a father. Dianne S. Sadoff points out that there is no mention of her real father in Esther's first-person accounts or any indication that she ever comes to terms with her own connection to Captain Hawdon (16). As far as Esther is concerned, he is "Nemo" or no one in the beginning of the novel and he remains so even after he has been identified. Whereas the third-person narrative voice willingly responds to the question, Where did Esther come from? the first-person child persists in disavowing the answer to the question that she, crucially, never herself poses.[16] From the moment she is presented with a mysterious guardian, Esther's fantasy is to make John Jarndyce her father, and the invented father is the one to whom she clings in the face of (in absolute denial of) the disclosure of the biological father. It seems to be critical for the child to play the agent of her own history instead of being history's passive "invention."

Early in her narrative, Esther confides: "My fancy, made a little wild by the wind perhaps, would not consent to be all unselfish, either, though I would have persuaded it to be so if I could. It wandered back to my godmother's house and came along the intervening track, raising up shadowy speculations which had sometimes trembled there in the dark as to what knowledge Mr. Jarndyce had of my earliest history—even as to the possibility of his being my father, though that idle dream was quite gone now" (95–96). Esther's apparent repudiation of the fantasy of Jarndyce as father cannot be taken any more seriously than her protracted refusal to admit to her affection for Woodcourt. Her godmother's house represents for Esther the space of absolute ignorance, of repressed origins and relationships. At the same time it marks a return to a "dark" place of "shadowy speculation" where Esther has unlimited opportunity for invention.

According to Esther's fantasy, Jarndyce has access to the source of her story; in endowing him with the power of invention, Esther invents him as inventor. It is telling, in this light, that Jarndyce calls the explicitly maternal Esther "Mother Hubbard." So, then, what is the origin of the child when the child originates its own story of origins? What conditions the origin of the "original" fiction? If the child parents the parent, as it were, so much so that Jarndyce is never released from the role of father into his own fantasied role of suitor, who might we say created the child? Certainly not Hawdon who is eliminated from Esther's narrative as less than "no one." Nor can we say that Lady Dedlock functions as a parent to the child on whose discretion her reputation hangs—whose position so clearly depends on the suppression of this child.

Laplanche and Pontalis contend that all primal fantasies (castration, seduction, the primal scene) are in fact fantasies of origin: castration refers to the origin of sexual difference; seduction treats the efflorescence of sexuality; the primal scene recapitulates the origin of the child itself. The question they consequently raise is: what then is the origin of fantasy when fantasy itself always structurally embraces its own origins? While we might easily account for both *Oliver* and *Bleak House* as, fundamentally, fantasies of origins, to what extent, however, can we distinguish between the textual fantasy of origins and the origin of textual fantasy?[17] If, on one level, we postulate that the inherent fantasy of both novels is the recapitulation of the primal scene, this is to say nothing really because all we know as a result is the name of a fantasy now dissembling as *origin* of fantasies.

Esther's desire for Jarndyce as a father in conjunction with the fatherly Jarndyce's desire for Esther as a wife suggests at first glance a fantasy of parental seduction distressing the specificity of roles. But Jarndyce is no more a father than Esther is his daughter and their masquerade of incestuous seduction underscores the infinite substitutive possibilities of the primary fantasy. Instead of simply father and daughter, they are playing out perpetually shifting roles of activity and passivity in the syntactic arena. Laplanche and Pontalis suggest that fantasy for the presubjective child is a setting in which the child can inhabit any of the syntactic elements: "'A father seduces a daughter' might perhaps be the summarized version of the seduction fantasy. The indication here of the primary process is not the absence of organization, as is sometimes suggested, but the peculiar character of the structure, in that it is a scenario with multiple entries, in which nothing shows whether the subject will be immediately located as *daughter;* it can as well be fixed as *father,* or even in the term *seduces"* (14). The specificity of the characters of Esther and Jarndyce is incidental to the overarching fantasy that "plays" them like so many syntactic elements. If the daughter in the fantasy "a father seduces a daughter" assumes the passive function, the Dickensian version produces a daughter who, although passive in her original submission to Jarndyce's proposal, actively positions him as father-agent of the sentence.[18] Moreover, Jarndyce's apparent activity is ephemeral: he has no control over the direction of Esther's affection and passively resigns himself to rejection at the same time (and here is the crux of the situation) that he offers a father/suitor to Esther in his stead. Woodcourt takes over the father function of the sentence not because the syntax of the fantasy is in any way altered. Rather, the change and exchange of roles among the characters occur according to the predetermined and inflexible structure of the fantasy.

When Jarndyce gives Esther to Woodcourt, she observes that "he tenderly raised my head, and as I clung to him, kissed me in his old fatherly way again and again. . . . 'My dearest,' [Jarndyce says to her,] 'Allan Woodcourt stood beside your father when he lay dead—stood beside your mother.' . . . 'Allan,' said my guardian, 'take from me a willing gift, the best wife that ever man had'" (860–61). The "old fatherly way," however, is rather the new fatherly style Esther has compelled Jarndyce to assume; Jarndyce, who dreamed of raising Esther to be his wife, never willingly inhabited the strictly fatherly position. In offering Esther to Woodcourt, the man who witnessed the dying moments of her parents (who oversaw the end, in other words, of those who produced Esther), Jarndyce at once fills the father and lover roles: he becomes the seductive father without himself seducing the daughter.[19] The fantasy enacted by the three players is that it is Jarndyce's desire that Esther and Woodcourt marry; Jarndyce goes so far as to offer Esther as a "gift." Further, in an extraordinary displacement of the sexual relations, it is Jarndyce, not Woodcourt, who repeatedly kisses the bride. Jarndyce's knowledgeable depiction of Esther as "the best wife that ever man had," implicitly positions Esther as a wife who has been *had* by Jarndyce himself in all wifely functions save the key one, which he now consummates through a kiss. Both men are intimately affiliated with Esther's story of origins; hence it is through these representatives of her origins that Esther finally finds a father and a husband of her own making. The point is that, in the long run, it does not really matter which man she chooses as husband and which as father because they are interchangeable insofar as they can signify for Esther her beginning and end (the beginning in terms of origin and the end as the solution to the origin-al question).

Oliver Twist as well is indeterminate as to the source of the child's production and, specifically, the child's agency vis-à-vis the adult. Not only is Oliver himself socially nameless, but the introduction of his mother to the reader emphasizes her analogous status—her social nonexistence. Her corpse is addressed by the surgeon as "Mrs. Thingummy," underscoring the kind of "death" associated with social extinction (46). Certainly Monks understands the value of the name (an understanding passed down to him from his father) inasmuch as his plot to besmirch the reputation of Oliver is at root an attempt to eliminate the child's name as heir; such a dissolution of paternity is akin to effacing altogether the child's name. The notion of "heir" itself suggests the consanguinity between property value and the value of being, the latter value an essential "property" of the constitutive name. Oliver's mother is introduced without a name because she is of no value, either in the social sphere, where she is effectively silenced, or in the realm of production. Having no sign-value, in other words, seems to invalidate her as a producer of signs (or children); in this sense, Oliver is motherless. Indeed, the disengagement of the mother's productive agency from the child-product is this novel's covert agenda that is nevertheless more pronounced than in the later *Bleak House*. Perhaps *Oliver Twist* strikes readers as the less successful novel precisely because its aggression is under lock and key. The mother of *Bleak House* is actively "killed" by the novel that acknowledges its ambivalence about the mother's power, whereas the discovery of the romanticized dead mother of *Oliver* does nothing toward restoring mortal form to her imperturbably "immaculate" child.

Parents and Children

The Freudian system fails to locate clearly the origin of Oedipal drives. The adult projects onto His Majesty the Baby his or her own narcissistic experience as a child with the concomitant childhood fantasies.

If we look at the attitude of affectionate parents towards their children, we have to recognize that it is a revival and reproduction of their own narcissism, which they have long since abandoned. . . . Thus they are under a compulsion to ascribe every perfection to the child . . . and to conceal and forget all his shortcomings. (Incidentally, the denial of sexuality in children is connected with this.) Moreover, they are inclined to suspend in the child's favour the operation of all the cultural acquisitions which their own narcissism has been forced to respect, and to renew on his behalf the claims to privileges which were long ago given up by themselves . . . he shall once more really be the centre and core of creation—"His Majesty the Baby," as we once fancied ourselves. The child shall fulfill those wishful dreams of the parents which they never carried out—the boy shall become a great man and a hero in his father's place, and the girl shall marry a prince as a tardy compensation for her mother. (*SE* 14:90–91)

The above passage especially shows how the relationship between forfeited fantasies of the past are reconceived as a future term. This fantasy of the child fulfilling the missed opportunities of its parents is a reversal of Freud's theory of the family romance in which the child imagines it is a lost or kidnapped progeny of exalted parents. While the child's fantasied omnipotence depends on idealizing its progenitors, the parents are similarly invested in conferred glory. The originary childhood fantasies of lost greatness are transferred onto the child, this child who is the representative of the past grandeur of the parents and the parents' parents—now sent forth as a future expectation. What Freud does not state outright, but which is nevertheless inevitable given the terms of his argument, is that such a projective mechanism must necessarily encompass the Oedipal system as well. The Oedipus complex is for Freud the foundation of the trajectory of the subject's desire and childhood is the scene of this pivotal moment; thus, what is implicit is that the child revivifies the parents' Oedipal desire along with their forfeited narcissism. In "suspend[ing] in the child's favour the operation of all those cultural acquisitions which their own narcissism has been forced to respect," the adult imagines the child as pure libido, or rather projects onto the child her or his own unfettered libido. Interestingly, Freud's account is paradoxical when it comes to the issue of childhood sexuality. For the adult, the child is perfect unsuppressed narcissistic libido; yet at the same time the parent imagines that the child is asexual—an astonishing feat of the imagination.[20] These apparently irreconcilable adult fantasies arise positionally according to whether the fantasying adult is identifying with the child or the adult. The

problem of the child-in-the-adult invariably tends to complicate identifications as well as their respective fantasies.

This paradox closely replicates Freud's reconsideration of the theory of seduction, when the child assumes the role of desiring subject. Julia Kristeva makes a remarkable connection between the shift
in Freud's point of view and his own status in the parent-child cycle: "Two events occurred: Freud ceased having children and his father died." It is after the death of his father that Freud, "a son who
is forced by the signifier to take his father's place," entirely reverses
the roles of agent and object in his theory of seduction. "The distress provoked by the discovery of that mistaken path was so great
that he wrote, 'Like Breuer, I almost gave up analysis. . . . At last came
the reflection that, after all, one had no right to despair because one
has been deceived in one's expectations; one must revise those expectations'" (274).

The revision of expectations reevokes the revision experienced by
the parent who is compelled to transfer onto the child desires previously directed toward her or his own original objects. The death of
his father not only relocates Freud himself as the father, but uncannily his children as well come to assume that space of "expectation"
vacated by the idealized father of childhood. Recall Freud's dream of
the bridge-children, discussed in chapter 4: The children are cast as
the "origin" of the father's route toward immortality; the adult skeletons are the remains of the idealizations invested in parental objects; it is across the bodies of the children that such idealizations
are transferred—onto the very children who facilitate the crossing.

The "family romance" characteristics of both *Oliver Twist* and *Bleak
House* are explicitly drawn but, in each case, with a twist. Both children gain idealized parents in terms of social rank (especially in Esther's case); yet these selfsame idealized parents are debased by the
crime of adultery. Meanwhile, their children perform their idealized
attributes. While Lady Dedlock is a noblewoman, her daughter is
noble and virtuous; if Edward Leeford and Agnes were both gener-
ous and kind, their son is equally so, minus the moral contamination. In many ways, Oliver's emergence unscathed from his sojourn
through London's criminal underside is the allegorical correction of
his parents' situation—the temptation by sin of the virtuous soul.
Oliver succeeds where they succumbed. Nevertheless, at the same
time that Oliver and Esther are the idealized end-products of fallen
parents, they are in part incarnations of sin, themselves living evidence of the debasement even as they transcend it.

"'Your mother, Esther,'" her godmother explains, "'is your disgrace and you were hers,'" a paradoxical statement in which the distinction between source and product is highlighted in the same instant in which it is erased (33). Even her use of tense is suggestive; the mother "is" while Esther is cast aside to the "were" of having been the source of her mother's disgrace. Her mother's contemporary position (in disgrace) is the end result of Esther as cause, as origin, as the child who somehow in the past produced her mother, not only as a disgraced mother, but as a mother at all—which constitutes the disgrace. Buried in all the rhetoric of parenting and the origins of the child is the sense that the child's arrival on the scene transforms the man and woman into "father" and "mother." To return to the epistemological predicament of Little Hans, the entrance of his sister (the baby) is, for him, the origin of the story of conception.

Esther's relationship to her mother is consistently marked by an inability to negotiate the assignments of past and future in the parent-child structure. The encounter with her mother at the church plunges Esther back into childhood recollections, specifically "even to the days when I had stood on tiptoe to dress myself at my little glass after dressing my doll," the selfsame doll Esther symbolically buries in the garden before escaping forever her dismal life at her godmother's (262). Seeing her mother for the first time is like looking in the mirror at herself as a child; yet that child-self is depicted in the maternal role of caring for the doll who is her double (like Esther herself, *both* mother and child).[21] Hence, while the face of the mother might recall the past for Esther, the mother is nevertheless construed fantasmatically as no more than a replica of the "original" mirror-face of the child herself.[22] Here we get a profound sense of the *mise en abyme* Lacan is negotiating in his work on the constitutive relationship between the subject and its image in "The Mirror Stage." The child points to its existence in the mirror image (there I am!) just as Esther finds herself in her mother's face (another mirror). But, as Dickens illustrates, the mother's face is no more than a mirror image of a mirror image.

Altered greatly by her illness, Esther claims that she was grateful "to the providence of God that I was so changed as that I never could disgrace her [Lady Dedlock] by any trace of likeness, as that nobody could ever now look at me and look at her and remotely think of any near tie between us" (516–17). In many ways, her illness affords Esther the final release from a tie that, as her godmother advised her, hitherto has been one of mutual disgrace—of nondifferentiation from the mother. Significantly, Esther repeats her godmother's language of "disgrace" that all along has bound Esther to her mother as a mirror image, preventing her independence as a subject in her own right. The vision of the child in the mirror recapitulated by the face of Lady Dedlock, the face that is at once parent and child, is smashed by the disfiguring illness that reconfigures the child as separate. Out of the near-death experience a different Esther reemerges (is "born"), released from the desubjectifying stasis of the mirror relation with her mother. It was a relation of stasis because, returning to Freud, the implicit contradiction of the parent's projections onto the child, as both past and future, fix the child in a liminal space that is nowhere, in no time whatsoever. While Dickens is undecided as to who is the subject of the mirror image, parent or child, twentieth-century fantasies increasingly have construed the child as the mirror to the adult gaze, as I will show in later chapters. Nevertheless, these fantasies find their earlier versions in Freud's confusion over the origin of narcissism and Esther Summerson's struggle to be liberated from the cycle of desubjectifying disgrace.

As Esther observes, "what this lady so curiously was to me, I was to her," a reiteration of the confusion of identity and origin, which repeats the mirror-alliance of the original encounter (328). For the child living the family romance, the fantasied parent is at once the omnipotent parent of the past and the heroic future that the parent achieves through the child. For the narcissistically doting parent, the child is the past of omnipotent narcissism and the future of unfulfilled potential. Both are simply productions of an ongoing fantasy transmitted generationally from parent to child. All this leaves us with the impression that if no children were born to the Smallweed family that is because no children are born *as* children. Jo is horrified by the *apparition* of Esther because he mistakes her for Lady Dedlock, a mistake that repeats one made on an earlier occasion in relation to Mademoiselle Hortense's masquerade as Lady Dedlock. In response to Hortense, Jo equivocates: "'It is her and it an't her,'" which is exactly the problem he confronts in the form of Esther, who is her mother at the same time that she is "Esther" (326). But "Esther" *is* her mother to the extent that she participates in her disgrace—created her *as* disgraced.

Oliver is the future perfect of his parents' debased but idealized relationship, the redemption of its flaws, just as he figures the past of their love for one another. Brownlow explains that Oliver's father trusted "that the child would share [his mother's] gentle heart, and noble nature," a confirmation not only of the hereditary transmission of character traits but also of the indistinction between the child and the mother (458). Leeford's logic seems to have progressed thus: the child gains the name of the father (assumes the title of heir) only if he becomes the mother, which is another way of saying that if Oliver can be (essentially) the mother he can be (socially) the father; he can "bear" the name of the father if he can prove he is the "born" child of his mother. In short, Oliver can function as the future of the line (father) as long as he replicates its past (mother—site of reproduction).[23] Oliver must carry on what preceded him and, in so doing, *is* his parents as much as they are him (all that remains of them). Further, the novel endorses Leeford's myth of parental reduplication in the form of the child. It presents us with a child who remains unaltered by a lifetime of hardship and cruelty, who clearly possesses an internal nature that is impervious to all environmental factors. Surely, the novel's manifest story is that children are the *products* of their parents at the same time that they *reproduce* them. Oliver has survived the test of environmental corruption and has come through with flying colors; he is rewarded with the paternal name of which he has proven himself worthy—a worth constituted precisely by his capacity for *being* the parent.

The corruption of Fagin's other children seems to bear out this premise that the children reenact the parent. Yet the others are no more Fagin's real children than is Oliver, while Oliver is as much Fagin's "child" as they are. Additionally, as I have already mentioned, Oliver is an improvement on the original version. Indeed, he does not share his mother's nature when it comes to resisting temptation. This makes of the father's exaction on the child, if taken to the letter, a double bind. If Oliver succumbs to temptation, is led astray by circumstances (as his mother was), then he is not fit to be her child and Leeford's heir. If, on the other hand, his innocence transcends his vicious circumstances, he is markedly different from his mother. His mission would seem to be unattainable even in the face of a narrative that presents him as successful.

What, then, we must wonder, is it that Oliver achieves that satisfies the text on one level while repudiating its directives on another? Even though Oliver fails on the level of the real, what the mother truly was, he succeeds in relation to the idealized parent. Here, we once again encounter a confusion between the narcissistic fantasies of the parent and the child because the mother Oliver plays is the idealized original parent of the family romance that is the *child's* fantasy and, likewise, the version of the mother Oliver has become is the parental fantasy of their own future perfect. We are flung back, consequently, into a *mise en abyme* of origins in which the child's fantasy and the parental fantasy converge in the stasis of the perpetual generational mirror. Oliver embodies the very contradictions he transcends; he emblematizes their reconciliation.

Subsequent to Oliver's disappearance from his house, Brownlow concludes that "'Oliver is an imposter'" (176). Oliver assuredly is an imposter in many respects, however unintentionally. Growing up as a poor friendless orphan in the workhouse, he is nevertheless the child of a well-to-do father, an essential blood relation that magically confers on him both perfect diction and gentlemanly manners. Forced to turn thief in Fagin's group, he is again appropriated by a false role. Moreover, it is the fact that the reader recognizes Oliver as an imposter, as a child who is not what he appears to be, that engages our interest in the first place. We require the inner Oliver to be better than his circumstances, in disharmony with them, in order to disburse willingly our compassion. What the novel counts on in fact is the general confidence in the child's (any child's) duplicity—the child's essential mutability that makes of it a tabula rasa charged with adult expectations.

Oliver is an imposter because he is a child and vice versa, because the child, as far as it is conceived by the adult imagination, inevitably masquerades in the service of adult fantasy. The psychoanalytic pursuit of the child in the adult is, from the outset, a confrontation with two children, a real child and an imposter, or a fantasmatic child. The fantasmatic child is the consciously recollected historical child the subject originally carries into analysis. The real child, on the other hand, is the ultimate goal of analytic inquiry. The real child stands behind the fantasmatic child in much the same way that the essential Oliver belies his contemporary circumstances. The fantasmatic child, which the subject freely presents to the analyst, is an imposter, the culmination of a series of distortions and omissions, a dummy-child elaborately erected by the subject according to an acceptable adult system of consciousness. Analysis thus endeavors to draw out the real child, subject of infantile fantasy, urges that child to "speak" for itself. André Green writes: "This necessarily involves us in a discussion the terms of which were defined by Anna Freud: is the 'real' child the child that is constructed, or reconstructed by psychoanalysis? My answer is an unequivocal 'No'. But I would also add that it is not the role of psychoanalysis to reconstruct the real child. The mythical child, or the mythical childhood of the real child is, rather, the object of child psychology" (qtd. in Laplanche, *Foundations* 82). Yet this ostensibly "real" child is as predetermined by analytic motives as is the fantasmatic child by adult defenses. If that real child will eventually speak the analytic "truth" of infantile fantasies, these fantasies are fundamentally yet another story that the adult world tells about the child. How can the analyst ever truly credit the speech of the real child when that very speech is in many ways merely the response to analytic expectations? The subject of analysis, installed by the transference drama into the role of child vis-à-vis the parental therapist, is necessarily trying to give the therapist what she or he wants, just like any compliant child.

The analytic premise is thus: in order for the adult to outgrow the child, in order to be "cured," the adult must confront what it is that the real child wants, must allow the real child finally to speak its desire. Hence the real child in analysis is the representation of the child that assures a real adulthood, liberated from the childhood scene of inexorable repetition. This can only finally be a *representation*, however, because the real child is only accessible through adult recapitulation, specifically an adult recapitulation of a child's world of fantasy designed to please a parental therapist. Is the climax of psychoanalytic treatment, as a result, always the child's success in pleasing the parent? Is the goal ultimately the pleasure of the analyst, the analysand's feeling of well-being nothing more than a by-product of the monumental achievement of becoming the right child, the child his or her parents always wanted? Is there, finally, any child produced in analysis who is *not* simply that—a product, an imposter?

The fantasmatic child, according to psychoanalysis, is the product of adult repression while the real child is the fantasying subject hitherto denied. Nevertheless, it becomes virtually impossible to dissever the one from the other when we take into account the conviction that the neurotic (and ignorant) adult subject her/himself is locked into a child scenario she or he is bound to relive. If the adult is in effect bound by the child's eye view, then the false child is as much the real child of fantasy as is the supposedly real child. The screen child, in other words, the conscious recollection, *is* the real child as well, being itself the culmination of the adult-as-child. Perhaps Oliver is too compliant, like the dutiful child of analysis who gives the analyst whatever she or he demands; and perhaps we do not believe in Oliver precisely because his compliance reveals too clearly the fantasies staked on the body of the child—by the analyst, by the parents, by a society loathe to have its fantasies flung back in its face.

Melanie Klein focused on the treatment of actual children rather than the adult patient's reconstructions in an attempt to treat the real discourse of the child, the arena of play. Nevertheless, even in her effort to determine what the child truly is prior to adult distortions, Klein requires the child-subject to adapt to a given model of adult symbolization. In her famous treatment of the four-year-old autistic child, Dick, Klein precipitates the boy into what she considers to be phase-appropriate object relations by suturing him into Oedipal language. Having translated for herself the child's physical discourse into the language of Oedipal desire, Klein invites him into what is patently *adult* sexual discourse. She explains that his "interest in these things and actions had a common source: it really had to do with the penetration of the penis into the mother's body" ("Symbol Formation" 101). Klein holds that his illness stems from his living as real what should be symbolic.[24] "I took a big train and put it beside a smaller one and called them 'Daddy-train' and 'Dick-train'. Thereupon he picked up the train I called 'Dick' and made it roll to the window and said 'Station'. I explained: 'The station is mummy; Dick is going into mummy'" ("Symbol Formation" 102). What Klein does is to compel the child into the terms of what is, despite her efforts to recapitulate the child's worldview, an adult take on the Oedipal experience.

Although Klein's treatment professes to be congruent with the child's real experience, it remains bound to the adult perspective of the child: the child is inevitably a reproduction of adult definitions. Even this actual child, a far remove from Freud's reconstructions, is the subject of adult inquiry and, finally, adult creation in the sense that Dick's cure inheres in the adult analyst's understanding of what the four-year-old child should *be*.[25] About her clinical work, Klein writes: "I found it of great value from the clinical and theoretical point of view that I was analysing both adults and children. I was thereby able to observe the infant's phantasies and anxieties still operative in the adult and to assess in the young child what his future development might be" ("Play Technique" 52). At the same time that Klein collapses the distinction between adult and child, she resurrects it as a myth of developmental progress. While she is reminding us that the infantile persists in the adult, she is likewise implying that the two spheres of experience can be readily differentiated. Thus, she is not describing a merger of adult and child; rather we have *two* subjects inhabiting a single body. Moreover, in terms of the young child, she defines it as a blueprint for an adult final term. What is curious here, however, is the notion that the adult subject is always *reproducing* the infantile whereas the infant is always *producing* (developing toward) the adult, a historical asymptote that dislocates the child from the possibility of historical self-presence.

Go-Betweens

It is perhaps because of its transience, its destiny to be always marginal to the adult temporal arena and adult discourse, that the child is so naturally assigned the role of go-between. The very status of the child in terms of the adult whom it speaks through and is spoken by is to be always having been and always becoming, never present in its own right. Esther, Jo, and Oliver are all played as go-betweens by the adult world that, while it may depend on them, absorbs them into its own exigencies.

As in *The Go-Between,* the children traverse both social and sexual borders, as if to dissolve not only their respective limits but the very demarcations between the two spheres of organization. Outraged by the ascension of Mrs. Rouncewell's son to a higher social status, Sir Leicester Dedlock perorates against the breakdown of the class system: "'And it is a remarkable example of the confusion into which the present age has fallen; of the obliteration of landmarks, the opening of floodgates, and the uprooting of distinctions. . . . He is called, I believe—an—ironmaster.' Sir Leicester says it slowly and with gravity and doubt, as not being sure but that he is called a lead-mistress" (402–3). More than the disruption of a class system by the potential "obliteration of landmarks," and "uprooting of distinctions," the baronet's language touches on the effacement of gender difference. The culmination of this diatribe is the narrator's insinuation that Sir Leicester himself cannot altogether negotiate the gender hurdles of ironmaster and lead-mistress, thereby suggesting that in transcending his class the housekeeper's son has disturbed the law and order of another arena as well.[26]

Esther, Oliver, and Jo all function in their respective texts as focal points around which class discrepancies converge. As though to underscore his position in the text, Jo's given occupation is that of crossing sweeper, situating him where the classes and sexes intersect. For the novel, specifically, he acts as a social and informational linchpin, a position that eventually destroys him as though to emblematize the ontological depletion inhering in and ensuing from the go-between's service status. Jo is nameless and marginalized in a text that, while it compassionates him, nevertheless rejects him as less valuable (even as it condemns society for doing likewise). He haunts the story as the more realistic counterpoint to Esther's fairy tale history, a constant reminder to the reader of what Esther herself, without the aid of Jarndyce, might have become. His relegation to the position of minor character dissimulates by attenuating the text's dependence on Jo's pivotal role.

If the various characters impose upon the crossing sweeper to serve their own ends, so does the narrative itself, which demands from this minor character the exorbitant service of weaving together a multitude of otherwise unconnected plots.

> What connexion can there be between the place in Lincolnshire, the house in town, the Mercury in powder, and the whereabouts of Jo the outlaw with the broom, who had that distant ray of light upon him when he swept the churchyard-step? What connexion can there have been between many people in the innumerable histories of this world who from opposite sides of great gulfs have nevertheless, been very curiously brought together?
>
> Jo sweeps his crossing all day long, unconscious of the link, if any link there be. (232)

As unconscious of the link as he is of everything else about which he frequently claims to know "nothink," Jo himself *is* the link that vanishes into "nothing" in the very instant of its contrivance. Oddly, although Jo is the locus of connection, once the connections are made (as a result of the child) they are presented as existing before the child who was merely the vehicle for their reemergence. In terms of the narrative chronology, however, the relationships between Hawdon and Lady Dedlock, and Esther and her parents, are subsequent to Jo's intercession. In this respect, Jo functions as the link between human and textual chronology. Jo transforms narrative future into historical past.

Once the "gulfs" are collapsed, the space between (the link itself) dissolves as well, being no longer necessary or even, for that matter, desirable, standing as it does for the division it transcended. When Lady Dedlock passes Jo at his crossing, he "crosses with her and begs" (236); but she resists both his plea and the danger of his crossing-space—"she does not turn her head until she has landed on the other side," as though achieving the steadfastness of firm land amid an indeterminate ocean. Jo's "whereabouts," the locus of intersection, is the place that always threatens to destabilize the arena of nobility and respectability to which Honoria Dedlock clings; the crossing is a token of her former intersection with the other side, Hawdon and the debasement for which he stands. (Sexuality and social instability are curiously commingled in Lady Dedlock's history; her choice of an aristocratic husband is tantamount to the abrogation of her sexual life.) Her precipitous move to the other side of the crossing suggests a fear of entrapment in the intersection even as she contracts with its denizen. But Jo has already "crossed with her," contaminated her, as it were, with his go-between status, condemning her to reinhabit, despite herself, the gulf of "intersection" she hitherto has denied. The other side to which Lady Dedlock hastens is rendered precarious by the abyss of the intersection to which she haplessly returns. Her return to the crossing dooms Lady Dedlock. As Bucket later explains to Sir Leicester, "'She is the pivot it all turns on,'" a function that infected her through her association with this go-between (729).

Jo is dismissed to the periphery of the narrative circle he unwittingly generates, swept aside as though by his own broom with which he sweeps away the traces of the horrific in-between-place of the crossing he at once asserts and strives to efface. This is the situation par excellence of the go-between child who must occult the traces of his own intersecting role.

For the sake of his "congregation," Chadband endeavors to "'so employ this instrument [Jo] as to use it to your advantage, to your profit, to your gain, to your welfare, to your enrichment,'" an appraisal of Jo that precisely defines his function in the novel (367–68). Many people profit from Jo, who is "delivered over unto" the imbricated narrative relationships not by divine power, as Chadband would have it, but rather by a text that requires the instrumentality of the child in order to "gain" (literally) its own end. Yet the text must consume the vestiges of its own device in order to maintain the pretense of itself as structurally continuous with the real life it reflects according to the inverse sequence of fantasy. In order for the end of the narrative, the reconstruction of origins, to look like the end instead of the beginning, the child who executes the transmutation must be "outlawed" from the law of origins he imperils in his enactment of their solution. About Jo the narrator asserts: "He is not of the same order of things, not of the same place in creation. He is of no order and no place, neither of the beasts nor of humanity" (645–46). He is the go-between. He marks the intersection between a series of binary orders (rich and poor, good and evil, narrative and historical time), none of which can accommodate him. And even as the narrator laments society's repudiation of its Jo's, the text repeats the repudiation. "Kill him," Dickens declared in his notes, as though the death of this particular child is effected by premeditated murder on the part of the author (*Working Notes* 235).[27]

It has been frequently observed that *Bleak House* is a detective story, the final revelations all dependent on the stratagems of Inspector Bucket.[28] Jo himself is the original object of Bucket's pursuit, and, significantly, Bucket is presented in an unsympathetic light insofar as he plagues the dying child. He steals Jo from his retreat at Jarndyce's, presses the child for further information, then orders him to stay away from London. Later, in the novel's effort to redeem the now likeable Inspector, Bucket explains to Esther that he removed Jo for the sake of her mother's reputation (Jo in the wake of his death is reconceived as dangerously loose-tongued). Dickens needs to exonerate Bucket in order to cast his job of detection in a positive light. Yet the Jo the reader knew was hardly prolix, in fact took pains to avoid committing himself verbally. Furthermore, even though the Inspector is at the end promoted to protector of Esther's sensibilities and would-be savior of her mother, was he not previously Tulkinghorn's own unscrupulous agent? In other words, the situation he attempts to remedy ensues in large part from his own agency.

These two Inspectors (for certainly they are two different personalities) characterize the novel's ambivalence about the work of detection itself. And what does this work discover? Two children—Esther and Jo; Esther as her mother's daughter, and Jo as the dangerous informational linchpin. The reason Bucket must dispose of Jo is not because the child speaks too freely, but instead because he unwittingly has become privy to information desired by others. The detective recognizes that Jo needs to be silenced, just as the text itself, a text of detection, of illuminating concealed identities, silences permanently the child who talks too much about "nothink," a nothingness that might momentarily unravel all the tenuous connections of identity on which the text is founded. Whereas Jo knows "nothink," Bucket, according to Karen Chase, "stands as a knowing center around which the novel's diversity may be organized" (110); Jo figures as the horrific underside of Bucket's revelations that finally obscure as much as they unveil. Jo is the "nothink" on which all the connections and identifications are premised, the child who is always liable to dismantle the systematizing and unifying efforts of a Bucket.[29] The distinction between these two examples of intermediaries can be found in their relation to the space between—that Jo measures and Bucket disguises. In the aftermath of all the impasses in the text left in the wake of the go-between child, all the irreconcilable questions about origin and end, subjectivity and desubjectification, Bucket rushes in to impose a formal logic on the whole (to make it whole). Where Jo imperils the text, Bucket rescues it. In contrast to Jo's inarticulateness (raising the possibility that there is something in excess of discursive solution), Bucket fluently explains all. Bucket is the final adult term that secures the world against the child.

Freud, too, has been characterized as a detective by himself and others[30] and, like Bucket, the object of his pursuit is invariably a child. These two narratives, the Dickensian and the Freudian, intersect at this point to suggest the extent to which the child must pay for the "crimes" (or neuroses) of adults, "crimes" whose origins are relocated in the child. Like Bucket, the analyst hunts down the child in the adult in an effort to "silence" its neurotic voice, the voice that repeatedly destabilizes and fragments adult psychic cohesiveness. Like the analyst, Bucket, who is identified by the text as the purveyor of truth, suppresses the child (the Jo-voice) as the heedlessly and ceaselessly repeated origin of the story of crime. With the strains of the child in full force (as long as Jo survives, as long as infantile fantasy ruptures the adult sphere), neither of these detectives is able to cure their textual and analytic subjects, a "cure" that would entail resolution into a harmonious self-identical subject. Their "reconstructions" (of crimes, of traumata) are simply containments of crimes that are unsolvable and traumata that are interminable; their reconstructions are inscriptions into a system of cause and effect whereby the crime and the trauma emerge finally as "curable" insofar as their origins have been identified.

Like Jo, Esther Summerson interlinks classes and sexes, herself the visible emblem of the repressed relation between Hawdon and Lady Dedlock, at the same time that she freely traverses the upper, middle, and lower classes—all of which accept her right of entry. Her journey culminates in the coalescence of Jenny with Lady Dedlock, those denizens of opposite extremes of the social spectrum who exchange roles as a result of Esther. Jenny is willing to exchange clothes with Lady Dedlock because of the debt she feels to Esther, while Lady Dedlock is led to Jenny via her daughter's trail. Mistaking her mother for "Jenny, the mother of the dead child," Esther finds instead her own mother, "cold and dead," cementing the connection between the two women—which is a dead child—Jenny's dead baby and Esther herself, for many years presumed dead by her mother (814). In fact Jenny's dead baby is the repressed nexus of the three whose lives are linked by the handkerchief with which Esther covers the dead infant,[31] the handkerchief Lady Dedlock presents to Esther when she reveals her identity, as though to suggest the "exposure" of the dead child (both the nakedness of the dead infant and the revelation of the "dead" child as alive). The gesture of covering the baby with the handkerchief finds its homologous completion when Esther lifts Jenny's hair to discover her mother beneath.[32] The concealment of the infant ends in the unveiling of the mother. Indeed, the dead infant Esther covers seems to have been transformed in the interval into her mother. Esther's mother is transformed into the subject who died in childbirth—at once the dead baby and the mother who more or less "dies" in her capacity as mother through the death of her infant. Esther's role, thus, is to express and seal the gap between the positions of mother and child, positions between which she all along has been captivated, a "Mother Hubbard" who has for so many years waited to be born. As Esther explains: "While I was very ill, the way in which these divisions of time became confused with one another distressed my mind exceedingly. At once a child, an elder girl, and the little woman I had been so happy as, I was not only oppressed by cares and difficulties adapted to each station, but by the great perplexity of endlessly trying to reconcile them" (495–96).

Jo's position in the text is to perform the go-between role that is more obliquely Esther's. Hawdon becomes more of a father to Jo than he ever could have been to his unknown daughter; and Jo's final wish is to be buried beside the closest thing to a father he has experienced. Moreover, via Jo, Esther contracts the smallpox that functions in the text as her metaphorical death, displaced onto the real death of Jo, who in all respects is Esther's alter-ego.[33] While Jo is always being ordered to "move on," continually being spatially disrupted as though to signify simultaneously his lack of social space as well as the menace his body poses to the stability of any space he occupies, Esther herself figures in her mother's fantasy as "the pattering of the little child's feet, ever coming on—on—on" (409). The nightmare step on Ghost's Walk, the place potentially haunted by a vengeful dead woman or a "man" (Tulkinghorn) who promises to real-ize a repressed (ghosted) past, is finally only the sound of the child's approach into Lady Dedlock's awareness, a child whose life figures the family scandal promised by the woman (the ghost) and the personal exposure guaranteed by the man (Tulkinghorn). Like Jo, Esther is a body that has been gotten rid of, "moved on" from being the child of someone to "no one's" daughter; like Jo, Esther imperils the space she inhabits. The disorder and ruin brought upon Lady Dedlock by the mere fact of Esther's existence is analogous to that with which Jo threatens the text itself. In gaining a birthright, Esther leaves behind her go-between counterpart, transcending the liminal status that Jo enacts for her. Conversely, Jo is "moved on" to an extratextual space. He is the social outcast and outlaw, the dangerous textual remainder, the exemplary go-between child.

Esther apologizes to the reader for her presence in her own story: "I hope any one who may read what I write will understand that if these pages contain a great deal about me, I can only suppose it must be because I have really something to do with them and can't be kept out" (126). This is the ultimate plight of the go-between child who willingly conspires in the deception that its status is marginal. It is because Esther can't be kept out that she overcomes her go-between function to become a character in her own right, more than the emblem of a repressed sexual relation. As distinguished from her counterpart, Jo, she "knows" who she is; she gains an identity that secures her place as heroine, while her go-between shadow (the place she outgrew) dies in her stead. Esther escapes the dangerous position of Jo through becoming for the novel an adult in place of a child. The death of her mother secures a coherent self-identical subjectivity with a narratable story that validates (rather than menaces) narration as a possibility.

Oliver Twist, another go-between, also has a counterpart who dies for him, young Dick from the workhouse, another intimation of what happens to the truly marginal, permanently nameless child. While Oliver overtly crosses the lines between virtue and vice and rich and poor and (like Hartley's Leo) eagerly volunteers to be a messenger for Brownlow, he also plays a large part in the union of Harry and Rose. Harry enlists Oliver as a correspondent between Rose and himself; moreover, it is in the revelation of Oliver's history that Rose finds her legitimate origins. It is through the assumption of her relationship (aunt) to Oliver that Rose herself is restored to social law and the reproductive economy (marriage). The relationship between Oliver and Rose in this light appears to be an earlier, and less satisfactory, version of Jo and Esther. Again, we have the near-death of the presumably illegitimate young woman. Whereas Dick dies for Oliver (just as Jo dies for Esther), signifying the death of the child who cannot be socially "born," the prelegitimate Rose figures as the obverse side of Oliver's social potential; the illegitimate child cannot grow up (like Dick), nor can it enter the reproductive arena (thwarted like the prelegitimate Rose), standing as it does outside of its conventions.

Before one is misled by the triumph of the illegitimate child as a token of the Dickensian text's acceptance of this particular position in society, we should not lose sight of the fact that other characters pay with their lives for the survival of these children, as though the novels exercise upon themselves a brand of self-punishment and self-containment as a mitigation of what they perceive as potentially disruptive. The "defect" of Oliver Twist, the "unreal . . . boy," who has been criticized as "a vacuum at the centre of the novel," ensues from making this empty vessel, this ideal go-between who evinces no resistance whatsoever to his position, the central character of the text—as though what is understood as inherently marginal has been reinscribed at the core.[34]

Arnold Kettle calls Oliver a "thin hero" and holds that his metamorphosis into the perfectly contrived end-world of the novel strikes the reader as false. About what remains useful for the reader in what he considers a flawed but powerful novel, Kettle writes, "Oliver himself does not survive; but the force he has set in motion does" (130, 138). The child himself is considered only a vehicle through which the social situation can unfold. One gathers that Kettle would have preferred, in the name of social and aesthetic realism, for the child to have died in the squalor from which he erupted. *This* would have been the culmination of his mission as social emblem.[35] Yet Kettle "kills" the child despite the text, by dismissing him as marginal to its social import—he does not "survive." J. Hillis Miller remarks that "there is little active volition in Oliver" (*Charles Dickens* 42). Rather, he is the object of forces external to him: "Once the decision is made that the outcast has no reason for existing, the world sets about deliberately to fill up the vacuum it has created by a legislative fiat. For even the space he takes up is needed. The world rushes violently in to bury him away out of sight, to take back the volume he occupied, and even to consume the very substance of his body" (37). Miller expertly accounts for not only the social response to the outcast child, but the text's necessity and, even more significantly, Kettle's reenactment of the general tendency to "bur[y the child] away out of sight." If the reader's response is to dismiss the child, this is not a failure on the part of the novel but rather of nineteenth-century fantasies of childhood that confuse childhood innocence with childhood emptiness. James Kincaid writes about the Oliver type: "This good child is, after all, so invitingly vacant that the goodness is utter blankness" (223). For Kincaid, such blankness in the child intensifies the adult's erotic response (175). Indeed, the numerous veiled threats to Oliver of castration would seem to corroborate Kincaid's position.

Perhaps because Oliver is so much like the typical idealized Dickensian heroine, or perhaps because of his interchangeability with Rose, Oliver is a markedly feminine little boy. In contrast to Fagin's boisterous group, Oliver makes an insipid appearance. Although Oliver is throughout the novel threatened with a hanging that sounds suspiciously like castration, the prediction comes as a gratuitous threat to this already emasculated child. Early on he is pronounced by a member of the workhouse board to be destined to hang, and Oliver is plagued by this prophecy throughout his adventures (58). Fagin especially relishes terrifying his ward with the details of "that unpleasant operation" (178). Monks cherishes the hope that Oliver will be permanently dissevered from his rightful name, a variety of social "castration" inextricably connected to the sexual inasmuch as Oliver cannot be a desiring subject until he has a social identity. Yet, the loss of masculinity, like the loss of a name, is prior to the threats that figure therefore as a confirmation of what we all along suspect. After Oliver is shot, Sikes complains, "'Damnation, how the boy bleeds!'" a description that, by virtue of being the most physical we have of this otherwise uncannily disembodied child, represents Oliver as at once in the process of being castrated and as post-castration—a girl (215). The threat of castration is neutralized by making Oliver already female. Certainly its receptivity to adult forces and desires makes of the go-between child a passive, feminized object.[36] Nell, another angelic Dickensian go-between, seems to cause far less gender trouble.

Miller calls Oliver "the real spy in the novel" (66). He points out that upon Oliver's entrance into the world of affluence and the socially enfranchised, he betrays the other underworld outcasts. In this sense, he figures as the denizen of the privileged class whose incursion into the criminal underworld is a form of espionage and betrayal. Instead of identifying with these other outcasts, he turns his back on them. The notion of Oliver as "spy" links him to Jo who is characterized as well as a type of spy, unwittingly privy to the secrets of the repressed relationship between the classes. In turn, one might say of Oliver that he is not betraying the outlawed element but is himself the conduit between two orders, a position that makes him appear to be a double-agent of sorts when in fact he is just "between," just a position. For that matter, all the go-between children treated in this study can be described as spies to varying degrees. In their travels between—sexes, classes, moral codes, and so forth—they are invariably caught in situations of repressing or disclosing information.

It is because the novel presents Oliver as qualitatively marginal, because it subscribes to a given ideology of the go-between child as utterly acquiescent, the linchpin of adult forces, that its attempt to pass him off as protagonist seems like a lapse in artistry.[37] In *Bleak House*, Oliver is resurrected in Jo; the vacuous go-between by now has been exiled from the center of the novel; the textual ideology is more nearly self-identical.

Curing the Family

Although the child is the vessel for a multitude of adult impositions and idealizations, in order for the fantasy to attain fruition, for
the adult to incorporate the idealized attributes of the narcissistically invested child, the child has to be eliminated. In part, the actual
child is eliminated purely by virtue of being perceived as no more
than a projection of adult desire; to be a go-between is to be nowhere,
to be nonexistent. Yet the instant the go-between child asserts its
presence as mediator, which is to say that the space "between" adult
players or between the adult and her or his object of desire is differentiated, the child figures instead as an obstacle to what it hitherto
fantasmatically provided.

Analysis itself, which depends on the intercession of the child,
seeks to destroy the child it covets. Subsequent to the dissolution of
Hans's phobia, Freud observes that "it may be that Hans now enjoys
an advantage over other children, in that he no longer carries within him that seed in the shape of repressed complexes which must
always be of some significance for a child's later life" (*SE* 10:143–44).
That "seed," however, is the child itself who, eventually overlaid by
the adult system, will *be* the neurotic origin the analyst essays to
uncover and purge. Given the psychoanalytic position that neuroses tend to originate in infantile stages, the resulting confusion between the child and the neurosis seems inevitable. The "seed" that
has been vanquished at its inception is the phobic child who will
never reemerge to plague the adult, the value of the child thus being negated in expectation of the adult it gestates. In *On Tue un Enfant,* Serge Leclaire goes so far as to assert that analysis involves the
repeated destruction of the omnipotent and idealized child in the
adult: "It is requisite that psychoanalysis never ceases to act out the
murder of the child, for it to understand that it must accomplish this,
in order to reckon with the omnipotence of the child. Psychoanalytic practice is based on bringing to light *the constant activity of a
death-bound force: that which consists of killing the fantastic (or terrifying) child who, from generation to generation, witnesses the dreams and
desires of its parents"* (11, my translation).[38] Psychoanalysis lures the
fantasmatic child into the analytic arena in order to destroy it—again
and again; for, according to Leclaire, the omnipotent child is repeatedly reborn in the subject even in the process of its annihilation. It
is the child of adult narcissistic longing Freud describes in "On Narcissism," the child ever receding into an idealized future that is real-

ly a lost and idealized past. It is also the child internalized as the ever-vigilant "witness" to adult desire, the primal-scene child who, like an-other subject being harbored by the adult, is repeatedly traumatized by the spectacle of its own adult desire; hence the prohibition imposed on adult desire originates in its own internal and traumatized child through whom the relationship between child and parent endlessly is replayed. Here, again, we find the conflation of the real child the adult subject once was with the fantasmatic child who lingers on in the subject as a regressive and disabling voice. The infantile relationship between the child and the adult sphere is internalized in the relationship between the adult subject and her or his child self. No wonder that the real child is often confused with the internalized child, thus becoming the object of both idealizations and destructive impulses.

The incestuous character of the perfect family with which Dickens frequently closes has been treated at length elsewhere.[39] As discussed above, Woodcourt is a father-substitute for Esther, substituting for the father-substitute Jarndyce. The two families with which the novel concludes, Esther's family, and the Jarndyce, Ada, young Richard arrangement, both install themselves in Bleak Houses, the smaller version a substitute for the original as if to suggest that the familial constellation is reproduced intact from generation to generation. In *Dombey and Son,* Florence Dombey and Walter Gay are an incestuous sibling couple (like Estella and Pip) whose children, little Florence and little Paul, provide Florence with the corrected version of the flawed family with which she began.[40] The marriage of Amy Dorrit and Arthur Clennam is a father/daughter arrangement that realigns the tortuous displacements of *Bleak House.*

Many of these characters are the products of unhappy family situations or illegitimate unions (or both); circumstances are resolved by closures that insert them into the happy families to which they all along aspired. If they find their ends in their beginnings, their novel-length journeys leading them "back" to what they never had in the first place, if the novels are narrativized pursuits of the idealized family into which one can, at the end, be born, then the incestuous family seems less like a reenactment of the family than an original family (the only "original" the texts have to offer)—an origin that seems accessible only through substitution and displacement. Whereas Woodcourt takes the place of the father figure, Jarndyce, Jarndyce himself is a substitute for a "real" idealized father who is—Hawdon, "Nemo," no one—the reality who cannot live up to the ideal, who has been therefore disfranchised of the paternal role. There is no actual ideal father for the substitutive ideal to emulate, no real origin for the ending to recuperate.

The incestuous family pursued and realized in Dickens is the same family with which the subject of analysis is reunited. In purporting to "cure" the subject's defective Oedipal constellation, the analyst leads the subject back to the family both to bring conflicts to light and to resolve them. Object-relations analysts go so far as to offer the therapy as a compensation for the pre-Oedipal deficit in adequate nurturing; the analyst heals the familial wound, reconstructs the internalized family into something intact and self-sufficient—not unlike the Dickensian incestuous family that, through its illusion of a restoration of what never was, functions as an idyllic and imperturbable space carved out of an unstable adult scene.

The analytic subject who endlessly repeats problematic familial configurations in her or his adult relationships is invited nevertheless to repeat, transferentially, the defective relation in therapy, thereby recognizing in its therapeutic actualization the original repressed scenario. It is by the therapeutic repetition itself that repetition as a way of life will be surmounted. Yet, if the end of repetition is reached through this final repetition that releases the subject from cyclical into linear existence, the final episode (that final de-immobilizing transaction, the instant at which the analysand can asseverate, like the protagonist of *The Snake Pit*, "Doctor, I'm not in love with you anymore") seems to entail fundamentally a permanent ascension into a perfected family. This substitutive family is designed to recreate in its own image the original defective family that, because it is always defective, can be nothing *but*—is now repudiated as origin.

The defective family is discarded in favor of a family reconceived as unimpaired. Hawdon, the failed father, is restored to Esther in the guise of Jarndyce so that now she is free to marry another idealized father, the right father that analysis offers to the patient hitherto fixed in a repetitive cycle of the wrong choice. It isn't that repetition is at an end; rather, it is frozen into the positive scene with which analysis forestalls the negative. Roy Schafer criticizes the cyclic tendency of psychoanalysis that conspires with potentially "comic" fantasies of the analytic subject. He writes that comedy's

> view of cyclic return implies that the past can be redone, if not undone. Thereby it implicitly denies the passage of time. It cancels out its pastness. Its perspective is timeless. . . . Yet have we not, by engaging in the analytic enterprise, based ourselves at least partly on the assumptions of the timeless cycle? After all, it is part of our technique to work back and forth over the analysand's life as if al-

most all parts of time are potentially recapturable, redo-able, im-
provable, even though they may not all be equally so in the particular case. In this respect we proceed as if time were not time at
all. (*New Language* 29)

Schafer urges, conversely, resignation to the tragic, linear model of
human history. Nevertheless, much of his vocabulary of the comic
spills over into his own professed tragic realism. Thus, he aims for a
self-coherent subject who learns to organize her or his past into a
unified narrative. Yet, as Schafer himself explains, such organicity is
typical of the comic mode. The increasing interest expressed by the
psychoanalytic community in the relationship between the analytic
process and narrative strategies (a trend founded, of course, by Freud's
case histories) leads me to ask what it is about narrative that appeals
to psychoanalytic thinking. Is it perhaps that narrative is structurally "comic" inasmuch as it offers an *aesthetic* resolution to a series of
otherwise discrete significations? Donald Spence's argument in favor
of the aesthetic merit of an interpretation (over its strict relationship
to the truth) suggests that there is less difference than one might
imagine between the Dickensian project of reconciling the irreconcilable and the psychoanalytic project of establishing the analysand
as an active narrator of a life history retrieved as coherent. Spence
asserts that "an interpretation satisfies because we are able to contain an unfinished piece of reality in a meaningful sentence; that is
part of what we mean by finding its narrative home" (137). D. A.
Miller, however, questions the success of such a narrative resolution:
"When reading [*Bleak House*] . . . one never feels quite at home; perhaps, having finished it, one knows why one never *can* feel at home"
(106). Yet, the permanence of "home" is exactly what drives the Dickensian narrative. The psychoanalyst as well is committed to the
"home" built by the analytic enterprise. If, as Spence seems to believe, narrative can provide the security of closure, a home as it were,
this then may account for psychoanalysis's fascination with narrative as a trope that can "save" the analytic process from its own implicit structural interminability.

    While Dickens ends *Bleak House* with a picture of a blissful inces-
tuous union, the missed incest between Jarndyce and Esther is alluded
to by Esther in morbid terms, indicating either that there are quali-
tative differences between incestuous choices or that Dickens is ambivalent about the nature of the exemplary incestuous family whose
perfection he resists at the same time that he exalts it. The incestuous family threatens the utter collapse into desire that thus foreclos-

es desire itself. It would be a "short-circuiting," as Peter Brooks has put it, of desire's elaborate peripety. Upon reading Jarndyce's letter of proposal, a proposal that "came upon [her] as the close of the benignant history [she] had been pursuing," Esther remarks that it was "as if something for which there was no name or distinct idea were indefinitely lost to me. I was very happy, very thankful, very hopeful; but I cried very much" (617). What Esther imagines she will have forfeited in marriage to Jarndyce is the sexuality she recognizes as a central component of Ada and Richard's relationship. Additionally, and perhaps more significantly, Esther foresees marriage to her father-substitute as a kind of death, her historical closure.[41] Although marriage is experientially always a prefiguration of death, one might posit in Dickens an attempt to differentiate right and wrong ends (deaths). The ending offered by marriage to Jarndyce appears to replicate too nearly the incestuous alliance that characterizes Esther's final choice. The more identifiable incestuous union with Jarndyce threatens to collapse into the immobility of literal incest, precluding any progress whatsoever, the most extreme manifestation of which is the Dedlocks' "dying of their own family gout" (231).[42] But the symbolic incestuous union with Woodcourt is implicitly infected by its correspondence to the "wrong" choice and, furthermore, the ideal closure is undercut by Dickens's hesitancy about endings of any kind.

Peter Brooks contends that both Dickensian plots and analysis attempt to achieve a "'cure' from plot" (114). But, conversely, I would argue that the drive toward stasis in the Dickensian novel and in analysis manifests not as a transcendence of plot but rather a permanent entrenchment in a perfected plot (the imperturbably happy family) elaborately wrought in the novels and the analytic encounter. Brooks draws his notion of the "cure from plot" from Freud's theory of the death drive, the goal of which is the release from the imperatives of motion that "plot" entails. Thus "the finding of the right end" of the narrative, as Brooks explains it, is akin to the human subject's drive toward the "right end" of life (140). The problem with calling this "end" *outside* plot, in both the Freudian schema and Brooks's narrative paradigm, is that the "right end" can only be imagined from the perspective of a subject immersed in life, whose end is interior rather than exterior to plot. Further, Brooks's argument about the progressive nature of the Dickensian and analytic repetitions arises from a confidence in that rather fine analytic distinction between repetition and transcendence of repetition that I suggest we must question. Interestingly, contemporary reviews of *Bleak House* attack precisely the novel's construction of plot (or lack thereof). "Plot it has none," remarked one reviewer, while others lamented the multiple subplots that undermine the reader's attempt to locate a central narrative trajectory (Collins 295). While the twentieth century has celebrated Dickens as a master craftsman *because* of his ability to weave together diverse plots, it is worth considering the hesitation expressed by his contemporaries. One might argue that it is Dickens's resistance to plot's insistent drive toward closure that expresses itself in a compensatory overabundance of plots.

The Chancery case of Jarndyce v. Jarndyce is oppressive because of the depleting effects of the family's interminable internal reproduction (the case "ends" because the legacy is exhausted). Jarndyce v. Jarndyce is an infinite mirroring of the family name, figured in the novel's closure with a family that threatens endlessly to recapitulate "bleak house," the "versus" at the same time standing for the fissure that divides the family from its own self-completion as a self-identical edifice. It is here that we find the kernel of the problematic of endings; while the text fears interminability, the infinite repetition of the Chancery case, it concurrently fears the end as a prevision of stagnation and death. In reference to the Chancery case, Richard insists, "'Well . . . everything has an end'" (696). But what the Chancery case suggests is the opposite possibility, that nothing has an end, especially not itself that does not actually end but rather is left hanging.[43] In the incestuous resolution we have an end that is at once the termination of the cycle of the text's pursuit, the happy family origin having been recovered and fulfilled, and the denial of the possibility of ending, when the end is the beginning. Again, however, the incest is displaced (from Jarndyce to Woodcourt) to look like progress instead of repetition, while the text's indeterminacy as to the merit of its own self-resolution all the while undermines its attempt at an idyllic vision. Like Esther's marrying Woodcourt instead of Jarndyce, perhaps the point of analysis is to train the analysand to accept substitutes *as* substitutes, no more than that. Yet, what if all the substitutes, like Woodcourt for Jarndyce, wind up being no more than equivalences? In other words, why bother with feeble substitution, Dickens seems to be asking, when you can have the real thing? Certainly, inasmuch as Dickens offers the more nearly incestuous ending in *Little Dorrit,* he seems to have answered the question he raises in indecision and despair in *Bleak House.*

Whereas there are too many wills in *Bleak House*'s Chancery case, a proliferation of possible endings, in *Oliver Twist* the sole will has been destroyed and the "'only proofs of the boy's identity lie at the bottom of the river'" (363). The closure of *Oliver* is reported in the conditional, as a story Dickens "would" tell if he could "weave, for a little longer space, the thread of these adventures," as though reluctant to close at all (479). We are given an incomplete closure, therefore, rendered in the conditional, that presents the end point as a future position on the horizon toward which the textual events strive but never actually meet.

In the Dickensian tale, the convergence of the synchronic and diachronic perspectives arrives at a kind of stalemate, the synchronic level of a perpetual present inhibiting the text's own immersion in history.[44] While it is essential for the illegitimate child to gain historical valence through a name and a story of origins, the period of namelessness in which it exceeds historical dimensions holds a certain fascination, a sense of infinite potential in which all stories are available to the child. Like the children at the burial orchestrated by Sowerberry who jump "backwards and forwards over the coffin," the Dickensian illegitimate child offers to the Dickensian text the possibility of an extratemporal space beyond origins and closure (84). Yet, this space is at the same time, horrifically, a space of nonexistence, the social limbo of nonsignification (namelessness) accentuating the problem of signification in the psychical arena. One must consider, furthermore, that the options presented are those of actual desubjectification or, with the insertion into historical time, an apprehension of a past and future desubjectification at the boundaries of the life of the subject. While Esther cannot enter the reproductive historical chain through marriage before she herself is historicized, the marriage she enters into is figured as an inflexible present that resembles death by virtue of its changelessness. The family into which Oliver is finally "born" presents closure as origin and end—there is nothing further beyond the idealized and permanent beginning. Oliver's "birth" into a real past gives him access to a real family;[45] nevertheless, structurally, his history only begins (and ends) in the family he needed to be born into in order to be "born."

It is in light of these narratives that demand the historicization of the subject in order to fix the subject for all time, that I postulate a bifurcation of textual desire.[46] The eruption of the family at the end of the Dickensian novel appears to inaugurate history, the reproductive life cycle, and mortality, on one level while, on another, we have families who structurally deny all the above. The transcendence of the transference constitutes no more than another repetition. Jo, in consequence of his resistance to diachrony, his refusal to "know," to be embedded in the knowledge that marks the birth of the historical subject, is expelled from the text as the intransigent factor that threatens to explode the myth of resolution, the fantasy that repetition is progressive.

Like *Bleak House*'s Jarndyce v. Jarndyce, *What Maisie Knew* opens with an image of the repetition ensnaring the family's reproductive agenda: Farange v. Farange. While Jarndyce v. Jarndyce revolves around the question of inheritance (and culminates with the revelation that parents have nothing to leave their children), the Farange case represents the child ("the bone of contention") both as the prize and the punishment for what James recognizes as an ultimately "incurable" family.

Notes

1. This is a term I import from Jean Laplanche and J.-B. Pontalis, "Fantasy and the Origins of Sexuality" (13).

2. In *Little Dorrit,* it is now the young woman who desires the older man who in turn loves elsewhere—as though Esther Summerson, recast as Amy Dorrit, is being punished for her earlier failure to recognize the best man. When Arthur Clennam finally marries Amy Dorrit, there is a sense of triumph in the novel. Additionally, I would propose that Florence Dombey's "real" love-object is her father whom she has lured into her family circle by the end of the novel.

3. In the "Wolf Man" case, however, Freud's objective was to prove the historical truth of the traumatic events; his investment here, nevertheless, seems to be in disputing Jung's denial of childhood sexuality. See *SE* 17:1–71.

4. Freud is emphatic on this point in analysis: in order for the analysis to be thorough and effective, it must be an infant analysis.

5. Laplanche discusses at length this particular case of Emma as an example of the impossibility of locating a single event or fantasy as the site of trauma. Rather, he explains, it is the convergence of the two. Hence, when the pubescent Emma returns to the store, the original sexual assault only now relates to feelings on her part of sexual excitation. It is her own sexual fantasy of a repetition of the original event that, in conflict with social prohibitions, traumatizes her. Laplanche argues that the sexual arena is particularly fruitful for the analyst because "sexuality alone is available for that action in two phases which is also an action 'after the event.' It is there and there alone that we find that complex and endlessly repeated interplay—midst a temporal succession of missed occasions—of 'too early' and 'too late'" (*Life and Death* 43).

6. The reversal of roles between adult and children in Dickens is treated extensively by Dickens scholars. Particularly, J. Hillis Miller's "young-old," "old-young" distinction clarifies the dynamic (183). The "young-

old" characters are those adults who refuse to grow up, whereas the "old-young" are the elderly children.

7. In reference to Mrs. Jellyby's activities, Arthur A. Adrian comments: "What are foreign missions, asks Dickens but an evasion of immediate responsibilities, if not even an exploitation of primitive people who would be happier left alone," suggesting that Mrs. Jellyby's imposition on these primitive people (read children) is analogous to the typical Dickensian parent's exploitation of his or her own children (125).

8. Frank Donovan remarks that although Dickens always discussed childhood itself as an idyllic time of life, "it is hard to find a happy child in Dickens" (15). This confusion, between a fantasy of a lost paradise called "childhood" and childhood as Dickens actually portrays it, disrupts as well the very stability of the term "child" in Dickens.

9. Philip M. Weinstein points out that Dickens "is in the awkward position of sympathizing spontaneously with the frustrated child, yet sharing his culture's cautionary fear of that child's attempts to redress his situation" (70).

10. In a curious analogue to the Dickensian reversals, Freud's description of the development of the superego indicates the extent to which the confusion between adult and child is developmentally inevitable. In *Civilization and its Discontents,* he explains the situation thus: "By means of identification [the child] takes the unattackable authority into himself. The authority now turns into his super-ego and enters into possession of all the aggressiveness which a child would have liked to exercise against it. The child's ego has to content itself with the unhappy role of the authority—the father—who has been thus degraded. Here, as so often, the [real] situation is reversed: 'If I were the father and you were the child, I should treat you badly.' The relationship between the super-ego and the ego is a return, distorted by a wish, of the real relationships between the ego, as yet undivided, and an external object" (*SE* 21:129). The internalization of the parent/child relationship in terms of the ego/superego conflict is standard Freudian theory. What is important to consider, however, in light of the subject at hand, is the way in which this internalized confusion is transmitted generationally. If the child cannot entirely distinguish the difference between its parents and itself, it grows up into an adult who repeats the reversal vis-à-vis his or her own children.

11. In "The Theme of the Three Caskets," Freud suggests that the mother's body, the site of birth, becomes imaginatively associated with death as well (*SE* 12:301). Compare this passage in the case of Hans to Winnicott's Gabrielle, discussed in chapter 4, where "birth" and "death" days become significant for the child in *relation* to one another.

12. See Sigmund Freud, "Instincts and Their Vicissitudes."

13. See Sandor Ferenczi, "The Confusion of Tongues between the Adult and the Child," for his treatment of the distinction between the child's sexuality and that of the adult, and the ensuing sexualization on the part of the adult of the child's affectionate behavior.

14. In play, Hans frequently enacts the role of progenitor of his play-mates; becoming mothers and fathers is typically a component in children's make-believe world.

15. Laplanche and Pontalis write that the child's "pre-history, located by Freud in phylogenesis, can be understood as a pre-structure which is actualized and transmitted by the parental fantasies" (17). Although this prestructure seems, at first appearance, to be a far cry from Freud's race memory, in fact the authors are falling into the same assumption of an inherent structure conditioning the emergence of developmental phases.

16. It is telling that Esther never encourages Guppy in the pursuit of her origins.

17. In raising the issue of the origin of textual fantasy, I am not referring to the realm of personal fantasy in the life of the empirical author but rather to the cultural pervasiveness of the fantasy that the texts merely reinvoke.

18. Most critics take for granted that Jarndyce would have been the wrong choice for Esther, an assumption that I believe ensues from identifying with Esther's point of view in the fantasy.

19. It is furthermore important to recall that Woodcourt is indirectly responsible for the death of Esther's father. Woodcourt provided Hawdon with the lethal dose of opium.

20. It is worth comparing Freud's unrepressed child to Peter Coveney's hypothesis that the abundance of Victorian literary deaths of children were metaphors for repression of "the instinctual self" (285).

21. Susan K. Gillman and Robert L. Patten, in "Dickens: Doubles:: Twain: Twins," convincingly argue that "with Esther, Dickens thoroughly develops 'ontogenetic' doubling . . . in which a character lives through a variety of selves externalized as alternatives and internalized as possibilities" (446).

22. For extensive discussions of the mirror theme in *Bleak House,* see Lawrence Frank, Alex Zwerdling, and Helena Michie. Michie treats at length the emergence of Esther's subjectivity in her disidentification with her mother.

23. Peter Garrett writes: "Fidelity to the past is rewarded, falsification or denial of it punished; indeed, in these terms, the rescue of Oliver Twist appears as a reward for the unconscious fidelity to his origins implied by his adherence to 'the principle of Good,' just as Monks is punished for his attempts to destroy Oliver's connection with that past" (55). Garrett is referring to Dickens's assertion in the Preface that his ambition is to "show, in little Oliver, the principle of Good surviving through every adverse circumstance, and triumphing at last" (*Oliver* 33). Garrett argues that it is Oliver's father whom the child revivifies. Alternatively, I suggest that while it is the father's law the child repeats and cements, it is his mother's essence that makes him subserve the patriarchal law.

24. Lacan describes the situation thus: "Now this anxiety is exactly

what is not generated in the subject in question. Dick cannot even engage in the first sort of identification, which would already be an essay in symbolism. He is, paradoxical as it may seem to say it, eyeball to eyeball with reality, he lives in reality. In Melanie Klein's office, there is neither other nor ego for him, just a reality pure and simple" (*Seminar* 1:82).

25. About Lacan's recognition of the significance of Klein's treatment of Dick, Shoshana Felman writes: "The constitution of Dick's unconscious (the mental functioning necessitating and enabling the substitution of objects of desire) is coincident, moreover, with Dick's own introduction into language—a language that precedes him and that comes to him from the Other (represented, here, by the therapist); a language that articulates a preestablished sociocultural symbolic system governed by a Law that structures relationships and into which Dick's own relations must be inscribed" (124). This Law that the therapist represents is the adult law of symbolic relations in which the child must be inserted.

26. Taylor Stoehr maintains that one finds in Dickens that, "the sexual and the class content have somehow been quarantined from each other. . . . Because the impact of one world upon another is not felt, there can be no final integration for these novels, but only a trumped-up ending. . . . The concentration on superficial unity of plot merely intensifies the split, by drawing attention to connections which could not be made were there no gap to be bridged" (97–98). Actually, the go-between child negotiates the relationship between the two arenas, which is precisely what is so menacing about it. If they seem to remain in separate spheres, it is as a result of the repression of the child who emblematizes their convergence. Consider, for example, that in the very idea of the illegitimate child one finds a salient consolidation of social and sexual plots.

27. It is curious that nowhere else in his notes does Dickens refer to a character's death in such terms.

28. See Karen Chase (92–93); Christine van Bonheemen (128–31); Gordon D. Hirsch (132–52); and Peter Garrett (33, 38, 60).

29. Weinstein makes an excellent case for the ways in which Dickens's "work manages . . . to assimilate—by out-maneuvering, by disguising, by blinking—its own fissures" (19). I thoroughly concur with Weinstein and see Jo as an instance in which the text reveals its own process of disguise.

30. To his friend and colleague, Wilhelm Fliess, Freud described his patient, "Dora," as "an eighteen-year-old girl, a case that has smoothly opened to the existing collection of picklocks" (Letter to Wilhelm Fliess, 14 October 1900, *Complete Letters* 427). Laplanche and Pontalis compare Freud to "a detective on the watch" (8).

31. Peter Garrett writes that the handkerchief "becomes the focus of a continuing minor plot line, a strand connecting rich and poor, mothers and children, living and dead" (65).

32. Christine van Bonheemen and Lawrence Frank both point out that

the gesture of lifting her mother's hair corresponds to Esther's own self-revelation in the mirror subsequent to her illness (*Family Romances* 120; "'Through a Glass Darkly'" 110). Albert D. Hutter explores Dickens's fascination with viewing the dead bodies at the morgue: "One challenge in looking at a body with the life gone out of it—a challenge of the most disturbing kind—is to allow into consciousness the opposing sense of life in us and death in the mirror we face. We look, but the gaze cannot be returned" (13–14). This then is the culmination of Esther's relationship with her mother's mirroring gaze—as a gaze that now reveals to her the future annihilation of her own gaze. Note that Woodcourt is her final and permanent mirror who tells her what she looks like (more beautiful than ever). Esther, trusting her husband's ability to create her, has no need to look for herself.

33. In his notes Dickens wrote: "JO—begin illness from him," as if to suggest that it is Jo himself who is the "disease" in the novel, that which threatens to expose irremediably the breakdown of social and familial roles (*Working Notes* 225). Immediately following his reference to Jo as the origin of the illness, on the same line in fact, Dickens noted "his disappearance," which refers specifically to Bucket's abduction but, in light of what precedes it, implies that Jo is the scapegoat for textual and social illness who must be removed—must disappear. Significantly, it is from the rat scurrying from Hawdon's grave in Tom-All-Alone's that Jo contracts the illness he passes on to Esther, suggesting that the real cause of dissolution is not the child but the failed father whose "disease" is "inherited" by the child. What is additionally revealed by this progression of the disease from Hawdon's grave to Jo to Esther is that Jo functions not only as Esther's go-between counterpart but also as an intermediary between Esther and her father. The only other contact Esther has with her father is via the letters from Kenge and Carboy written in Hawdon's hand, which reduces Hawdon's status to that of Jo's—a receiver and messenger of other people's words, incapable of being themselves producers of signs. Dianne Sadoff shows that Hawdon never accedes to the paternal function vis-à-vis his daughter, never gains that patriarchal "authority" (16–19). As the instance of the letters to Esther amply illustrates, Hawdon cannot even speak in his own voice to his own child, but rather records another indifferent law (note that Kenge and Carboy are attorneys).

34. Angus Wilson, in his introduction to the Penguin Edition, sums up the critical response to the novel (26). See also reviews of *Oliver Twist* in Philip Collins (42–46).

35. As James Kincaid points out: "One of the most baffling of the many mysteries of Victorian culture is this split between little Oliver Twist in the novel and little Oliver Twist in life" (74).

36. In his working notes for *Bleak House*, Dickens crossed out the name "Joe" and replaced it with "Jo" (215). Jo is sexually ambiguous, more appropriate for the gender slippage characteristic of the go-between.

Gordon Hirsch notes that Esther herself is sexually indeterminate (138–39).

37. Although the go-between Leo is the central character of Hartley's novel, his self-recognition as go-between in conjunction with his defiance makes him a go-between in function but not in nature, an important distinction.

38. "Il faut que le psychanalyste ne cesse de perpétrer le meurtre de l'enfant, de reconnaître qu'il ne peut l'accomplir, de compter avec la toute-puissance de l'infans. La pratique psychanalytique se fonde d'une mise en évidence du travail constant d'une force de mort: celle qui consiste à tuer l'enfant merveilleux (ou terrifiant) qui, de génération en génération, témoigne des rêves et désirs des parents" (11).

39. See especially Sadoff (52); Albert J. Guerard (69–108); Mark Spilka (51); Peter Brooks (128); and Thomas A. Hanzo (27–47).

40. Given the fact that Dickens originally did not have Estella and Pip unite at the end of *Great Expectations,* one might postulate that among his "dark" visions of the later novels is the insight that the idealized family is unattainable in any form.

41. Nina Auerbach discusses "those forced happy marriages that look so much like deaths in [Dickens's] novels" (113).

42. In "Repetition, Repression and Return in *Great Expectations,*" Peter Brooks calls the overtly incestuous choice of a love-object a short-circuit of the deferred route to death (128). If the marriage plot in the Dickensian novel is a kind of death, it must be the "right" death, whereas the incestuous choice represents the short-circuiting of the narrative that progresses directly from the preorganic to death. Again, we confront a distinction between acceptable and unacceptable manifestations of incest.

43. Projected titles for *Bleak House* included "The Solitary House / That was always shut up," and "The Ruined House, / That got into chancery / and never got out," both connotative of imprisonment in repetition (*Working Notes* 189, 201). The idea of being "always shut up" in the house and never getting out is vividly depicted by Esther's progress from one Bleak House to another. But again, if this is a negative ending, it is the only positive one.

44. Van Bonheemen remarks on the temporal ambivalence apparent in the very first paragraph of *Bleak House:* "It is the absence of beginning that the narrator seems to stress" (106).

45. Note that he cannot prove the past events of his criminal experience until he is in possession of his own historical past as a vantage point from which he can narrate reality.

46. John Kucich theorizes that Dickensian novels repeatedly work out the relationship between passion and repression, which are not antagonistic drives but rather "two different forms of desire itself" (203). Kucich shows that in the earlier novels the dichotomy emerges in discrete characters; thus, we have, for example, the repressive force of Monks and the

unharnessed passion of Bill Sikes. We find what Kucich calls entirely "self-negating" characters like Oliver juxtaposed with consuming self-interest. Such dichotomous representations of what is truly nondichotomous in Dickens eventually are transformed into characters like Esther who is both "self-negating" *and* self-interested, whose strategies of repression function as an inextricable *component* of her desire; repression in fact conditions her desire.

6

Maisie Farange: Damaged Child

> But the recognition of this reversal of roles get us no
> further; the practice of child analysis seems to be always
> in danger of filling with guilt either the adult or the child.
> —J.-B. Pontalis, *Frontiers of Psychoanalysis*

"Well, you ain't a myth, my dear . . ."

If she isn't a "myth," as Mr. Perriam declares, certainly Maisie, this "interminable little *Maisie*," as James called the child/novel, is a fantasy (*Notebooks* 167). It is not her existence that is in question; rather, it is her position, the where and the why of her, her relationship to internal social arrangements as well as her role vis-à-vis a reader whose core alliance, with the adult scene or the child's experience, remains uncertain. James's decision not to let his child narrate her own story is not only related to the concurrent development of a psychoanalysis that derives its theory of childhood from adult recollections but also is critical thematically in a story that is about using the child to serve adult ends. In *What Maisie Knew,* we are offered the child's eye view of the nasty machinations of a fashionable but immoral adult set whose complicated sexual regroupings seem to proceed from the presence of the child it is their business to blame. Thus, like Leo Colston, Maisie is not the product of the sexual relation but its origin. Like Hartley and Dickens, James is caught in the psychoanalytic bind of simultaneously trying to differentiate the child from the adult and collapse the two positions.

Writing the child in light of the mechanism of deferred action, the fantasy that the child is growing toward adult discourse, which will make good on previously unarticulated experience, characterizes James's mismanagement of the child's position. My position as reader, as a result, is destabilized by this novel that asks me to overlook the question of my own situatedness and my allegiances—with the child or the abusive parent, with a misguided and misguiding narrator, or with the child served up as paradigm of virtue or corruption. The critical response to *Maisie* tends either to take sides (over Maisie's "knowledge," complicity, and so forth) or to rise above such limited debates. Yet, one cannot help but choose a side, as it were, in this novel that, from its own inability to declare itself as situated (in the adult or the child), produces a commensurate fantasy in the reader who tries valiantly to read "outside" of perspectives, outside, further, of the question of our relation to our own constitutive child's narratives.

It is because there is no legitimate child's perspective anywhere in this novel about the child, and, as a result, no grist for the mill of "knowledge," for which there is no legitimate vessel, that *Maisie* is a story about an adult relationship to a "knowledge" suppressed as "primal" and a scene that can only be revivified under the anesthetic of adult discursive appropriations. Hence, any "knowledge" Maisie might gain is crucially subordinated to adult knowledge, which is necessarily greater than the child's. To identify knowledge with traumatic knowledge and to submit adult insights to the evocative tangents of an unharnessed child's "voice" with all its desperation and force would be to plummet into the very mouth of horrific primal experience that it is the novel's purpose to avert—a detour that it is the reader's pleasure to repeat. It is the novel's and the reader's business to *limit* the potentially excessive, "interminable," knowledge of the child.

J. Hillis Miller goes to great lengths to prove that, ethically, "we are by no means free to make *Maisie* mean anything we want" (*Pygmalion* 79). We are not "free" in this way, he argues, because the text restricts our transmuting interpretations. Yet, as Juliet Mitchell points out, "freedom" is overdetermined in the novel (183). For Mrs. Beale and Sir Claude freedom means liberation from their marital partners; for Maisie, it means choosing her future; for Mrs. Wix, it is equated with the immoral activity of the sexually "free" couple—just as "free talk" in *The Awkward Age* refers to sexual conversation. Thus a relationship to the novel expressed in terms of "freedom" instantly is complicated by the semantic overload of this hypercathected Jamesian usage. It is inevitable, however, that we as readers should fall prey to characterizing our own response in such terms, inevitable because the novel seduces us into the terms of its fantasy.[1] We can be too "free" with Maisie, making of her an adult sexual object, or we can choose her future for her—how many critical futures have been chosen! Moreover, we can imagine, like most critical readings of this text, that we are "free" from the oppressive question of situatedness, a question the novel compels us *into,* set up by James in the adult/child dichotomization of 'perspective.

The questions posed throughout *What Maisie Knew* are: How much does Maisie know about the relational complexities surrounding her? Does she manage to resist the contaminating depredations of such knowledge of her "moral sense"? James offers as though actual the distinction between a deadly contamination and a steadfast innocence. Nevertheless, for James to locate textually such a faith in the truth of the either/or in Mrs. Wix and her moral "straighteners" suggests a certain debasement of the text's central questions inasmuch as Mrs. Wix is characterized as ultimately naive and self-motivated. How to evaluate Mrs. Wix becomes, as a result, as hotly debated critically as is the moral sense of which she is the final arbiter.

This question of Maisie's final status—as morally damaged or inviolate—is posed relentlessly in Jamesian scholarship that winds up trying to solve James's dilemma as though somehow the text offers conclusive data as well as incontrovertible delineations between these two possibilities.[2] Such critical responses cannot help, as a result, but repeat the Jamesian double fantasy of a child who is altogether differentiated from adult input and the child as a symptom of the adult relation. It is in the narrative structure itself, the ostensible child's vision that is "translated" by an adult narrator who lends words to the perception of an otherwise inarticulate central consciousness, that we find the exposure of the impossibility not only of answering the moral question—but even of raising it. As James explains in the Preface:

> Small children have many more perceptions than they have terms to translate them; their vision is at any moment much richer, their apprehension even constantly stronger, than their prompt, their at all producible, vocabulary. Amusing therefore as it might at the first blush have seemed to restrict myself in this case to the terms as well as to the experience, it became at once plain that such an attempt would fail. Maisie's terms accordingly play their part—since her simpler conclusions quite depend on them; but our own commentary constantly attends and amplifies. This it is that on occasion, doubtless, seems to represent us as going so "behind" the facts of her spectacle as to exaggerate the activity of her relation to them. The difference here is but of a shade: it is her relation, her activity of spirit, that determines all our own concern—we simply take advantage of these things better than she herself. (x)

What Maisie may or may not experience is rendered at once obscure and dependent on the translating vocabulary of the narrator who, it seems, has special access to a child's perspective that can only unfold within discourse—specifically, the discourse of an adult who commands the child's experience as narrative property. Merla Wolk has gone so far as to assert that the course of the novel shows us Maisie's consciousness developing *toward* the narrator's until, by the end, Maisie no longer depends on the narrator's intercession; she has, in other words, quite literally acceded to the epistemological position of the narrator. Her insights and intellect increasingly converge with those of a narrator now rendered obsolete inasmuch as he is replaced by his perfect double-in-consciousness—the spectating child who is simultaneously inside and outside the purview of a story that is never really hers. If, as Wolk suggests, Maisie can now adequately assume the narrative position the narrator all along has been "raising" her for, it is because the novel at heart tolerates no distinction between the insights of the adult and the child other than this issue of vocabulary that the child experiences but cannot speak. It is critical for the text both to define the limits of the child's consciousness and to stabilize them through the speech of the adult. For what the child suggests is not too few "terms" but too many sensory and experiential registrations that exceed adult language. Thus, the only defense against the child's potential excess is a "vocabulary" that defers like an anodyne emotional impacts from their intellectual(ized) registration.

James's concern that the narrator will seem to be "going so 'behind' the facts of [the child's] spectacle as to exaggerate the activity of her relation to them" replicates in the narrator/child relationship the relationship between the child and her adult caretakers.[3] The ambiguous use of "spectacle" in this context casts some doubt on the spectator/spectated patterns in the novel where Maisie is characterized repeatedly as a spectator of adult events that seem only to "happen" as a consequence of her observation; and perhaps (this is James's true fear) nothing will take place, will further the action of the narrative, without the intercession of a child. Yet the child in this instance is herself presented as a "spectacle" that the reader is invited to watch, that the narrator can travel behind—materializing this spectacularized child's consciousness as an entity with boundaries (before and behind, inside and outside). These boundaries sustain the possibility of entering the child and hence violating her or being warded off at the portals of sacrosanct territory, a "literary" rape that will be acted out on the plot level in *Lolita*.

All the interest of the novel accrues as a result of the reader's intersections with the child's consciousness. Sometimes we wonder what Maisie knows, at other times what we know; such is the discrepancy between speculation and narrative absolutes, of which, when it comes down to it, there are so very few. At times the distinction between Maisie's knowledge and our own is empowering; finally, such power leads us to formulate the child's knowledge of events in terms of what we ourselves have gleaned from the oblique narration. Thus, what the child knows, necessarily, is no more than what the highly particularized adult reader knows. Maisie's perceptions, her intuitions, her chain of associations are all interpreted by the reader; what Maisie knows is what the reader has determined to "make" of all this—which suggests that either the text is the ultimate "child" or the child is the ultimate "text." The child, of course, can hardly speak about what it does not know. On the subject of trusting the "vocabulary" of the child Freud stated: "An analysis which is conducted upon a neurotic child itself must, as a matter of course, appear to be more trustworthy, but it cannot be very rich in material; too many words and thoughts have to be lent to the child. . . . An analysis of a childhood disorder through the medium of recollection in an intellectually mature adult is free from these limitations" (*SE* 17:8–9).[4] On loan, as it were, from the adult sphere (which is always in the process of initiating the inarticulate adult-in-the-making) are the "words and thoughts" imputed to the child by the adult analyst. Like James, Freud prefers the adult's consciousness as "medium" for the thoughts that the child simply did not know it had. There is a great danger involved in these analyses (Freudian) and interpretations (Jamesian) in that one can never really know how much was *there* to begin with and how much was superadded by an adult imagination. Freud, notwithstanding, resolves this little dilemma quite neatly when he characterizes the adult analytic activity in terms of a loan the child will make good on—will grow up to, in other words. The process seems inevitable. Why not, he reasonably deduces, *start* with the adult whose childhood experiences presumably remain historically intact?[5] James as well denies that he is wholly altering the story through his appropriation of the child's point of view. His "own commentary" merely "attends and amplifies" the child's "conclusions." He "simply take[s] advantage" of her relationship to her experience better than she inasmuch as he has access to a knowledge she does not yet possess. This distinction between the child's insights and the adult's recapitulation, as well as the distinction between a child's capacity and that of an adult who can think for her, repeats the Jamesian moral dilemma between the child who is an empty vessel contaminated permanently by her vicious relations and the child who resists all such incursions. Maisie's double is the recollected child of analysis, the child who is either created anew in analysis, or the child who is revived like Sleeping Beauty, frozen in the moment of her descent into slumber.

In a notebook entry on *The Turn of the Screw*, James wrote that "it is a question of the children 'coming over to where they are,' referring literally and figuratively to the relationship between the children and the ghosts" (109). Yet the description applies perhaps even more nearly to Maisie's situation because in her we find a child who is throughout the novel coming over to where they are—to adulthood, adult knowledge, perhaps even pernicious influences that seem finally in the Jamesian program to mean nothing more than adulthood itself.[6] Although some of James's adults, like Lambert Strether, Milly Theale, and Isabel Archer manage to sustain an undiminished innocence into adulthood, one could argue that it is their innocence that renders them so utterly incapable of negotiating the social world that preys upon them. One might even go further to suggest that it is this inexplicable and imperturbable innocence that makes these characters so problematic and even, especially in the case of Strether, incredible. Where in *The Turn of the Screw* James inflates the distinction between adults and children into a tale of horror, such a distinction might obtain as well in his ostensibly realistic work.[7] Perhaps it is this very difference James erects between the inviolate and Edenic child's vision (consider the governess's original perception of the angelic children at Bly) and adult social experience that threatens to transform *Maisie* as well into a tale of horror.

What we learn, what the texts illustrate against their will, is that there is no outside of the social space, that it is never really a matter of the child coming over because the child is always already there— on the "other side" of which there is no "other side." This is the governess's dilemma in *The Turn of the Screw*: if the possession she suspects is real, then it has already occurred and all her efforts are in vain. Such contradictions inhere as well in the question of the adult's versus the child's perspectives. If adult vocabulary and adult knowledge are superimposed on the child (by James and Freud), their mutual fantasy might be that their distinctions are meaningful—their faith in an essential difference between the child's experience and the adult's. Thus while it appears that their mistake is in imagining a usable congruence between the two subject positions, one could equally question their confidence in a distinct child position that is "outside" of and different from adult understanding. It is indeed paradoxical that both Freud and James should be so immensely interested in the very child-subject that they represent as lacking just what it would take to make it interesting. One cannot help but wonder why they would take on the child at all when its interest so clearly resides in adult mediations. Maud Mannoni's account of "deficient" (retarded or psychotic) children suggests some possibilities as to why the child is required by texts that take such pains to exclude its voice.

In contrast to Freud and James, who use adult mediators to access the child, Mannoni exploits the child's symptomatology to betray the otherwise silent parental fantasies. Mannoni believes that the child functions on both physical and discursive levels as a mouthpiece for the mother's unconscious. "For it is often the mother's fantasies," Mannoni points out, "that give direction to the child's future destiny" (*Backward Child* xxii). At the same time that Mannoni takes for granted the "deficient" child's role vis-à-vis parental (specifically *maternal*) fantasy, the analyst's own relationship to the child becomes one of always privileging the absent (parent) over the presence of the analytic subject (the child). This is no more than to repeat what she sees as the structure of the parent/child relation—the child used in the service of what is absent (from consciousness)—the otherwise unsignifiable. In *The Child, His "Illness," and the Others*, Mannoni explains, "Clinically, it is clear that the Oedipus complex (the introduction of a Symbolic order) is above all the expression of an unsolved problem of the parents in regard to their own parents, of which the child, by his symptom, has become the representative signifier" (vii). To suggest, as I think this does, that the child is bound to recapitulate its preexisting circumstances reduces the child to a narrative vehicle that merely repeats in distorted form the stories of adults, of adults as children, of adults as the children of parents who produced a "deficiency" that gets played out in an interminable generational transmission of symptoms.

In both James's fictional text and Mannoni's psychoanalytic theory insist their own fantasies of the child as a vessel for aggressive parental fantasies. However, whereas Mannoni never addresses her own complicity in (re)producing the child as a subject of adult fantasy, the Jamesian text is ambivalent about whether the child resists adult influence or is an empty vessel. Further, James more overtly confesses his vilification of the mother whereas Mannoni's ideologically blind account locates the mother as the representative and purveyor of gender rules—gender rules that, as we will see, are bound to reveal her as failed.

While Mannoni's child speaks the otherwise silent "question" of the parental couple (*Backward* 175), in contradistinction to the child who must be spoken for in James and Freud, in none of these accounts do we find a child being listened to qua child. The defective child "serve[s] as the prop of adult fantasies and voyeurism" (*The Child, His "Illness"* 32)—not only the parents', as it turns out, but the analyst's as well. The analyst uses the problem child as a telescope down a generational corridor, but in so doing she sees best what is far removed and misses the object close at hand. Such "tunnel vision" on the part of the analyst tends to reproduce the victimization of the child by the parents. Like the parents, Mannoni confuses the "presence" of the child with a disavowed past that can only be "seen" or "recognized" where it is not. Whereas James looks to the future of Maisie's knowledge and Freud charts the past of the adult that would have expressed the same sentiments if only the words had been available, Mannoni and the parents of her analysands strip from the child both past and future. For the parents, insofar as Mannoni characterizes them, the child's past and present are the interactional catastrophe of their own histories and the child's future is spelled out on a slate in an unconscious world where fate slumps in wait for a solution that no conscious question has solicited.

For Mannoni, the child's past is always the story of parental failure and its future is the explosion in their faces of their own guilt. The child, thus, is the means whereby the parents can be punished and know it; to be punished with a "deficient" child and not know why is unsatisfactory for the analyst who refers remorselessly to her balance sheet of guilt and retribution. There will be payment exacted from these failed parents, payment in the form of a monstrous progeny, payment for analytic services rendered, and finally the finger isolating the guilty parties, who are always the same old parents, any parents; it is always the same old story. Only the child, the go-between who negotiates the parent/analyst relation, does not profit from its own intercession. Well, perhaps its IQ goes up several notches and it manages contentedly in a low-paying job—but this child never really gets back in kind all that the analyst has borrowed. It gave her the story of "deficiency," a theory of how parental fantasy is reproduced in the form of a child whose body and mind are no more than symptoms. In return, Mannoni converts the child into a symptom of her own theoretical grid, a proof of what she told us from the start.

All the "interest" in Maisie's story as well lies in what the adults are about, what ever more extravagant sexual exchanges and configurations they can invent before running out of partners, money, pretexts—even Maisie herself, who will no longer intercede. She finally is permitted to refuse the role of pretext because the text itself no longer requires her; all the complications have been explored ad nauseam; this story has run its course. And thus (James has Maisie do it for him), James exits quickly and gracefully from a world now thoroughly picked over for sexual possibilities. James's notebook entry underscores the extent to which he counted on the child as a vehicle through which the sexual complications might escalate in intensity and narrative effect: "Might not something be done with the idea of an odd and particular relation springing up 1st between the child and each of these new parents, 2d between one of the new parents and the other—through the child—over and on account of and by means of the child? . . . Best of all perhaps would be to make the child a fresh bone of contention, a fresh source of dramatic situations, *du vivant* of the original parents" (71).[8] It is difficult to gauge James's intention here, whether the sexual relations are his primary concern, and the child simply facilitates them, or if in fact he is centered upon the child whose personality is "enhanced" by the interest generated by her circumstances. In short, is it the child or the adult who garners the author's (and the reader's) attention? Once again, we are left with a distinction (between the child and the adult) that dissolves in its very elaboration. If the adult relations are primary and the child is merely the pretext that allows them to unfold, at the same time she augments their value. Likewise, if the adult complications are marginal insofar as they offer the child's perspective a more interesting landscape, we must conclude that the child's perspective minus the adult machinations is too quotidian to motivate a novel.

The sexual landscape of *What Maisie Knew* certainly steams for a nonpornographic novel of the period. While the profusion of affairs and sexual regroupings might seem lurid if perceived through an adult consciousness, the filter of Maisie's perspective renders it all somehow less obvious—even as the insertion of a child into this *mise en abyme* of adult concupiscence lends force to the scandalousness of the plot. This combination of better and worse, allowing the novel to pass itself off as a "moral" tale even as it delights in abundant immoralities, is precisely the mix the child facilitates. As James tells us, she "keep[s] the torch of virtue alive in an air tending infinitely to smother it" (viii)—or rather, she is the pretext whereby adult improprieties can flourish, "the centre and pretext for a fresh system of misbehaviour" without seeming to be interesting in and of themselves (vii). Thus, both James and the reader can deliciously engage the promiscuities without claiming such pleasures as intentional. Both reader and text offer their concern for the child's moral development as pretext for participation in *adult* fantasies. If Maisie has the sense that "it was as if the whole performance had been given for her," this is precisely how the reader can enjoy the text without feeling indebted to moral guilt (9). While it is difficult for me entirely to inhabit the guilt experienced by a contemporary reader of a nineteenth-century version of soft-core pornography (which the plot events surely constitute),[9] I recognize my own late twentieth-century guilt in the exploitation of a child for the purpose of my own pleasure; without doubt, such pleasure remains utterly taboo. To emphasize what Maisie knows is at once to do too much and too little; there is a kind of overcompensation in the form of the pretext of the *child's* knowledge as opposed to the reader's. Indeed, no agreement can be found among adult readers as to what Maisie *should* know, what there is to know *about*.

The structure of the relationship between the reader, the text, and the child-intercessor is reenacted internally in relationships that repeatedly ignite and develop as a result of Maisie herself. The constant refrain, that she "brought them together," the "them" signaling an absurd game of fill-in-the-blank, prevails among the sexual couples as a mitigating circumstance; the child's role, the pervasive assumption of her innocence, legitimizes the sexual pairings with a sense of their own fatedness. Like the text and the reader, the sexual partners are brought together over the "body" of the child who assumes considerably more agency (in terms of plot development and reader "interest") than her minor status would warrant. "'What in the world's our connexion,'" exclaims Mrs. Beale, "'but the love of the child who's our duty and our life and who holds us together as closely as she originally brought us?'" (358–59). The "love of the child" signifies not only their mutual concern for the child's welfare but the fact that their "connexion" *is* the "love of the child" who creates them as connected.

One wonders what will become of Sir Claude and Mrs. Beale without the ruse of parental responsibilities to legitimize their relationship in the eyes of the world. Their expectation of Maisie is a perverse variation on Mrs. Wix's theme of the salvific child, who will "save" them not from the moral fall foreseen by the straighteners but rather a social fall from respectability. As Mrs. Beale remarks, "'I daresay you *will* save us—from one thing and another'" (129). While Maisie is that which maintains as superficially virtuous an illicit alliance, her novelistic function is to defend the text against charges of prurience disengaged from moral purpose—pleasure without payment in the form of corrective seriousness. But one must consider the possibility (surely Sir Claude considers it) that it is Maisie's involvement in the affair that renders it so especially unsavory. Without the element of exploitation, Sir Claude and Mrs. Beale's relationship figures as yet another tedious affair that would hardly disturb the cream in one's morning coffee, their spouses having absconded. It is, however, the forced participation of Maisie (who, like Leo Colston, cheerfully represents her involvement as voluntary) that lends their romance an additional odor of unredeemable sin. This is what Sir Claude perceives. It is his resistance to "mixing up" the child in the adult sexual scene, hence "compromising" her reputation, that I suspect has won for Sir Claude some favorable critical response (167–68).[10]

Like mutually concerned parents and analysts, who come together for the sake of a child's psychical defect, Mrs. Beale and Sir Claude pretend to save Maisie from her hitherto defective caregiving environment. At the same time, Mrs. Wix urges Sir Claude to live alone with Maisie and herself, all in the name of salvaging the child's endangered moral sense. The possible "deficiency" or miraculous imperviousness of this moral sense generates enormous interest among all these adults, including the reader who reads in search of the salvation of the child. But such interest among the profit-conscious (whether the profit be a "cured" child, or financial security for an aging and underqualified governess, or an illegitimate alliance "subsidized" by a dependent ward) is supplemental, always in excess of the originally extended credit. Such interest speaks of desires without sufficient resources, of having to pay a bit extra to compensate for having come up short in the first place. "Interest" accrues when desire gets beyond itself and seeks what it cannot pay for. Like the child's consciousness, borrowed "on time" (the child's anticipated future) by adult exigency (Freud's, James's), the "interest" is a superaddition to original value. In other words, we all get more than we bargained for. What we in fact do bargain for, a sustaining confidence in the inviolate sensibilities of the child, gratification of our prurience, whatever, no longer seems to matter, supplemented as it is by an economy of accumulation and pretence—that what one paid is what one gets in return.

But what then is the original value and what is the interest? Is the child the value supplemented by the sexual divergence, or is the sexual scene "amplified" (to use James's own word) by the child's gaze? Is it Maisie's voyeurism, cloaking both the author's and the reader's, that adds spice to otherwise ridiculous and improbable adult sexual escapades? "Our business," James explains, "is to extract from her current reaction whatever it may be worth; and for that matter we recognise in it the highest exhibitional virtue" (xi). The "worth" of

Maisie's "reaction" is certainly inflated by its "exhibitional virtue," meaning the tale's moral qualities that, according to the standard nineteenth-century American prerequisite, raise its interest above pure sensation. If Maisie's "reaction" is the object of interest, the thing placed on exhibition, at the same time she is reacting to what she herself sees. Thus, we as reader watch Maisie watching. Our voyeurism seeks direction from her gaze and, in cleaving to it, enjoys the simultaneous rapture of seeing and not understanding (pure sensation) and understanding without really seeing (pure knowledge). Perhaps it is in the dramatic disjunction of the sensational from the epistemological that we reap our reward, our ultimate transgressive pleasure of credit without interest and without value lost.

My conversion of Jamesian "interest" into a financial metaphor is not without precedent for a novel that depicts relationships that confuse sexual desire with financial necessity.[11] The issue of money, who is getting what from whom, and the sound of the miserably few shillings Miss Overmore has in her pocket, becomes a chronic worrisome theme in a novel whose final concern is how Maisie will be provided for. Miss Overmore's graduation to the rank of Mrs. Beale is, on her part, surely financially motivated while her husband's eventual abandonment of her seems to ensue more for the sake of pursuing women who will support him than from any kind of sexual boredom. Ida Farange involves herself with fellows with names like "Perriam"[12] and "Tischbein," for James a not-so-subtle anti-Semitism directed at upstart Jews with all their bad manners and new money. Mrs. Wix's dedication to Maisie repeatedly is undermined by her plaintive inquiries about what should become of her without this means of employment. In response to Mrs. Wix's assertion that Mrs. Beale is a prostitute of sorts to Sir Claude, on whom she "lives," Maisie observes that Mrs. Wix lives on Sir Claude as well (206).

While the question of money tends to complicate further the nature of amorous relations in the novel, the sexualization of money makes it impossible to isolate mercenary from sexual agendas—or even love from profit. While Mrs. Beale blithely "makes love" to all who might serve her agenda, Maisie as well is characterized as "deriv[ing] great profit" from the relationship she precipitates between Mrs. Beale and Sir Claude (300, vii). At the same time, Maisie is a "great gift" that has come to Mrs. Beale for the sake of "handling" her romantic "complications" while Mrs. Wix lauds her capacity to "'repay [Sir Claude] a thousand-fold'" for his parental investment in her (124, 106).

Thus, Maisie alternately figures as *agent* in the game of profit and payment and as an *object* of exchange value. She circulates both actively and passively, and the text's indeterminacy as to whether Maisie can herself profit or can only *be circulated* as desired or despised, a gift given or a debit noted, ends up representing the love relation itself (whether it be between sexual partners or parent and child) as something quantifiable in dollars and cents. This obsession with the quantity of love and its remorseless insufficiency fuses at a certain point with the insufficiency of each parental couple, which never has enough left over for the child who benefits them only insofar as she returns more than she receives. This is why Mrs. Wix's injunction to Sir Claude to take care of a child who will repay him is absurd in light of the kind of payment (sexual) Sir Claude demands. But, in a novel that confuses sexual with financial profit, it is not surprising that readers would assume that at the end Maisie is offering Sir Claude her virginity.[13] Again, we return to the question of love that is never enough. Not for Beale who needs to pursue more profitable sexual partners than his pretty but portionless wife. Not for Sir Claude whose eyes rove ever in search of other women. This core dissatisfaction that catalyzes every character in the novel finds a startling reversal, however, in the child. Despite her superabundance of parents, by the end Maisie is left stranded with a governess, facing a financially tenuous future, as Mrs. Beale sharply notes. Yet, she is never, save once, presented as consciously wanting more than she receives;[14] ironic, indeed, since it is Maisie who winds up having the least, unless of course we count her possibly thriving moral sense.

Sir Claude's repeated assertions of his terror of Mrs. Beale (as well as Mrs. Wix's concern for his safety in the clutches of this deadly femme fatale) reveal the monumental task involved in wrenching free from the appalling power of the sexually attractive adult female. In contrast, his androgynization of Maisie, whose potential womanhood is explicitly negated by calling her "old boy" and "old man," suggests why Maisie's moral status remains so ambiguous. Maisie's prepubescence is trotted out frequently as a reminder to the reader of just what it is that the text finds at once so appealing about Maisie (she is not a woman) and troubling (she will be). "Mrs. Wix spoke not only as if Maisie were not a woman, but as if she would never be one," and she never is in a story that ends prior to her growing up (314). Exactly because Maisie will never be a woman, the text affords her a certain moral potential denied to the adult women who are all characterized as predators of various degrees of charm and attractiveness but enormously dangerous withal.

Regardless of how horribly Beale and his male companions tease the child, it is the women, her mother's friends, whom she most fears. While the men are outspoken about their exploitation and indifference (they are represented as so many carnivores who might at any moment tear what little "fat" there is from Maisie's toothpick legs), the women mask with concern their own lethal curiosity about the child and her circumstances. It is the "lie" that inspires dread in Maisie. And it is the "lie" that these adult women have elevated to an art form. This "lie" is finally no more than the lie that the adult woman has anything to offer either male sexual partners or children, the inhabitants of their reputed sphere. As Sir Claude remarks, "'Besides, there *are* no family women—hanged if there are! None of them want any children—hanged if they do!'" (61). He explains to Mrs. Beale that the type one marries is the attractive woman of fashion, suggesting that he gets what he bargained for. But Mrs. Beale appeals to him (beyond her physical attractiveness) through her purported dedication to Maisie, misrepresenting herself from the start as a "family woman," his avowed heart's desire. Thus, it is not only Maisie's intercession on the purely functional level of introducing them that is significant; it is also her status as child, that object whose interest they claim to share. To the extent that Maisie has been for quite some time giving her what she craves, Mrs. Beale does not prevaricate to Sir Claude her attachment to the child.

As Mrs. Wix has led Maisie (and the reader) to understand, "the essence of the question was that a girl wasn't a boy: if Maisie had been a mere rough trousered thing, destined at the best probably to grow up a scamp, Sir Claude would have been welcome" to raise her by himself (302). If the adult woman is the incarnation of all that is shameful, deviant, deathly, the prepubescent female child is the overcompensating emblem of virtuous dedication to the needs of others. The manipulations and self-aggrandizements of adult women look even more blameworthy in contrast to Maisie's winsome obligingness. I say "overcompensating" because if the adult women are too awful, Maisie is simply too good.[15]

J. Hillis Miller has argued that the gender identifications of both the narrator and the reader are neutralized and depersonalized in the novel (73). On the contrary, the novel is about nothing if not about the construction of the ostensibly neutral or impersonal as essentially masculine, as a protest in fact against the depredations of an appalling femininity that threatens to unravel the entire late nineteenth-century Victorian social fabric. The Jamesian protest is lodged in his account of the mother-child relation.[16] Like Mannoni, James isolates and represents the source of social and familial disease in the figure of the child who is "deficient" in the very thing that makes the child a potential social whole: namely, adequate nurturing by an appropriately gender-submissive mother. It is interesting, as many readers have observed, to consider why James inverts a story that revolts against the sociological probabilities—tells of the child who transcends her "vicious" circumstances instead of acquiescing. In a sense, Maisie's "deficiency" is precisely in the arena of the predictable; she does not really turn out as one would expect. We cannot help but wonder how many children subject to Maisie's experience would emerge quite so complacently nonneurotic.

Maud Mannoni insists that deficiency in children intersects with the mother's repressed fantasies. Such fantasies are invariably transgressions against the paternal order, a usurpation by the mother of the father's phallic prerogative in the familial constellation. The "backward child" suffers from the "neurosis of a mother who finds it difficult to accept a true triangular situation, in which the father plays the role of guardian of the Law" (*Backward* 53n). The child's deficiency, in other words, is a concretization of the mother's own deficiency vis-à-vis the paternal order. She has the effrontery to transgress the familial hegemony that operates as the normative system for rearing gender-adequate children. She must embrace her *essential* incapacity to speak any law other than the father's. "'Daddy is the big boss,'" Mannoni explains to a child patient. "'Mummy and Paul take orders from Daddy'" (*The Child, His "Illness"* 134).

The backward child symbolizes the collapse of the triangle propped on a faith in the value of the phallus. Such a phallus is only potent if the mother is submissive. As Mannoni complains about one couple: "The Father represented the law in his Nazi uniform; but at home it was the mother who actually *was* the Law, and this is a characteristic to be found in all psychotics and most feebleminded children" (*Backward* 141). For the mother to usurp phallic power in the family is necessarily to reveal the very thing it is her function to conceal, the weakness of the phallus whose status depends on her support. Thus, I would argue that Mannoni is correct about the causative relationship between such gender anarchy and the deficient child. However, the deficiency that the child stands for is as much the logical lapse in a system that converts weakness into strength and castration into an absolute as it is the mother's failed articulation of paternal dominance. Julia Kristeva as well describes the kind of women who deny their castration "because for them the child is the cork that stops, seals the community of the species, and allows for the usurpation of the father's place while refusing to recognize it" (279).[17]

This is how blame is displaced from the mother to the child, the pre-text that "allows" the mother to persist in her phallic transgressions. The deficiency that the child becomes is the revelation of a faulty Oedipal system, the horrific exposure of its fragility in the face of the resisting mother.

Maisie sees herself as "deficient in something that would meet the general desire," a deficiency that is inevitable, given the impossibili-ty of fulfilling an adult desire that produces its own disruption (10). What has gone awry in the Jamesian system, as in Mannoni's, is the mother's refusal to subserve the father's law. Correspondingly, James fantasies that the child will set in order the very relation the child reveals as insufficient, an insufficiency the child herself represents despite how indefatigably she tries to overcome the impasses stud-ding her go-between path.

"From conception, the child plays a very definite role for the moth-er on the fantasy plane; his destiny is already marked out; he will be an object without desires of his own, whose sole purpose will be to fill the maternal void" (*Backward* 61). This highly particularized child is the phallic child who restores to the mother a phallic intactness she denies ever being without. It is in the mother's refusal to acknowl-edge her insufficiency as such as well as her subsequent, postconcep-tion, refusal to relinquish that which she denies having missed, that produces a child compelled to function at once as the restoration of the lost phallus and the proof that no restoration was required for that which has always inhered in the mother as her phallic poten-tial. Despite the proliferation of such fantasies, however, the child by virtue of its very being cannot help but signal to the mother on some level her disavowals. The birth of the child, its literal emergence and separation from her would-be intactness is a constant (albeit sup-pressed) reminder of the disjunction between fantasy and reality, between possession of the phallus and her "actual" castration.

Oddly, Mannoni never targets the father in her guilt-assigning pro-gram. His fantasies are relevant only to the extent that they lead him to marry a particular kind of phallus-depleting woman. The process of analysis, hence, entails not only the child's eventual refusal to be the support of maternal fantasy but also the mother's acceptance of her "true" role vis-à-vis the male purveyor of the phallus. If Manno-ni's fathers repeatedly come off as ineffectual in counteracting the force of the mother's fantasy, this seems to be because the mothers will not let them assume their proper roles.

The Jamesian father is as ineffectual as Mannoni's father; he rou-tinely falters under the influence of the powerful phallic mother who

damages her offspring through her repudiation of her legitimate function. Where Beale is simply a scoundrel and a cad, egotistical and childlike, a happy-go-lucky kept man, Ida is a horror of feminine ruthless-
ness. She is characterized as monstrously tall, a mother whose sharp
embrace threatens to wound her child. Beale is indifferent to his daughter, but Ida might kill her—this is the impression we are left with. Projectively, Ida confides to her daughter, "'Your father wishes you were
dead,'" a remark more deathly to Maisie than any of her father's care-
less asides (220). Of course, it is Ida herself who would like Maisie dead,
this child she perceives as an obstacle to her sexual freedom. What
she really despises about her daughter, however, is the proof she offers of Ida's maternity, a position intolerable to Ida's phallic self-esteem.
Maisie recognizes that while Mrs. Beale falls short of the role of mother,
this is "something (strangely, confusingly) that mamma was even less"
(24). The Jamesian textual expectations, like Mannoni's, are simply less
demanding of the father than they are of the mother. The condemnation of the Jamesian mother ensues from the impossibility of an actual mother ever being commensurate with the idealized mother. It is
the failure to be the ideal that manifests in James as monstrosity and
in Mannoni as neurotic. Ida and Mrs. Beale are caricatures, puppet
women whose narcissism is represented as boundless simply because
they have any narcissism at all. Just as Mannoni's mother should dutifully forfeit her narcissism (always read by Mannoni as phallic pre-
tensions), so should the Jamesian mother divest herself of personal
demand. Failure to be "nothing" escalates into megalomania. Failure
to be an adjunct to husband and child is reconfigured as potentially
catastrophic to the family the woman is obliged to sustain through
her own self-abnegation.

From the beginning, the novel foregrounds the problem of maternity. If Beale and Ida were equally adulterous parents, the court
judged the mother more blamable and hence awarded custody to the
father. The mother's sexual transgressions, her resistance to the patrifocal family, are treated as considerably more deviant (dangerous?)
than the father's incidental peccadilloes. Mrs. Beale is worse than Sir
Claude, moreover, because a woman's exploitation of the child is registered in the text as pure exploitation, as opposed to the subtleties
of the man's moral and ethical indecision. In fact, it is Mrs. Beale
who lures this otherwise considerate fellow along the path of gross
self-interest (hers). As a result, Sir Claude comes across as a positive
(albeit weak) character because he resists capitulating altogether to
the feminine trap. Mrs. Wix as well is an ambiguous character because at the same time that she holds out as a possibility the symbi-

otic promise of maternity, her own chronic neediness undercuts the selflessness of James's idealized fantasmatic mother who hovers at the margins of Maisie's blighted universe.

The bad mothers in this novel are by far more pernicious than *The Go-Between*'s phallic mother, Marian, precisely because of their refractoriness in light of this understood but unrepresented maternal ideal. It is the dedication to the ideal, in fact, that catalyzes a host of defense mechanisms in the wake of her nonappearance. Some critics, desperate for the right kind of mother in this motherless novel, choose Mrs. Wix. Pelham Edgar commends the "warmth of her motherly tenderness" (120), while Joseph Wiesenfarth notes that she "has no interest but the child's" (57). Juliet Mitchell remarks on Ida's "terrifying arbitrariness" and her failure to "reflect her child," which is seen as a "major deprivation" in light of the object-relations (specifically Winnicottian) model of "symbiotic security" (179). In contrast, Mitchell notes, Mrs. Wix is "ultra-possessive" (185). Yet Mitchell, like the novel, persists in advancing an idealized mother-child relation out of the materials the text offers as possibilities. Given the representation of the women in *What Maisie Knew*, however, all of whom fail as mothers to various degrees, the text proves what Mitchell and, I suspect, most readers resist—the impossibility of being even a "good-enough mother," itself a spurious formula whereby normative status is attributed to idealizations.

This novel that casts its heroine's sordid environment as a force that can be "resisted" is itself subject to this defense mechanism: "This was the quite different question of the particular kind of truth of resistance I might be able to impute to my central figure—*some* intensity, some continuity of resistance being naturally of the essence of the subject. Successfully to resist (resist, that is, the strain of observation and the assault of experience) what would that be, on the part of so young a person, but to remain fresh, and still fresh, and to have even a freshness to communicate?" (xi). The possibility of the child's resistance to the debasement of everything from her moral to her ethical sensibilities is held up by many critics as the key issue.[18] However, we should reconsider here the meaning of resistance in its Freudian sense, which consequently recasts Maisie's experience (as well as the reader's relationship to that experience) as a resistance to the very knowledge the text purveys as desirable. According to Freud resistance is that which impedes analysis, either in gesture or word. Failure to keep one's analytic appointment, for example, constitutes a form of resistance. Transference is a form of resistance to the extent that the neurosis is reiterated in its own terms. Because the analytic subject achieves secondary gains from the neurosis, resistance is offered to anything that attempts to part the subject from her or his neurotic gratifications. In "Analysis Terminable and Interminable," Freud remarks that "the defensive mechanisms directed against the former danger recur in the treatment as *resistances* against recovery. It follows from this that the ego treats recovery itself as a new danger" (*SE* 23:238). Resistance is only a phase apart from repression. There are dangers indeed for Maisie, James, and the reader in overcoming resistance to the horrors of the nuclear family the novel elaborates. Displacing the horror, however, from the revelations about love and parenting ("the assault of experience") onto the question of what Maisie *understands* about her experience, constitutes a form of resistance. The novel invites a kind of antiknowledge in that it involves the reader in a circuitous route around the struggles that it denies, finally, are significant.

The way in which the novel generates resistance in its readers can be found in reader efforts, against all odds, to fashion from textual evidence a localizable good mother. Despite the absence of any adequate mother in this story, somehow critics are compelled to create one for Maisie. Either they select Mrs. Wix as a reasonably devoted parent; or the good mother is hunted down in the margins of the text, the mother who is everywhere remembered, if not actually represented (Mitchell); or the narrator is made to stand in as Maisie's good mother (Merla Wolk). Carren Osna Kaston goes so far as to suggest that Maisie "give[s] birth to herself" (135). Self-creation is a core fantasy of psychoanalysis as well. In the event that one's own parents prove inferior, the analytic subject gives birth to her/himself *as* her own parent, the only parent who is fit to take care of the subject. Subtending the analytic situation of self-parenting and self-creation is the persistent and uninterrogated faith that someone somewhere has material access to parents like those one must create for oneself. William Nance effuses over the way in which the golden Virgin in Boulogne "symbolizes Mrs. Wix as well as Maisie and hence also the union of the two" (97), neglecting both the narrator's description of the Virgin as "gilded" (198) as well as James's own acknowledged ambivalence about some of Catholicism's formal "manifestations."[19] The Virgin of *What Maisie Knew* is a false idol, as are all Maisie's mothers, Mrs. Wix most notably perhaps because she, far more than Ida or Mrs. Beale, fulfills vestigial prerequisites of the good mother.[20]

But mothers, in James, tend to kill and/or ruin their children. Dolcino of "The Author of *Beltraffio*" is killed by his mother to protect his innocent soul from contamination by his father's vile fiction. Effie Bream, in *The Other House,* is killed by her father's would-be second wife, who is closely identified with Effie's dead mother. Young Miles of *The Turn of the Screw* dies in the embrace of the governess, who could be seen as yet another example of deadly motherhood in the Jamesian canon. Even though she herself dies at the end, Eustace's mother in "Master Eustace" unwittingly has destroyed her son's life. Fernanda Brookenham of *The Awkward Age* effectively ruins her daughter's chances for marriage. Muriel Shine sees Maisie as yet another of James's sacrificial children. These children are routinely "killed off in order that adults may fulfill themselves. . . . It would appear [that], for James, parents and children could not live comfortably together in the same fictional world and most often the child is expendable" (29–30).

I agree with Shine about the child's victimization by James's adults as well as its expendability; however, she misses the pivotal role of the "mother" (natural or surrogate) in the Jamesian "phantasmatic"[21] of the family as well as his repeated treatment of maternal failure that becomes an essential structural component of the emotionally abused child. The fantasy of the innocent child inevitably coexists for James with the fantasy of the failed and self-interested mother.[22] What the Jamesian child most emphatically is not is self-interested. Like Lambert Strether, these young go-betweens are committed to never getting anything for themselves.[23] Set this utterly self-sacrificing creature alongside the self-absorbed mother and we have a suggestive reversal of the received relationship between mother and child. The mother, in this scenario, inhabits the place of the egoistic child and the child assumes the status of selfless caregiver. This reversal of mother-child positions constitutes a frank *resistance* to the egoistic child of Freudian and Kleinian psychoanalysis. Like non-Kleinian object-relations theory, however, which restores the child to its original innocence and loudly proclaims its victimization at the hands of mothers who are always selfishly immersed in their own neurotic stories, the reversal occurs to protect the child in the adult. This "child" cannot tolerate, in light of its adult-level guilt, the record of its sins.

Critical responses seem to engage unconsciously the text's unconscious complaint. Alfred Habegger, for example, develops an elaborate argument about the novel's moral schema that winds up being a homologue for mother-child symbiosis. "At the bottom of [Maisie's] soul," writes Habegger, "and of her creator's, lies a strange insistence, which is essentially aesthetic, on parallel arrangements in which one part answers to another. In Maisie's final choice, where she agrees to leave Mrs. Wix if Sir Claude gives up Mrs. Beale, she reveals her preference once again for matching parts. This feeling for symmetry underlies her sense of reciprocity, for reciprocity is a kind of symmetry in giving (The contract, on the other hand, is symmetry in getting)" (472). "One part [that] answers to another" sounds a good deal like symbiosis, e.g., the original mother-child relation. Yet symmetry is also the most salient fantasmatic characteristic of the sexual relation. This metaphor of symmetry, embracing both the mother-child relation and the sexual relation, suggests how nearly these two relations are equated in the novel. The inadequacy of each sexual partner to the other is a mirror held up to the inadequacy of Maisie's many mothers to their child. The reciprocity (giving) Habegger opposes to the contract (getting) is premised on the infant's experience in which the mother plays inexhaustible provider to the child's inexhaustible appetite. In the Jamesian (and Habeggerian) inversion of the mother-child relation, however, it is the parents who know how to get and the child how to give, confirming what I argue above is bound to happen when the maternal fount runs dry.

Osborn Andreas proclaims that Maisie chooses to go with Mrs. Wix because she "is complete within herself, while Sir Claude and Mrs. Beale are, insofar as they need each other, incomplete" (119), a somewhat "wild" reading that nevertheless emerges from the novelistic fantasy that Andreas succumbs to almost in its own terms. This brand-new, trumped-up Mrs. Wix who is "complete within herself" (a truly startling view of Mrs. Wix) is produced by a desperate attempt on the part of the critic to project onto one character the novel's fantasy about the undisrupted extension of the mother into the child. Interestingly, it is Mrs. Wix's little needs (for surely they are paltry) that invite such wrath from other critics. Greedy hag that she is, she is using Maisie for her support (hardly criminal) or she is desperately in love with Sir Claude and using Maisie to hang on to him (a fairly extreme exaggeration).[24] By way of summarizing the critical reception of Mrs. Wix, one might say that when she is the good mother, she is very very good and when she is bad—she is horrid. Yet Mrs. Wix is the natural receptacle for all the unresolved feelings about motherhood the novel agitates in the reader. It is the resistance to recognizing the textual fantasy as only fantasy that generates in readers these highly resistant readings.

Such resistance is an essential component of the reader's position in the text. In fact, what the text invites is the reader's participation in its own novel-long fantasmatic elaboration of just what such a mother must be: none of the above. Because the Jamesian notion of adequate mothering is founded on negative examples, the novel leaves us with nothing positive out of which to construct the paradigm. Although we know what makes the "bad" mothers so bad, we have practically nothing to go on to map her excellent counterpart. Such a dilemma for the reader winds up being profoundly traumatic, because it arises from a disjuncture between fantasy and reality in nineteenth- and twentieth-century representations of the Western family. If Maisie's mothers are awful, so are ours, all of them, without exception. They are awful simply because they are never "good-enough." The "good- enough" mother of object-relations theory is a fraud inasmuch as Winnicott's term feigns a tolerance for imperfection in what is actually an impossible paradigm.[25] Unfortunately, his paradigm records perfectly the communal fantasies of an entire culture.

"Enjoy being tuned-in and almost in love with yourself," Winnicott enjoins the new mother, "the baby is so nearly part of you" (*Child and the Family* 14). The baby who is so "nearly part of" the mother is the Oedipalized male fantasy that gives rise not only to a culture- wide horror of maternity (the dread of eviction, the even more fear- some prospect of the child's reincorporation) but to both Winnicott's and James's simultaneous excoriation and prediction of maternal fail- ure. In fact Winnicott frequently reveals just how little confidence he has in the mother's innate capacity to be "good enough." In meet- ing with a mother and her child, for example, he leaves a spoon on the table for the baby to investigate: "At this point I will probably have to tell mother what to do, because otherwise she will help too much, or hinder as the case may be; so I ask her to play as small a part in what happens as possible" (*Child and the Family* 34). She knows, natively, as if by instinct how to raise her child, this "ordi- nary devoted mother," yet somehow she needs her pediatrician to monitor her potential interference. The child is "nearly part of" her, yet she is advised to play "as small a part in what happens as possi- ble" as though the part that is the child needs to become superven- ing while the part that is the mother increasingly recedes. The selfless mother, the mother who enjoys an indivisible communion with her child, the attuned and empathic caregiver who wards off any intru- sions from the outside world that might disrupt the mother-infant continuity—this is the mother celebrated by the Winnicottian for- mula and received as normative by the Western family.

Winnicott believes that the mother experiences a psychosis-like "primary maternal preoccupation" for the first few weeks of her child's life, at the end of which she should dust away the cobwebs of her postpartum insanity. Joyce McDougall points out that the failure of the mother to separate adequately from her child after the first year compromises the future of the child's mental health (*Body* 82). This perfectly timed mother whose initial overinvestment and subsequent detachment produce as structural necessity in the infant the combination of edenic plenitude and self-sufficient ego, this notable adjunct to a child whose phases she facilitates in perfect harmony, is the mother of whom James offers a partial vision via her failed representatives: Ida and Mrs. Beale, the self-interested mothers whose needs override those of the child, and Mrs. Wix who does not know when to let go. What is so particularly unnerving about Mrs. Wix is how clearly she reveals the sickness of "primary maternal preoccupation," the implicit threat being that the mother will permanently "occupy" the soul of the child.

Good mothering is expected to make the child a happy representative of the sexual relation; but just as the sexual relation is flawed from the outset, grounded as it is in a fantasy of indivisibility, so too is mothering that cannot possibly produce the very child-emblem of the sexual relation. James all the while pretends to blame the mothers for Maisie's predicament, when it is really Maisie herself who is the problem, just as Ida will insist.

It is not just our treasured and uninterrogated fantasies of mothering that James disturbs, as well as the relationship between mothering and the patrifocal regime of the family; our complacency about the nature and objective of romantic love is undermined. Thus, the neat formula that proclaims the goal of gender difference romantic love and the product of romantic love the child not only is dysfunctional in *What Maisie Knew* but is thrown into irrevocable disarray. Just as the novel invites us to imagine a child whose moral structure survives intact amid corrupting influences, it treasures a fantasy that there abides some relationship, some familial term, some *scene* outside the horrid social mess. Again, we return to the issue of the tale of horror in which the most appalling element is the absence of any respite, any place beyond the place where evil happens.

Although Maisie is touted as the link on which adult relations depend, her presence renders such relations difficult if not impossible. While she brings together Mrs. Beale and Sir Claude, she also keeps them apart because, as Sir Claude observes, she should not be "mixed up" in a relation that "compromises" her virtue. She is the "bone of contention" (5) between Ida and Beale Farange, who use her to extend beyond the boundaries of a legitimate (married) relation the defining characteristic of that relation: "They felt indeed more married than ever, inasmuch as what marriage had mainly suggested to them was the unbroken opportunity to quarrel" (6). The question, then, haunting the text is: If Maisie functions as a go-between that cements sexual relations between adult partners, why is it that her intercession tends to produce conflict more often than reconciliation? Throughout the novel, we are reminded of the interdependence of the child and the sexual couple; yet, at the end, we learn that while the couple needs the child in order to thrive, the child's existence threatens to separate them. This impasse is spelled out explicitly in the plot. Although Mrs. Beale and Sir Claude require Maisie's presence to legitimize their scandalous relationship, it is Maisie's presence (the possibility that her social virtue will be "compromised") that lends moral urgency to an otherwise banal illicit affair. While Maisie is the child who brings together the adult sexual partners, not only initially, but as a chronic pretext for meeting, she is also that which divides them. In fact, at one point, when her introduction of Sir Claude and Mrs. Beale precipitates the rupture of their respective marriages, her go-between function is absolutely identified with her role as the child of divorce.

Maisie's role as go-between constitutes a reversal into its opposite of what she most clearly is for the novel, the term of divorce. The interminable refrain, "you brought us together," "I brought you together," overcompensates for the beginning, the novel's "truth," where the child is introduced as the term that daily revivifies the sexual couple's hatred for one another. "It would have been hard to say," we are told, "if the child, between [Sir Claude and Ida], more connected or divided them" (213). What we end up with are two scapegoats for the failed nuclear family and its host of imperatives—mother *and* child—which is hardly surprising when we consider that, at least as far as psychoanalytic discourse is concerned, these subjects are almost indistinguishable. This is what both the novel, with its interminable assignments of blame, and the criticism reveal. Just as critics alternate between accusing bad mothers and fabricating good ones out of whole cloth, they vacillate between the depraved scion of an ignominious family and the ultimate proof that the child can fashion spontaneously its own inviolate spirit from the wreckage of the family's dissolution. John C. McCloskey tellingly emphasizes the "similarity of child and parent [Ida], so that Maisie's final decision is quite consistent with the character inherited from her attractive, though consciously immoral, parents" (499–500). Like the narcissistic phallic mother, Maisie is flawed by "a regard for self" (500), which has escalated into being "selfish, self-regarding, demanding" (506).

We are introduced to Maisie as a remainder of a failed union; she is the term that survives the finality of the split. She persists as an indefatigable emblem of the failure of the dream of romantic love. Hence, Maisie is not presented to the reader as the fruit of union but rather the signal of its failure. Instead of coming into the textual world to represent the romantic connection that created her, she emerges as the nexus of "the struggle she appeared to have come into the world to produce" (48). Ida accuses her of having "made most of the trouble between [her and Sir Claude]," which means both that Maisie has profited from their separation and that Maisie herself is the source of the trouble she has "made."

"'A child cuts you off from your husband, it's never the same again,'" explains the mother of one of Mannoni's feebleminded analysands (*Backward* 23). Expressed in the language of castration, this mother tells the dreadful truth of the idealized child, what ends up being so especially painful for the parents, for the writer, for James, for everyone who reads this novel that, depending on one's perspective, may be the most honest or dishonest treatment of the child in literature. The child does cut the sexual partners off from one another in the sense that they are forcibly wrenched from the fantasied other they hitherto blissfully had internalized as part of the whole. "Thus the over-all retardation of maturity in this child could not fail to be experienced by both parents with a dramatic intensity equivalent to the castration experience, since they knew, even before the medical tests were carried out, that this child would symbolize what had always been *lacking* in them" (*Backward* 20–21). Ironically, the child wants to bind the parents; she wants to find for them the love they blame her for losing. "'Oh do you love her?'" Maisie cries out to the Captain whose few kind words about her mother prompt in Maisie a prevision of romantic bliss (152). But instead, Maisie can only "'make each feel so well how nasty the other wants to be'" (128). She herself is the weapon; she inflicts pain with her reprehensible presence that speaks everything she cannot be and must be. "The child is . . . the living pledge of a lie at the level of the couple" (*Backward* 54). The child is the last laugh, the joke on us who shows us all too clearly all our blind spots patched over with the ends of fantasies we couldn't dispose of anywhere else. This child was our final hope; we thought this might do it for us, give us the proof we had always needed that everything we have ever believed in, from why we wake up in the morning to our immortal soul, is grounded in truth.

The child tries; Maisie offers herself with "her little instinct of keeping the peace" (182). She offers to save us and, as Mrs. Beale agrees, "'I daresay you *will* save us—from one thing and another,'" which is of course the problem—that we don't know what we want to be saved from or what we want saved (129). She wants to keep the peace, to make everything right somehow, but she is trained instead as a "messenger of insult" to convey back and forth Ida's and Beale's vicious attacks (15). Only through her professed stupidity can she refuse this ambassadorial service. As a result, she is denounced as the "'perfection of a dunce'" as even Sir Claude, her supposed ally, calls her, when she proves unwilling to inform against her mother's lover (157). She emerges as deficient: she is a stupid refractory messenger, she doesn't have enough fat on her "toothpick" legs, she doesn't really have parents or a "moral sense" or even a home to call her own. Maisie worries about the time when "with two fathers, two mothers and two homes, six protections in all, she shouldn't know 'wherever' to go" (99):[26] "Society confers a special status on the child by expecting him, all unknowing, to fulfill the future of the adult. It is the child's task to make good the parents' failures, to make their lost dreams come true. The complaints of parents about their offspring thus refer us first of all to their own problems" (*The Child, His "Illness"* 3–4). Of course the child cannot accomplish any of this, which marks the child from the start as deficient. Sir Claude has such high expectations: "'You've done us the most tremendous good, and you'll do it still and always, don't you see? We can't let you go—you're everything'" (334). But Maisie proves unequal to his hopes, like any child. The service he demands from her, to sustain as uncomplicated his relationship with Mrs. Beale, is impossible in a novel that shows the sexual relation as inevitably complicated and unsatisfying.[27]

In James's unfinished short story, "Hugh Merrow," a couple comes to an artist requesting that he paint for them the child they cannot have. "'All we want,'" the husband explains, "'is that he should be such a one as we *might* have had.' 'Oh, better than that,' the young woman interposed. 'We might have had one with some blot, some defect, some affliction. We want her perfect—without a flaw'" (103). The presence of the real child demystifies the fantasmatic child, the copula of a make-believe union. This real child is always defective in its incapacity to live up to the fantasmatic child. "In the case of feeblemindedness, the mother will be so preoccupied by mental deficiency that, before others, the child's lack will always be objectified by her. (It is in the child that something is lacking, and as long as the other remains convinced of this, the child's illness will conceal the mother's illness)" (*Backward* 63). Mannoni offers the parenthetical comment as an ironic emphasis on the mother's defensive strategy. Yet, the mother is right; it *is* in the child that something is lacking—everything that would satisfy parental desire. "She puzzled out with imperfect signs, but with a prodigious spirit, that she had been a centre of hatred and a messenger of insult, and that everything was bad because she had been employed to make it so" (*Maisie* 15). Not only is the child at fault in its incapacity to repair the parents and make good their treasure hoard of fantasy, where reality incessantly retreats in the face of inarticulable "romantic longings," she herself is the fault, her own body localized as the site of failure.[28]

"Formulate *to* the child—," James observes in a notebook entry, "*for* the reader, *through* Mrs. Wix or Sir Claude, this charm so complicating and entangling for others" (166), the child's charm that complicates textual and parental plots and always threatens to seduce adulthood into its fantasmatic, idealizing snares. It is the child who is the complicating and entangling factor inasmuch as she gives rise to expectations she cannot fulfill. She cannot compensate for maternal fantasies anymore than she can forge an adult sexual relation. She cannot live up to the reputation of her innocence and is thus resigned to the role of fraud (hence the plethora of critical vilifications of Maisie's part in all this); she cannot restore the phallus to Mannoni's frantic mother nor can she restore normative gender roles to the family careening dangerously away from a patriarchal grid. She is an implacable site of refusal. She *is* the lie that produced her. Like the actual child, she is less than the fruition of parental and social fantasy and more than deficient in their accomplishment.

Notes

1. For the landmark essay on the extent to which textual fantasies are repeated by readers, see Shoshana Felman's "Turning the Screw of Interpretation."

2. For a summary of the virtue/corruption debate preceding 1965, see Joseph Hynes; for subsequent contributions to this discussion, see Thomas L. Jeffers, John C. McCloskey, and James W. Gargano.

3. Some critics accuse James of participating in just the kind of child abuse he represents. See, for example, Lee E. Heller (82–83).

4. In "Dora's Secrets, Freud's Techniques," Neil Hertz compares James's narrative appropriation of Maisie to Freud's analytic appropriation of Dora. As Hertz points out, Freud, like James, describes his enterprise as one of "translation": "With the exercise of a little caution all that is done is to translate into conscious ideas what was already known in the unconscious" (66).

5. The issue of the historical accuracy of analytic reconstructions remains unclear in Freud. In his account of the "Wolf Man," Freud insists that his reconstruction is reliable, but here he is motivated by a latent agenda to disprove Jung's theory that childhood sexual memories tend to be reprocessed through *adult* fantasy. In the later "Constructions in Analysis" Freud minimizes both the importance and the possibility of historical accuracy. See also Donald Spence on this topic.

6. J. A. Ward writes that "personal evil can be avoided only by a retreat from the world—the ultimate course for Maisie and Nanda" (88), suggesting that through exiling these two heroines, James is protecting them from an inevitably corrupting adulthood.

7. Certainly, Marius Bewley treats Maisie as a horror story (138).

8. James calls Maisie the "bone of contention" in the novel as well (5). Further, "bone of contention" is how Mrs. Maudsley refers to a letter being fought over by Marian and Leo in *The Go-Between* (280). Here we have a metonymy (in *both* novels) where the message-bearing child becomes confused with the message and vice versa.

9. Sallie Sears calls *What Maisie Knew* "a latent pornographic novel" (27). Margaret Walters as well refers to James's "connoisseur's pleasure in the violation of [Maisie's and Nanda's] innocence, the 'death of her childhood'; a pleasure detached, voyeuristic, almost pornographic" (197).

10. See especially McCloskey (505n).

11. Others have noted the financial metaphor. See J. Hillis Miller (52–54, 64, 74) and Thomas Jeffers (172).

12. Harris Wilson recognizes this character as a "Jewish financier" (280).

13. See, for example, Edward Wasiolek (170–71); Cargill (257); J. Hillis Miller (60). Harris W. Wilson writes of Maisie that "her greatest asset opposed to Mrs. Beale's lush worldliness is her virginity, and that she is prepared to offer" (281).

14. The one time Maisie directly wants money is during and after the final encounter with her mother when she considers at length the amount she loses as a result of her poor performance.

15. Sharing wholeheartedly the textual horror of adult femininity, John C. McCloskey sees Sir Claude as barely escaping Maisie's greedy clutches: "In her first meeting, as a child, with Sir Claude, Maisie felt that he belonged to her, and it is this possessiveness intensified by the years of his kindness and responsible devotion modified by Maisie's increasing maturity that defeats her now, for Sir Claude refuses to be possessed" (511).

16. More than the family is in question in the late nineteenth century. As James shows everywhere in his fiction but delineates especially clearly in the figures of Ida's Jewish paramours and Beale's brown Countess, the inner circle of the privileged classes is being invaded by people whose ethnic and racial backgrounds once would have excluded them. The chronic concern with money in James's middle and late fiction seems

to be James's explanation for the debasement of social hierarchy, a debasement that is a correlative for the dismantlement of reliable familial categories.

17. Recall that "cork" is precisely how Joyce McDougall's patient imagines himself vis-à-vis his mother. Judith Butler criticizes Kristeva's representation of "the maternal body as bearing a set of meanings that are prior to culture itself. She thereby safeguards the notion of culture as a paternal structure and delimits maternity as an essentially precultural reality" (80). Kristeva's reification of motherhood is not at all a rebuttal to Lacan, as some have argued, but rather it is entirely in keeping with his phallogocentric, and latently essentializing, system.

18. Kenny Marotta suggests that "the reader's resistance is not merely parallel to Maisie's resistance to the assault of her experience: it is the same act" (495), an argument with which I entirely concur. I would add, moreover, that such resistance on the part of both Maisie and the reader is specifically antagonistic to "knowledge."

19. See Leon Edel for an account of James's attitude toward Catholicism (115).

20. See Edwin Bowden's reading of the Madonna symbolism in the novel (84–85).

21. I am importing Kaja Silverman's use of this term in relation to James. Drawing on Laplanche and Pontalis's definition of a phantasmatic as "an unconscious phantasy or group of related phantasies which underlie dreams, symptoms, acting out, repetitive behavior, and daydreams," Silverman goes on to explain: "As I have already proposed with respect to cinema, it can also be seen to organize artistic production, and indeed to be the best way into the whole question of authorship. Authorial subjectivity, in other words, is constituted at least in part through the repeated inscription of a particular phantasy or group of interconnected phantasies within a textual corpus" (171).

22. Another Jamesian child, Nanda Brookenham, likewise suffers at the hands of a self-serving mother. J. A. Ward observes that Nanda's "selflessness is an ironic contrast to the destructive egotism of her mother" (101).

23. Most readers of *What Maisie Knew* agree that, at the end, she is making a plea for what *she* wants as a subject in her own right, outside, finally, the circuit of adult selfishness. Thus, her offer to Sir Claude that he run away with her is interpreted variously as giving herself to him sexually (Wilson) or simply as the emergence of her own demands (see, for example, Kaston). However, this offer should be reconsidered in light of the fact that James's ambassadorial characters (especially when they are children) do not gain personally from their services; it is another example of her desire to "save" him. Even the money that she covets from her mother (and fantasizes about at length) is revealed eventually to be something she would be able to offer to Sir Claude in his straitened circumstances.

24. See, for example, J. A. Ward (90).

25. Jane Flax treats the central problem with Winnicott's character-ization of mothering: "Nonetheless the concept of the good enough mother, although meant to capture and validate what women do as child rearers, also reflects deeply ingrained social fantasies about women. For example, the culturally prevalent splits between the 'good,' pure, self-effacing and the bad, sexual, selfish, self-determining woman are repli-cated within this concept. The good enough mother seems to have no life apart from her relation with the baby—no other work or pleasurable activity, no independent sexuality, no relations to other adults or even to the baby's siblings. She is utterly and exclusively devoted to one child" (125).

26. J. Hillis Miller comments on Maisie's relationship to James's own deficiency. He contends that "the use of the scenic method in *Maisie* is a way of compensating for [his] failure [as a dramatist]. . . . In this way too the creation of Maisie can be seen as a compensation for a failure and a lack" (*Versions* 52).

27. Jonathan Gathorne-Hardy describes pre-twentieth-century children as "really little adults, but adults with defects who must be trained and taught as quickly as possible to be true adults" (45).

28. *Romantic Longings* is the title of Steven Seidman's book about the sexualization of love in the late nineteenth and twentieth centuries.

7

Nabokov's *Lolita* / Lacan's Mirror

> This half man or half god begets, if one can use the
> expression, more of the same kind. Narcissus, who also
> thought he was self-sufficient, is not far away. . . .
>
> —J.-B. Pontalis, *Frontiers of Psychoanalysis*

> I just reread "Lolita." . . . I love him, of course. But I
> found it pretty difficult to read the second time because
> of what he did to that girl.
>
> —Sally Mann, quoted in "The Disturbing Photographs
> of Sally Mann"

Maisie's spectating role excludes her from the social scene
that she apprehends as though from the other side of a window. As
James describes it, her "sharpened sense of spectatorship . . . gave her
often an odd air of being present at her history in as separate a manner as if she could only get at experience by flattening her nose
against a pane of glass" (107). His representation of the child divided from adulthood by an obstacle that is at once transparent and implacable suggests that the child's identity remains distinct from that
of the adult scene she appraises. At the same time, however, Maisie
functions as a mirror that reflects adult society. In a notebook entry
on the novel, James called the child a "mirror, the plate, on which
it [adult activity] is represented as reflected" (150).[1] There is quite a
difference between the transparency and double-access of the window and the one-way reflectiveness of the mirror. It is Maisie's role
as social mirror that reveals the window motif as yet another pretext in a novel that pretends the mirror can be a window, that what
one sees can look back—or that the adult subject even wants to see
more than a self-image.[2] *Lolita* casts aside all such pretexts and reduces the child to the surface of a mirror that I would argue has been
all along the go-between child's central function.[3]

Lolita poses a challenge to psychoanalytic inquiry for the simple reason that Nabokov repeatedly ridiculed Freud and his paradigms of human sexuality for what he considered their stultifying reductiveness.[4] I could say in my defense that I will not be so naive as to classify Humbert as a repressed homosexual (like his doctors at the mental institution) nor will I cleave to the Oedipal blueprint for the novel's "parody of incest" (*Lolita* 289). Nevertheless, to rationalize the introduction of a psychoanalytic approach into the inviolate Nabokovian territory is self-defeating insofar as one would allow the Nabokovian defense to remain unexamined. I am not after a reading that would please a dead author, an immaculately subtle wordplay euphemizing (or altogether excising) the seaminess that Humbert himself skillfully tidies up in his rhapsodic and aestheticized descriptions of pedophilic escapades.

It strikes me as noteworthy that the psychoanalytic theory most suited to the Nabokovian sensibility, the theory that most admirably reclaims psychoanalysis from the would-be Freudian dungheap, is that of Jacques Lacan, a purveyor of word-play par excellence. It is moreover significant that fundamentally Lacan's is a theory of narcissism, an exhumation, an explication, and a celebration of the narcissistic worldview. It is this emphasis on narcissism that gives Lacan such a sympathetic psychoanalytic style for the Nabokovian subject, which is always narcissism to some degree. Lacan's preference for the linguistic structures undergirding the psyche in place of genitals and anality and Oedipal lust, his articulation of a desire depleted of passion, a cold hollowed-out space between need and demand is not dissimilar to a novel that presents child molestation as a tour through literary history and lepidopterist lore. If Lacan gives us the syntax of human love and its concomitant neuroses, Nabokov gives us the parody of pedophilia. "I've only words to play with," muses Humbert in a text that reiterates throughout that it is only a text, not to be taken seriously, not to be confused with a "real" life it repudiates— which is the point, after all.[5] If texts are always self-referential, in imitation of a "reality" that can only live in quotes, then the play/ serious controversy surrounding this novel is incidental, when one considers that such a dichotomy can only hold in a world divided between the real and the text.[6] Whether or not we are meant to take the child molestation theme seriously or we *are* meant to take the novel seriously as a serious parody of the novel form are questions that are invalidated in light of the text's emphasis on the fatuity of all such distinctions. So let us not bother about morality, because this parody of pedophilia—which molests and is molested by other texts (literary parent figures) as much as it recounts the dim history of the debauching of one Dolores Haze—merely replicates the parody of reference we tend to call real life that, like the novel, is no more than a palimpsest of outmoded narrative conventions.

Lacan, despite his self-proclaimed "return to Freud," like Nabokov, clearly finds the old-fashioned Freud straight up a bit silly—perhaps a bit too realistic, too concerned about real body parts and real parents. Freud turns the psychic life into a vast roman à clef; he reveals the sordid underside of things, the closest we come to what we call the real. So the "real," the impossible for Lacan, strung up by Nabokov in inverted commas, the real is the space of contention in the narcissistic economy and one would like to know just why it is that this real is intolerable in both the fictional and the psychoanalytic systems, and what it is about their relationships to the real and to narcissism that make of Lacan and Nabokov such mirror images.

Narcissistic Bedfellows

In *Narcissistic Narrative,* Linda Hutcheon argues that the most remarkable feature of twentieth-century metafictions is their explicit inclusion of the reader in the imaginative process. Whereas the narrative form always has been narcissistic to the extent that it is self-reflexive, recent metafictions both emphasize the process of writing and actualize the role of the reader (27–34). "Whatever the reason," she writes, "the novel from its beginnings has always nurtured a self-love, a tendency toward self-obsession. Unlike its oral forbears, it is both the storytelling and the story told" (10). Hutcheon stresses that she uses "narcissism" in its nonpejorative sense; rather, she uses it in Freud's sense of a primary state through which we all pass in infancy and which remains a psychic mode in all of us to varying degrees. Contrary to Hutcheon, however, I see Nabokov's work as ultimately manipulative of the reader and his brand of narcissism as pathological rather than "healthy."

Christopher Lasch has complained that people tend to use narcissism too generally, invoking it descriptively when they mean simply vanity and so forth (*Narcissism* 71–75). My own use of narcissism is in the sense of self-sufficiency sustained through the absorption of external objects whose alterity is denied. Narcissism produces identificatory specular relationships that mistake themselves for object relations.[7] What is most disturbing about these manifestations of narcissism is that they range from misrepresenting themselves as object-love to celebrating narcissism as the only undeluded posture. Denis de Rougemont called *Lolita* a "Tristan manqué" because all that is missing is Lolita's reciprocal passion (54). But the point is precisely this distinction between Humbert's infatuation and relationships that have *two* desiring agents. Like the Lacanian subject gazing at her or his specular counterpart and mistaking it for an-other, intrasubjectivity is mistaken for intersubjectivity. Lolita merely facilitates the specular encounter between Humbert and Quilty. Not only is the child, Lolita, a mirror, the textual *Lolita* as well is the mirror Nabokov holds up to the reader who is either dutifully swallowed by the Nabokovian imagination or is threatened with a fight to the death (like Quilty and Humbert).[8]

Worse than the pretense of object-love, moreover, is the denial of the aggressivity toward the child (who is throughout threatened with murder in the allusions to the story of Carmen) as well as toward the reader who is forcibly silenced. Brian McHale discusses the "aggressive stance" of the postmodernist text toward its reader (225). He holds that "postmodernist representations of sadomasochism function as models of the 'sadistic' relation between text and reader" (226). The sadistic relationship, according to Freud, is structurally specular inasmuch as its force derives from the dual identifications of both the masochist and the sadist, whose experiences of each other's subjectivities spill over into the subjectivity of their mirror opposite, their partner in crime, their hurt/hurting object that produces an identification with pain/causing pain. The masochist's pain belongs to the sadist; the sadist's gratification belongs to the masochist. In this sense, the individuated subjectivity of the "other" of the sadomasochistic relation is preempted because the subject imagines her/himself in *both* roles; at the same time, one's own subjectivity is no more than a truck stop for the other's fantasy. Similarly, *Lolita* is a contest for mastery. The text's one-way desire for the reader tries to foreclose reciprocity—even though the text loathes precisely its dependence. It is the hate generated by the indebtedness to an external object that induces the text to suppress aggressively the reader; such is the text's attempt to master that which otherwise might master it.[9] As I will show, the Lacanian model is equivalent strategically to the Nabokovian to the extent that they are both premised on a narcissistic relationship with their audiences—and both enterprises depend ultimately on a child in the mirror.

The author's rivalry with the reader is established from the outset. The rivalry between the reader and the text, one-sided as it is, is reproduced internally by the conflict between Humbert and Quilty, one-sided as it is. The stake, which is *Lolita,* is recast as the stake which is Lolita. Yet the text and the child are not equivalent because the narcissistic cathexis of the text is serious while the investment in the child is merely a ruse. As in any parody, there is something here that is serious and something here that is play. The serious needs to be denied as important, however, just as the play is specifically play-acting—at object-love. More than Nabokov perhaps suspected, his whole endeavor reenacts the structure of child-molestation in its one-sided account of power. At the same time, this is just what the novel argues is not true. The child is accused of being the molester.

My reading of Nabokov occurs within the context of a long critical debate over whether the novel identifies with Humbert's perspective (aestheticism and solipsism) or disidentifies and reveals his perspective as reprehensible. I would never dispute Nabokov's thorough recognition of Humbert's affair with the child as a moral transgression. Nevertheless, his narcissistic perspective is apparent in both the content and structure of his novels as well as in various statements he made on his relationship to writing. The fact that the narcissism acts out egregiously upon a child (both within the text and between the reader and the text that offers up the child's body for delectation) is at once an illustration and analysis of twentieth-century Western culture's narcissistic investment in the child. Intriguingly, Nabokov's mirror-child looks a great deal like Lacan's mirror-child who is the cornerstone of Lacan's theory of the narcissistic structure of the human subject.[10]

In addressing these issues, I have been compelled to come to terms with what I acknowledge is my own antipathy to the kinds of self-reflexivity we find in Lacan and Nabokov, my intolerance of the position they carve out for me as a reader, specifically as a woman reader for whom issues of mastery necessarily are overdetermined. In many ways it is in response to my oppositional reaction to authorial narcissism that my argument unfolds. In the face of overtly narcissistic strategies, I find myself forced into the position of identifying with the child, specifically the sense that I am being controlled by an incomprehensibly powerful adult authority whose estimation of me depends on my concessions to just this authority.[11]

Let us, for the moment, turn to three accounts of the relationship between primary narcissism and the emergence of the ego ideal in order to understand better both psychoanalytic and novelistic fantasies about the subject's primordial experience of fusion as well as the emergence of correlative specular structures. It is in the subject's relationship with the ego ideal that one finds the prototype for all further substitutions for primary narcissism. Elaborating upon the ego ideal in "On Narcissism," Freud observes:

This ideal ego is now the target of the self-love which was enjoyed in childhood by the actual ego. The subject's narcissism makes its appearance displaced on to this new ideal ego, which, like the infantile ego, finds itself possessed of every perfection that is of value. As always where the libido is concerned, man has here again shown himself incapable of giving up a satisfaction he had once enjoyed. He is not willing to forgo the narcissistic perfection of his childhood; and when, as he grows up, he is disturbed by the admonitions of others and by the awakening of his own critical judgement, so that he can no longer retain that perfection, he seeks to recover it in the new form of an ego ideal. What he projects before him as his ideal is the substitute for the lost narcissism of his childhood in which he was his own ideal. (*SE* 14:94)

Thus, to retain a simulacrum of his originary narcissism, the subject is bisected into the reality-serving ego and an idealized ego that has become the reservoir of his infantile self-love. Thereafter the subject is drawn toward this separated image of himself as both an ideal he subserves as well as an alterity with which he longs to reunite.

Drawing on Freud's discussion of the ego ideal, Janine Chasseguet-Smirgel theorizes that the subject's relationship with her or his ego ideal is founded upon the mother-infant dyad when mother and infant were imaginatively fused, a symbiotic bond that the subject will ever after strive to recapitulate. The maternal object is conjoined inseparably with the infant who is, as far as the infant can know, both consumer and consumed, sucking and suckled, both demanding and demanded, needing and needed with no vestige of unappeasable desire intruding on the symbiotic system—the giver and taker, predator and preyed upon being for the first few months of life merely alternate syntactic positions of one and the same being.

Lacan coined the term the "mirror-stage" to describe the period of primary narcissism he located between the ages of six to eighteen months. This mirror-stage is formative of the "I" coincidental with the emergence of the ideal ego.[12] The baby apprehends in the mirror the vision of the future unification and motor coordination of its own body which is "fragmented" and "sunk in his motor incapacity" (4, 2). The infant henceforth longs to "be" its own reflection, the reflection that will assume the role of the linguistic and social "I" in the foundation of the infant's subjectivity. In becoming the ideal ego (or ideal I) in the mirror, the infant hopes to regain the experience of totality it lost in its demotion from the status of the mother's desired object. This emerging subject confuses the ideal ego in the mirror with what it learns to call "I." Thus for Lacan the ideal ego is the origin of the ego itself, shaped by a mirroring relation that produces the *image* of what was only an imaginary unity (between the mother and child) and will *be* only an imaginary coherence of the subject. He distinguishes between the ideal ego and the ego ideal, which he points out are mirror opposites, the former leading in the direction of the past and the latter in the direction of the future. The ideal ego is the initial elaboration of the ego as an "other," whereas the ego ideal is related to future idealizations including social and parental objects. Chasseguet-Smirgel's ego ideal, on the other hand, although it too points to a lost and impossible union, is more clearly differentiated from the ego proper. Her version is a composite of the ideal ego, whose origins are the infant's lost and regretted omnipotence, and the ego ideal, which is the projection of the earlier ideal onto parental and societal models.

For Lacan, the child's relationship with its mirror image is the prototype for all future relationships with "real" objects. The split that the mirror-stage inaugurates and constitutes, the rivalry entrenched between the subject and her or his idealized ego, will be the groundwork for all future adversarial and identificatory relations. Foremost among these relations is the Oedipal constellation measuring identificatory and adversarial parental objects against the mirror paradigm—which reverses the expected order of perception, does it not? In Lacan's schema the "real" imitates the representational—the parents are no more than shades of the ego's relationship with itself. Moreover, instead of the superego inheriting parental and social laws, it seems that parental laws are heir to the mirror ideal.[13] And behind the mirroring edifice resides the lost aspect of the eternally elusive union of mother and child who together are nothing more than an omnipotent, self-sufficient, intact neonate. There is no (m)other on the horizon of the pre-mirror-stage child, the child who is that mother's desire.

Lacan writes that the child sees itself "in a symmetry that inverts it, in contrast with the turbulent movements that the subject feels are animating him" (*Écrits: A Selection* 2).[14] The fact that it can *see* *itself* reverses the child upon itself, sets it *en opposition* with an "I" that, externalized, becomes deadly. The mirror ideal will fight "me" to the death for mastery of point of view, specifically, of position—looking out from or into the mirror.[15] What this symmetrical inversion is all about then seems to be the question of the gaze and its object and the contest between the two for the position of mastery. "It is this moment that decisively tips the whole of human knowledge into mediatization through the desire of the other," an "other" who will henceforth be the introjected mirror image (*ES*, 5). Thus, the object of desire will thereafter be, after this split in position, a space of contention marked out by competing perspectives, between the mirror-image and the gaze, between the subject and the internalized other.

Lacan's advice that the reader "observe the role of the mirror apparatus in the appearances of the *double*, in which psychical realities, however heterogeneous, are manifested" (3) suggests that the familiar literary motif of the doppelgänger is based on the internalized mirror experience the double figure revivifies for both writer and reader. Nabokov's use of "the mirror apparatus" in all his novels has been commented on widely.[16] Most of his work to some degree touches on the mirror image or the double, characters that, although superficially differentiated, figure as alter egos. The culmination of the mirror metaphor in Nabokov occurs in *Ada* in which the incestuous brother and sister possess symmetrical birthmarks on their hands and feet, and the specular sibling offers the only possibility of romantic satisfaction. Diverging in this instance from the tragic outcome of many incestuous or near-incestuous literary liaisons,[17] Nabokov leaves his couple happy, together and still in love in their nineties, coauthoring the book. In fact *Ada* celebrates narcissism in a way that *Lolita* cannot—perhaps because the narcissistic relation in *Lolita* is between two men, Humbert and Quilty, whereas in the later novel the heterosexuality serves to mitigate the homoerotic implications. I use the word "homoerotic" advisedly, however. Although the relationship between Quilty and Humbert is a narcissistic attachment between individuals of the same sex, Humbert desires Quilty not as a sexual partner but instead as his mirror complement.[18]

As Joel Whitebrook argues, it is a profoundly disturbing feature of Chasseguet-Smirgel's work that she represents homosexuality as a narcissistic perversion. In fact antinarcissists like Christopher Lasch and Chasseguet-Smirgel who see the efflorescence of narcissistic disturbances as the apocalyptic signal of the decline of Western society tend to be homophobic as well. The homosexual relationship for these writers figures the narcissistic relationship par excellence. While Lasch more covertly refers to the "pansexual[ism]" of the gross narcissist (*Narcissism* 86), Chasseguet-Smirgel depreciates the pervert,[19] unmotivated by an ego-ideal, who overestimates his anal-level (inferior) objects. Yet, as Humbert's relationship with Quilty indicates, it is not solely the homoerotic relationship that is narcissistic here; rather, it is the insertion of the mirror-child into the relationship between two men. It is the strategy whereby object-love is corralled in the service of narcissism that creates the destructive effects. It is the false attribution to the ancillary object (the child) of the position of central object of desire that creates *not* homosexual object-love but narcissistic gropings in the dark for which *both* the false object (Lolita) and the double (Quilty) must die so that the solipsistic subject survives intact. The fact that Nabokov also has Humbert die, as though to suggest the ultimate failure of the narcissist, does not mean that Nabokov or his novel have surmounted the narcissistic position. The text takes over the role of the solipsistic subject. The reader the text engineers is the final term of the self-complacent narcissism that persists in the face of its own introspection. Indeed, instead of being self-revelatory, such introspection is yet another instance of the text's obsessive self-involvement.

What is most curious about the ostensible encomium to the girl, Lolita, the "light of [Humbert's] life" (11), is that while the first two-thirds of the novel recount Humbert's efforts to get her and then keep her, the last third, when he has lost her, is really about his pursuit of Quilty. At the end of the novel, when Humbert sees Lolita for the last time, what he most wants from her is the name of the man for whom she left him. It is Quilty's name he coaxes from her soon after his arrival; only subsequently does Humbert invite Dolly to go away with him. The gun in Humbert's pocket is for Quilty, not for Lolita, a confusion the novelist goes so far as to highlight for the reader who by now has been strung along on *Carmen* references for nearly three hundred pages: "I could not kill *her,* of course, as some have thought. You see, I loved her. It was love at first sight, at last sight, at ever and ever sight" (272). And then, as if to frame allusively the scene, as he parts from Lolita for the last time, the narrator tells us: "Then I pulled out my automatic—I mean, this is the kind of fool thing a reader might suppose I did. It never even occurred to me to do it" (282). Of course, the reader has supposed Humbert murdered Lolita precisely because of the kind of aggressivity that here he avows and denies in the same instant.

> "Come, his name!"
> She thought I had guessed it long ago. It was (with a mischievous and melancholy smile) such a sensational name. I would never believe it. She could hardly believe it herself.
> "His name, my fall nymph."
> It was so unimportant, she said. She suggested I skip it. Would I like a cigarette?
> "No. His name. . . .
> She said it was really useless, she would never tell, but on the

other hand, after all—"Do you really want to know who it was? Well, it was—" And softly, confidentially, arching her thin eye-brows and puckering her parched lips, she emitted, a little mockingly, somewhat fastidiously, not untenderly, in a kind of muted whistle, the name that the astute reader has guessed long ago. (273–74)

None of this is dissimilar to Quilty's own style. As Humbert says of him, "His main trait was his passion for tantalization. Goodness, what a tease the poor fellow was!" (252). Ever the self-styled minx, what Lolita serves up to Humbert this time around is not her body but a name, the name of his rival who is to be killed in her stead and whose name is now (again, in place of Lolita's) the object of desire. Humbert's narrative opens with a long, delirious palpation of the name of the girl—and now suddenly, it is the name of the man that becomes paramount. In an odd shift of the expected sequence, the girl stands in between two men, playing the role of the pander who literally has to trade the man for money.[20] It is Quilty who now inspires far more passion in Humbert than the ruined nymphet whom he claims he loves. It is to Quilty's destruction that he will now dedicate himself with all the obsessiveness that earlier characterized his pursuit of nymphets. He now desires Quilty as much as he once desired Lolita, and the two men end up tussling with one another in a burlesque of a homosexual embrace: "We rolled all over the floor, in each other's arms, like two huge helpless children. He was naked and goatish under his robe, and I felt suffocated as he rolled over me. I rolled over him. We rolled over me. They rolled over him. We rolled over us" (301).

If we try to read the triangle in this novel as a flawless illustration of Lacan's formula that "man's desire is the desire of the Other," in which Humbert's shares the object of the Other's desire, at the same time that Quilty desires to be desired by Humbert *as* the Other, we cannot help but stumble over the question of whose desire is being imitated.[21] In other words, Humbert's desire for Lolita is imitated *by* the very mirror ideal, Quilty, his trajectory emulates. We learn, for example, that Quilty admired Lolita when she was ten years old, long before Humbert's own infatuation. Yet throughout the novel, Quilty shadows Humbert, repeating both Humbert's relation with Lolita, his general nympholepsy, and his travel route—a route that, in yet another twist, Humbert will subsequently attempt to retrace. Nevertheless, certain stops along Humbert's last journey with Lolita have been prearranged by Lolita and Quilty, which makes of the trip an inextricable tangle of imitations, throwing into question the very boundaries between Humbert and Quilty, imitator and imitated, the representational and the real—like the fusion of mother and child, the text (re)presents the prediscursive landscape, before language splits the subject into halves that ever after pursue one another. It is not that there is a wholeness from which we "fall"; instead, the alienating emergence of the subject in language intimates a prior unmediated relationship with the real. In the mirror encounter, the representational mirror image is imitated by the subject who is the model for the mirror—in this *mise en abyme,* a "primary" subject is irretrievable. Nabokov tantalizes us with a mirage of prediscursive or primary narcissism only to leave us stranded in an infinitely receding chain of mirrors.

Janine Chasseguet-Smirgel writes that the human subject "is involved in a constant quest for that part of his narcissism that was wrested from him at the time of the primary loss of fusion" (7). What the child loses is the part that is at once infant and primary object. The ego ideal is the heir to this loss of fusion and henceforward entices the ego ("I") with what "I" could "be" once again if "I" stepped through the mirror and regressed into primary fusion. The loss of primary fusion and the consequent substitution of the ego ideal (the representative of both the past union and its dissolution) precipitates the future fight for sovereignty between the two fragments (ego and ego ideal) left after the explosion. What is most interesting in Lacan's particular formulation of the child's relation with the mirror-ideal is his emphasis on the anticipatory nature of the child's response, that what the child (fore)sees in the mirror is the vision of its future physical and psychical unity. Yet, at the same time, the subject's relation with the ego ideal anticipates a future premised on a lost past. This is the origin of what Lacan calls "that paranoiac structure of the ego" (*ES* 20). Built into the very fabric of the ego, as it were, is this counterpart, at times similar, at times superior, at times adversarial, who haunts the subject. It seems more critical, however, that the rivalry proceeds most directly from the *historical* divergence, the discrepancy in point of view (looking out from or into the mirror) being reduplicated (mirrored) and intensified by the directional antagonism (past or future) of desire.[22]

What learning the name of his rival does for Humbert is pull together not only the tail ends of clues but a *series* of men he imagined to be potential threats to his affair with Lolita, having variously mistaken Quilty for other admirers and detectives. The point is that what hitherto has been fragmented into diverse characters is in an instant for both the reader and Humbert resolved into a single rival. Like the idealized mirror image apprehended by the infant as the future coherence of its own fragmented body, Quilty at once plays the threat of fragmentation, the jubilation of the discovery (just one man, just one body), and the parodic reversal of the ideal. Thus, to call Quilty the simple manifestation in the text of the ideal ego in relation to Humbert's subject is to miss the point altogether. Quilty figures all stages and both sides of the mirror in the narcissistic economy, and Humbert Humbert "solipsizes" his own doubleness, both the self-love and self-loathing that constitute the subject's relationship with the mirror. Further, we must remember that the "ideal," if we locate Quilty as such, is a "pervert." In the inversion between the subject and the mirror image as well as the subject's recognition of her/himself in reverse we find not simply a narcissistic reduplication but a sense of the futility of the narcissistic effort; the "other" subject will never be perfectly aligned, it will always be heading in the opposite direction

The Seductive Child

One could posit that Quilty externally mirrors the internal mirroring of Humbert, but this would be to overlook the pivotal role of Lolita because it is she who keeps them apart, then brings them together. Having such influence, then, is Lolita empowered by the text or rather is she disfranchised utterly? And even if we can determine in the end that, no pawn she, Lolita is responsible for the deaths of two men, volition nevertheless remains indeterminate to the extent that like Helen of Troy, the activity arises in the face that lures the gaze, that semantically attributes initiative to the passive object. Yet somehow, when the stakes are "real" (and everyone always imagines she or he knows the essential from the superficial), when for instance this trifle about semantics confuses the "real" rapist from the "real" victim (wearing those clothes, she asked for it), then we can see illustrated just how determinate is the confusion. As Humbert explains to Lolita: "'A minor female, who allows a person over twenty-one to know her carnally, involves her victim into statutory rape'" (152).

In many respects *Lolita* narrates the problems of transitivism; the central scene of the novel gives us the child seducing the pedophile. Lacan describes the following pattern of behavior by children between the ages of six months and two and a half years as "normal transitivism": "The child who strikes another says that he has been struck; the child who sees another fall, cries. Similarly, it is by means of an identification with the other that he sees the whole gamut of reactions of bearing and display, whose structural ambivalence is clearly revealed in his behaviour, the slave being identified with the despot, the actor with the spectator, the seduced with the seducer" (*ES* 19).[23] The child has difficulty distinguishing between pronouns, whether it is occupying the first or the third person, the "I" being only in its tentative formation; the me and not-me are not yet rigidly divided. In each instance the would-be subject of the verb is passivized (or demoted to a by-phrase) while the object of the verb is promoted to the position of subject. One might say, "John hit Mary," or one might say instead that "Mary was hit by John." In the first instance, the verb has what are called two arguments—the agent and the object. But in the revision, John has been passivized to a by-phrase, hence no longer a central argument of the verb. Mary has become the subject while the object of the action has been removed now that "John" becomes instead a component of a prepositional phrase. In short, in the phrase "Mary was hit by John," the verb has a subject but no object. The transition is so pronounced that some languages cannot even articulate the "by John" and would strand Mary, having been hit, all alone in the sentence. Further, in an uncanny shift of logic coincidental with the shift in Mary's status vis-à-vis the verb, Mary, in her newfound activity, seems to assume responsibility for having been hit.

When Humbert confides to the reader that "I am going to tell you something very strange: it was she who seduced me" (134), he is merely expressing a fact that has been all along semantically latent. The object of his desire, Lolita, has been seducing him in the sense that his desire has been ignited by the sight of her or (by way of another description) she has *caused* him to desire. If Humbert craves the nymphet, it is only because she "attracts" him. Indeed, Robertson Davies has argued that the novel explores "'not the corruption of an innocent child by a cunning adult, but the exploitation of a weak adult by a corrupt child'" (qtd. in Boyd 230). Although Humbert insists that he was the object of her subjective volition ("it was she who seduced me"), it is clear that Lolita is instead "subjected" by the lust she unwittingly provokes.[24]

In a precursor to the scene at the Enchanted Hunters, Humbert, concealed by a thick robe, masturbates beneath Lolita's frolicking legs, showing just how irrelevant is Lolita to the relationship Humbert has created and enacted. Although she participates to the extent that the combination of her presence qua nymphet and the pressure elicited from her hapless body "conspire" in the action, it is a brand of participation fashioned and controlled by Humbert who exults that Lolita has been "safely solipsized" (62). What has changed between the time of the masturbation scene and the seduction at the Enchanted Hunters is simply that the narrative has literalized the metaphorical and shown the captive for the despot she is. "Like some predator that prefers a moving prey to a motionless one," Humbert projects activity onto Lolita (44). There are some languages that would leave Lolita out altogether from the sentence "Humbert was seduced by Lolita."

What is so intriguing about the scene at the Enchanted Hunters is that the seducer's fantasy is fulfilled with no culpability on his part because what was hitherto no more than linguistic sleight of hand has leaked into the "real" life of the narrative. Despite his protestations, however, Lolita refers to "the hotel where you raped me" (204), which makes for a vertiginous imbrication of fantasy and "reality." Here the "real" fictional girl repudiates the fantasmatic level and insists on the real positions of prey and predator. Throughout the novel, the child character will make these stabs at a subjectivity apart from the pedophilic dream, yet her efforts have the effect of no more than a different literary convention (e.g., social realism) in a text that parodies all literary conventions.

The very name of the pivotal hotel, the Enchanted Hunters, concentrates the dilemma. The hunting predators (read Humbert and Quilty) who prey on nymphets are acted *on* by the nymphets who enchant them into hunters. And isn't the very mystery of the Enchanted Hunters the question of whether it is referring to hunters who have been enchanted or rather men who have been captivated into the hunting position? Is the nymphet enchanted into an art object by the pedophile on whose heart she preys?[25] When Humbert presents Lolita with a suitcase full of new clothes (a scene that occurs fittingly at the Enchanted Hunters), the child is transformed into the predator stalking her bait: "Then she raised by the armlets a copper-colored, charming and quite expensive vest, very slowly stretching it between her silent hands as if she were a bemused bird-hunter holding his breath over the incredible bird he spreads out by the tips of its flaming wings" (122). "As if she were" Humbert himself entranced by the beauty of the girlchild he has trapped, this child has caught him. The following morning Lolita will be grasping what Humbert calls his "life" as though it were the deceptively lovely bird (of prey) that seduced her into seduction. The outlines of predator and prey dissolve amid the tangle of the sexual aim and the object of desire. There is no way to *speak of* the difference.

The headmistress of Lolita's school inadvertently transposes the name of the play in which Lolita has been cast into "The Hunted

Enchanters," a reversal that foregrounds the question of agency. The play itself offers a specular capsule of the novel's central paradox: "Dolores Haze was assigned the part of a farmer's daughter who imagines herself to be a woodland witch, or Diana, or something, and who, having got hold of a book on hypnotism, plunges a number of lost hunters into various entertaining trances before falling in her turn under the spell of a vagabond poet (Mona Dahl). . . . but a seventh Hunter (in a *green* cap, the fool) was a Young Poet, and he insisted, much to Diana's annoyance, that she and the entertainment provided . . . were his, the Poet's, invention" (202–3). Like Humbert, the hunters are "lost" in the nymph's wood where she can do as she likes with them (enchant them perhaps into a pedophilic obsession from which there is no release). But at the same time, the nymph is at the mercy of the Poet's invention, the pedophile's lust, the confessionalist's encomium to her, the novelist's whim. Her "art" of enchantment is invented by the object of her sorcery who has imagined her into being the object of his desire, who has desired her to "be." For if she enchants the hunter, he only hunts her as the object of his fantasy. The "play's profound message" is supposed to be "that mirage and reality merge in love," which exactly repeats the "message" of *Lolita*, where love is a mir[ror]age and the "reality" of the love-object is its "mirror-age" (203). Meanwhile, the readers, all along worried that we are implicated in the pedophilic escapades we voyeuristically observe, are surprised to discover that ultimately the novel positions us next to Lolita, as a facilitating agency en route to a primal self-embrace.

In defining the difference between the sexual object and the sexual aim, Freud writes: "Let us call the person from whom the sexual attraction proceeds the *sexual object* and the act towards which the instinct tends the *sexual aim*" (*SE* 7:135–36).[26] What is crucial here is the implicit double role played by the sexual object. While it is clearly acted on by the subject's desire, at the same time it "emanates . . . the sexual attraction" that ensnares that subject of desire who is, unavoidably as it were, *subjected* by the aura of attractiveness exhaled by the object. The "sexual attraction" seems to emanate through its own self-sustaining agency. In part, one might posit the anthropomorphism of the sexual attraction through which *it* gains both agency and intentionality, leaving to one side the volition of the object that, thereafter, merely subserves the sexual attraction. Seen in this light, Humbert's predicament becomes more sympathetic—what else can he do but respond when Lolita invites him to play a special child's game she has herself just learned (isn't that the technique of the sexual attraction, to coax the subject into a state of desire?); when she teaches him the sexual game he tells her he knows nothing about (because isn't it true that the sexual attraction prompts the subject in what and how to desire?), what else can he do when the sexual attraction emanating from Lolita preempts his will, when his desire becomes the passive instrument of Lolita's sexual attraction? Humbert exults: "I . . . had her have her way" (136).

Freud theorized at length on what he called the "vicissitudes" of the instincts (or drives) and observed that the drive always partakes of its opposite. As discussed above, masochism is sadism turned inward on the subject in which the subject identifies with the aggressor and the sadist likewise identifies with the pleasure of the masochist. Similarly, the exhibitionistic subject identifies with the voyeurism imposed on the one who views his genitals while the scoptophiliac fantasizes her/himself the object of another's gaze.[27] Freud notes that in the shift from sadism to masochism, "the active aim (to torture, to look at) is replaced by the passive aim (to be tortured, to be looked at)" (*SE* 14:127). Although he often denies as much, Freud implicitly equates passivity and activity with femininity and masculinity respectively, associations that are culturally pervasive.[28] Yet at the same time, the "passively" penetrated female could be said to entrap the phallus, like the condition on which Humbert allows Lolita "to take part in that play. Provided male parts are taken by female parts" (98). As far as Humbert is concerned, his "male part" has been "taken" by Lolita's femininity. One might speculate that to be at once female and a child is the ultimate position of passivity, yet still somehow the girlchild is construed as grasping and predatory and emphatically *active* in the experience of her own appropriation. What is appropriated as thoroughly as her body and her mind is her status vis-à-vis the textual action.[29]

The mechanism of reversal inhering in the partial drives, the question of how pleasure is achieved, is fundamentally about the vicissitudes of point of view; the aim of the drive inevitably raises the question of origin and direction. Whether the *aim* be active or passive, the drive is active. Jean Laplanche and J.-B. Pontalis write of masochism that it "is the expression of a response to instinctual demands—in other words, it is an activity aiming to get him into a situation that provides satisfaction. Yet the final stage of this behavior is not attained unless the subject manages to take up a position in which he is at the mercy of the other" (Laplanche and Pontalis, *Language* 9). Masochism is active then in the sense that the subject actively aims at passivity, at *taking up* the position of being mastered.

There is no room in this system for the position of the victim, who is obviated. There are only the sadist who acts upon the victim with whom she or he identifies and the masochist on whom the sadist relies for his or her position of mastery. The rape victim has *involved* the rapist in the crime of statutory rape, an involution from which she or he will never be disentangled or acquitted. Lolita has seduced Humbert into committing an act for which she is culpable—in his eyes as well as for the reader who is told, and believes faithfully: "it was she who seduced me."

Beside the sleeping Lolita in the Enchanted Hunters, Humbert observes that "now and then it seemed to me that the enchanted prey was about to meet halfway the enchanted hunter" (133). Gone is the distinction between desiring subject and its object; instead we find both child and adult overwhelmed by an enchantment that exceeds them, Humbert's lust having been transmogrified into the magic of a fated love. Of course one might concede that the prey invariably meets halfway the hunter—it lures the hapless man into a desiring hunter.

Nevertheless, the "real" enchantment, the putative sleeping pill Humbert feeds Lolita to drug her insensate, never takes effect. It seems that Humbert has been deceived by a physician who gave him placebos in place of the potent barbiturates he sought. Moreover, he is deceived by Lolita's ensuing exhaustion, mistaking her ordinary fatigue for the potency of the drug. Lolita refuses the fairy tale role in which he has cast her as a Sleeping Beauty who will fall asleep (under his magician's spell) instead of awakening to the kiss of a prince. So, when Lolita is alerted by his touch, should we take this to mean that Humbert is really the prince (albeit in frog disguise)? Does the prince merely evaporate the haze of sexual latency from the sleeping princess—who is more than willing to enter his arms? Although the pills do not fulfill their putative function, something has happened between the time when Humbert sent Lolita off to bed and her waking up. The would-be fairy tale princess must wake her groom who dissembles sleep (Humbert acting the coy mistress?) and urge him into sex. Humbert's expectations have been simultaneously defeated and fulfilled. The pill that fails to induce a profound fairy tale sleep instead charms the nymphet into acting out her fantasmatic role—a reversal that raises the question of what exactly is "fake" about the purple pills that "drug" the child into adult concupiscence. The virginal princess is really an experienced lover. Something has changed.[30]

It is in the room at the Enchanted Hunters, asleep beside Lolita, that Humbert's "confusion . . . metamorphos[ed]" Lolita from the passive object of his lust into an active sexual subject (134). The figurative potential of the object of seduction has been realized. Lolita has been transfixed into the permanence of the metaphor—a metamorphosis, ensuing from Humbert's "confusion"—he cannot determine who has seduced whom and, more importantly, neither can the text that lives the transitivism.

As Alfred Appel, Jr., points out, Nabokov was "not unaware that a 'nymph' is also defined as 'a pupa,' or 'the young of an insect undergoing incomplete metamorphosis'" (*Lolita* 340).[31] While Appel reads Lolita's transformation as that of the "nymph" into the butterfly, the metaphor for art to which Humbert has elevated her, we should consider as well her metamorphosis into a metaphor that tacitly dismisses the "reality" of violation. If the metaphor of active passivity has metamorphosed the subject of passivity into the seductress, so then does the text metamorphose the very question of violation into a conundrum. When Lolita declares to Humbert that she has already lost her virginity, the text intimates that there is no such state as virginity—the deflowering always precedes the debaucher, who is irrevocably following in the steps mapped out by his victim. The "real" victimization of Lolita occurs in her petrifaction into a metaphor, in the insistence that she be a butterfly tantalizing the folds of a net. Describing one of his butterfly hunting expeditions, Nabokov exults: "I stooped with a grunt of delight to snuff out the life of some silver-studded lepidopteron throbbing in the folds of my net" (*Speak Memory* 138). It is the butterfly who shapes the folds of his net, whose ensnared and quivering wings "create" the ecstasy in its captor and produce the net designed in its service. In the Nabokovian universe, onto the butterfly is projected primary agency; its loveliness and desirability are determinative.

About Narcissus's fascination with his own image, Ovid writes: "He wants himself; the loved becomes the lover, / The seeker sought, the kindler burns" (3.425–26).[32] It is not without relevance that the story of Narcissus is told by Tiresias who "know[s] / what love [is] like, from either point of view," both male and female, because the metamorphosis Narcissus experiences is the transposition from the object of desire (the lovely youth for whom everyone longs) to the desiring subject (3.326). Moreover, the vehicle of metamorphosis, that which puts Narcissus in the transitivistic relationship with himself, is the pool of water—the mirror. It is within the mirror that the transformation occurs, the reflection creating not only Narcissus's object but his desire. What the mirror enacts and reveals is both the separation and the dissolution of the boundaries, for, while the mirror offers the self as an object of desire, it is itself the boundary flung up between self and other. "When my lips go down / To kiss the pool, his rise, he reaches toward me. / You would think that I could touch him—almost nothing / Keeps us apart" (3.449–52). Almost nothing "but a thin film of water," the very reflecting surface that ignites and focuses desire in the first place, that shows desire where to look (3.448).

Recall that the mirror offers the subject to himself in "a symmetry that inverts it," analogous to the inversion experienced by the linguistic subject who becomes the agent of her or his own victimization. The subject of the sentence "Humbert seduced Lolita" gazes at itself in the mirror, which reflects it back to itself as "Lolita seduced Humbert."[33] The text performs the mirroring function inhering in all relationships between subjects and objects of desire by transferring the agency of the child molester to the child. The metamorphosis of the nymph into the butterfly has conferred on her the activity of adulthood. What the infant apprehends in the mirror is its own temporal leap into its future of motor capacity, just as the child in this instance has been granted an adult sexuality. In the textual mirror that sanctions through replicating the linguistic metamorphosis, the seduced becomes the seducer in concert with the child becoming the adult.

The site of the metamorphosis of Lolita from object of seduction to agent is in the mirror that Lolita herself is—because what Humbert recognizes in or through Lolita is not the child but his rival for her love, the rival that confers value on her. If in his pursuit of Lolita Humbert transforms her into the image of himself (the seducer), we might say that the subject always finds himself in the mirror just as the mirror always shows nothing but the subject. Humbert never does in fact see Lolita, the real child, because he is captivated by his mirror image in her place, inserting himself into her space, thereby collapsing her space into the "almost nothing" intervening between himself and the reflection she serves up (like any mirror), the name he exacts from her, his "brother" in desire, the "brother" he desires, Quilty.

Two Dollys

Chasseguet-Smirgel points out that the "ego ideal is a substitute for primary narcissistic perfection, but a substitute from which the ego is separated by a gulf, a split that man is constantly seeking to abolish" (4–5). Like the "thin barrier of water" between Narcissus and his image, the gulf is what has created the ego ideal inasmuch as, without the split between the subject and the mother, a substitute is unnecessary. At the same time that the ego ideal replaces primary narcissism, the pool into which Narcissus stares (the barrier, the mirror) substitutes for the original rupture. Like the mirror that tantalizes the subject with an imitation of what has been lost, the mirror whose space ("almost nothing") imitates the originary separation as well, Lolita functions as the split between Humbert and his idealized image—the ideal with whom he longs to reunite. The only route to the reflection is to eliminate the mirror barrier, just as Humbert attempts to preempt Lolita by incorporating or "solipsizing" her.

> A full-page ad ripped out of a slick magazine was affixed to the wall above the bed, between a crooner's mug and the lashes of a movie actress. It represented a dark-haired young husband with a kind of drained look in his Irish eyes. He was modeling a robe by So-and-So and holding a bridgelike tray by So-and-So, with breakfast for two. The legend, by the Rev. Thomas Morell, called him a "conquering hero." The thoroughly conquered lady (not shown) was presumably propping herself up to receive her half of the tray. How her bed-fellow was to get under the bridge without some messy mishap was not clear. Lo had drawn a jocose arrow to the haggard lover's face and had put, in block letters: H.H. And indeed, despite a difference of a few years, the resemblance was striking. Under this was another picture, also a colored ad. A distinguished playwright [Quilty] was solemnly smoking a Drome. . . . The resemblance was slight. Under this was Lo's chaste bed. (71)

The emphasis on various kinds of mirroring is marked—the ad "represented" a husband (who bears a "striking resemblance" to Humbert) "modeling" a robe, which is an allusion to (a mirroring of) the purple robe worn by both Humbert and Quilty, whose "resemblance" is apparently only "slight," Humbert observes as though he scans all men in search of degrees of resemblance. The robe "by So-and-So" inserts the "and" like a mirror between "So" and "So," which are linked and sundered by the "and" that functions like Lolita whose space (her bedroom) brings together Humbert and Quilty face to photograph. "Under this" encounter is the bed of the absent Lolita ("the thoroughly conquered lady [not shown])" who sustains the specular structure. The "conquering hero" has occulted his lady, his Lolita, from the landscape where she nevertheless persists in the vestigial form of a conjunction, a "slight" barrier pronouncing the minimal "resemblance" binding. Humbert's belief that the resemblance is only "slight," however, is akin to his later denial of a confraternity with a rival who disgusts him. The image of the robe-garbed model he selects as more nearly like is closer to his own self-appraisal as a "hero." Adjacent to the picture of the model whom Lolita has designated "H.H." is the picture of the "crooner" Humbert later will insist was the one who reminded Lolita of himself, a metonymic slippage repeated in the leap from the look-alike model to the double, Quilty.

Humbert cannot figure out how the lover negotiates the bridge-like tray in pursuit of his lady "without some messy mishap." Nor can Humbert attain his own lady without the "messy mishap" of—what? Charlotte's death? A very messy mishap, indeed. Sex with the nymphet? Messy in the sense that it debases the "magic" of his attachment to Lolita with the coarser features of human "animality" (136). Quilty's murder? A gory affair. But again, in another metonymic sleight of hand, Lolita is herself the bridge Humbert must pass beneath. "Under all this" lurks the mirror-child who supports the bridge, the "and" expanding between "So" and "So"—the child who has erected the bridge that provides the mirage of a route to what lies *beyond* the frame of the picture, to the space where an imaginary lady (mother?) awaits "not shown," not visible, merely imaginary. If there is a "lady" anywhere in this scene, she is "not shown" in the picture, which only implies her, and she is not in the bedroom Lolita has vacated. There are only men here. The child, who is ostensibly what is at stake in bridging the gulf yawning between what is within the picture and without, is herself the gulf that Humbert must "messily" vanquish in his effort to escape the confines of the frame. Thus Humbert needs to destroy Lolita in order to recover that thing she represents. She becomes "the small ghost of somebody I had just killed" (142) because, and make no mistake, the victim of murder in the text is Lolita, only Lolita. It is not Quilty, who is no more than a parodic reflection of Humbert; his very death cries sputter and chortle like a laugh track minus the joke. It is Lolita, the mirror who bridges and bars the passage between Humbert and himself; it is Lolita who must disappear (*"Dolorès disparue"*) (255).[34]

Dilating upon "nymphet love," Humbert explains that the "beastly and beautiful merged at one point, and it is that border line I would like to fix, and I feel I fail tó do so utterly" (137). But what Humbert never recognizes is that the very borderline he longs to fix itself bisects the beastly and beautiful into separate spheres. The nymphet he manipulates into a passage back into the past of narcissistic merger hangs in space and time between himself and the former space in the other time. Like a mirror, the borderline between reality and the fantasmatic, Lolita "fixates" the insuperable gulf, because the border-line by definition reveals not merger but difference—the line between. The borderline insists upon the discrepancy between the beastly and the beautiful. And while Lolita holds up the possibility of an ulti-mate reconciliation, she is in truth only the "dead end (the mirror you break your nose against)" (227).

After a clandestine meeting with Quilty during her second cross-country trip with Humbert, Lolita lies to Humbert that she ran into an old school friend. "'Her name please,'" Humbert demands, like the name of his rival he will later exact—the same name in both in-stances—Clare Quilty. Finally, Lolita tells him:

> ". . . Dolly, like me."
> "So that's the dead end" (the mirror you break your nose against). . . . "What did the two Dollys do?" (227)

As though in imitation of Humbert's name (two Humberts) and his double, Quilty, whom he will finally discover at the other end of the question only Lolita can answer, Lolita presents him with herself in duplicate—the mirror he breaks his nose against, another Lolita, yet another mirror. For a moment, Humbert sees only Dolly (the only name she offers, no Quilty in sight); he sees only the surface of the mirror he cannot transcend. As though to underscore the mirage-like aspect of Humbert's goal, he is confronted by not one Dolly, or doll, not just one representation of a person (a mirror image of the child?) but two representations, the mirror looking at itself. Deceptively, Lolita installs her body as mirror in the space where Humbert expects to find access to himself/his double—the image of the rival and broth-er he seeks.

Later, she will teasingly reveal to Humbert a glimpse of what he seeks. "And as I looked at his oval nut-brown face, it dawned upon me that what I had recognized him by was the reflection of my daughter's countenance—the same beatitude and grimace but made hideous by his maleness" (239). Here, Quilty, who is the mirror *im-age,* mirrors the mirror (Lolita, whose body is also "nut-brown," the mirror-color the same as the mirrored color). If Quilty imitates Hum-bert's "daughter's countenance," then Quilty is imitating an impos-tor because Lolita is only a fake daughter as much as she is a fake fairy tale princess and a fake virgin; while she might be assigned var-ious roles, she always resists them to some extent, exposing in her resistance the fraud. This is the other "Dolly," the Dolly who can leave, go her own way. She is always a threat to the narcissistic econ-omy. The mirror cannot *be* the subject; and if it only reveals an imitation, it always reflects what it "sees." Just as Lolita intractably will not yield to Humbert's impositions of daughter or untried virgin or Sleeping Beauty, what she shows him on the surface of the mirror she enacts is not what he hoped to see: instead she shows him either the pervert's "hideous grimace" or the impenetrable "boundaries" of the mirror itself. What Humbert in fact perceives in Quilty is Quilty looking at Lolita, a reflection of Humbert looking at Lolita—his "hideous maleness" imposed on the translucent surface, distorting with his presence (his maleness, his possession of the phallus) her feminine specularity.[35]

The mirror-child necessarily has no presence of its own that would disrupt the perfect impression of the subject on her surface. While she must be full of her model, she lacks her own subjectivity. Lacan, that expert on the narcissistic impulse, writes: "Just as the senseless oppression of the superego lies at the root of the motivated imperatives of conscience, the passionate desire peculiar to man to impress his image in reality is the obscure basis of the rational mediations of the will" (*ES* 22). If the superego oppresses the subject with the "imperatives of conscience," the subject oppresses reality with the superfluity of his or her image, "impressing" all reality, as it were, into specular service. The reciprocity of the two parallel trends is itself a brand of specularity. For, if the subject is imposed on from outside her/himself by the culture-inflated baggage of the superego, the subject responds by extruding the psyche, converting outside reality into a reflection of the intrapsychic. From the narcissistic perspective, "reality" is draped in quotes—"one of the few words which mean nothing without quotes," as Nabokov said—in order to underscore its self-referential basis. Thus the "reality" of Lolita, the child who develops crushes on "crooners," argues with her mother, and converses in the most up-to-date slang, is bypassed in the creation of another Lolita whose reality can be harnessed by the quotation marks of the perceiving subject. The novel itself reads in many ways like a protracted struggle between two competing views of Lolita, the two "Dolly's," the "outside" Dolly, the "realistic" child of twelve, and the "inside" Lolita, product of the novelist's vision, stamped with the desire of the text. Like a parodic reflection of author-ity, Humbert strives for creative control, author-ity being no more than the parodic reflection of the child molester. In Quilty's play, Diana kisses the poet "to prove to [him] that she was not a poet's fancy" (203), but Lolita's kiss only further cements Humbert's fancy, and the child who "sobs in the night—every night, every night" (178) sobs in vain for a reality hardly attended to by solipsistic Humbert, or the narcissistic text, or the reader badgered into a narcissistic paranoia of entrapment in an author's delirious game.

When the child molester looks in the mirror, he sees of course another child molester, not the girlchild on whom he has impressed himself, whose undeveloped (impressionable) femininity is merely the literalization of what femininity is (not) in the face of the implacable phallus that sees only itself. The place where the phallus is not, the emptiness of the mirror, the castrated girl, nonetheless *reflects* the phallus back to Humbert who impresses upon all "reality" his "hideous maleness." How different, in fact, is Humbert's self-referential delusion from that of the psychoanalytic conceptualization of gender difference, having the phallus or being castrated, the having and not having premised on the primacy of the phallus that apprehends in femininity the lineaments of the missing phallus? As though viewing itself in a mirror, the phallus "sees" only itself in a "reality" that depends on its presence. When Freud asserts that all children, both male and female, believe in the universality of the phallus, and Lacan claims that "the woman will reject an essential part of femininity, notably all its attributes through masquerade" ("Meaning of the Phallus" 84), certainly both theorists are acting like Humbert insofar as what they designate as reality is only a mirror of their "maleness." The novel, however, recognizes the maleness superimposed upon Lolita's countenance as a perversion, a perception missed by the analysts who take the mirror of their maleness as the picture of reality. Although Lolita is a tool whereby Humbert pursues his idealized male ego, the text at least senses the appropriation and distortion (into "hideous maleness")—unlike psychoanalytic theory that mistakes its specular female for the real woman.[36]

Chasseguet-Smirgel contends that the psychoanalytic theory of the phallic mother, the superimposition of a phallus on the vagina, is akin to the denials of the pervert.[37] The small boy, as a result of his frustration that his small penis is insufficient vis-à-vis the mother's adult vagina, denies his insufficiency by ignoring the vagina and imagining in its place a phallus. Where Freud postulates that the fetish of the pervert functions as a substitute for this mythical maternal phallus as a defense against castration anxiety, Chasseguet-Smirgel argues that what the male child fears is not organ loss but rather organ inadequacy, or generational difference. He perceives the difference between his father's organ and his own and hence the impossibility of an incestuous union with the mother. Thus the fetish elides not castration anxiety but generational difference: "it seems to me that the necessity to maintain the illusion of the lack of difference between the sexes, which corresponds to a denial of the difference between the generations, the one governing the other, which is common to all perversions, would explain why fetishism can be found in all the perversions" (17–18). The male child desires to grow up and be the father who can satisfy the desire of the mother, thereby re-fusing with her. Consider the tension evidenced here between the narcissistic impulse to return to the state of infantile fusion and the longing to grow up into the person of the father. Chasseguet-Smirgel seems to overlook specifically the potential internalized conflict ensuing from these competing trajectories. If the child longs to grow up into sexual maturity, it is only in order to regain the past relationship with the mother. Like the idealized mirror image the subject longs to grow up into (to fuse with), it is also the vision of that to which one longs to return.[38] Surreptitiously, Chasseguet-Smirgel's theory of the ego ideal reproduces the inconsistency plaguing Freud in his discussion of anaclitic love. Even the object relation that ostensibly surmounts the narcissistic economy is no more than a detour en route to a satisfaction the narcissist finds instantly. It is perhaps because of the implications of her argument that Chasseguet-Smirgel needs to overstress not only the inferior quality of the pervert's sexual style but the pervert's unconscious recognition of his inferiority. Humbert's idealization of the pervert, as well as his backward trend into the "future" of his desire, reveals the temporal complications that Chasseguet-Smirgel's self-complacently future-centered theory overlooks.

Unlike that of the inadequate little boy, Humbert's organ is really too large for Lolita. "While eager to impress me with the world of tough kids, she was not quite prepared for certain discrepancies between a kid's life and mine" (136). And later, she "said I had torn something inside her" (143). In a sense, this interchange epitomizes the narcissistic fantasy, the son's phallus being too large for the mother. He fills her up better than the father, leaving the mother more replete with, more connected to, the son (the core fear subtending Freud's Oedipal program). The "discrepancies between a kid's life and mine," between a kid's penis and Humbert's, are commensurate with the discrepancies between the mother and child as well as those between Humbert and Lolita, who in the maternal position has somehow digressed into childhood as the "son" grew toward her, missing each other yet again—the generational gap remains unbridgeable.

So, the question then is not only whether the son can grow into the father according to Chasseguet-Smirgel's formula but rather if, in attaining the father's adult adequacy, he has not even further removed himself from the fusion he was after, if his pursuit of adulthood is not simply the mirror inversion of his recession into the past of infantile symbiosis. Has Humbert headed the wrong way? Is the nympholepsy actually a grotesque evocation of the generational misconstruction on the part of the child who follows the reversed path into adulthood figured by the ego ideal, receding ever further from his goal? Where the male child desires to copulate with the mother, the adult male Humbert seeks the girlchild—an utter reversal of the expected (normative) order of events. Chasseguet-Smirgel elaborates:

> When the child is obliged to acknowledge the difference between the sexes and their complementary genitality, he finds himself obliged at the same time to acknowledge the difference between the generations which, for the pervert, is equivalent to being consigned to the void. Everything possible must therefore be done to avoid this awful awareness. Pregenital sexuality, its erogenous zones and part objects, must itself be subject to a process of idealization. (18)

Strangely, in her effort to parallel sexual and generational differences, Chasseguet-Smirgel makes it sound as though the recognition of sexual complementarity is concurrent with the recognition of generational complementarity; the generations fit together like the sexes. In light of such a construction, it seems almost inevitable that the generations would pursue each other as objects of desire—or at least in the case of the pervert, whose aim is to mask the generational as well as the sexual gap, by pinning a phallus on the mother, by cementing child and adult. The result is to make everyone the same sex and the same age, for the phallic mother is a denial of feminine difference, just as the pedophilic relationship confers adulthood on the child and quasi-childhood on the adult. Where Lolita gains the semblance of adulthood by her initiation into adult sexual practice, Humbert literally wears the mask of the child by invading her body.[39]

Perversion literally means to turn away from. In the case of human sexuality, it refers to turning away from the normative heterosexual procreative relationship. Inversion, on the other hand, means to turn into or toward; in psychoanalytic parlance, this refers specifically to homosexuality because, according to a narcissistic model of homosexuality, the homosexual turns *toward* the self-image. Turning away from the adult aspect of the mirror ideal, Humbert retreats back into childhood, turns away, is perverted, into pedophilia. At the same time, he proceeds toward the mirror in pursuit of his homoerotic counterpart, Quilty. His perversion/inversion, his detour back into the child and his progression into the man are paradoxes that are correlates of the temporal ambiguity reflected in the mirror that shows both where you are going and where you have been, especially when one considers that the future towards which Humbert aims (in the figure of Quilty) is yet another digression into perversion. "To be their own ideal once more," writes Freud, "in regard to sexual no less than other trends, as they were in childhood—this is what people strive to attain as their happiness" (*SE* 14:100).

"It will be marked," Humbert explains, "that I substitute time terms for spatial ones. In fact, I would have the reader see 'nine' and 'fourteen' as the boundaries—the mirrory beaches and rosy rocks—of an enchanted island haunted by those nymphets" (18). The substitution in this instance, however, seems double-edged. Just as time becomes in Humbert's system a figure for space, temporal terms are replaced by spatial images—a double superimposition that emblematizes the text's pervasive paradox. For while the child seeks its future in the mirror, it is a future defined by the space the mirror carves out. Humbert's rendezvous with his "Riviera darling," Annabel, was a seaside affair that mirrored (in both her name and the location) Edgar Allan Poe's earlier, seaside Annabel Lee from not only a different century and another "kingdom by the sea" but a different *textual* space. But the mirror image alters the "original" text as much as it is in-formed by it. Humbert marries the mother in order to be close to the daughter—a mirror reversal of Poe's marriage to his young cousin in order to be with his aunt. While Poe seems to be caught in the past of prepubescent sexuality, he is in truth progressing into the "future" offered by the older aunt, another take on a "parody of incest." Although Humbert manifestly situates himself in an adult sexual relationship with Charlotte, he sees in the mother only her connection to the daughter, the link to her own history *as* daughter (Humbert calls her "Lottelita"). Freud has written that "the finding of an object is in fact a refinding of it," perfectly capturing the temporal and spatial distortion of desire (*SE* 7:222).

Humbert complains that "we do not, as dignified Orientals did . . . use tiny entertainers fore and aft between the mutton and the rose sherbet. . . . the old link between the adult world and the child world has been completely severed" (126). While the tiny prostitutes were used "fore and aft" their bodies (the spatial element), they were likewise employed between the beginning and the end of the meal (the temporal element) somehow through their presence unifying the meal from beginning to end, from birth to death as it were. The "fore and aft" of the female child's body is almost undifferentiated, the prepubescent uniformity preceding the bisection into the physically distinct fronts and backs attendant on maturation, as well on the separation from the fore-pleasure of the child to the death-adumbrating end-pleasure of the adult.[40] That ancient time before the link between the adult and child was severed is very specifically when the infant and mother blended in an undisrupted whole, the severance connoting umbilical disjuncture. Chasseguet-Smirgel observes that the ego ideal "represents a link-concept between absolute narcissism and object relatedness, between the pleasure principle and the reality principle, because it is itself a product of the severance of the ego from the object" (28). Thus, if the subject, subsequent to the rupture, pursues her or his ego ideal, she or he seeks in fact the very emblem of the division she or he longs to heal. After the fact, after the plunge into separation and subjectivity, there is no turning back— desire chases the chimera of its own inception, that inception by definition being *subsequent* to the paradisiac time, a "beginning" that is the "end," a "fore" that is "aft."

Perhaps the figure of child appears to offer a solution to the temporal aporia because the child is progressing forward (growing up) while at the same time evoking the past of the adult. Perhaps the child, denizen of both worlds, is the "key" to the riddle.[41] Or at least Humbert imagines that the possession of the child will transport him back (or forward?) into that mythical time-transcendent "enchanted island." Yet how can one really speak of such a mission in temporal terms when it is precisely these boundaries the lover of children wants to escape? Lolita is not a child to Humbert but a nymphet, a mythic emanation of an otherworldly immortal realm. Half-goddess, Lolita is half-buried from his desperate probe. Like the picture she shows him of "a plaster replica of the Venus di Milo, half-buried in sand" (60), the enchanted part of Lolita lurking beneath the smirking preteen is obscured from view. She is the "key (342!) . . . half-shown to [Humbert] (magician showing object he is about to palm)" (120), but Humbert, not the hotel clerk, is the magician who can turn a plaster replica into the "real" representation of the "real" goddess or a key (any key) into the key to 342, to Lolita's home, or Lolita's body, which he yearns to "turn . . . inside out and apply voracious lips to her young matrix, her unknown heart" (167).

At the same time that Lolita figures as the enchanted treasure hoard Humbert strives to unlock with his magic key, she is herself the key that will unlock the ineffable hoard, or the solution to the indecipherable text she images as nymphet, as *Lolita*. If she is the door she unlocks or the code she cracks, the door is in another dimension and the code is secreted in an unknown tongue. "The key was in my fist, ... she was mine," Humbert effuses, before he understands that he has locked his keys inside the car, the locked object being now the keys that have supplanted the car as object of desire (127).

To believe that he is a suitable partner for a twelve-year-old girl and to perceive the girl as sexual object is to deny the generational taxonomy conditioned by temporality. Although Chasseguet-Smirgel theorizes that the child's denial of generational difference results from its desire to unite incestuously with the mother, perhaps the denial of generational difference is primary—in that the recognition of the disparity precipitates the child from the apparent permanence and boundlessness of everlasting fusion with the mother into time and death. But instead of drawing him back into prehistory, the child conveys Humbert into the "future" pledged by his mirror-image, a future now reeking of death as much as primary fusion.

Quilty is his "successful" successor, alternately labeled his "predecessor," who captures the heart of the nymphet who refuses Humbert her love (119). Humbert desires Lolita's desire as much as her body, but this she reserves for his more "perfect" (desirable?) idealized self in the form of Clare Quilty, the preeminent pedophile. Not only is the ideal a pervert, he is more successfully and elaborately perverted. Both Humbert's future and his past, Quilty shows Humbert where Humbert wants to be and what Humbert has lost. "The gray car slowing up before us, the gray car catching up with us" (230) is how Humbert experiences the shadow that wavers fore and aft, constitutive of "the enchanted interspace" separating Quilty, Lolita, and himself (221). But the child is only a decoy—a plaster replica, a useless key—a fake mother figure propping up a sagging Oedipal triangle that stands in for the pre-Oedipal narcissistic duality between two males grandstanding in the mirror. And the division is no more than the forced and artificial entrance into a fantasmatically intersubjective system on the part of what is radically the solipsistic infant. Humbert requires Lolita to lead him to the "rival devil or influential god" whom he kills in an effort to recapitulate himself as One. Because the only access to the rival/ideal is through the mirror, the mirror must be destroyed (as surely as Humbert destroys Lolita). The destruction of the mirror marks an attempt to vanquish the other side where the other abides—hence the elimination of all otherness. Upon killing Quilty, Humbert drives away on the wrong side of the road, "the queer mirror side" (308); it is not that he merely has become the mirror image but rather that he imagines he has exceeded all mirrors and the world of relationships they inaugurate and reflect.

Gentle Reader

Adulation for the master thus goes along with contempt for his
disciples.
—François Roustang, *Dire Mastery*

The only object relationships *Lolita* recognizes are those between
the subject and his mirror image. With the conquest of the mirror
comes the attainment of the psychotic goal implicit in the imaginary
captivation by the mirror image, the evaporation of the ego and its
boundaries. "And do not pity C.Q.," Humbert remarks. "One had to
choose between him and H.H. . . . " (311), just as Nabokov had to choose
between "mesmer mesmer," "lambert lambert," and "otto otto" for the
name of his character whom he conceived as a prisoner of a duality
only art, only *Lolita* (the lure with which he traps the reader and assimilates us in his solipsism), could collapse. It is in the "refuge of art"
that inheres the fantasy of the single text playing the world, creating
both itself and the reader, reducing everything to the solitary imagination, self-conceived and self-sustaining. With the elimination of the
rival for the object's affections, Humbert imagines that the gap between
himself and the object will dissolve forthwith, along with the very
desire that erupted from the distance. Unwilling to live in the frustration of desire generated by primary rivalry, Humbert attempts to destroy the rival—one had to choose "so as to have [Humbert] make [Lol-
ita] live in the minds of later generations . . . the only immortality you
and I may share, my Lolita" (311). Like "Petrarch's Laura and Dante's
Bea" the desired object is ingested as muse, as an artistic inspiration
inseparable from the artist. Everything, all objects, all not-me reality,
recedes into the totalizing mind of the creator.

Thus the text culminates in a celebration of the narcissistic fantasy, not only acting it out but valorizing the narcissistic perspective
as the unadorned truth. With the death of the rival comes the regression from the ego and the world of not-me objects and the ascension into the euphoria of what is not pre- or posthistory (time
having been shed with the habiliments of the ego) but the extrahis-
torical arena of the narcissistic universe.

Nabokov has written of himself (posing as his pseudonymous Si-
rin) that "the real life of his books flowed in his figures of speech,"
explicitly denying a real beyond the letter (*Speak* 288). But if the word
stands in for the thing, in fact designates the absence of thing, then,
according to Nabokov's formula, the substitute is exalted into the

prototype for the real. Moreover, when the real life pulses very specifically through the "figure" that transforms the purely referential into the metaphorical, in a sense being the metaphor of the metaphor (the word standing in for the thing is the metaphorical imperative of any speech), then the real is dislocated even further from the material. Like Lolita, the substitute for her "prototype,"[42] Annabel, who is yet another substitute in a different dimension (literary history), like Lolita who is merely a figure of speech, the creative work assumes primacy over the disavowed arena of the real.[43] The author consequently is transfigured in his figurative landscape into the creator and purveyor of "real life," the position of the deity to which the narcissistic fantasy at root aspires. In response to Alfred Appel, Jr.'s question whether his characters ever took over the novel, Nabokov said: "No, the design of my novel is fixed in my imagination and every character follows the course I imagine for him. I am the perfect dictator in that private world insofar as I alone am responsible for its stability and truth" (*Strong Opinions* 69). In another interview, he refers to his characters as "galley slaves" (*Strong Opinions* 95).

For a period of time it became somewhat unfashionable to read the pedophilic component of *Lolita* as anything other than an extended metaphor.[44] Thus, Julia Bader eschews the literal content altogether in favor of a purely aesthetic interpretation. For her, Quilty is the epitome of the bad artist. Paul Bruss, in contrast to Bader, claims that Quilty is the real author, and Humbert is merely his editor. Mark Lilly points out that the novel's "main purpose is not to replace one form of morality with a new one, but to direct us away from morality altogether, and towards the specially enchanted world where the logic and delight of games replaces everyday reality" (96). David Packman insists that *Lolita* is all "play," but that play is a valid theme in itself without the moral support of "seriousness." *Lolita*, according to Packman, is about meaninglessness, and the cryptogrammic paper chase is a replication of the writer/reader relationship. In short, Nabokov is a Quilty who leaves the reader a series of meaningless clues. Lucy Maddox goes so far as to asseverate that "child rape and murder . . . can be disturbing but convincing metaphors for a desire for moral and aesthetic perfection" (67). This particular trajectory in the critical reception, that treats the pedophilia theme as incidental to the "real" project of the novel, which is either a metaphor for artistic creation or the thematization of the process of reading itself, shows the degree to which the scholarship colludes with the narcissistic fantasy of the novel.[45] Yet such a strategy might well be the critic's sole defense in the face of a novel that would swallow us whole, would exact from us a mirroring of its matrix and brutalize us for our failure to *be* what we read.

At one point, Humbert describes himself as "with Lolita," just as in his autobiography Nabokov referred to the creation of *Lolita* as a "painful birth" (*Speak* 65). Certainly the comparison of artistic creation to motherhood is a familiar metaphor, but one imagines that most of us know the difference between the text and the real child. In this instance, however, in which a child is at stake as much as a novel, in which the child *is* the novel *Lolita,* and the child in the novel is given life by a self-styled poet of nymphets who creates her *as* nymphet, then the difference between the natural child and the literary child is eerily elided. Always implicit in the maternal metaphor is the artist's capacity for independent reproduction, but *Lolita* attempts to metamorphose into "real life" this "figure of speech." Simply, Nabokov has given "life" to the metaphor by transforming (or metamorphosing) it into the "real," at the same time that the "reality" of the child, any child, is superseded by her mission as artistic property. Because, make no mistake, *Lolita* is defiantly Nabokov's property, a property he jealously defends against the reader's appropriative glance with his armament of tricks and traps.

In the Afterword, Nabokov writes: "The first little throb of *Lolita* went through me . . . when I was laid up with a severe attack of intercostal neuralgia" (313), pains Humbert will mirror in the form of heart disease. Where Nabokov's imitation of heart disease, of unrequited desire, sates itself in the production of a novel, Humbert's heart pangs evolve into the birth pangs of labor, metonymically enacted by Lolita's pregnancy.[46] But Lolita's child is stillborn in the sterile wasteland that "real life" has become in the Nabokovian system, the "real life" that has been transcended successfully by the solitary paradise of the text. Only the master can produce—his chest pains into heart disease and his heart disease into art. There is no place for the other of reproduction in the narcissistic economy. There is no place for the child of reproduction when the product is merely a reiteration of the self. There is no place for the reader when the text is its own superior reader. "'The tour of your thigh,'[Humbert cautions Lolita,] 'should not exceed seventeen and a half inches. More might be fatal (I was kidding, of course)'" (211). Of course, growing up for Lolita does prove fatal. She is barred entrance into the reproductive chain in which she would have become a producer of images in place of the produced image, the progression entailed by the transformation from the child to the adult. Because the parent reproduces her/

himself in the child who in this sense reflects its creator, the post-pubescent Lolita marks the end (the death) of Lolita as pure image, the death of Humbert's Lolita. Like the "joke" inhering in the phrase "to be seduced," Humbert's humor in this case transpires in the "real" of the narrative. Although he is only "kidding," all his fantasies are bound to be realized by a text that actualizes figures of speech.

Although Lacan repudiates the mirror-stage (imaginary) distortions of the ego, the mirror-stage is nevertheless the paradigm in his system for all subsequent object relations. Lacan invites the subject to overcome the barrier posed by the mirror by recognizing it *as* mirror. In other words, we should embrace the mirror as the only ontological "truth" available. Even Lacan's accounts of intersubjective relationships suggest his inability to distinguish between the specular and the truly intersubjective. Thus, he says of the sadomasochistic relationship: "In the mirage of play, each identifies himself with the other. Intersubjectivity is the essential dimension" (*Seminar* 1:215). Although such intersubjectivity is constituted on the Imaginary plane (in other words, premised on a specular relationship between a subject and an image), Lacan for some reason insists on the necessity for more than one subject. Rather, we should say that the sadomasochistic relation requires more than one *body* and it is just this distinction between subjects and bodies that is missing in Lacan. He writes, "The object relation must always submit to the narcissistic framework and be inscribed in it" (*Seminar* 1:174), which is at first glance no different from what Freud implied in "On Narcissism." We should pay close attention to his language, however. His characterization of the object relation as that which "submits" recalls the master/slave paradigm in which there can be only one master and one slave. Thus it is that each subject, in all object relations, strives for mastery. This is how we end up with child molestation that looks like love. This is how we end up with a fight to the death that looks like homosexual embraces.

Geoffrey Green argues that Nabokov's relationship with the reader is characterized by transference effects obtaining between the analyst and patient: "The author's reader becomes the image in the mirror" (34). In this narcissistic embrace, however, the refractory analyst/reader is vilified for any distortion—hated in advance for even the threat of difference. This is not a transference that will lead from repetition to change; this is the end of the line. Lacan's audience as well must submit to the narcissistic framework he elaborates. Throughout his texts, he leaves a trail of clues, the vaguest possible references to the work of other analysts, generally unnamed. In part, he is a Nabokovian gamemaster teasing the reader into the quiz, which is the text. Repeatedly, we are interrogated by his narcissistic grandiosity that positions the reader as always less knowledgeable; yet, at the same time, Lacan seems to imagine that we do indeed share his mind. Lacan's disciples will have difficulty elaborating their own theories because, as François Roustang writes, "A system based exclusively on recognition by Lacan inexorably leads to the sterility of his disciples" (28). Like Lolita, the disciples cannot bear fruit; entering the economy as a producer rather than a mirror image will prove fatal—just as it does for Lolita, for the mirror-child. Like Nabokov's reader, Lacan's disciples will strive to reflect the mind of the master.

To see *Lolita* as a creative transcription of the Lacanian point of view renders both the creative and psychoanalytic texts suspect. In *Lolita* the import of the child molestation is attenuated in light of the self-reflexivity that suggests a text can only be about itself. Any "outside" object is transformed into a metaphor for the text itself, a mere reflection of the textual subject, just as for the mirror-bound subject of Lacanian psychoanalysis all objects are metaphors for the relationship with the mirror image. Nabokov's metafictional narcissism is only troubling insofar as it feigns a partnership with the reader ("Imagine me; I shall not exist if you do not imagine me") when the reader suggested by the text is really even less than a spectator (131). Rather, we are the game show contestants earnestly trying to catch the allusions, solve the riddles strung out by the author-cum-gamemaster.[47] We are the sentimentalists pathetically disposed to hover over the dashed sensibilities of a ruined girl-child—plunging into the trap of the wrong end of the mimetic endeavor. For the reader to condole with the girl is to fall prey to what Hutcheon calls "mimesis of product," the text's would-be representational world, instead of remaining steadfastly in touch with the "mimesis of process," the "real" concern here, the act of writing itself, to which we should all pay deferential attention as the narrative pyrotechnics act out (40).

When *Lolita* first appeared in print in the United States, many librarians noted that their borrowers never finished the novel, a fact Alfred Appel, Jr., adduces in favor of the *reader's*, not of the text's, prurience ("Springboard" 113). Yet it is subsequent to the seduction scene that the novel reveals itself (disrobes?) for the self-involved metafiction it truly is. Having discarded altogether the pretense of representation, it leads us along the cryptogrammic paper chase, its own tortured psyche being served up as so much literary detritus. (Was this the seduction all along? To seduce the reader into the narcissistic worldview?) I suggest that the librarians' statistic did not ensue from the readers' prurience; rather, readers grew bored—just as we do in the company of any narcissist. Such immense self-involvement winds up, contrary to Hutcheon's premise, *excluding* the reader who is no more than a Lolita-like route into the interior of the narcissistic economy.

Both Lacan and Nabokov urge us to concede to the "reality" of our narcissistic constraints and our captivation in a universe populated by specular emanations. But to regard the narcissistic experience as the only reality seems nevertheless to validate the omnipotent infant's point of view, seems in fact to be a philosophy bent on sanctioning (even soliciting) regression. The ego-psychology Lacan condemns as strengthening the root of distortions (the ego being that agency that mistakes its narcissism for object relations) certainly suffers from an immobilization of the subject by a tyrannical normativity. Yet the alternatives Lacan offers us are between a self-deceived and a self-aware narcissism, inverted mirror images of one another—and one cannot help but wonder if this catch-22 impasse he proposes is not itself a self-projection, the "mirror he breaks his nose against." Jane Flax puts it best. Lacan, she writes, "transforms Freud's concept of narcissism into an ontological and incontestable theory of human nature" (91).[48]

Humbert's fatal error is represented as his refusal to see Lolita as nothing more than a mirror and Quilty as a mirror image. The recognition of the narcissistic predicament, however, which is the prerogative of the text, seems to condone the appropriation of the child as inevitable, whether it be deluded or enlightened. Curiously, the fantasy implicit in the recognition of a pervasive mirroring is the denial of alterity. Inherent in both Lacan's and Nabokov's points of view is the assumption that there is no "real" other within our ken beyond incorporeal self-reflections. If the other is only a distorted mirror image seen as though in a mirror of our own device, we do in a sense transcend the mirror that bars access to a recuperation of an inviolate narcissism.

Both Lacan and Nabokov induce in their audiences a paranoid desire to avoid what seems to be our inevitable denigration. Lacan's work has the effect of making his audience privilege his word as the "truth." Surely, as Jane Gallop has suggested, Lacan assumes the role of the phallus, the one supposed of knowledge (*Daughter's Seduction* 33–42).[49] Nabokov-as-author describes himself as "someone . . . in the know"—yet both analyst and author come to believe in the very fallacy that sustains their respective "arts" (*Bend Sinister* xii).[50] For Lacan, analytic knowledge, the originary delusion of the patient, is validated; for Nabokov, artistic control is actualized. Interestingly enough, Nabokov's knowledgeable "someone" is set in contrast to the "Viennese Quack," Freud and his intrusive gaze—yet here we find Nabokov and Lacan (another analyst) equally committed to having the very knowledge they otherwise represent as unachievable. Lacan's disciples, many of them analysts themselves, take issue with some of his points in the seminars, only to be silenced by his supremely self-complacent wisdom. When, during one lecture, Lacan cited Descartes, Octave Mannoni attempted to correct him: "It was Pascal who said that, not Descartes." Lacan: "There is a passage in Descartes on the progressive purification of the ego beyond all its specific qualities. But you aren't wrong, in so far as Pascal tries to take us beyond the creature." Mannoni: "He said it explicitly." Lacan: "Yes, but it was a gesture of rejection" (*Seminar* 1:276). Time and again, in his encounters with his audience, Lacan cannot be wrong, even if, as shown here, he is *in fact* wrong. Simply, Lacan revises Pascal's intention.

Lacan's *Écrits* challenges the reader to comprehend what seems self-consciously too difficult and, by virtue of its turgidity (like the phallus), must be superior to the reader's understanding. This is the typical strategy of what Gear, Hill, and Liendo call the sadistic narcissistic personality. Such an analysand "provokes an impotent countertransference: the analyst feels that he is a powerless, helpless, hopeless servant of the powerful analysand who has the analyst's professional future in his hands" (29). The following is an extract from the beginning of the first session between an analyst and a sadistically narcissistic patient. The analysand has requested permission to use the analyst's phone to call his wife, even though he admits that this is a violation of the analytic "contract." The analyst, uncertain whether this is transference material or a necessity, hesitates.

> Analysand [after waiting for a few moments]: Well? What do you say? Will you lend me your phone or not? [Pause] I see. You're like many other analysts, cold, inhuman . . . ridiculously rigid. . . . I must remember that before asking you any special favor. I might have known that you wouldn't understand. It's too complicated for little minds.
> Analyst [disoriented]: (Silence)
> Analysand: At least you might know that you're making my poor wife unhappy with your "technique" [sarcastically]. You need to be smart to be flexible. . . . But I understand your position. You're afraid of doing something wrong. The poor thing . . . [At this point the analyst interrupts angrily, with an interpretation]. Don't get angry, doctor. You should keep yourself under control.

It seems that you don't understand that I'm not violating our agreement. It seems, moreover, that you understood literally that I was asking you for your phone. That's not true. I'm just associating about asking you for the phone. I didn't really mean that I really wanted to use your phone. As a specialist, you should know the actual meaning of your patient's words [sarcastically]. (30)

To encounter this type of narcissist one risks a masochistic countertransference; one risks devaluing oneself at the same time that one succumbs to the narcissist's demand for idealization. Because of our countertransferential need to be valued by the text, we read in search of the text's approval instead of for its meaning. We will be punished if we attempt interpretation; we will be informed summarily that we took literally what was only an association—or a metaphor. Perhaps Pascal did write about the progressive purification of the ego, but, of course, you are missing the point if you take his words literally. "Then I pulled out my automatic—I mean, this is the kind of fool thing a reader might suppose I did. It never even occurred to me to do it" (282). We need to be better readers—as specialists, we should know the actual meaning of the writer's words. We need to be "astute." Then we will know the "name that the astute reader has guessed long ago." He said he wanted to phone, and we thought he wanted to phone—I mean, this is the kind of fool thing a reader might take seriously. The kind of transference this "patient" desires is a mirroring transference through which the patient is revealed as ideal and the analyst is the defective patient. Like Hermann in Nabokov's novel *Despair*, the sadistic narcissist accuses the audience not only of stupidity but also of narcissism: "And a damned good fool I *have* made of someone. Who is he? Gentle reader, look at yourself in the mirror, as you seem to like mirrors so much" (34). The devalued reader, the analyst who has become a patient, countertransferentially needs to be idealized; we want to be as good as the patient—who wants us to want just this. We want to master Lacan's ambiguities as well as his extensive and ill-contextualized references to other analytic theories, just as we want to catch the literary allusions in the cryptogrammic paper chase—we want our knowledge to pass muster. In all instances, in the Lacanian text, in the Nabokovian universe, in the encounter between the narcissistic personality and the analyst, the analyst/reader has an examination to pass or fail. Is it a real phone he wants? Or is it a metaphor for aesthetic creation? Is it a child or a mirror?

This narcissistic worldview that for both Nabokov and Lacan emerges as the child in the mirror/the child as mirror has found an analogue in the uses of the child by contemporary culture. As the final chapter will make clear, this mirror-child has sustained a transmogrification into derealized children of all kinds, from the legal arena's fetishization of the origins of life to the self-recovery movement. The "inner child" is the self-contained speculum, the view from within of adult desire—the child disembodied into the adult turned inside out.

Notes

1. Juliet Mitchell treats the ironic intersection of Maisie as both mirror and window (178, 188).

2. Addressing this double-role of the child, James Kincaid writes that "the child is constructed as a mirror that is also a window, reflecting back to the adult viewer a child, a true child" (195). This "true child" is of course the "form of our own self" (196).

3. Barbara Eckstein (185) and Robert Gregory remark on the similarities between *Lolita* and *What Maisie Knew*.

4. Certainly psychoanalytic readings have been performed nevertheless. For the most important of these see W. W. Rowe, *Nabokov's Spectral Dimension;* G. M. Hyde, *Vladimir Nabokov;* Margaret Gullette's "The Exile of Adulthood"; and Jeffrey Berman's *The Talking Cure.* Berman suggests that Nabokov's repugnance to Freud and Freudianism arose as a result of Freud's Germanic background, which Nabokov unconsciously equated with fascism. Page Stegner believes that Nabokov disliked Freud because Freud said that the artist is controlled by her or his art (35). J. P. Shue sees a battle for power waged between Nabokov and Freud, who threatens to appropriate the author's texts with his psychoanalytic hermeneutic. In light of my argument about Nabokov's narcissistic investment in his sole possession of his text, I certainly concur with Shue. Geoffrey Green, in *Freud and Nabokov,* explores the profound similarities between Freud's and Nabokov's worldviews; indeed, Green shows that despite Nabokov's attacks on Freud's simplifications, Freud had a far less rigid notion of the distinction between reality and fiction than did Nabokov.

5. In the Afterword to *Lolita,* Nabokov observes that "reality" is "one of the few words which mean nothing without quotes" (314). In *Strong Opinions,* he elaborates: "I tend more and more to regard the objective existence of *all* events as a form of impure imagination—hence my inverted commas around 'reality'" (154).

6. For the long-running battle over whether the novel is to be taken seriously (i.e., serious moral purpose) or as a rhetorical game, see: John Hollander; F. W. Dupee; Page Stegner; and Alfred Appel, Jr.

7. Even though Lasch attempts to employ narcissism in its "correct" sense, he is fighting a losing battle. Certainly, there is no agreement among psychoanalysts. For elaborations of the narcissistic personality

disturbances, see Otto Rank's 1911 account; Freud's "On Narcissism: An Introduction"; Otto Kernberg's *Borderline Personality Disorder and Pathological Narcissism*; Heinz Kohut's *Analysis of the Self* and *The Restoration of the Self*; and Ernest Wolf's *Treating the Self*. Richard Chessick's *Psychology of the Self and the Treatment of Narcissism* offers a useful history of the evolution of this term in psychoanalytic theory.

8. Hutcheon notes the concurrence of phenomenological accounts of reader-response and metafiction. This brand of reader-response criticism, despite the protest that it is reader-centered, reduces the reader to a vessel served up at the whim of the supervening textual consciousness. Thus, Wolfgang Iser's "implied reader" is limited to the role assigned her by the text, just as Poulet's reader is an empty vessel inhabited by the text. Stanley Fish's text-construing reader is, as well, a compliant social product who is produced by the textual assumptions as much as she or he produces the text. Coincident with the emergence of these structuralist/ phenomenological descriptions of the reader's position vis-à-vis the text was the influence of Lacan's structuralist theory of psychoanalysis. Here, like the reader who is a linguistic contrivance of the text, the psychoanalytic subject is "born in the field of the Other," an inhabitant of a language that predetermines subjectivity. Not even the unconscious is private and idiosyncratic in the Lacanian system. The unconscious is no more than an effect of the habits of metaphor and metonymy that act out in the "other scene" universal linguistic laws. What is curious about metafiction, its related critical theories, and the structuralist psychoanalysis of Lacan is their relationship to narcissistic strategies.

9. J. P. Shue holds that, paradoxically, the parodic features in Nabokov's work suggest an *"hors-texte"* that necessarily "undermine[s]" the Nabokovian text's professed "independence" (649). "Far from articulating an absolute freedom, they inscribe instead the horizons of a particular historical moment and the limits of authorial power" (649).

10. Like Humbert, Nabokov imagines he has access to the "reality" of the child, which certainly marks a reversal for a writer so noisily resistant to "reality." In his Cornell University lecture on *Bleak House* Nabokov discussed how "the false childishness of [Skimpole] throws into splendid relief the virtues of authentic childhood in other parts of the book" (*Lectures* 83). As I argue in chapter 5, however, the confusion between adults and children in *Bleak House* is precisely what dismantles the received distinction. Skimpole's betrayal of Jo is described by Nabokov as "the false child betraying the real one" (*Lectures* 91), yet the Dickensian text is more concerned with articulating positions of innocence and guilt than it is invested in corporeal adults and children. At the same time, Nabokov resists his sentimental response to the Dickensian child by assuring his audience that such effects are purely stylistic; thus he distances sentimentality through aestheticization. Richard Rorty discusses the degree to which Nabokov needed to fantasy an extraworldly space of art where one could rise above social ugliness and cruelty (141–68).

11. A number of critics have referred to the pivotal scene at the end of the novel, when Humbert hears the sounds of children playing and recognizes that "the hopelessly poignant thing was not Lolita's absence from my side, but the absence of her voice from that concord" (310). For examples of readings that argue quite specifically in favor of the novel's moral investment in revealing Humbert's cruelty, see David Rampton, Leona Toker, Ellen Pifer, Brian Boyd, and Richard Rorty.

12. Freud used these terms interchangeably. See Laplanche and Pontalis's account of various writers' uses of the term "ideal ego" in *The Language of Psycho-Analysis* (201–2). For Lacan's distinction between the ego-ideal and the ideal ego, see "Ego-ideal and ideal ego" in *The Seminar of Jacques Lacan, Book I*.

13. According to Freud it is in the dissolution of the Oedipus complex, as a result of castration anxiety, that the superego is formed. Henceforward the subject assumes the paternal law as his or her own.

14. *Écrits: A Selection* is Alan Sheridan's English translation, hereafter cited as *ES*. Lacan's original reads: "*sous une symetrie qui l'inverse, en opposition à la turbulence de mouvements dont il s'éprouve l'animer*" (*Écrits* 95).

15. Humbert laments the "perilous magic of nymphets" while Van Veen refers to his relationship with his sister, Ada, as "perilous," like all encounters with the mirror in which the subject is threatened with extinction (*Lolita* 136; *Ada* 100).

16. Consider Kinbote's reading of Shade's poem "Pale Fire" as a reflection of his own exile from Zembla and, furthermore (like a mirror within a mirror), his commentary on the poem intricately interweaves the movements of Shade's future assassin with Shade's own routine to indicate some sort of preternatural synchronicity between the two men. This is no subtle leitmotif on the part of Nabokov. He repeatedly refers to mirrors and underscores the self-referential nature of his projects. David Packman calls Quilty Humbert's "mediator, the other who stands between the self and the desired object," after Rene Girard's theory of the mediation of objects of desire (38).

17. Including those of his own device in *Lolita* and *The Enchanter*, where the stepfather/stepdaughter relationships lead to death.

18. Certainly narcissistic mirroring can structure the heterosexual relation as well.

19. Under pressure from gay alliances in the United States, the American psychiatric community finally removed homosexuality from its list of perversions in the DSMIII-R. See David F. Greenberg's *The Construction of Homosexuality* for an account of this conflict (429–30). Under no such constraints, Chasseguet-Smirgel's antagonism to homosexuality and her assumption of its perverse structure underscore her theory of the ego ideal.

20. Humbert makes it clear that, without the name, he will leave without giving her the financial assistance she requested. "I said I had better go, regards, nice to have seen her" (273).

21. Derived from Freud's description of the unconscious as "another

scene," Lacan's Other refers alternately to the personal unconscious, the reservoir of language, and systems of social exchange and kinship relations. While Freud represents the unconscious as a component of the subject, Lacan's use of Other indicates the extent to which the unconscious (by virtue of being "another scene") is also another subject. In short, the "Other" emphasizes the instability of identity by virtue of the fact that we are never certain where "I" is located when "I" speaks. As a result, the "Other" seems to be the site of "truth" about the subject. The small-o "other" is the identificatory counterpart who can at times be idealized, hence the intersection with "Other." This idealized "other" is the ego-ideal.

22. I would argue that the sense of nostalgia so many critics attribute to Nabokov, even going so far as to treat the theme of pedophilia as a metaphor for the return to a lost and blissful Russian childhood, is not a nostalgia for anything nearly so concrete.

23. Appel writes that "Humbert is both victimizer and victim, culprit and judge" ("Springboard" 127). In this sense, Humbert is the Lacanian transitivistic child who remains experientially undifferentiated from objects.

24. Page Stegner writes that "judging from the come-on that Lolita gives [Humbert] while he is a boarder in her mother's house, his statement that it is she who seduced him seems very possibly true—although it can never be forgotten that all this is reported by Hum" (109). Unbelievably the reader seems to collaborate with the seducer's perspective in this instance. The child is here represented as the source of *adult* concupiscence.

25. In *The Enchanter*, Nabokov's precursor to *Lolita*, it is the pedophile who is the title character.

26. In "Instincts and Their Vicissitudes," Freud explains: "If the object becomes a source of pleasurable feelings, a motor urge is set up which seeks to bring the object closer to the ego and to incorporate it into the ego. We then speak of the 'attraction' exercised by the pleasure-giving object, and say that we 'love' that object" (*SE* 14:137).

27. Freud originally believed that sadism was primary and masochism was always the effect of the subject's sadism turned inward. In "Instincts and Their Vicissitudes" Freud notes that although the scoptophilic drive is premised on the subject's looking at his own sexual organ, "a preliminary stage of this kind is absent in sadism, which from the outset is directed upon an extraneous object, although it might not be altogether unreasonable to construct such a stage out of the child's efforts to gain control over his own limbs" (*SE* 14:130). In formulating the "death instinct," Freud came to terms with the existence of a primary masochism and held sadism to be instead the rerouted manifestation of the desire to destroy *oneself*. See *Beyond the Pleasure Principle* (*SE* 18:3–64).

28. See, for example, his comment on these equations in "Femininity" (115).

29. In the Afterword, Nabokov remarks that the novel's critics alternately read it as "'Old Europe debauching young America' and 'Young

America debauching old Europe,'" as though to allegorize the young girl being cast in the role of the middle-aged man (316).

30. Basing her reading on Christina Tekiner's "Time in *Lolita*," where it is proved that the dates Nabokov gives the reader render impossible Humbert's final visits to Dolly and Quilty, Leona Toker argues that Humbert's visits are purely wish-fulfillment, a textualization of wishes that cannot happen in real time (209–19). Such a wish-fulfillment pattern, in which Humbert's fantasies transpire in the "real" life of the narrative, would account for Lolita's acting the seductress. Consider Humbert's fantasy about Hourglass Lake: "The Quest for the Glasses turned into a quiet little orgy with a singularly knowing, cheerful, corrupt and compliant Lolita behaving as reason knew she could not possibly behave" (56). No sooner imagined than it happens in this novel where a wife dies at the convenience of a husband's whim and a twelve-year-old seduces a forty-year-old stepfather and even paranoid fantasies of betrayal and intrigue become reality. In short, much of what Humbert imagines (both good and bad) comes to pass.

31. Appel writes: "Just as the nymph undergoes a metamorphosis in becoming the butterfly, so everything in *Lolita* is constantly in the process of metamorphosis, including the novel itself—a set of 'notes' being compiled by an imprisoned man during a fifty-six-day period for possible use at his trial, emerging as a book after his death, and then only after it has passed through yet another stage, the nominal 'editorship' of John Ray, Jr." (*Annotated Lolita* 340).

32. In the tale of Actaeon, the change is described similarly: "Actaeon, once pursuer / Over this very ground, is now pursued" (3.226, 3.227).

33. Lacan refers to "each great instinctual metamorphosis" in describing the movement between activity and passivity in the instincts (*ES* 19). In a similar vein, Anna Freud writes that "there are many children's games in which through the metamorphosis of the subject into a dreaded object anxiety is converted into pleasurable security" (*Ego and the Mechanisms of Defence* 111). This strategy, what Anna Freud calls the "identification with the aggressor," serves to *protect* the child.

34. In reference to *Lolita*, Nabokov called himself "the kind of author who in starting to work on a book has no other purpose than to get rid of that book," as though the novel itself in some way interferes with the novelist and what he expects to gain through the writing process (*Lolita* 313).

35. Thus it is critical that Lolita is both child and girl. As discussed in earlier chapters, the child is the social vessel par excellence of adult narcissistic projections and appropriations. Further, as Luce Irigaray has argued at length, phallocentrism constructs (and depends on) the woman's status as speculum. See *This Sex Which Is Not One* and *Speculum of the Other Woman*.

36. Interestingly, Lacan treats the ego as the seat of distortions, yet ignores the distortions that his own ego projects on the figure of woman.

37. Chasseguet-Smirgel writes: "One might, at this point, wonder to what extent the whole conception of the male oedipal position, as described by Freud, needs to be revised (and many have been the attempts) in the following light: to assert that at the time of the Oedipus complex the male child has no desire to penetrate the mother (having no awareness, even unconsciously, of the existence of the vagina) seems to me to be confirming male defences generally and that of the pervert in particular" (17).

38. Lacan holds that the child learns from the lacking and desiring mother to desire the phallus. When the child cannot be the phallus that would satisfy her, then it wants to have the object of her desire. In Chasseguet-Smirgel's terms, the male child cannot satisfy the mother because his organ is too small; according to Lacan, the problem is that he only possesses a penis (not a phallus). Note how parallel their arguments are; only, she is speaking in literal terms, whereas Lacan's rhetoric seems decorporealized.

39. Humbert refers to his "adult disguise," which describes simultaneously the adult facade veiling the child and his obsession with the world of girlchildren disguising the adult he is (41).

40. Michael Balint treats extensively the distinction between the forepleasure of the child and the end-pleasure of the adult in *Primary Love and Psychoanalytic Technique*. I should also draw the reader's attention to Kaja Silverman's essay on *What Maisie Knew*, in which she explores at length what she calls James's "'pederastic identification'" that surfaces in his often used references to "going behind" his characters (189). Recall that his whole narrative enterprise in *Maisie* is characterized as "going so 'behind' the facts of her spectacle"—going behind, specifically, a Lolita-like girl-child (x).

41. It is worth comparing the key imagery in *Lolita* to other examples of children either functioning as keys or being perceived as mysteries subject to the intrusion of a male "key." In Henry James's novel *Watch and Ward*, two adult male characters compete to fit their keys into the child Nora's "diminutive timepiece," a manifestly sexual description, although at the same time implying that Nora suggests more than sex to their inspection (109). Jane Gallop offers a remarkable reading of Freud's analytic probe of Dora with his "collection of picklocks" (*Daughter* 132–50).

42. Humbert tells us that "Lolita was to eclipse completely her prototype" (42).

43. Chasseguet-Smirgel emphasizes that access to reality, the development of the ego, and the secondary processes are only possible in the absence of total satisfaction of desire. This ego, however, the formation of which impels the subject into desire, is the target of Lacan's repeated attacks. Specifically, he condemns a psychology that strives to reinforce what he derogates as the seat of distortion. According to Lacan, the ego obfuscates the object of desire and cure consists of the subject's recognition that what she or he desires is merely a signifier without a signified—

that there is nothing that can satisfy her or him. Yet the ego's function is to mediate between pleasure and reality, reality imposing itself on the subject's pursuit of pleasure. With the dissolution of all distortions, therefore, with the disavowal of the not-me world in conflict with the "integrity" of the preindividuated subject, necessarily would come the dismantling of the ego and the eruption of the subject back into the originary boundlessness of the purely pleasured being, the predistorted subject of narcissism.

Lacan says that "the erectile organ comes to symbolize the place of *jouissance*, not in itself, or even in the form of an image, but as a part lacking in the desired image" (*ES* 320). The place it symbolizes, the place where the phallus fills the gap in the desired image, is the site of the incestuous fusion of mother and son when her desire is preempted by the phallus that completes her. Chasseguet-Smirgel writes that the "'psychic death' [ensuing from mother/son incest] . . . is the result of the destruction of the ego's development which had been initiated by the impossibility of union with the mother. The coincidence of ego ideal and ego that thus occurs sweeps away the acquisitions of the process of developing manhood, now rendered useless and inconvenient for the realization of this fusion, and culminates in serious distortions of the ego" (33). Could one argue that the distortions in the "ego" of Lacan's text are precisely what obsess the text with primal fusion—*jouissance?* And isn't it telling that the very ego that rescues the subject from this "psychic death" in which all alterity is self-referential is the object of Lacan's vituperations? Like Lacan's psychoanalytic text, Nabokov's literary text argues in favor of the narcissistic or self-referential text that doesn't see beyond its own borders.

44. David Rampton holds Alfred Appel, Jr., accountable for this trend (102).

45. The debate seems to come down to moral/immoral (or aestheticism) readings that repeat the division Nabokov himself sets up. In a letter to Edmund Wilson, Nabokov urged his friend to think of the novel as "a highly moral affair" (298); yet in the Afterword to the novel, he says most explicitly that *Lolita* "has no moral in tow" (316). We need to underscore the word "affair" in the letter to Wilson because Nabokov is marking a difference between the "affair" between the pedophile and the child and the text/reader relationship. Nevertheless, critics have been unable to overcome the Nabokovian terms that "play" us indefinitely. I am reminded here of Shoshana Felman's analysis of the critical reception of *The Turn of the Screw*, where we find rehearsed over and over again the novel's central question: is the governess hysterical or are there really ghosts? Are we being told a serious story about child molestation and cruelty or is this merely good literary fun?

46. Nabokov said that "Lolita didn't have any original. She was born in my own mind. She never existed" (*Strong Opinions* 16). This echoes his emphasis on his domination of his characters, his fantasy of solitary

procreation. His statement that she "never existed" is double-edged, suggesting that she was wholly a product of his own mind (the author's jealous attachment to his character?) and emphasizing the point I have all along been making—that Lolita herself is curiously absented from a novel that does not consider her altogether relevant.

47. Unlike Thackeray's depiction of the narrator as a puppet-master in *Vanity Fair*, *Lolita*'s narrator wants to control the readers as much as it controls the characters.

48. Stuart Schneiderman criticizes the American habit of calling Lacan a narcissist. He argues that "his flaw was hubris, and hubris has nothing to do with what is now called the grandiose self" (16). I hope that my comparison of Lacanian and Nabokovian strategies will do something toward refuting Schneiderman's claim.

49. Jane Flax points out: "Like any narcissist's universe Lacan's writings often seem to be a series of self-referential and opaque images" (92).

50. Interestingly, Lacan accuses Michael Balint of inducing in his patients "a terminal narcissistic trance" (*ES* 246).

8

Special Deliveries: The Speculative Children of Contemporary Culture

The child is the mirror of the adult, the fairy-mirror that gives the right answer.
—Hélène Cixous and Catherine Clément, *The Newly Born Woman*

It's Midnight—Do You Know Where Your Inner Child Is?
—*New Woman*

Now that many of us know the sex of our children long before they are born (via amniocentesis and ultrasound), the identity of the child originates in utero. At twenty weeks gestation, the child has a gender, a name—a fully projected subjectivity. We read to it, play music to it. We are harassed, even arrested, if we do anything (drugs and alcohol) to compromise it because when we are pregnant we become the perceived guardian of what is imagined to be a full-fledged human subject. As a result of this projected subjectivity, the child increasingly becomes a repository of both individual and social fantasy. Not only do adults overlook the difference between themselves and living children, the unborn as well are stamped with specular logic. This is Lolita's final term, and Humbert has gotten what he wants; he has attained her matrix. The speculum in search of the core of Lolita is the adult's path toward self-invention.

Notwithstanding the difference between the child and the adult, this difference is co-opted by the adult who once was a child. Laplanche elaborates on the relationship thus: "Given that the child lives on in the adult, an adult faced with a child is particularly likely to be deviant and inclined to perform bungled or even symbolic actions because he is involved in a relationship with his other self, with the other he once was. The child in front of him brings out the child within him" (*Foundations* 103). Such of course is the problem involved for the adult who takes the child as a subject of inquiry. The fact that all observers/theorists of children have been children inevitably complicates the relationship between the observing and observed subjects. It is also what makes the subject so compelling; because of the overtly fantasmatic nature of any construction of the child, such constructions tend to show more clearly just how ideology is produced. Because the child is the linchpin of psychoanalytic theory at the same time that it is a preeminent fictional subject for the nineteenth and twentieth centuries, over the course of this study I have invited these two disciplines to meet over the body of the child on which their self-representations rely. The fictional child has led the way in exposing its psychoanalytic versions for the fictions they are.

What emerged in the eighteenth century as the investment in a site named "childhood" (of the nostalgically lamented preindustrial pastoral scene—of the justification of the nuclear family of capitalism—of the encoding of woman's body as a site of production[1]—of the articulation of desire's modern trajectory) has been flattened into rhetorical device used to call up a wealth of associations having to do with powerlessness, loss, deprivation, isolation. To assume the role of "adult child" in the society is to be exonerated of responsibility for a life's worth of wrong choices. Here we find a despair that exults in its acknowledgment. Material children, meanwhile, hover at the periphery of the adult's delirious encounter with her or his "true self," personified as the hitherto rejected inner child to whom one must now devote one's life. The recuperation and reparenting of the inner child is a monumental task; no time is left for children external to the solipsistic embrace. This recovered child is a celebrity, the toast of talk shows, journalism both serious and tabloid; this child is the darling of the society that commiserates with aplomb the "children" adults have regained.

While the diverse contemporary fantasies about the child share much in the way of their necessity for the child to serve a symbolic social function, they trace different trajectories in the construction of childhood. Thus, where the concern with the repressed child of abuse (Lolita's sisters and brothers) has to do with repositioning oneself in relationship to agency and victimization, an increasing social investment in the new children of technology compensates for despondency over the perceived dissolution of the nuclear family and social decay. Finally, the widespread influence of "inner child" popular psychologies is the most recent offshoot of what I have shown to be psychoanalysis's indeterminacy as to the site of its inquiry, the adult or child. All these trends in the production of fantasied children are ominous portents for women in the sense that not only do we find woman's reproductive agency being increasingly expropriated by the state, but also the relationship between the maternal body and the child is being dissevered in the effort to "produce" a child men can "bear."

Repressed Child Syndrome; or, Surviving Our Mothers

Astonishing numbers of adults (particularly women) are recovering long suppressed memories of childhood sexual abuse. The law is accommodating the trend. Invoking the use of delayed discovery,[2] courts are allowing the clock on the statute of limitations (anywhere from one to three years) to start running as of the date of the recovered memory. Before the invocation of delayed discovery, the statute of limitations on filing charges for child sexual abuse began when the child attained majority, eighteen years old. In most other instances, the law defines the event as the material event. The judicial system's encounter with childhood amnesia, however, has relocated the "event" from the material to the psychical. The boundaries of childhood expand. This therapeutic recovery is the recovery of the long suppressed child who awakes from a kind of hibernation as it were, asleep but still viable. This child-in-the-adult is taken seriously as a material witness. The memories, often solicited by the therapist who looks for certain "trademarks" of the abused child—protracted childhood amnesias, repetitions of abusive patterns in adulthood, and so forth—are advanced as reliable reconstructions. As one analyst urges: "Knowledge of both the prevalence of sexual abuse and amnesia for it, as well as the knowledge that some patients may not identify themselves as sexual abuse victims, should result in the analyst 'listening for' a history of the event of sexual abuse" (Alpert 429).

In a reversal of everything Freud theorized about the relationship between the original event and the emergence of trauma, specifically, the tendency of trauma to operate according to the principle of *nachträglichkeit* (deferred action) whereby original events and their sequelae interact in ways that irremediably problematize cause and effect, these recollections are sustained by the patient, the therapist, the legal system, talk show hosts, as transparent and self-identical.[3] In fact, Freud is a popular scapegoat for those who target him as the explanation for why people have dismissed for so long the child's story as fantasy.[4] By contrast, these days, the child's word is taken as the unimpeachable truth. In many cases, children have incorporated as truth the fantasies adults impose on them.[5] Thus, if parents are trying to determine if their child has been abused at, say, a day care center, inadvertently they might suggest details the child then assimilates as its own memory.

Although recent legislation in some states is trying to prevent such prompted testimony from being accepted into court, in many states the assumption remains that the child is ultimate truth-teller.[6] What is important here is the interaction between the adult's and the child's fantasies. The child comes home from day care with a rash. A parent, influenced by the nationwide fear that her or his child will be abused, asks if the child has been burned at school—and so on. The problem is that the etiology of the parent's fantasy is multifold. In part, the parent might be identifying with the child who becomes the blank slate for her or his own Oedipal impulses and their guilty repression. In part, the parent might be identifying with the desiring adult whose desire for the child is likewise complicated by identifications with the child. Meanwhile, the child's sexual and aggressive fantasies are being stimulated by parental questioning. It is not only the parent's fear that emerges; it is the collision of fear with desire that generates the hysterical response. In the end, there are no unconditional adults in this story and there are no genuine children; there is only a morass of identifications and disidentifications, guilt, denial, defense mechanisms, projections, transitivisms—at the end of which no one subject can be distinguished from another, let alone their fantasies.

Why do we want to believe that so many children were victims of sexual abuse? Are we impelled by counterphobia or desire? Why are patients hesitantly asking their therapists about the possibility of psychically repressed molestation? (In fact, this very question signals in the minds of many therapists the reality of the abuse.)[7] What is the relationship between the adult therapeutic subject and the child either recollected or haunting the patient as a potential revelation? Not only is this recollected child received as a subject entirely individuated from its adult mediator, but it also inheres in the adult subject as a threat to her or his relationship to history. This child is dangerous: to the abusive parents who now confront the dreadful combination of the child's rage deployed by adult capacity; to the adult subject who lives in fear of the child's emergence as a disruptive voice. But, at the same time, this child is being courted by a society that finally handles much better these deferred children who mark everyone as essentially a victimized child struggling amid the upheavals of the Western family.

Donald Spence offers some insight about why these "resurrections" might be useful: "To be told that his present behavior is a consequence of some earlier event about which he has no recollection can be, for some patients, a great relief. The fault, as it were, is taken out of his hands" (167–68). Beverly Engel, author of *The Right to Innocence*, a book that encourages recovering memories of one's suspected childhood sexual abuse, quotes a patient's assessment of her "recovery": "'I didn't even know I had been sexually abused when I first started therapy, but finding out explained so much of my behavior to myself. Even though the recovery process was often difficult, the more I understood myself, the more encouraged I felt. It feels so wonderful to no longer be a mystery to myself'" (85). The solved "mystery" involves unveiling a child's sensational story to the hitherto confused adult. The child's story corrects through reframing a narrative otherwise lacking a beginning (sexual abuse), a middle (surviving the abuse), and an end (recovery).

Like Oliver Twist's nightmarish and originally unverifiable account of his abduction (molestation) by Fagin and Bill Sikes (criminal parent-figures), the abuse survivor needs to convince others of the reality of the crime. Exculpation of the child (Oliver *was* kidnapped; the abuse survivor *was* abused) proves to be the founding moment of the child's narrative of innocence. The central theme of self-help books on childhood sexual abuse is that "you," the victim/survivor, did not participate in your victimization. While no one would argue that a child is in any way accountable for its abuse, we can see why a history of abuse might become desirable for others wanting to recast themselves as passive victims of lives gone awry. The childhood sexual abuse narrative strips the subject of all agency—hence its benefits. We want to be Oliver, the child who emerges blameless for events in which his participation was forced. Indeed, Audrey Jaffee has shown that such projection of guilt is typical of Dickensian narrative practice whereby the narrating subject refuses centrality (hence agency) in her or his own story. "David [Copperfield] and Esther suggest that the villain of one's life—if one is recounting it—is necessarily someone else" (113). To assume the narrator's role in relation to one's victimization might at first glance appear to be an effort to wrest power from one's history of disempowerment. Yet, ironically, agency is compulsively repudiated when the victim-narrator projects outward the origin of her or his life story. As long as the narrator cleaves to the child's position, responsibility will be located elsewhere. It is because of their identification with this child's position that Esther and David resist the role of agency; it is in the story of Oliver

Twist that we find the transparent account of the child's perpetual victimization that is later reworked and disguised in *Bleak House* and *David Copperfield*.

Such a no-fault trend in therapy, establishing the patient's regime as child—who, as a result, is permanently the blameless victim—seems to provide a solution to the awkwardness of the endlessly protracted psychoanalytic "cure."[8] Because compassion for the child has become a knee-jerk response on the part of a culture fixated on a greeting card brand of the imaginary (not real) child, the adult subject's self-representation as child (along with the therapeutic collusion) necessarily displaces the responsibility (and agency) outside the therapeutic subject—the child is never at fault.

In February 1992, a parental group was organized in response to these delayed accusations. The False Memory Syndrome Foundation is devoted to countering the spontaneous memories and subsequent legal proceedings of their children. Elizabeth Loftus, a cognitive psychologist who specializes in memory, is the leading witness for the defense.[9] She argues that memory is highly mutable and that it is possible for a therapist to engender fictive memories in patients who previously had no recollection of abuse. For example, because some therapists believe that all women with eating disorders experienced childhood sexual abuse, these therapists encourage their patients to "create" memories that not only conveniently become the origin of all their woes but gratify the therapist. Additionally, just what constitutes sexual abuse is unclear. If you respond affirmatively to whether you were "objectified and ridiculed about your body," according to the authors of *The Courage to Heal* (what Carol Tarvis calls the current "bible" of child abuse), you were a victim of childhood sexual abuse (*Courage* 21; "Beware" 21).

The statistics of childhood sexual abuse are altered vastly according to the scope of the criteria. It seems that if you were "fondled, kissed, or held in a way that made you uncomfortable," you too are as much a victim of childhood sexual abuse as those who were molested more directly (21). *The Courage to Heal* tells the story of a woman who defines her relationship with her father as "emotionally incestuous" (82). Even though she has never been able to retrieve a single memory of physical contact, she is convinced that such experiences occurred and she is grateful that the incest groups she attends consider her a bonafide club member. The authors of *Courage* encourage faith in one's instincts: "Assume your feelings are valid. So far, no one we've talked to thought she might have been abused, and then later discovered that she hadn't been. . . . If you think you were abused and your life shows the symptoms, then you were" (22). Beverly Engel insists that she has "never worked with a client who initially suspected she was sexually abused but later discovered she had not been" (2). Bass and Davis tell their readers: "One practical way to validate your abuse is to look at your life. If you see the effects of abuse and then, as you begin the healing process, you see your behavior change, even slightly, you can trust that your belief is sound" (88). Note the language: suddenly it becomes urgent to "validate your abuse"—no longer a stigma, it is a relief to appeal to this hideous childhood secret as the answer to your problems, now classified as no more than "symptoms" of your original victimization. Of course, it is more than relevant that these symptoms could have multiple alternative etiologies. But the abuse-mongers long for the "validation" of their problem-histories that would shape into a narrative of child abuse what otherwise reads as a lifelong series of disconnected and unexplained "troubles."

Where childhood begins and ends is a question that coincides with the question of child abuse. Throughout this study I have emphasized the difficulty we all have in locating the boundary between child and adult, especially since we remain the children of parents, no matter what our ages. The authors of *Courage* do not seem to find this question complex. They stress the parent's culpability, regardless of the "child's" age. "Even if a sixteen-year-old girl walks into her living room naked and throws herself on her father, he is still not justified in touching her sexually. A responsible father would say, 'There seems to be a problem here.' He would tell her to put clothes on; he'd discuss it with her, get professional help if necessary" (107). Because I have been reared in the same culture as the authors, I share their moral and ethical assumptions. Nevertheless, I cannot help but think about what is being demanded of the adult in this instance. Even though the entire recovery movement, of which "adult survivors" are a part, depends on calling adults "children," the particular adult portrayed here must be steadfastly "adult" with no remnant of the vulnerable error-prone child. The sixteen-year-old is innocent because she occupies the role of child; the father is unspeakably vicious if he acts upon her misguided invitation. In this deceptively uncomplicated relationship, two positions are articulated, adult and child—and you can only inhabit one or the other, according to what has been called by one critic the "sex abuse industry" (Taylor). If you play the child, you are exonerated promptly regardless of your crime/ infraction—and regardless of your physical age. Perhaps you are allowing your husband to abuse your daughter; if you are merely repeating your own trauma, you cannot help it. You remain psychically that helpless child at the mercy of daddy. If you play the adult, however, you must be error-free, unconscious-free. You cannot appeal to childish failings because you are not allowed to be the child; there is room for only one child in this picture. Thus, the father of the sixteen-year-old is not permitted to have his own unresolved issues with his own parents. He is not accorded an "inner child" because this would muddy unduly the allocation of blame and responsibility.

The child abuse "industry" needs a scapegoat and that scapegoat is the fantasied adult who is either unimpeachably good or irredeemably monstrous. Taking parents to court is simply the final term in the story of vengeance complete with heroes and villains and happy endings in which the villain pays the hero a huge amount of money from his or her home owner's insurance. It even has been argued that it is preferable for adult children to take their parents to court because juries find the testimony of adults more credible than that of children. Additionally, I would contend, the testimony of adult children is more compelling than that of young children because our society is not particularly invested in the real child who, if the statistics remotely reflect reality, is being abused routinely. In fact, given the rate of child abuse, it is more likely than not that at least one of the jurors is an abuser. Take, for example, the case of the FBI agent who specialized in child abuse cases; he was regularly abusing his own daughters who took him to court years later ("Damages"). No, it is not children who are being protected here. Rather, our society is re-enacting on a grand scale the plot of a Dickens novel, with its sentimental representations of blameless children, the victory of the oppressed child, and the punishment of unambiguous evil.[10] These performances, just like Dickensian narratives, demand identifications and disidentifications. The "reader's" identification with the child is enhanced when the child is an adult. We can feel vulnerable (like a child) at the same time that we feel powerful (we are punishing mommy and daddy).

Thus, the identification is simultaneously with the child's *position* and the adult's body, just as we disidentify with the adult's position (the predator). We are infantilized in our relationship with the "child" of abuse. The narrative of child abuse installs the "reader" in the child's space and we conform to the imperatives of the space we occupy. Even if the "reader" is himself or herself an abuser of children, for the time we fulfill our prescribed role the identification is invariably with the child. As Georges Poulet has argued, in the "reader's" encounter with the "text": "I am on loan to another, and this other thinks, feels, suffers, and acts within me" (45). The reading experience entails the "invasion" of the reader's consciousness by another's (44). What Poulet does not address, however, is the issue of the reader's susceptibility to textual ideology. Part of the reader's complicity depends on the extent to which she or he shares certain cultural assumptions.[11] James Kincaid has analyzed at length the trials of the McMartin Preschool staff for the sexual molestation of children in their care. Arguing that Raymond Buckey's indictment was premised on hysterical responses to the mere whisper of abuse, Kincaid asks: "Isn't this trial staged so we can tell the pedophiles from the rest of us?" (352).[12] Thus, even if the "reader" of the courtroom drama is a molester, the understood moral and ethical centers are shared by the reader-as-social product, as opposed to the reader as idiosyncratic subject. Given the role of "child" in our society, the site of no fault, an identification with the child is likely. But the child with whom one identifies is never a real child; it is always an adult child, which is all adults can or want to know of children.

E. Ann Kaplan notes the "new centrality being given to the foetus in film comedies, and . . . the general prevalence of foetal imagery in literature, television and recent journalism" (203). It is important to note that representations of the fetus exclude the body of the mother. Kaplan concludes that in large part it is male fear and envy of the mother's reproductive power that drives men to try to control it. I agree with Kaplan, but at the same time we need to consider the fact that before attention to the child, the womb was hardly a sentimentalized site of contestation. Rather, the womb (and the woman's chastity) was embedded in a discourse of patrimony, of keeping estates intact through primogeniture. It is in relation to the value placed on what she produces that woman's reproductive function is valued. With industrialization came a commitment to progress and a potentially utopic future as well as increasing emphasis on individual achievement. As a result, the mother is not only responsible for the future of the race but with her resides as well the source of the individual's life story. Nancy Pottishman Weiss puts the story of mothering in its postindustrial context: "The mother, not only literally the original producer, is more importantly its refiner and packager" (302). It is this postindustrial investment in the child (along with all the metaphors of production that consequently devolve upon the body of the mother) that transforms motherhood into a such an overdetermined site of social interest. Her reproductive "power" seems to grow in relation to the desperate social fantasies reposed in the child. When children cannot fulfill the fantasies they subserve, someone needs to pay. Adults blame the child and "adult children" blame the mother. Further, I worry about embracing the discourse of "womb envy" from Karen Horney and Erich Fromm through current versions. The problem for feminists is that the reversal from penis to womb does not do us any good in the end because we remain invested in the language of envy. It is not Freud's theory of "penis envy" per se that proves so oppressive to the relationship between women and their sexuality; rather, it is the introduction into gender difference of a preferential marker—the having and the not having—and, implicitly, a battle over the desired marker. As the theory of castration anxiety so clearly illustrates, the narrative of penis envy does not establish the male as self-sufficient; rather he is the monarch only recently and tentatively enthroned who lives in chronic fear of deposition.

As I showed in chapter 3, psychoanalysts condemn the mother for everything from faulty attunement to her infant (Stern) to her child's eventual gender-identity (Stoller and Chasseguet-Smirgel). The mother's primary responsibility haunts as well the story of the child's sexual abuse. Engel (who excoriates her own mother for walking around the house naked) explains that "when a child is unable to get the type of nurturing relationship with her mother that she needs, the child often seeks this emotional connection elsewhere" (104).[13] The ostensibly feminist survivor-recovery guides in popular literature wind up conspiring with the hostile masculinist psychoanalytic accounts of bad mothering. Accused of being on "the side of those who provide support for 'molesters, rapists, pedophiles and other misogynists,'" by author E. Sue Blume[14] (27), Carol Tarvis offers a different angle on what has been primarily feminist support for the daughter-victims: "We might ask why so many therapists don't believe the *mothers* who tell a different story about their daughters' therapeutically induced memories" (*NYT* 27). In her book on the daughter-centered plots of women writers, *The Mother/Daughter Plot*, Marianne Hirsch contends that feminist theory and criticism have remained remarkably daughter-centered as well; mothers are linked to the rejected forms of patriarchal power and the continued victimization of women. "In this feminist family romance, sisters are better mothers, providing more nurturance and a greater encouragement of autonomy. In functioning as mutual surrogate mothers, sisters can replace mothers" (164). The emergence of a countrywide network of support groups for survivors of childhood sexual abuse seems to be a popular variation on the desire for a motherhood refashioned out of the relationships among sisters.

The necessity for the daughter to evade the patriarchal victimization of her mother is represented in the childhood sexual abuse literature as the mother's complicity; she is seen as herself an abused child who facilitates a repetition of the pattern in the life of her daughter. Engel's study makes clear that without the mother's participation, the daughter would not be at risk. In "The Fantasy of the Perfect Mother," Nancy Chodorow and Susan Contratto show how the mother comes to represent the origin of her daughter's victimization at the hands of patriarchy: "The victim-mother creates a victim-child" (61). Typically, the survivor accounts of repressed memory syndrome cast as virulently antifeminist any speculations as to their authenticity. As Tarvis suggests, however, these accounts may themselves be deeply antifeminist in their need to join forces with the grand old patriarchal story of failed mothering. Chodorow and Contratto put it this way: "The fantasy of the perfect mother . . . has led to the cultural oppression of women in the interest of a child whose needs are also fantasied" (71).

Nicholas Lemann proposes that the adult survivor of child abuse syndrome is part of a large scale "'recovery' movement, an offshoot of the American self-help tradition" (119-20). Thus the recovered drug addict or alcoholic finds a new incarnation in the adult survivor of child abuse, another tribulation which not only has made one a stronger human being but also reverses the stigma into a badge of honor, club membership and all that it entails. Lemann wryly notes that the protagonist of Patti Davis's novel, *A House of Secrets*, "is an 'adult child' literally: the subject of every aspect of her adult life is her childhood" (122). On the page facing Lemann's article is an advertisement for Nordic Track. The headline reads: "Discover that thin person inside of you" (123). Whether we discover a child or a thin person becomes irrelevant in the story of discovery and recovery of some purified essential (but long buried) self. Sometimes this self is the thin and beautiful body genuflecting to its mirror image. At other times, the self is the child who offers the possibility of beginning again, starting from scratch to make an even better version. The "child" plays two roles in this sense; it is the original flaw, what went wrong, the culprit in the sordid account of one's error-strewn history. It is also the trope par excellence for transformation—to return to the child is to begin again.

This bifurcation of the child suggests why the child is the object of aggression at the same time it is the privileged site of the disappointed adult. Let us also consider the distinction between pedophilia (which literally means child-*love*) and abuse. Indeed, the term pedophilia is now rarely used, perhaps because we want to bury the relationship between love and aggression signaled by sex with children (especially one's own). To love the child *is* to hate it. It is not that the love is related to the hate; rather, the emotional investment in the child mobilizes two different affective trajectories.

In his account of the origins of love and hate, Freud explains that despite their frequent coincidence in a single object, they have altogether different origins (*SE* 14:136–40). Hate is more primitive than love, the narcissistic ego's response to the influx of external stimuli. Hate is premised on original self-preservative responses of the organism. Love, on the other hand, is the transference of one's original narcissism to an external object. "Being in love consists in a flowing-over of ego-libido on to the object" (*SE* 14:100). "At the higher stage of the pregenital sadistic-anal organization, the striving for the object appears in the form of an urge for mastery, to which injury or annihilation of the object is a matter of indifference. Love in this form and at this preliminary stage is hardly to be distinguished from hate in its attitude towards the object" (*SE* 14:138–39). In the case of the child who, as Nabokov has shown us, has been appropriated by the nuclear family and the culture of sentiment as the narcissistic vehicle par excellence, one can see that the self-preservative instincts and the narcissistic ingestion of the object would interact in explosive ways. To the extent that the child induces in the parents indeterminacy as to their physical and emotional boundaries, the adult's narcissism spills over rapturously into this other who is the self. Like Poulet's desubjectified reader who acts out the textual self-consciousness, the adult's relationship with the child throws into turmoil the subject's otherwise self-complacent status as self-identical. This other is not the self, which intimates mutiny to the ego that hoards its territory like a nation-state. If the child is the most perfect love-object because of its revivification of a tenuously renounced narcissism, it is also the object most dangerous to the territory of the ego. We can see once again why the mother is targeted not only as the only parent but as a miscreant parent because her physical relationship with the child, the fact that it is quite literally part of her for nine months, corporealizes the ego's investment in its offshoots. Further, we can see why children are overestimated (the overestimation common to the love object) in sentiment but not in reality. The real child is invariably a transgressor not only of ego-boundaries but also of the sentimental narrative itself that never holds up in the face of the patently refractory child. As a result, we need to go back earlier, prebirth, before the child can even begin to define its own subjectivity.

Immaculate Conceptions

The unconceived children of the Norplant controversy seem to meet the criteria for perfection inasmuch as they induce sentimental identifications without the inconvenience of existing. Unlike the child of abortion, whose material existence remains a factor, these wholly speculative children reveal more clearly the neurotic underside of our society's relationship to the child. When Judge Howard Broadman ruled that the abusive mother, Darlene Johnson, could, as an alternative to three years in prison, undergo a surgical procedure in which the hormone-dispersing device Norplant would be implanted in her forearm, he based his decision on the rights of the unconceived child. This unconceived child is a fictional subject who has assumed legal status. Far more than the abused children, the welfare of the child Johnson was carrying as well as her "unconceived children," garnered Broadman's concern ("California").

Johnson had been found guilty on three counts of child-abuse. Broadman determined to keep her in jail for the remainder of her current pregnancy because of his suspicion that she would harm her fetus with drugs, even though there was no evidence that she had ever used drugs while pregnant.[15] Additionally, he threatened her if she continued to smoke cigarettes: "I also ordered her not to smoke cigarettes as a condition of her being on probation, granted probation. I told her that since she was pregnant, if she got caught smoking, I was going to send her to prison and take away the baby" (*People v. Johnson*, judgment 4). As for the mandatory condition of three years on Norplant, Judge Broadman "ruled that the rights of Johnson's unconceived children were paramount" (*People v. Johnson*, appellant 12). As noted in the appeal, the judgment was unrelated to rehabilitation. "How does forcible implantation of a hormonal contraceptive device promote that goal? There is no reason to think that a woman with Norplant in her arm will be a better mother than a woman without the Norplant implant" (46–47).

Both in opinions responding to the judgment and newspaper articles, the concern was that the court was trying its hand at social engineering, suggesting a reemergence of a hitherto defunct eugenics. Yet, Judge Broadman's logic derives as much from the status of the child in contemporary culture as it does from the urge to restrict burgeoning welfare rolls. The fact that the living children of Darlene Johnson were accorded less consideration than children who, according to Broadman's judgment, should not be born only serves to show the degree to which the fantasmatic "child" has superseded the material child in the cultural imaginary. These fictional children serve adult agendas while by-passing the intrusive exigencies of actual children in the self-celebratory social fantasy.[16]

The failure of Broadman's judgment to meet rehabilitative criteria (the proximate relationship between the crime and its cure) suggests that Johnson's crime resonates for our culture in an emotional arena altogether removed from that of the physical victimization of children. Like the repressed child of the incest survivor, the unconceived child has no existence that is not conferred upon it by adult (re)constructions. The individuated subjectivity of the child, always so disturbing to adult fantasy, is collapsed entirely with the emergence of this child who is solely a vehicle of adult motives. The speculative children of contemporary culture provide a correction to the material child who cannot help but languish in the wake of this idealized adult alter-ego. In light of a lengthy review of children's rights laws, Martha Minnow determines that "children simply are not the real focus of the varied laws that affect them" (5–6). Rather, Minnow argues at length, laws seemingly related to children tend to serve "other powerful social goals," among which is policing women's bodies.

The use of Norplant to keep the "wrong" kind of women from bearing children has gained a great deal of approbation countrywide. Kansas state representative Kerry Patrick (self-described as "pro-life") wants to mandate Norplant for any woman of childbearing age who is convicted for possession or distribution of crack, cocaine, or heroin. Additionally, he wants to offer financial incentives to encourage poor women to use Norplant. Argues Patrick: "It's time we stopped worrying about the rights of the mother and started worrying about the rights of the children she's bringing into the world" (Rees). Nevertheless, according to Patrick's program the "rights" of children would be protected most effectively by making certain they never *are* brought into the world. A writer for the *New Republic* suggests that "the children born of drug-abusing and violent women deserve our attention. And right now, Norplant may be the only practical option we've got" (Rees). Again, the argument suggests that the best way to attend to the needs of children is to prevent their being born. Judge Broadman has explained that "what I did was I found that there were constitutional rights of the children, the born children and her unconceived children. And I balanced their rights against her rights and they won" ("California"). How has it happened that "unconceived children" have rights and that, moreover, the best way to protect their rights is to preempt them as subjects? In response, Johnson's defense attorney, Charles Rothbaum, pointed out: "I really don't understand this idea that he's protecting unborn. How do you protect somebody if you don't even allow that person to be born? . . . What he's doing is preventing somebody from having life" ("California").[17] Apparently, Harry Bodine, an antiabortionist who shot at Judge Broadman in his own court, shared Rothbaum's viewpoint. Bodine was angry at the judge for his ruling on a device that would "'kill innocent babies'" ("Controversial Judge"). If we dismiss Bodine as insane, then we need to see Broadman as equally deluded. Their fantasies about the status of unconceived subjects are eerily compatible. For Broadman, this "innocent baby" has legal rights that entitle it *not to be born* into an unsatisfactory environment (specifically, *not to be conceived*). For Bodine, the right to *be conceived* is supervening.

What we find here is the abortion controversy distilled into its most extreme elements. As in the case of Maisie's parents who "wanted her not for any good they could do her, but for the harm they could, with her unconscious aid, do each other" (5), the needs of the child are exploited in the service of conflicts between adults. The concern is never with living children—it is only with speculative children who are the ideal locus for adult projections. Moreover, these speculative children are the fully mythologized product of the male metaphoric relationship to reproduction. It is not coincidental that in the showdown over the rights of the unconceived we have two men—a judge setting himself up as the purveyor of woman's right *to* conceive and an extremist casting himself as the superhero of (perhaps his own?) unfertilized sperm. It is the hostility, now fully unleashed, to the metaphoric divide between the man and the offspring that is counter-invested in a speculative child conceived imaginatively (is this not what the metaphoric relation has always come down to?) and deployed as a juridical subject. For the judge to interdict conception officially is to arbitrate the woman's reproductive economy with his socially empowered prerogative, a power used in the service of disidentifying the woman's womb from her subjectivity.

Inner Children

The problem of course, even with unconceived "children," is that they persist in having a separate identity, if only potentially. The fact that they are the site of such fervent debate (read transferences) renders them almost as problematic as living children. It seems the best child might be the "inner child" not only because it is safely stored *inside* the ego but because it will never contest the past the adult revises arbitrarily. Its beatific and imperturbable silence is precisely why it is accorded a "voice."

The notion of a "true self"/"false self" dichotomy, elaborated by Winnicott as the felt discrepancy between an "essential" self and the perceived duplicity of its social compliance, was reduced by Alice Miller to a version in which the "true" remains isolated utterly from the "false" that the therapist can strip away like so much wrapping paper. Charles L. Whitfield's *Healing the Child Within* has generalized this "false self" into a societywide pathology, arguing that most caregivers simply are not caring enough. Such purveyors of the "inner child" address a dual subject—an adult in body who carries intact a developmentally thwarted child. This child needs to be "reparented" by the therapist who now speaks only to the "child," any notion of adult subjectivity having been dismissed as an unauthentic suppression of the creative, vital essence. Adulthood itself is under fire; socialization is reconceived as social oppression.

To start with, it is the actual parents who ruin their children. In contradistinction to the Freudian developmental schema in which the parents figure positively as internalized civilizing agencies, such "civilizing" structures are reassessed as incarcerating. The superego is bad. The id—site of the liberated subject—is good. The adult subject her/himself subsequently reenacts on her own "inner child" the abusive neglectful authority of the parents. Adults are bad, period. The inner child suffocates beneath the weight of adult demands, that false subject who is no more than a repressive superaddition; children, especially inner children, are essentially good. The inner child signifies that the essence of the adult *is* the child, one's *essential,* albeit buried, goodness. But children are not adequately nurtured; this is the therapist's job, then, to dissect the adult and repair the child within, like carving open the wolf in pursuit of Red Riding Hood. Whitfield offers his readers the opportunity to find out if they too are wounded children who require his help. You can take a test. Regardless of what you answer, it seems that you need his advice. If you respond "occasionally," "often," or "usually" to *any* of his questions (including "Do you seek approval and affirmation?" "Do you ever find it difficult to express your emotions?"), then "you may find it useful to continue reading" (3). "If you answered mostly 'Never,' you may not be aware of some of your feelings" (4).

Given this catch-22 model, it would seem that almost all readers need to read this book; but of course, this only serves to support Whitfield's initial observation that "from 80 to 95% of people did not receive the love, guidance and other nurturing necessary to form consistently healthy relationships, and to feel good about themselves and about what they do" (2). Mothers, for Whitfield, are in general selfishly absorbed with their own needs at the expense of the child. "In fact, getting pregnant and carrying a child to term is sometimes primarily for the mother's needs" (22). This raises a curious point: how might it be otherwise? Is the good mother, conversely, thinking about the welfare of the species? James's fantasy of the universally deplorable mother is validated as social theory.

John Bradshaw's *Homecoming* has received popular attention for its profile of the "inner child" who, if unattended to, menaces the adult subject.[18] Loosely invoking Jungian archetypes of the child, Bradshaw distinguishes between the wounded child and the wonder child who emblematizes the adult subject's creative essence. Coming to terms with one's "inner child," for Bradshaw, means essentially ridding oneself of one's destructive "childish" features. Indeed, as it turns out, each adult harbors two "inner children," one useful and the other worse than useless. Recapitulating the fairy tale strategy of dividing an ambivalent maternal figure into idealized fairy godmother and wicked stepmother, Bradshaw responds to his ambivalence by isolating into distinctive subjectivities the conflicting features of the child.[19] "In the child archetype, the positive child is vulnerable, childlike, spontaneous, and creative. The negative child is selfish, childish, and resists emotional and intellectual growth" (253). Like Solomon, he advises splitting the child down the middle. Such ambivalence to the child, as Paula Heimann observes, resides in language itself:

> The Anglo-Saxon languages offer an easy distinction between the factual and the hostile reference to the child. The first is "childlike" ("kindlich"), the second "childish" ("kindisch"). I may say to a child, when irritated, "Don't be childish!," and meaning, "Do not pretend that you are stupid, just because you are a child." I should not say, "Don't be childlike." The pejorative use of the word "infantile" betrays the ambivalence to children of those who are no longer children. They either denigrate childhood or sentimentally idealize it by attributing creativity exclusively to the child. (340–41)

To nurture and "reparent" one's inner child is to preempt the child as an independent and divisive subject-within-the-subject. Bradshaw's theory and program ultimately are passively hostile. While he professes to esteem the child as essentially creative and joyful, at the same time he vilifies the incursions of the "wounded child" who "contaminates our adult life" (xiii). The goal is to heal the wounded child (and hence eliminate it) in order to let the "wonder child" re-emerge. This "wonder child" is a near relative of Serge Leclaire's "marvelous child" (discussed in chapter 5), the child of fantasy who must, over the course of psychoanalytic treatment, repeatedly be "killed." Bradshaw's extreme rendition of this fully actualized inner being highlights the fantasmatic component in Leclaire's account. The inside/outside paradigm that they share merely reiterates theoretically a pervasive confusion about the child's boundaries; since I was once a child, is the child in here or out there? Such a model is itself a rather dramatic spatialization of affects and agencies.[20] As we can see in Whitfield, the id is the baby while the superego is played by the overbearing parent. The typology of intrapsychic agencies, in conjunction with the personification of the characteristics associated with the child, leads to enormous confusion about not only distinctions between adult and child, material child and fantasmatic child, but, even more troubling, a scotomization of material children who inevitably prove to be less useful (usable) for the narcissistic subject who plays *all* children in this solipsistic reverie. In summarizing Leclaire's theory, Daniel Gunn writes: "Everyone has a child within. Indeed one has not so much a single child as several children: the child one once was; the child one was—and even more the 'marvelous child' one *was not*—for one's parents; the child one might want to have; and the child one is still, every day, when one thinks of what one might have been and done" (45). To overemphasize an inner child, to assign this child a distinctive subjectivity, is to respond to adult subjective indeterminacies with a story that ironically only further dismantles boundaries never sufficiently erected in the first place.

This subject-within-the-subject, the child within the adult, is akin to Hartley's method of distinguishing the child's subjectivity from that of the adult. Consider, for example, Bradshaw's injunction to have the two "subjects" correspond. One patient did not want to go to an amusement park but "reluctantly honored his inner child's request" (209). Like big and little Leo, these adults and children coexist and communicate as individuated subjects. Such contrived individuations of one's *own* ego, however, only serve to underscore the extent to which encounters with truly individuated subjects are intolerable. The central fantasy here seems to be that the child never grows up; while it physically disappears, its "voice" remains frozen at some evanescent transitional moment when the transformation from child to adult only appeared to occur. If the transformation is a fantasy, so too is the imagined resistance to it.

"On that day I made the decision to reclaim and champion my inner child. I found him frightened to the point of terror. At first he did not trust me and would not go with me" (xvi). Try sending him a letter.[21] "[Right-handed, "more controlling, logical side" (91–92)] Dear Little John: I'm so glad you were born . . . Love, Big John" (91). "[Left-handed, "nondominant side" (91)] Dear John: I want you to come and get me I want to matter to someone. I don't want to be alone. Love, Little John" (92). The pronouns begin to float, unanchored in any subjective specificity: "You [adult] can be there as a wise and caring adult to help this child come into the world. You [adult] can be there when you [child] were born. . . . Your child will also need *your* nurturing support. . . . you [adult] were not *actually there* the first time your inner child went through these stages [but isn't it a *you* who was born? Is "you" the adult or the child or some combination of the two?] . . . as you [adult] learn to champion your inner child, you [adult?] can find nurturing people who will give you [adult?] what you [child?] needed then, and what your inner child needs now in order to grow" (56). Later, we are advised to "see the grown-up you and hear your grown-up self giving you the affirmations of nourishing love" (98). In Bradshaw's desperate effort to rupture the inner from the outer, the child source from the adult end-product, his object-world shatters into entirely subjectified fragments of a single self all loosely inhabiting a solitary "you." This "you" proves unfit for what (impossibly) amounts to both a totalizing and a segregating task. To the extent that these various you's are historically consanguineous, they cannot be differentiated altogether; their paths must converge. Their difference, nevertheless, insists in their disparate trajectories and origins, related but asymptotic. The child begins before the adult; the adult is predicated on a child whom the adult nevertheless enfolds as a subcategory of the final (adult) term.

The problem is that this fantasy of inner children, the war between the "fantasy-child" (the child one was supposed to be) and the "real child" (the child one was), eventuates in a conflict between "depraved" versus "good" children—the fantasy-child of difference who endangers the adult it inhabits as opposed to the integrated child whose desires are congruent with those of its adult "mentor." As Bradshaw cautions, "Your wounded inner child complicates your life" (57). Complication is bad. Conflict is bad. It is important to note the social discordance between the fantasy of the inner child, the child contained within the adult, and the external child with a refractory subjectivity all its own. Bradshaw's account of the child is merely a simplified repetition of what have been for over a thousand years dichotomous representations of the child.[22] The child is either essentially depraved (now revised to wounded) or essentially innocent (the wonder child).[23]

The wonder child is the inner child who *can be* contained, whose subjectivity is finally always subordinated to the adult container; the wounded child is the external (real) child, the child with needs in conflict with adult exigencies, the child who makes trouble for us simply by virtue of being an individuated subject. In each case that I have addressed, the actual child is subordinated to the fantasmatic child. To date, adult survivors of incest who all along have recalled the abuse (the Type One plaintiff) have not been allowed to invoke delayed discovery; conversely, the Type Two plaintiff (suffering from amnesia of the events until recently) has been afforded this option.[24] Why is it that the Type Two plaintiff is so much more compelling than the Type One plaintiff whose "child" witness lacks the fantasmatic component necessary to enthrall judge and jury with her "truth?" Truth needs to be sufficiently aestheticized (and anesthetized) as narrative. The child-witness of hitherto repressed memories is the child of fiction—the very child for whom we long. This is the child who fulfills our need for a coherent subjectivity, the "inner" correspondent with the "outer," the past swallowed by the present. At the same time, this is the child who makes of our despondent unfulfilled adulthood the tail end of the child's pathetic story. It is always the fault of someone else—the wounded child perhaps—and the wounded child is the victim of abusive parents. Nevertheless, the solution of the adult mystery is always the child as source. If parents seem to catch all the blame—look again. These abusive parents are motivated, it turns out, by yet more untreated wounded children in Bradshaw's version of a world populated by "children."

Although these corporealized wounded inner children of Whitfield and Bradshaw appear to be a light distance away from the foundational imperatives of psychoanalysis with its emphasis on psychical reality, the notion of an inner child finds its roots in both psychoanalytic anthropomorphizations (specifically the structural paradigm of ego-psychology) and the inability of psychoanalytic inquiry (to date) to address adequately the site of the analysand. In one of the few direct responses to the question of this site, Roy Schafer minimizes the historic component of the analytic process; rather, analytic reconstructions are important to Schafer only insofar as they relate to present issues (*New Language*). Nevertheless, for Schafer what is supremely "present" about the analysand is the transference, a process inextricably embedded in the complications of the historical subject. Schafer employs a cyclical as opposed to linear model of time to metaphorize analysis, thereby attempting to cement the *relationality* between past and present. He tries to avoid privileging the reconstructive aspect of analysis at the expense of its curative program, a problem he contends plagues psychoanalytic practice. Yet Schafer's own argument suggests the impossibility of dissevering the one space (historical) from the other (transferential), both of which depend for their very significations on the other scene. Although Schafer suggests that we can simply reassign priority in the analytic enterprise, to say the least, it is not so simple.

As I discuss in chapter 5, the confusion in regard to who is being treated (the adult final term of the traumatized child or the child within an adult) persists in psychoanalytic doctrine and practice as a scotomization of not only the subject of psychoanalysis but also the nature of subjectivity itself. It is not that this confusion can be resolved—I doubt it—but as long as such an indeterminacy is ignored, psychoanalytic inquiry cannot help but repeat both the structure of and the motive for its repression. The psychoanalytic interminability lived out in both the incompatibility and the indistinction between "adult" and "child" reiterates the neurotic structures without surpassing them. If the goal of psychoanalysis is to precipitate in the analytic subject just on the verge of repetition a transcendence of the pattern, psychoanalysis itself remains fixated in self-sustaining and self-confirming repetitions.

Curiously, it is what psychoanalysts consider pathological that the "inner child" movement converts into an objective—the tendency to split child and adult personae. Where psychoanalysis strives for integration, Whitfield, Bradshaw, and the rest want us to fashion whole subjects out of the stuff of fantasy. Nevertheless, it is in the contradictions obtaining in psychoanalytic theory that one discovers the roots of "inner child" thinking. Despite the theoretical assignment of splitting to pathology, one finds a tendency on the part of analysts to conspire with the patient's fantasy. For example, the analyst Litza Guttieres-Green describes one analysand thus: "The split deepened between the respected adult he was on the surface and the impotent child he brought along to me to care for. For this reason, he concealed everything that made up his adult life from me, showing me only the wounded child he hid from everyone else" (452). While Guttieres-Green treats the splitting as illness, her own account colludes with the split inasmuch as she resorts to the selfsame terms of an adult/child division fantasied by her patient. In fact, it seems that she herself might be responsible for invoking such personifications. To collude with the very fantasy that she agrees is pathological is what psychoanalysis has been doing since Freud. Winnicott as well personifies the inner "child": "In time it could be said that he brought himself to analysis and talked about himself, as a mother or father might bring a child to me and talk about him. In these early phases . . . I had no chance of direct conversation with the child (himself)" (*Holding and Interpretation* 20). It is psychoanalytic theory that is fixated in the position of a pathological splitting—casting the adult/child distinction as fantasmatic at the same time that it is acted out verbally. Although the "inner child" movement might be dismissed as a debasement of psychoanalytic theory's more complex descriptions of intrapsychic experience, one might equally argue that the movement simply reveals what has all along been a latent problem in theory and practice.

Conclusion

The child in its manifestly go-between status is so terrifying to the adult because of the way in which the child throws into question the organization of the adult subject who sees in the child "me" and "not-me," the child I was and the adult I am, an inexorable and appalling resurrection of an internal bisection. If the child so often functions as a literary tool whereby differences are eradicated and forged in the same moment, it is because the child is the ultimate representative of the instability and impermanence of categorical knowledge. Such fantasies about the child ultimately depend on the disappearance of any material child from the landscape of adult knowledge. To the extent that the actual child resists adult appropriations, this child must quietly follow the path of all transgressors into exile. What we finally come to realize is that by virtue of functioning as a go-between, the child has no space to call its own. Inserted between two realms, it inevitably partakes of both. While the go-between child is bound to reconcile disparate arenas or experiences, it ends up being infused as well as confused with elements of both arenas, incapable of being either, or what would be its idealized culmination in a fusion of the two. The go-between child becomes the vessel of social, sexual, and conceptual remainders, what is in excess of categorical markers. Crossing the divide, the child is contaminated not only by the arenas on either side but also by the mark of division itself, that essential and essentializing edifice that is at once affirmed and denied, perceived as an obstacle but at the same time necessary for the maintenance of illusory categories of material and metaphysical knowledge. In denying the space between through the excision of its textual representative, the text can negotiate division as such without any threat to its internal system of similarity and difference. Just as the bliss of solipsism is restored to the adult living alone with her or his inner child, textual divisions are fantasmatically reconciled.

As I have argued throughout this study, the go-between always winds up being more adept at exposing the failure of human relationships than it is at restoring them—a consequence that ultimately, in the masculinist economy, points to the failure of the womb's promise. Leo Colston's efforts result in the final dissolution of the central sexual couple. The Dickensian families culminate in intact generational reproduction—change that is defied by the interminability of the closed circle. Maisie proves to be the child of divorce in all senses of the term and Lolita's mirror function underscores the narcissistic compulsion motivating the human relationships it is the child's duty to subserve—collapse back into the same. This economy of the same is based on the fantasy that is reposed in the relationship between the mother and the infant. In psychoanalysis, the theory of mother-child fusion ensues from a male fantasy that is twofold. First, there is a need to create in the past a unity that is unachievable in the present, a history of desire itself, as it were. Second, the motivation for a fantasy of nondifferentiation between mother and child proceeds from the resistance to more than one sexed subject.

In light of the male Oedipal paradigm of the family, with its furtive agenda to repudiate the life-giving capacity of the womb, what we have seen from these children who accomplish precisely the opposite of their putative missions is an underlying antagonism to the womb itself. If the child is a fraud, so is the womb that produces it. The fraudulence of the womb sanctions diminishment of the woman and ambivalence toward the child she cannot produce—*as* the site of adult male fantasy—*as* the site of fusion, of a perfectible future, of a harmonious past of the sexual relation. This is the sexual relation that cannot happen for just the reason Lacan adduces—there is just one sex here. But what Lacan does not account for, and what is resisted by the entirety of psychoanalytic thinking, is the *participation* by psychoanalytic accounts of the child in denying a feminine subject. While I hope that my feminist account of the child offers a corrective to a culturewide investment in controlling both materially and narratively the mother's reproductive body, I by no means imagine that female fantasies of the child are more accurate, more in touch with actual children, than male fantasies. Indeed, female fantasies of the relationship between the mother's body and her child are equally caught up in assumptions about self and other, inside and outside—merger and separation. Moreover, I believe that essentialistic representations of mothering that currently pervade certain feminist political alternatives[25] are ultimately as oppressive as the masculinist strategies I have charted; to the extent that they idealize mothering, they merely sustain the masculinist vision.

In my analysis and assessment of the relationship between the child of fiction and the child of psychoanalysis, I have urged the fantasies to encounter one another and, in the course of that encounter, unveil each other as fantasies. Nevertheless, that leaves us with the question of what then, what next? Where might such "negative" insights lead? To a reevaluation of the patriarchal nuclear family and the ways in which its deployment of the go-between child repeat social deployments of the child—or vice versa? To a consideration of the relationship between what George Boas has called the "cult of childhood" and the psychoanalytic community's increasing emphasis on narcissistic personality disturbances? Or finally, and most crucially, to persist in finding strategies whereby women can take back the child wrested from them by male narrative fantasies of all kinds? Certainly, we must continue to interrogate the received relationships between the psychological and the social subject, between the tenuous drive-fragmented subject of Freudian psychoanalysis and the false coherences proffered by both recent psychoanalytic models and the inner child movement, between the body and its social and sexual performances.

Notes

1. For an analysis of the economy of the womb, see, for example, Gayatri Spivak's "Feminism and Critical Theory."

2. Delayed discovery refers to the time lag between the event and the plaintiff's cognizance of personal injury; hence, the statute of limitations is recast according to the date of discovery. Clearly, in the case of a repressed memory, the victim would not file charges until the event was consciously recovered. This particular type of adult survivor of abuse is labeled Type Two. Type One, on the other hand, never repressed the event(s) but nevertheless argues on the basis of a delay in relating current emotional problems to the traumatic episodes. For Judge Plunkett's original distinction (1367), see *Johnson v. Johnson* and Clevenger's analy-

sis of Type One and Type Two cases in "Statute of Limitations." Delayed discovery is a strategy borrowed from malpractice cases where the plaintiff often is unaware of medical consequences until after the date of the statute of limitations. For legal articles on this subject, see Hagen, "Tolling the Statute of Limitations"; Bickel, "Tolling the Statute of Limitations in Actions Brought by Adult Survivors of Childhood Sexual Abuse"; Thomas, "Adult Survivors of Childhood Sexual Abuse."

3. One writer, outraged by Carol Tarvis's attack on the "incest-survivor machine," compares her argument to "the old Freudian position of not believing anything the patient said" (Janov). Another response to Tarvis's article notes that she "sounds a bit like Freud when he claimed that reports of incest were merely the fantasies of hysterical women" (Malek). Here we find a disintegration into the very extremes—patient as truth-teller or hysterical liar—that both Freud and Tarvis try to avoid. The abuse industry has made it a point to blame Freud for minimizing the validity of these accounts. Because the abuse industry has no understanding of the subtleties of the relationship between psychical and material realities, they convert into either/or what for Freud was never so clear. Ironically, psychologists hostile to repressed memory syndrome hold Freud's theory of repression accountable. See Richard Ofshe and Ethan Watters, "Making Monsters" (5–6).

4. See, for example, Sylvia Fraser.

5. See Ceci and Bruck, "Child Witnesses," for their research on the unreliability of children's memories as well as some solutions for using child testimony.

6. See Hollida Wakefield and Ralph Underwager, *Accusations of Child Sexual Abuse* (xiv).

7. Throughout *The Courage to Heal,* the authors contend that the suspicion would not arise without legitimate historical basis.

8. Certainly the emergence of self psychology in psychoanalytic theory and practice is related to and encourages the increasing desire to identify with the victim. Marshall A. Greene, who argues that self psychology is not a form of psychoanalysis, highlights this central difference from classical psychoanalysis: "In self psychology, any disruption of the treatment, i.e., some sign of discomfort or withdrawal by the patient, is seen as being caused by a failure in empathy on the part of the analyst (Goldberg 1978). The genetic reconstructions are also focused on the failures of the parents, the original selfobjects. In either case, the ultimate cause of pathology is outside the patient: he is not responsible for it because his real needs were not met. The psychoanalytic view is far more complicated. While psychoanalysis does not ignore the influence of the environment, its clinical focus is on the intrapsychic conflict, particularly the defenses. The patient is accountable for his own behavior even if the analyst's judgment is suspended" (46–47).

9. For the best criticism to date of repressed memory syndrome, see Elizabeth F. Loftus's "The Reality of Repressed Memories." Loftus suggests

that the psychoanalytic theory of repression has inspired this popular hunt for buried sexual traumata.

10. Wendy Kaminer, in censuring the recovery movement, invokes the Dickens analogy as well to illustrate the fantasy subtending "inner child" thinking: "Inner children are always good—innocent and pure—like the most sentimentalized Dickens characters, which means that people are essentially good and, most of all, redeemable: Even Ted Bundy had a child within" (18).

11. Although what I am talking about sounds somewhat like Fish's notion of "interpretive communities," the role of affect is considerably more important in this model. See *Is There a Text in This Class*. To an extent, my model is closer to that of Steven Mailloux, who treats the necessity for shared conventions in his book *Interpretive Conventions*.

12. Kincaid regards the recent plethora of child sexual abuse trials as distillations of the more widespread fantasmatic cultural narratives about the child. I am particularly interested in the strategies of identification and disidentification that make such narratives "good reads."

13. In *Aliens in the Home*, Sabine Büssing notes that parental "carelessness and indifference" tend to be at the root of the "disaster" that befalls their children (89).

14. Blume is herself an author of one of the survivor-recovery manuals, *Secret Survivors*.

15. Johnson did in fact take drugs, thereby violating the terms of her probation. As a result, she was remanded to prison and the appeal was moot. Since the Johnson case, however, several women have been implanted with Norplant as a condition of probation (see Henley 735–47). Broadman offered mandatory birth control as the condition of probation in an earlier case, *People v. Zaring*, where the rationale was not that the defendant abused her children but that, because she was convicted of drug use (and had already given birth to five children no longer in her custody), she had the potential to give birth to "a cocaine or heroine-addicted baby" (qtd. in Henley 727). Broadman has quite a reputation for handing down "creative" decisions. In the case of divorcing parents with a small child, he required that instead of the child being moved back and forth between the parental homes, the child remain in one house while the *parents* move in and out (Arthur 34). In Broadman's extremist emphasis on the child's rights (whether the child be born or "unconceived"), we find an astonishing example of the extent to which adult needs get projected onto the child.

16. Indeed, Broadman specifies that while the state will pay for Norplant, Johnson herself (already on welfare!) is responsible for the cost of parenting classes. Madeline Henley recounts the case of Lisa Smith, convicted of child abuse, who will be implanted with Norplant after her jail sentence. "Media reports," writes Henley, "have not indicated that Smith will receive any counseling or parenting classes. If Norplant is ordered without therapeutic intervention, its truly punitive intention becomes

more obvious" (738n). Certainly, favoring the needs of the "unborn future children" seems to predominate in all sectors. Many states are now devising policies that will offer welfare mothers financial incentives to use Norplant; not only will the state pay for implantation, women will be paid simply for using the device. See Henley for extensive documentation of state policies regarding Norplant and sterilization; one Senate proposal was to pay women on welfare ten thousand dollars to undergo sterilization (752). Such strategies constitute an example of our society's willingness to allocate resources to the unconceived while funding for living children remains insufficient.

17. Stacey L. Arthur finds a similar paradox in an opinion on an earlier case involving child abuse, *People v. Pointer.* Arthur writes, "In unambiguous language, it [the opinion] refers to preventing injury to the unborn as serving a 'salutary purpose,' and goes on to evaluate the efficacy of birth control as a means of achieving that end" (43).

18. For a less popularized account of the treatment of the "inner child," see Christine A. Courtois's *Healing the Incest Wound* (202–3).

19. Bruno Bettelheim describes such splitting in *The Uses of Enchantment.*

20. For an important consideration of this spatialization metaphor in psychoanalysis, see Roy Schafer, *A New Language for Psychoanalysis* (chap. 8).

21. Like Fairbairn, Bradshaw finds it critical to excuse at length his use of the male personal pronoun for both sexes. Again, we find an anticonflict theory to which gender difference would pose the most insurmountable obstacle.

22. See Robert Pattison's *The Child Figure in English Literature* in which he traces the roots of this distinction to what was originally a religious controversy between Pelagius's representation of a humanity born innocent and good and Augustine's emphasis on an originally sinful subject who must be saved through conversion.

23. As Peter Coveney has written, the child is the reservoir of cast-off instincts or the avatar of presexual innocence. Furthermore, Philippe Ariès treats the tendency to dress children in outmoded adult fashions (56–57). Thus, the fact that cast-off and repudiated instincts are attributed to them not only by adults generally but by psychoanalytic theory in particular suggests using the child as a receptacle for that which the adult "outgrows."

24. See Norrie Clevenger, "Statute of Limitations," 453.

25. See, for example, Sara Ruddick's *Maternal Thinking,* where an idealized mother-child relationship is submitted as a paradigm for nationstates, or Jessica Benjamin's *The Bonds of Love,* where the interaction in the mother-child dyad offers a way out of strategies of domination and subordination.

Works Cited

Adrian, Arthur A. *Dickens and the Parent-Child Relationship*. Athens: Ohio University Press, 1984.

Aletti, Vince. "Child World." *Village Voice* 26 May 1992: 106.

Alpert, Judith L. "Retrospective Treatment of Incest Victims: Suggested Analytic Attitudes." *Psychoanalytic Review* 78 (1991): 425–35.

Andrade, Mary Anne. "Wake into Dream." *The Dickensian* 86 (1990): 17–28.

Andreas, Osborn. *Henry James and the Expanding Horizon: A Study of the Meaning and Basic Themes of James's Fiction*. Seattle: University of Washington Press, 1948.

"Answering a Child's Call for Help." *Atlanta Constitution* 23 Nov. 1992: A16.

Appel, Alfred, Jr. "*Lolita:* The Springboard of Parody." In *Nabokov: The Man and His Work*. Ed. L. S. Dembo. Madison: University of Wisconsin Press, 1967: 106–43.

Ariès, Phillipe. *Centuries of Childhood: A Social History of Family Life*. Trans. Robert Baldick. New York: Vintage, 1962.

Arthur, Stacey L. "The Norplant Prescription: Birth Control, Woman Control, or Crime Control?" *UCLA Law Review* 40 (1992): 1–101.

Bader, Julia. *Crystal Land: Artifice in Nabokov's English Novels*. Berkeley: University of California Press, 1972.

Balint, Alice. "Love for the Mother and Mother-Love." *IJPA* 30 (1949): 251–59.

———. *The Early Years of Life: A Psychoanalytic Study*. New York: Basic, 1954.

Balint, Michael. *The Basic Fault: Therapeutic Aspects of Regression*. London: Tavistock, 1968.

Balint, Michael, and Alice Balint. *Primary Love and Psychoanalytic Technique*. New York: Liveright, 1965.

Baranger, Madeleine, et al. "The Infantile Psychic Trauma from Us to Freud: Pure Trauma, Retroactivity and Reconstruction." *IJPA* 69 (1988): 113–28.

Bass, Ellen, and Laura Davis. *The Courage to Heal*. New York: Harper and Row, 1988.

Benedek, Therese. "Parenthood as a Developmental Phase: A Contribution to the Libido Theory." *Journal of the American Psychoanalytic Association* 7 (1959): 389–417.

Benjamin, Jessica. *The Bonds of Love: Psychoanalysis, Feminism, and the Problem of Domination.* New York: Pantheon, 1988.

Berman, Jeffrey. *The Talking Cure: Literary Representations of Psychoanalysis.* New York: New York University Press, 1987.

Bernays, Anne. Letter. *New York Times Magazine* 18 Oct. 1992: 12.

Bersani, Leo. *A Future for Astynax: Character and Desire in Literature.* New York: Columbia University Press, 1984.

Best, Joel. *Threatened Children: Rhetoric and Concern about Child-Victims.* Chicago: University of Chicago Press, 1990.

Bettelheim, Bruno. *The Uses of Enchantment: The Meaning and Importance of Fairy Tales.* New York: Knopf, 1976.

Bewley, Marius. *The Complex Fate: Hawthorne, Henry James and Some Other American Writers.* London: Chatto and Windus, 1952.

Bickel, Lisa. "Tolling the Statute of Limitations in Actions Brought by Adult Survivors of Childhood Sexual Abuse." *Arizona Law Review* 33 (1991): 427–53.

Bien, Peter. *L. P. Hartley.* University Park: Pennsylvania State University Press, 1963.

Blum, Harold P. "The Value of Reconstruction in Adult Psychoanalysis." *IJPA* 61 (1980): 39–52.

Blume, E. Sue. Letter. *New York Times Book Review.* 14 Feb. 1993: 27.

Boas, George. *The Cult of Childhood.* London: University of London, 1966.

Bollas, Christopher. *Forces of Destiny: Psychoanalysis and Human Idiom.* London: Free Association Books, 1989.

Bowden, Edwin T. *The Themes of Henry James: A System of Observation through the Visual Arts.* New Haven: Yale University Press, 1956.

Boyd, Brian. *Vladimir Nabokov: The American Years.* Princeton: Princeton University Press, 1991.

Bradshaw, John. *Homecoming: Reclaiming and Championing Your Inner Child.* New York: Bantam, 1990.

Brenner, Charles. "Some Contributions of Adult Analysis to Child Analysis." *Psychoanalytic Study of the Child* 40 (1985): 221–33.

Brody, Sylvia. *Patterns of Mothering: Maternal Influence during Infancy.* New York: International Universities Press, 1956.

Brooks, Peter. *Reading for the Plot: Design and Intention in Narrative.* New York: Vintage, 1984.

Bruss, Paul. *Victims: Textual Strategies in Recent American Fiction.* Lewisburg, Pa.: Bucknell University Press, 1981.

Burlingham, Dorothy. "Empathy between Infant and Mother." *Journal of the American Psychoanalytic Association* 15 (1967): 764–80.

———. "The Pre-Oedipal Infant-Father Relationship." *Psychoanalytic Study of the Child* 28 (1973): 23–47.

———. "Simultaneous Analysis of Mother and Child." *Psychoanalytic Study of the Child* 10 (1955): 165–86.

Büssing, Sabine. *Aliens in the Home: The Child in Horror Fiction.* Westport, Conn.: Greenwood, 1987.

Butler, Judith. *Gender Trouble: Feminism and the Subversion of Identity.* New York: Routledge, 1990.

"California: Constitutionality of Requiring Norplant." Abortion Report. *American Politcal Network.* State Report. 12 Nov. 1991. Available in LEX-IS, Nexis Library.

Cargill, Oscar. *The Novels of Henry James.* New York: Macmillan, 1961.

Casey, Edward, and S. Melvin Woody. "Hegel, Heidegger, Lacan: The Dialectic of Desire." In *Interpreting Lacan.* Ed. Joseph H. Smith and William Kerrigan. New Haven: Yale University Press, 1983: 75–112.

Ceci, Stephen J., and Maggie Bruck. "Child Witnesses: Translating Research into Policy." *Social Policy Report* 7 (1993): 1–30.

Chase, Karen. *Eros and Psyche: The Representation of Personality in Charlotte Brontë, Charles Dickens, and George Eliot.* New York: Methuen, 1984.

Chasseguet-Smirgel, Janine. *The Ego Ideal.* Trans. Paul Barrows. New York: Norton, 1984.

Chessick, Richard. *Psychology of the Self and the Treatment of Narcissism.* Northvale, N.J.: Jason Aronson, 1993.

Chodorow, Nancy. *The Reproduction of Mothering: Psychoanalysis and the Sociology of Gender.* Berkeley: University of California Press, 1978.

———, and Susan Contratto. "The Fantasy of the Perfect Mother." In *Rethinking the Family: Some Feminist Questions.* Ed. Barrie Throne and Marilyn Yalom. New York: Longman, 1982: 54–71.

Cixous, Hélène, and Catherine Clément. *The Newly Born Woman.* Trans. Betsey Wing. Minneapolis: University of Minnesota Press, 1986.

Clément, Catherine. *The Lives and Legends of Jacques Lacan.* Trans. Arthur Goldhammer. New York: Columbia University Press, 1983.

Clevenger, Norrie. "Statute of Limitations: Childhood Victims of Sexual Abuse Bringing Civil Actions against Their Perpetrators after Attaining the Age of Majority." *Journal of Family Law* 30 (1991–92): 447–69.

Coe, Richard N. *When the Grass Was Taller: Autobiography and the Experience of Childhood.* New Haven: Yale University Press, 1984.

Collins, Philip, ed. *Dickens: The Critical Heritage.* New York: Barnes and Noble, 1971.

"Controversial Judge Steps Aside." *Washington Post* 15 Apr. 1991 (final ed.): A6.

Coveney, Peter. *Poor Monkey: The Child in Literature.* London: Rockcliff, 1957.

Curriden, Mark. "'I Thought Police Told the Truth.'" *Atlanta Journal Constitution* 10 Oct. 1992: A1.

———, and Bill Torpy. "Parents Turned In for Drugs by Son Win Court Ruling." *Atlanta Journal Constitution* 19 Nov. 1992: A1 and A16.

Dally, Anne. *Inventing Motherhood: The Consequences of an Ideal.* New York: Schocken, 1983.

"Damages Are Awarded to 2 Sisters for Abuse." *New York Times* 18 May 1990: D16.

Davidson, Richard Allan. "Graham Greene and L. P. Hartley: "The Basement Room" and "The Go-Between." *Notes and Queries* 13 (1966): 101–2.

Davis, Walter A. *Inwardness and Existence: Subjectivity in/and Hegel, Heidegger, Marx, and Freud.* Madison: University of Wisconsin Press, 1989.

Davis v. Davis. 842 S.W.2d 588, Tenn. Sup. Ct. 1992.

Delbaere-Garant, Jeanne. *Henry James: The Vision of France.* Paris: Société d'Éditions, 1970.

Degler, Carl N. *At Odds: Women and the Family in America from the Revolution to the Present.* New York: Oxford University Press, 1980.

DeMause, Lloyd, ed. *The History of Childhood.* New York: Psychohistory Press, 1974.

de Rougemont, Denis. *Love Declared: Essays on the Myths of Love.* Trans. Richard Howard. New York: Pantheon, 1963.

Deutsch, Helene. *Neuroses and Character Types: Clinical Psychoanalytic Papers.* New York: International Universities Press, 1965.

Dickens, Charles. *Bleak House.* New York: Signet, 1964.

——. *Great Expectations.* Harmondsworth, U.K.: Penguin, 1965.

——. *Little Dorrit.* Harmondsworth, U.K.: Penguin, 1967.

——. *Oliver Twist.* Harmondsworth, U.K.: Penguin, 1966.

——. *Dickens's Working Notes for His Novels.* Ed. Harry Stone. Chicago: University of Chicago Press, 1989.

Dickstein, Susan, and Ross D. Parke. "Social Referencing in Infancy: A Glance at Fathers and Marriage." *Child Development* 56 (1988): 506–11.

Donovan, Frank. *The Children of Charles Dickens.* London: Leslie Frewin, 1969.

Donzelot, Jacques. *The Policing of Families.* Trans. Robert Hurley. London: Hutchinson, 1979.

Dugger, Celia W. "Welfare Agency Took Missing Boy, Police Say." *New York Times* 18 May 1993: B3.

Dupee, F. W. Review of Vladimir Nabokov's *Lolita.* In *Nabokov: The Critical Heritage.* Ed. Norman Page. London: Routledge and Kegan Paul, 1982: 84–91.

Edel, Leon. *Henry James: The Untried Years, 1843–1870.* New York: Harper and Row, 1953.

Edgar, Pelham. *Henry James: Man and Author.* Boston: Houghton Mifflin, 1927.

Ehrenreich, Barbara, and Deirdre English. *For Her Own Good: 150 Years of the Experts' Advice to Women.* Garden City, N.Y.: Anchor Press, 1978.

Engel, Beverly. *The Right to Innocence: Healing the Trauma of Childhood Sexual Abuse.* New York: Ivy Books, 1989.

Erikson, Erik. *Childhood and Society.* 1950. New York: Norton, 1963.

Escalona, Sibylle K. *The Roots of Individuality: Normal Patterns of Development in Infancy.* Chicago: Aldine, 1968.

Fairbairn, W. Ronald D. *Psychoanalytic Studies of the Personality.* London: Routledge and Kegan Paul, 1952.

Faulkner, William. *Absalom, Absalom!* 1936. New York: Vintage, 1972.

Feldman, Sandor S. "On Homosexuality." In *Perversions: Psychodynamics and Therapy.* Ed. Sandor Lorand and Michael Balint. New York: Random House, 1956: 71–96.

Felman, Shoshana. *Jacques Lacan and the Adventure of Insight: Psychoanalysis in Contemporary Culture.* Cambridge: Harvard University Press, 1987.

———. "Turning the Screw of Interpretation." In *Literature and Psychoanalysis: The Question of Reading: Otherwise.* Ed. Shoshana Felman. Baltimore: Johns Hopkins, 1982: 94–207.

Ferenczi, Sandor. "The Confusion of Tongues between the Adult and the Child (The Language of Tenderness and of Passion)." *IJPA* 30 (1949): 225–30.

———. *Thalassa: A Theory of Genitality.* Trans. Henry Alden Bunker. New York: Psychoanalytic Quarterly, 1938.

Field, Andrew. *Nabokov: His Life in Art.* Boston: Little, Brown, 1967.

———. *Nabokov: His Life in Part.* New York: Viking, 1977.

———. *VN: The Life and Art of Vladimir Nabokov.* New York: Crown, 1986.

Fish, Stanley. *Is There a Text in This Class? The Authority of Interpretive Communities.* Cambridge: Harvard University Press, 1980.

Flax, Jane. *Thinking Fragments: Psychoanalysis, Feminism, and Postmodernism in the Contemporary West.* Berkeley: University of California Press, 1990.

Fraiberg, Selma. *Selected Writings of Selma Fraiberg.* Ed. Louis Fraiberg. Columbus: Ohio State University Press, 1987.

Franks, Lucinda. "The War for Baby Clausen." *New Yorker* 22 Mar. 1993: 56–73.

Fraser, Sylvia. "Desperately Wanting Not to Believe. . . ." *Toronto Star* 28 May 1992: B1. Available in LEXIS, Nexis Library.

Freud, Anna. *The Ego and the Mechanisms of Defense.* New York: International Universities Press, 1966.

———. *Normality and Pathology in Childhood: Assessments of Development.* London: Hogarth, 1966.

———. *The Psycho-Analytical Treatment of Children: Technical Lectures and Essays.* Trans. Nancy Procter-Gregg. London: Imago, 1946.

———, and Sophie Dann. "An Experiment in Group Upbringing." *Psychoanalytic Study of the Child* 6 (1951): 127–68.

Freud, Sigmund. *The Basic Writings of Sigmund Freud.* Trans. and ed. A. A. Brill. New York: Modern Library, 1938.

———. *The Complete Letters of Sigmund Freud to Wilhelm Fliess, 1887–1904.* Trans. and ed. Jeffrey Moussaieff Masson. Cambridge, Mass.: Belknap, 1985.

———. *Die Traumdeutung über Den Traum. Gesammelte Werke.* Vols. 2 and 3. London: Imago, 1942.

———. *The Standard Edition of the Complete Psychological Works of Sigmund Freud.* 24 vols. Trans. James Strachey et al. Ed. James Strachey. London: Hogarth, 1953–66. Referred to here and in the text as *SE.*

————. "Analysis of a Phobia in a Five-Year-Old Boy." 1909. *SE* 10:1–149.

————. *Beyond the Pleasure Principle.* 1920. *SE* 18:1–64.

————. *Civilization and Its Discontents.* 1930. *SE* 21:59–145.

————. "Constructions in Analysis." 1937. *SE* 23:257–69.

————. "Family Romances." 1909. *SE* 9:235–41.

————. "Femininity." 1933. *SE* 22:112–35.

————. "Fetishism." 1927. *SE* 21:149–57.

————. "From the History of an Infantile Neurosis." 1918. *SE* 17:1–71.

————. *Inhibitions, Symptoms, and Anxiety.* 1926. *SE* 20:75–174.

————. "Instincts and Their Vicissitudes." 1915. *SE* 14:109–40.

————. *The Interpetation of Dreams.* 1900. *SE* 4 and 5.

————. "On Narcissism: An Introduction." 1914. *SE* 14:67–102.

————. *On the History of the Psycho-Analytic Movement.* 1914. *SE* 14:1–71.

————. *An Outline of Psychoanalysis.* 1940. *SE* 23:141–215.

————. *Project for a Scientific Psychology.* 1895. *SE* 1:281–397.

————. "Theme of the Three Caskets." 1913. *SE* 12:289–301.

————. *Three Essays on the Theory of Sexuality.* 1905. *SE* 7:123–245.

————. "The Relation of the Poet to Day-Dreaming." *On Creativity and the Unconscious: Papers on the Psychology of Art, Literature, Love, Religion.* New York: Harper Torchbooks, 1958.

Friedman, Gloria. "The Mother-Daughter Bond." *Contemporary Psychoanalysis* 16 (1980): 90–97.

Gable, Sara, Jay Belsky, and Keith Crnic. "Marriage, Parenting, and Child Development: Progress and Prospects." *Journal of Family Psychology* 5 (1992): 276–94.

Gallop, Jane. *Reading Lacan.* Ithaca: Cornell University Press, 1985.

————. *The Daughter's Seduction: Feminism and Psychoanalysis.* Ithaca: Cornell University Press, 1982.

Garcia, Emanuel E. "Freud's Seduction Theory." *Psychoanalytic Study of the Child* 42 (1987): 443–68.

Gargano, James W. "*What Maisie Knew:* The Evolution of a Moral Sense." *Nineteenth-Century Fiction* 15 (1960): 33–47.

Garrett, Peter. *The Victorian Multiplot Novel: Studies in Dialogical Form.* New Haven: Yale University Press, 1980.

Gathorne-Hardy, Jonathan. *The Rise and Fall of the British Nanny.* London: Hodder and Stoughton, 1972.

Gay, Peter. *Freud: A Life for Our Times.* New York: Norton, 1988.

Gear, Maria Carmen, Melvyn A. Hill, and Ernesto Cesar Liendo. *Working through Narcissism: Treating Its Sadomasochistic Structure.* New York: Aronson, 1981.

Gill, Richard. "Letter from L. P. Hartley." *Journal of Modern Literature* 5 (1976): 529–31.

Gillman, Susan K., and Robert L. Patten. "Dickens: Doubles:: Twain: Twins." *Nineteenth-Century Fiction* 39 (1985): 441–58.

Ginzberg, Janet F. "Compulsory Contraception as a Condition of Probation: The Use and Abuse of Norplant." *Brooklyn Law Review* 58 (1992): 979–1019.

Girard, René. *Deceit, Desire, and the Novel: Self and Other in Literary Studies.* Baltimore: Johns Hopkins University Press, 1965.

———. *Violence and the Sacred.* Trans. Patrick Gregory. Baltimore: Johns Hopkins University Press, 1977.

Glover, Edward. "Examination of the Klein System of Child Psychology." *Psychoanalytic Study of the Child* 15 (1960): 75–118.

———. *On the Early Development of Mind.* New York: International Universities Press, 1956.

Goux, Jean-Joseph. "The Phallus: Masculine Identity and the 'Exchange of Women.'" *Differences: A Journal of Feminist Cultural Studies* 4 (1992): 40–75.

Green, André. *The Tragic Effect: The Oedipus Complex in Tragedy.* Trans. Alan Sheridan. Cambridge: Cambridge University Press, 1979.

Greene, Geoffrey. *Freud and Nabokov.* Lincoln: University of Nebraska Press, 1988.

Green, Graham. "The Basement Room." *Collected Stories.* New York: Viking Press, 1972: 457–89.

Green, Martin. *Children of the Sun: A Narrative of Decadence in England after 1918.* New York: Basic, 1976.

Greenacre, Phyllis. *Emotional Growth: Psychoanalytic Studies of the Gifted and a Great Variety of Other Individuals.* 2 vols. New York: International Universities Press, 1971.

———. *Trauma, Growth, and Personality.* London: Hogarth, 1953.

Greenberg, David F. *The Construction of Homosexuality.* Chicago: University of Chicago Press, 1988.

Greene, Marshall A. "The Self Psychology of Heinz Kohut: A Synopsis and Critique." *Bulletin of the Menninger Clinic* 48 (1984): 37–53.

Grosz, Elizabeth. *Jacques Lacan: A Feminist Introduction.* London: Routledge, 1990.

Grubb, W. Norton, and Marvin Lazerson. *Broken Promises: How Americans Fail Their Children.* New York: Basic, 1982.

Guerard, Albert J. *The Triumph of the Novel: Dickens, Dostoevsky, Faulkner.* New York: Oxford University Press, 1976.

Gullette, Margaret. "The Exile of Adulthood: Pedophilia in the Midlife Novel." *Novel* 17 (1984): 215–32.

Gunn, Daniel. *Psychoanalysis and Fiction: An Exploration of Literary and Psychoanalytic Borders.* Cambridge: Cambridge University Press, 1988.

Guntrip, Harry. "My Experience of Analysis with Fairbairn and Winnicott (How Complete a Result Does Psycho-Analytic Theory Achieve?)." *International Review of Psycho-Analysis* 2 (1975): 145–56.

Guttieres-Green, Litza. "Evolution of the Transference in a Case of Homosexuality Declined." *IJPA* 72 (1991): 445–61.

Habegger, Alfred. "Reciprocity and Market Place in *The Wings of the Dove* and *What Maisie Knew.*" *Nineteenth-Century Fiction* 25 (1971): 455–73.

Hagen, Ann Marie. "Tolling the Statute of Limitations for Adult Survivors of Childhood Sexual Abuse." *Iowa Law Review* 76 (1991): 355–82.

Haggard, Rider. *She.* 1887. New York: Oxford University Press, 1991.

Hanzo, Thomas A. "Paternity and the Subject in *Bleak House.*" In *The Fic-*

tional Father: Lacanian Readings of the Text. Ed. Robert Con Davis. Amherst: University of Massachusetts Press, 1981: 27–47.

Hartley, L[esley]. P[oles]. *The Go-Between.* New York: Stein and Day, 1953.

———. *The Novelist's Responsibility.* London: Hamish Hamilton, 1967.

Hartmann, Heinz. *Ego Psychology and the Problem of Adaptation.* Trans. David Rapaport. New York: International Universities Press, 1958.

Heimann, Paula. *About Children and Children-No-Longer: Collected Papers, 1942–80.* Ed. Margret Tonnesmann. London: Tavistock/Routledge, 1989.

Heller, Lee E. "The Paradox of the Individual Triumph: Instrumentality and the Family in *What Maisie Knew.*" *South Atlantic Review* 53:4 (1988): 77–85.

Hellman, Ilse. "Simultaneous Analysis of Mother and Child." *Psychoanalytic Study of the Child* 17 (1972): 359–91.

Henley, Madeline. "The Creation and Perpetuation of the Mother/Body Myth: Judicial and Legislative Enlistment of Norplant." *Buffalo Law Review* 41 (1993): 703–77.

Henry, George W. "Psychogenic and Constitutional Factors in Homosexuality; Their Relation to Personality Disorders." *Psychiatric Quarterly* 8 (1934): 243–64.

Hertz, Neil. "Dora's Secrets, Freud's Techniques." *Diacritics* 13 (1983): 65–76.

Hess, Elizabeth. "Snapshots, Art, or Porn?" *Village Voice* 25 Oct. 1988: 31–32.

Hewison, Robert. *In Anger: Culture in the Cold War, 1945–60.* London: Methuen, 1988.

———. *Under Siege: Literary Life in London, 1939–1945.* New York: Oxford University Press, 1977.

Hiner, N. Ray, and Joseph M. Hawes, eds. *Growing Up in America: Children in Historical Perspective.* Urbana: University of Illinois Press, 1985.

Hirsch, Gordon D. "The Mysteries in *Bleak House:* A Psychoanalytic Study." *Dickens Studies Annual* 4 (1975): 132–52.

Hirsch, Marianne. *The Mother/Daughter Plot: Narrative, Psychoanalysis, Feminism.* Bloomington: Indiana University Press, 1989.

Hoffer, W. "The Mutual Influences in the Development of Ego and Id: Earliest Stages." *Psychoanalytic Study of the Child* 7 (1952): 31–41.

Holland, Norman. "Massonic Wrongs." *American Imago* 46 (1989): 329–52.

Hollander, John. Review of Vladimir Nabokov's *Lolita.* In *Nabokov: The Critical Heritage.* Ed. Norman Page. London: Routledge and Kegan Paul, 1982: 81–91.

Holmes, Mary J. *Homestead on the Hillside.* New York: J. H. Sears, 1923.

Homans, Margaret. *Bearing the Word: Language and Female Experience in Nineteenth-Century Women's Writing.* Chicago: University of Chicago Press, 1986.

Horney, Karen. "The Flight from Womanhood: The Masculinity Complex in Women, as Viewed by Men and by Women." *IJPA* 7 (1926): 324–39.

Hughes, Judith M. *Reshaping the Psychoanalytic Domain: The Work of Melanie Klein, W. R. D. Fairbairn, and D. W. Winnicott.* Berkeley: University of California Press, 1989.

Hunt, David. *Parents and Children in History: The Psychology of Family Life in Early Modern France.* New York: Basic, 1970.

Hutcheon, Linda. *Narcissistic Narrative: The Metafictional Paradox.* London: Methuen, 1984.

Hutter, Albert D. "The Novelist as Resurrectionist: Dickens and the Dilemma of Death." *Dickens Studies Annual* 12 (1983): 1–39.

Hyde, G. M. *Vladimir Nabokov: America's Russian Novelist.* London: Marion Boyars, 1977.

Hynes, Joseph A. "The Middle Way of Miss Farange: A Study of James's *Maisie.*" *ELH* 32 (1965): 528–53.

In Re Clausen. 442 Mich. 648, 502 N.W.2d 649, 1993.

Isle, Walter. *Experiments in Form: Henry James's Novels, 1896–1901.* Cambridge: Harvard University Press, 1968.

Jaffe, Audrey. *Vanishing Points: Dickens, Narrative, and the Subject of Omniscience.* Berkeley: University of California Press, 1991.

James, Henry. *The Complete Notebooks of Henry James.* Ed. Leon Edel and Lyall H. Powers. New York: Oxford University Press, 1987.

———. *The Novels and Tales of Henry James.* 26 vols. New York: Charles Scribner's Sons, 1907–17. Referred to here and in the text as *NT.*

———. "The Author of *Beltraffio.*" 1909. *NT* 16: 3–73.

———. *The Awkward Age.* 1908. *NT* 9.

———. *The Turn of the Screw.* 1908. *NT* 12.

———. *What Maisie Knew.* 1908. *NT* 2.

———. *The Awkward Age.* 1899. New York: Penguin, 1966.

———. "Hugh Merrow." *New York Times Magazine* 26 Oct. 1986: 55, 102–5.

———. *The Other House.* 2 vols. London: William Heinemann, 1986.

———. *Watch and Ward.* London: Rupert Hart-Davis, 1960.

Janov, Arthur. Letter. *New York Times Book Review* 4 Apr. 1993: 34.

Jeffers, Thomas L. "Maisie's Moral Sense: Finding Out for Herself." *Nineteenth-Century Fiction* (1979): 154–72.

Johnson v. Johnson. 701 F. Supp. 1363; 1367, N.D. Ill. 1988.

Jones, Edward T. *L. P. Hartley.* Boston: Twayne, 1978.

Kahn, M. Masud R. *Hidden Selves: Between Theory and Practice in Psychoanalysis.* New York: International Universities Press, 1983.

———. "Introduction." In *Through Paediatrics to Psycho-Analysis,* by D. W. Winnicott. London: Hogarth, 1975: xi–l.

Kaminer, Wendy. *I'm Dysfunctional, You're Dysfunctional: The Recovery Movement and Other Self-Help Fashions.* Reading, Mass.: Addison-Wesley, 1992.

Kaplan, E. Ann. *Motherhood and Representation: The Mother in Popular Culture and Melodrama.* New York: Routledge, 1992.

Kaston, Carren. *Imagination and Desire in the Novels of Henry James.* New Brunswick: Rutgers University Press, 1984.

Kerig, Patricia K., Philip A. Cowan, and Carolyn Pape Cowan. "Marital Quality and Gender Differences in Parent-Child Interaction." *Developmental Psychology* 29 (1993): 931–39.

Kernberg, Otto. *Borderline Conditions and Pathological Narcissism*. Northvale, N.J.: Jason Aronson, 1985.

Kettle, Arnold. *An Introduction to the English Novel*. 2 vols. London: Hutchinson University Press, 1951.

Key, Ellen. *The Century of the Child*. Trans. Ellen Key. New York: Putnam's, 1909.

Kincaid, James R. *Child-Loving: The Erotic Child and Victorian Culture*. New York: Routledge, 1992.

Klein, Melanie. *The Psycho-Analysis of Children*. Trans. Alix Strachey. London: Hogarth, 1950.

———. "The Oedipus Complex in the Light of Early Anxieties." In *Love, Guilt and Reparation and Other Works, 1921–1945*. New York: Free Press, 1975.

———. *The Selected Melanie Klein*. Ed. Juliet Mitchell. New York: Free Press, 1987. Referred to here as *SMK*.

———. "Early Stages of the Oedipus Conflict." *SMK*. 69–83.

———. "The Importance of Symbol Formation in the Development of the Ego." *SMK*. 95–111.

———. "The Psycho-Analytic Play Technique: Its History and Significance." *SMK*. 35–54.

———. "The Psychological Principles of Infant Analysis." *SMK*. 57–68.

Kofman, Sarah. *The Enigma of Woman: Woman in Freud's Writings*. Trans. Catherine Porter. Ithaca: Cornell University Press, 1980.

Kohut, Heinz. *How Does Analysis Cure?* Ed. Arnold Goldberg. Chicago: University of Chicago Press, 1984.

———. *The Restoration of the Self*. New York: International Universities Press, 1977.

Kreutz, Irving. "L. P. Hartley, Who Are U? or, Luncheon in the Lounge." *Kenyon Review* 25 (1963): 150–54.

Kris, Ernst (chair). "Problems of Infantile Neurosis: A Discussion." *Psychoanalytic Study of the Child* 1 (1954): 16–71.

———. "The Recovery of Childhood Memories in Psychoanalysis." *Psychoanalytic Study of the Child* 11 (1956): 54–87.

Kristeva, Julia. *Desire in Language: A Semantic Approach to Literature and Art*. Trans. Leon S. Roudiez. Ed. Thomas Cora et al. New York: Columbia University Press, 1980.

Kucich, John. *Repression in Victorian Fiction: Charlotte Brontë, George Eliot, and Charles Dickens*. Berkeley: University of California Press, 1987.

Kuhn, Reinhard. *Corruption in Paradise: The Child in Western Literature*. Hanover: Brown University Press, 1982.

Lacan, Jacques. *Les Complexes familiaux dans la formation de l'individu: Essai d'analyse d'une fonction en psychologie*. Paris: Éditions du Seuil, 1978.

———. *Écrits*. Paris: Éditions du Seuil, 1966.

———. *Écrits: A Selection.* Trans. Alan Sheridan. New York: Norton, 1977.

———. *The Four Fundamental Concepts of Psycho-Analysis.* Trans. Alan Sheridan. Ed. Jacques-Alain Miller. New York: Norton, 1978.

———. "God and the *Jouissance* of the Woman." *Feminine Sexuality.* Trans. Jacqueline Rose. Ed. Juliet Mitchell and Jacqueline Rose. New York: Norton, 1985: 137–48.

———. "The Meaning of the Phallus." In *Feminine Sexuality,* 74–85.

———. "The Neurotic's Individual Myth." *Psychoanalytic Quarterly* 48 (1979): 386–425.

———. "Of Structure as an Inmixing of Otherness Prerequisite to Any Subject Whatever." Trans. Richard Macksey and Eugenio Donato. In *The Languages of Criticism and the Sciences of Man: The Structuralist Controversy.* Ed. Richard Macksey and Eugenio Donato. Baltimore: Johns Hopkins University Press, 1970: 186–200.

———. *The Seminar of Jacques Lacan. Book 1: Freud's Papers on Technique, 1953–1954.* Trans. John Forrester. Ed. Jacques-Alain Miller. New York: Norton, 1988.

———. *The Seminar of Jacques Lacan. Book 2: The Ego in Freud's Theory and in the Technique of Psychoanalysis, 1954–1955.* Trans. Sylvana Tomaselli. Ed. Jacques-Alain Miller. New York: Norton, 1988.

———. "Some Reflections on the Ego." *IJPA* 34 (1953): 11–17.

Lampl-De Groot, Jeanne. "Considerations of Methodology in Relation to the Psychology of Small Children." *IJPA* 20 (1939): 408–17.

Langley, Dena Beth. "In Vitro Fertilization: Eliminating the Current State of Limbo between Pre-Embryonic Rights and the Fundamental Right to Procreate." *Wake Forest Law Review* 26: 1217–43.

Laplanche, Jean. *Life and Death in Psychoanalysis.* Trans. Jeffrey Mehlman. Baltimore: Johns Hopkins University Press, 1976.

———. *New Foundations for Psychoanalysis.* Trans. David Macey. Oxford: Basil Blackwell, 1989.

Laplanche, Jean, and J.-B. Pontalis. "Fantasy and the Origins of Sexuality." *IJPA* 49 (1968): 1–18.

———. *The Language of Psycho-Analysis.* Trans. Donald Nicholson-Smith. New York: Norton, 1973.

Lasch, Christopher. *Culture of Narcissism: American Life in an Age of Diminishing Expectations.* New York: Warner, 1979.

———. *Haven in a Heartless World: The Family Besieged.* New York: Basic, 1977.

Laslett, Peter, ed. *Household and Family in Past Time: Comparative Studies in the Size and Structure of the Domestic Group over the Last Three Centuries in England, France, Serbia, Japan, and Colonial North America, with Further Materials from Western Europe.* Cambridge: Cambridge University Press, 1972.

———. *The World We Have Lost.* London: Methuen, 1963.

Leavy, Stanley A. *The Psychoanalytic Dialogue.* New Haven: Yale University Press, 1980.

Leclaire, Serge. *On tue un enfant: Un essai sur le narcissisme primaire et la pulsion de mort.* Paris: Éditions du Seuil, 1975.

Lemaire, Anika. *Jacques Lacan.* Trans. David Macey. London: Routledge and Kegan Paul, 1977.

Lemann, Nicholas. "The Vogue of Childhood Misery." *Atlantic* Mar. 1992: 119–22.

Lilly, Mark. "Nabokov: Homo Ludens." In *Vladimir Nabokov: A Tribute.* Ed. Peter Quennell. New York: William Morrow, 1980: 88–102.

Loftus, Elizabeth F. "The Reality of Repressed Memories." *American Psychologist* 48 (1993): 518–37.

Long, Michael. *Marvell, Nabokov: Childhood and Arcadia.* Oxford: Clarendon Press, 1984.

McCloskey, John C. "What Maisie Knows: A Study of Childhood and Adolescence." *American Literature* 36 (1965): 485–513.

McDougall, Joyce. *Plea for a Measure of Abnormality.* New York: International Universities Press, 1980.

———. *Theaters of the Body: A Psychoanalytic Approach to Psychosomatic Illness.* New York: Norton, 1989.

———. *Theaters of the Mind: Illusion and Truth on the Psychoanalytic Stage.* New York: Basic, 1985.

———, and Serge Lebovici. *Dialogue with Sammy: A Psycho-Analytical Contribution to the Understanding of Child Psychosis.* Trans. Joyce McDougall. Ed. Martin James. New York: International Universities Press, 1969.

McHale, Brian. *Postmodernist Fiction.* New York: Methuen, 1987.

Mack, Dana. "War on Drugs? War on Parents." *Wall Street Journal* 17 June 1993: A10.

Maddox, Lucy. *Nabokov's English Novels.* Athens: University of Georgia Press, 1983.

Mahler, Margaret S. *On Human Symbiosis and the Vicissitudes of Individuation.* 2 vols. New York: International Universities Press, 1968.

Mailloux, Steven. *Interpretive Conventions: The Reader in the Study of American Fiction.* Ithaca: Cornell University Press, 1982.

Malcolm, Janet. "The Family of Mann." *New York Review of Books* 3 Feb. 1994: 7–8.

Malek, Ceil. Letter. *New York Times Book Review* 14 Feb. 1993: 27.

Mannoni, Maud. *The Backward Child and His Mother: A Psychoanalytic Study.* Trans. Alan Sheridan. New York: Pantheon, 1972.

———. *The Child, His "Illness," and the Others.* New York: Random House, 1970.

Marcus, Steven. *Freud and the Culture of Psychoanalysis: Studies in the Transition from Victorian Humanism to Modernity.* New York: Norton, 1984.

Marotta, Kenny. "*What Maisie Knew:* The Question of Our Speech." *ELH* 46 (1979): 495–508.

Masson, Jeffrey Moussaieff. *The Assault on Truth: Freud's Suppression of the Seduction Theory.* New York: Penguin, 1985.

"Maternal Rights and Fetal Wrongs: The Case against the Criminalization of 'Fetal Abuse.'" *Harvard Law Review* 101 (1988): 994–1012.

Mead, Margaret. *Male and Female: A Study of the Sexes in a Changing World.* New York: William Morrow, 1949.

———. "Some Theoretical Considerations on the Problem of Mother-Child Separation." *American Journal of Orthopsychiatry* 24 (1954): 471–83.

Michie, Helena. "'Who Is This in Pain?': Scarring, Disfigurement, and Female Identity in *Bleak House* and *Our Mutual Friend.*" *Novel* 22 (1989): 199–212.

Miller, Alice. *Prisoners of Childhood: The Drama of the Gifted Child and the Search for the True Self.* Trans. Ruth Ward. New York: Basic, 1981.

Miller, D. A. *The Novel and the Police.* Berkeley: University of California Press, 1988.

Miller, J. Hillis. *Charles Dickens: The World of His Novels.* Cambridge: Harvard University Press, 1958.

———. *Versions of Pygmalion.* Cambridge: Harvard University Press, 1990.

Minnow, Martha. "Rights for the Next Generation: A Feminist Approach to Children's Rights." *Harvard Women's Law Journal* 9 (Spring) 1986: 1–24.

Mitchell, Juliet. "*What Maisie Knew:* Portrait of the Artist as a Young Girl." In *Air of Reality: New Essays of Henry James.* Ed. John Goode. London: Methuen, 1972: 168–89.

Moi, Toril. "Patriarchal Thought and the Drive for Knowledge." In *Between Feminism and Psychoanalysis.* Ed. Teresa Brennan. New York: Routledge, 1989: 189–205.

Mulkeen, Anne. *Wild Thyme, Winter Lightning: The Symbolic Novels of L. P. Hartley.* Detroit: Wayne State University Press, 1974.

Murray, Lynne, and Colwyn Trevarthen. "The Infant's Role in Mother-Infant Communications." *Journal of Child Language* 13 (1986): 15–29.

Nabokov, Vladimir. *Ada or Ardor: A Family Chronicle.* New York: McGraw-Hill, 1969.

———. *The Annotated Lolita.* Ed. Alfred Appel, Jr. New York: McGraw-Hill, 1970.

———. *Bend Sinister.* 1947. New York: McGraw-Hill, 1974.

———. *Despair.* New York: Putnam's, 1966.

———. *The Enchanter.* Trans. Dmitri Nabokov. New York: G. P. Putnam's Sons, 1986.

———. *Lectures on Literature.* Ed. Fredson Bowers. New York: Harcourt Brace Jovanovich, 1980.

———. *The Nabokov-Wilson Letters.* Ed. Simon Karlinsky. New York: Harper and Row, 1979.

———. *Pale Fire.* New York: Berkley, 1962.

———. *Speak Memory: An Autobiography Revisited.* New York: Putnam's, 1966.

————. *Strong Opinions.* New York: McGraw-Hill, 1973.

Nance, William L. "What Maisie Knew: The Myth of the Artist." *Studies in the Novel* 8 (1976): 88–102.

Ofshe, Richard, and Ethan Watters. "Making Monsters." *Society* 30 (1993): 4–16.

Ohmann, Richard. "The Shaping of a Canon: U.S. Fiction, 1960–1975." *Critical Inquiry* 10 (1983): 199–223.

Ovid. *Metamorphoses.* Trans. Rolfe Humphries. Bloomington: Indiana University Press, 1955.

Packman, David. *Vladimir Nabokov: The Structure of Literary Desire.* Columbia: University of Missouri Press, 1982.

Page, Norman, ed. *Nabokov: The Critical Heritage.* London: Routledge and Kegan Paul, 1982.

Pattison, Robert. *The Child Figure in English Literature.* Athens: University of Georgia Press, 1978.

People v. Darlene Johnson. Appellant's Opening Brief. Cal. Sup. Ct. No. 29390, 1991.

People v. Darlene Johnson. Text of Judgment Proceedings. Cal. Sup. Ct. No. 29390, 2 Jan. 1991.

Peterfreund, Emanuel. "Some Critical Comments on Psychoanalytic Conceptualizations of Infancy." *IJPA* 59 (1978): 427–41.

Pinchbeck, Ivy, and Margaret Hewitt. *Children in English Society.* 2 vols. London: Routledge, 1969–73.

Pine, Fred. *Developmental Theory and Clinical Process.* New Haven: Yale University Press, 1985.

"Police Say Girl Turned in Parents for Drug Abuse." *Atlanta Journal Constitution* 23 Nov. 1991: B3.

Pontalis, J.-B. *Frontiers of Psychoanalysis: Between the Dream and Psychic Pain.* Trans. Catherine Cullen and Philip Cullen. London: Hogarth, 1981.

Postman, Neil. *The Disappearance of Childhood.* New York: Delacorte Press, 1982.

Poulet, Georges. "Criticism and the Experience of Interiority." In *Reader-Response Criticism: From Formalism to Post-Structuralism.* Ed. Jane P. Tompkins. Baltimore: Johns Hopkins University Press, 1980: 41–49.

Pritchard, R. E. "L. P. Hartley's *The Go-Between.*" *Critical Quarterly* 22 (1980): 45–55.

Pruett, Kyle Dean. "Oedipal Configurations in Young Father-Raised Children." *Psychoanalytic Study of the Child* 40 (1987): 435–56.

Radley, Alan. "Psychological Realism in L. P. Hartley's *The Go-Between.*" *Literature and Psychology* 33:2 (1987): 1–9.

Rampton, David. *Vladimir Nabokov: A Critical Study of the Novels.* Cambridge: Cambridge University Press, 1984.

Rees, Matthew. "Shot in the Arm: The Use and Abuse of Norplant; Involuntary Contraception and Public Policy." *The New Republic* 9 Dec. 1991: 16. Available in LEXIS, Nexis Library.

Roberts, Clay. Letter. *Wall Street Journal* 30 June 1993: A15.

Rorty, Richard. *Contingency, Irony, and Solidarity.* New York: Cambridge University Press, 1989.

Rose, Jacqueline. *The Case of Peter Pan; or, the Impossibility of Children's Fiction.* London: Macmillan, 1984.

Ross, John Munder. "Fathering: A Review of Some Psychoanalytic Contributions on Paternity." *IJPA* 60 (1979): 317–27.

Roth, Henry. *Call It Sleep.* 1934. New York: Avon, 1962.

Roustang, François. *Dire Mastery: Discipleship from Freud to Lacan.* Trans. Ned Lukacher. Baltimore: Johns Hopkins University Press, 1976.

Rowe, W. W. *Nabokov's Spectral Dimension.* Ann Arbor: Ardis, 1981.

Ruddick, Sara. *Maternal Thinking: Towards a Politics of Peace.* New York: Ballantine, 1989.

Sadoff, Dianne. *Monsters of Affection: Dickens, Eliot, and Brönte on Fatherhood.* Baltimore: Johns Hopkins University Press, 1982.

Schafer, Roy. *The Analytic Attitude.* New York: Basic, 1983.

———. *A New Language for Psychoanalysis.* New Haven: Yale University Press, 1976.

Schmidt v. DeBoer. Text of Testimony. Washtentaw County Circuit Court, 1993.

Sears, Sallie. *The Negative Imagination: Form and Perspective in the Novels of Henry James.* Ithaca: Cornell University Press, 1968.

Seidman, Steven. *Romantic Longings: Love in America, 1830–1980.* New York: Routledge, 1991.

Seltzer, Mark. *Henry James and the Art of Power.* Ithaca: Cornell University Press, 1984.

Shelley, Mary. *Frankenstein.* 1818. New York: Bantam, 1967.

Shine, Muriel. *The Fictional Children of Henry James.* Chapel Hill: University of North Carolina Press, 1964.

Shorter, Edward. "Comment by Edward Shorter." *History of Childhood Quarterly* 1 (1974): 593–97.

———. *The Making of the Modern Family.* New York: Basic, 1975.

Shue, J. P. "Nabokov and Freud: The Play of Power." *Modern Fiction Studies* 30 (1984): 637–50.

Silverman, Kaja. "Too Early/Too Late: Subjectivity and the Primal Scene in Henry James." In *Why the Novel Matters: A Postmodern Perplex.* Ed. Mark Spilka and Caroline McCracken-Flesher. Bloomington: Indiana University Press, 1990: 165–91.

Solnit, Albert J. "Developments in Child Psychoanalysis in the Last Twenty Years, Pure and Applied: A Vital Balance." *Studies in Child Psychoanalysis: Pure and Applied.* New Haven: Yale University Press, 1975: 1–13.

Spence, Donald P. *Narrative Truth and Historical Truth: Meaning and Interpretation in Psychoanalysis.* New York: Norton, 1982.

Spilka, Mark. *Dickens and Kafka: A Mutual Interpretation.* Bloomington: Indiana University Press, 1963.

Spitz, René. *The First Year of Life*. New York: International Universities Press, 1965.

Spivak, Gayatri Chakravorty. "Feminism and Critical Theory." In *Other Worlds: Essays in Cultural Politics*. New York: Methuen, 1987: 77–92.

Sprengnether, Madelon. *The Spectral Mother: Freud, Feminism, and Psychoanalysis*. Ithaca: Cornell University Press, 1990.

Stegner, Page. *Escape into Aesthetics: The Art of Vladimir Nabokov*. New York: Dial, 1966.

Stern, Daniel. *The Interpersonal World of the Infant: A View from Psychoanalysis and Developmental Psychology*. New York: Basic, 1985.

Stevenson, Ian, and Joseph Wolpe. "Recovery from Sexual Deviations through Overcoming Non-Sexual Neurotic Responses." *American Journal of Psychiatry* 116 (1960): 737–42.

Stoehr, Taylor. *Dickens: The Dreamer's Stance*. Ithaca: Cornell University Press, 1965.

Stoller, Robert J. *Presentations of Gender*. New Haven: Yale University Press, 1985.

Stone, Lawrence. *The Family, Sex, and Marriage: In England, 1500–1800*. New York: Harper and Row, 1977.

Tarvis, Carol. "Beware the Incest-Survivor Machine." *New York Times Book Review* 1 Jan. 1993: 1, 16–17.

———. Letter. *New York Times Book Review* 14 Feb. 1993: 27.

Taylor, Bill. "True or False?" *Toronto Star* 18 May 1992. Available in LEXIS, Nexis Library.

Thomas, Karen M. "Adoption: Laws and Emotions." *Dallas Morning News* 10 Aug. 1993: 1C. Available in LEXIS, Nexis Library.

Thomas, Rebecca L. "Adult Survivors of Childhood Sexual Abuse and Statutes of Limitations: A Call for Legislative Action." *Wake Forest Law Review* 26 (1991): 1245–95.

Toker, Leona. *Nabokov: The Mystery of Literary Structures*. Ithaca: Cornell University Press, 1989.

Treurniet, Nikolaas. "Psychoanalysis and Self-Psychology: A Metapsychological Essay with a Clinical Illustration." *Journal of the American Psychoanalytic Association* 31 (1983): 59–100.

Van Bonheemen, Christine. *The Novel as Family Romance: Language, Gender, and Authority from Fielding to Joyce*. Ithaca: Cornell University Press, 1987.

Von Hug-Hellmuth, Hermine. "On the Technique of Child-Analysis." *IJPA* 2 (1921): 287–305.

Wakefield, Hollida, and Ralph Underwager. *Accusations of Child Sexual Abuse*. Springfield, Ill.: Charles C. Thomas, 1988.

Walters, Margaret. "Keeping the Place Tidy for the Young Female Mind: *The Awkward Age*." In *Air of Reality: New Essays on Henry James*. Ed. John Goode. London: Methuen, 1972: 190–218.

Ward, J. A. *The Imagination of Disaster: Evil in the Fiction of Henry James*. Lincoln: University of Nebraska Press, 1961.

Wasiolek, Edward. "Maisie: Pure or Corrupt?" *College English* 22 (1960): 167–72.

Weeks, Jeffrey. *Coming Out: Homosexual Politics in Britain, from the Nineteenth Century to the Present.* London: Quartet, 1977.

Weinstein, Philip M. *The Semantics of Desire: Changing Models of Identity from Dickens to Joyce.* Princeton: Princeton University Press, 1984.

Weiss, Nancy Pottishman. "Mother, the Invention of Necessity: Dr. Benjamin Spock's *Baby and Child Care.*" In *Growing Up in America: Children in Historical Perspective.* Ed. N. Ray Hiner and Joseph M. Hawes. Urbana: University of Illinois Press, 1985: 283–303.

West, Nancy M. "Order in Disorder: Surrealism and *Oliver Twist.*" *South Atlantic Review* 54 (1989): 41–58.

Whitebrook, Joel. "Perversion: Destruction and Reparation: On the Contributions of Janine Chasseguet-Smirgle and Joyce McDougall." *American Imago* 48 (1991): 329–50.

Whitfield, Charles L. *Healing the Child Within: Discovery and Recovery for Adult Children of Dysfunctional Families.* Deerfield Beach, Fla.: Health Communications, 1987.

Wiesenfarth, Joseph. *Henry James and the Dramatic Analogy: A Study of the Major Novels of the Middle Period.* New York: Fordham University Press, 1963.

Williams, Raymond. *The Country and the City.* New York: Oxford University Press, 1973.

Wilson, Harris W. "What *Did* Maisie Know?" *College English* 17 (1956): 279–82.

Winnicott, D. W. *The Child and the Family: First Relationships.* Ed. Janet Hardenberg. London: Tavistock, 1957.

———. *Holding and Interpretation: Fragment of an Analysis.* Ed. M. Masud R. Khan. London: Hogarth, 1986.

———. *The Piggle: An Account of the Psychoanalytic Treatment of a Little Girl.* Ed. Ishak Ramzy. London: Hogarth, 1978.

———. *Playing and Reality.* London: Tavistock, 1971.

———. *Through Paediatrics to Psycho-Analysis.* London: Hogarth, 1975.

Wishy, Bernard. *The Child and the Republic: The Dawn of Modern American Child Nurture.* Philadelphia: University of Pennsylvania Press, 1968.

Wolf, Ernest S. *Treating the Self: Elements of Clinical Self-Psychology.* New York: Guilford, 1988.

Wolff, P. H. "Observations on Newborn Infants." *Psychosomatic Medicine* n.s. 21: 110–18.

Woodward, Richard B. "The Disturbing Photography of Sally Mann." *New York Times Magazine* 27 Sept. 1992: 28–52.

Zelizer, Viviana A. *Pricing the Priceless Child: The Changing Social Value of Children.* New York: Basic, 1985.

Zwerdling, Alex. "Esther Summerson Rehabilitated," *PMLA* 88 (1973): 429–39.

Index

VIRGINIA L. BLUM is an associate professor of English at the University of Kentucky. Her articles have appeared in *American Literature* and *Literature and Psychology*.